Pathologic Grief
Maladaptation to Loss

Pathologic Grief
Maladaptation to Loss

Selby Jacobs, M.D., M.P.H.
Professor of Psychiatry
Department of Psychiatry
Yale University School of Medicine
New Haven, Connecticut

Washington, DC
London, England

Note: The author has worked to ensure that all information in this book concerning drug dosages, schedules, and routes of administration is accurate as of the time of publication and consistent with standards set by the U.S. Food and Drug Administration and the general medical community. As medical research and practice advance, however, therapeutic standards may change. For this reason and because human and mechanical errors sometimes occur, we recommend that readers follow the advice of a physician who is directly involved in their care or the care of a member of their family.

Books published by the American Psychiatric Press, Inc., represent the views and opinions of the individual authors and do not necessarily represent the policies and opinions of the Press or the American Psychiatric Association.

Copyright © 1993 American Psychiatric Press, Inc.
ALL RIGHTS RESERVED
Manufactured in the United States of America on acid-free paper.
96 95 94 93 4 3 2 1

American Psychiatric Press, Inc.
1400 K Street, N.W., Washington, DC 20005

Library of Congress Cataloging-in-Publication Data
Jacobs, Selby, 1939–
    Pathologic grief : maladaptation to loss / by Selby Jacobs.
      p.   cm.
    Includes bibliographical references and index.
    ISBN 0-88048-531-0
    1. Bereavement—Psychological aspects. 2. Grief therapy.
  I. Title
    [DNLM: 1. Adaptation, Psychological. 2. Bereavement.
    3. Psychotherapy. BF 575.G7 J17p]
RC455.4.L67.J3 1993
616.85'2—dc20
DNLM/DLC   92-48695
for Library of Congress   CIP

British Library Cataloguing in Publication Data
A CIP record is available from the British Library.

*To
John Selby,
Maude Rae Campbell,
Ann Blinn,
Alicia Ann, and
Kyra Rae*

Contents

Acknowledgments ix

Foreword xi
    Beverley Raphael, M.D.

1   Introduction 1

2   Pathologic Grief 13

3   Defining the Range and Magnitude of the
Clinical Complications of Bereavement 39

4   Relationship Among the Clinical Complications
of Bereavement 59

5   An Adaptive Model 75

6   Social Networks and Supports 93

7   Adaptation to a Loss 115

8   Personal Risk Factors for Complications 141

9   Differential Diagnosis of the Complications of
Bereavement 173

10   Introduction to Treatment 201

11	Integrating the Treatment for Complications of Bereavement	235
12	Pharmacological Treatment of the Complications of Bereavement	253
13	Psychotherapy of the Complications of Bereavement	279
14	Mutual Support Groups	315
15	Prevention	335
16	Conclusions	349
	Appendix	363
	Index	371

Acknowledgments

Many persons contributed to the writing of this manuscript in various ways over the past 11 years. They collaborated in the conceptualization of the studies, discussion of problematic issues, implementation of the research, analyses of the data, writing of articles, treatment of bereaved patients with complications, reading and editing parts of the manuscript, or administrative support. These persons include Stephen Atkins, Boris Astrachan, Lisa Berkman, Sally Brown, Martha Bruce, Peter Charpentier, Charles Gardner, Fay Hanson, Stanislav Kasl, Thomas Kosten, Richard Lane, Barry Lebowitz, Paul Lieberman, Kathleen Kim, John Mason, Warwick Middleton, Craig Nelson, Adrian Ostfeld, Colin Parkes, Beverley Raphael, Edward Rynearson, Catherine Schaefer, Sanford Schreiber, William Sledge, David Snow, Jacob Tebes, Victor Wahby, and Sid Zisook. Thanks, once again, to all of them.

Also, I would like to acknowledge the support of NIMH Research Grants MH 32750, entitled "Neuroendocrine Aspects of Grief in Adults," and MH 32260, entitled "The Effect of Spousal Illness and Death in Older Families," that enabled much of the research that laid the foundation for this manuscript. Finally, I would like to make a final expression of gratitude to the bereaved participants who took part in these studies at a very difficult time in their lives.

Foreword

It is better to have loved and lost than never to have loved at all.
—Tennyson

The nature of human relationships, from the nurturing of mother-infants bonds to the passions of adult intimacy, is a source of intense interest to all—from the participants themselves to various scientific researchers. These attachments are seen to serve a critical function in the integration of social systems and the sustenance of individuals. The pain that occurs with a separation of these attachments or with their loss has been suggested as serving evolutionary functions (e.g., Averill 1968). All societies acknowledge this pain and most have evolved social rituals to deal with it. More recently its role in the genesis of more broadly based human suffering and ill health has made it a focus for medical research explorations and understandings.

In this scholarly and systematic exploration of pathologic grief, Selby Jacobs provides the most detailed and up-to-date integration of what is known in this field. This volume starts by reviewing the work of earlier researchers, including the classic contributions of Freud (1917), Parkes (1972), Bowlby (1969, 1973, 1980), and many others. Jacobs delineates the nature of normal grief and the variations seen by clinicians and researchers that have been deemed pathologic. The range and extent of these pathologies and the clinical problems they constitute are of significance to all clinicians, as they may lead to increased presentations for medical care, increased substance use and abuse, significant mental health problems, increased risk of death for some groups, and, for all, substantial human suffering.

The nature of adaptation to loss of a loved one is influenced by many variables, from the quality of the attachment and the coping styles of the bereaved person to environmental influences such as the quality of social networks and the social adaptations and role transitions that must be mastered.

This volume epitomizes the more rigorous scientific approach to the study of bereavement that has evolved in the last decade, extending the accepted truths of previous workers by intensive theoretical, epidemiological, and clinical research. Jacobs relies not only on a critical appraisal and presentation of the findings of other investigators, but on his own group's studies of the parameters of pathologic grief.

After an introduction and overview, the next three chapters provide a review of prior conceptualizations of pathologic grief and the range and magnitude of the clinical problems associated with it. Jacobs then presents his own model of a dimensional view of normal bereavement as involving dimensions of numbness and denial; separation distress; mourning and/or depression; and traumatic distress. This conceptualization is valuable in integrating current understandings and providing a framework for Jacobs's own research. The central role of separation distress in pathologic syndromes of delayed (or absent), inhibited, and chronic grief is also conceptualized. Jacobs goes on to highlight the risk of clinical complications, which include pathologic grief, major depression, panic disorder, and generalized anxiety disorder, and the overlap that may exist between them.

These conceptualizations integrate research and clinical material and provide a strong basis for the presentation of an adaptive model as optimal for understanding bereavement complications. The model integrates environmental and contextual elements (e.g., social supports), the nature of the agent causing the syndrome (the death and its circumstances), and personal variables (e.g., coping styles and strengths). This valuable framework then provides a starting point for more detailed exploration in Chapters 6, 7, and 8 of social networks and supports; the processes of adaptation to loss, including coping styles and ego defense mechanisms; and personal risk factors and complications.

It is in these chapters that the breadth and depth of Jacobs's research provides fascinating insights, particularly in terms of coping styles and ego defense mechanisms. More particularly, there is a rich and honest presentation of the multiplicity of influences on bereavement outcome, including the effects of different losses, different adaptations at different stages of loss, the uncertain yet significant role of personality, and the complex and as yet poorly understood biological components of bereavement.

These presentations are essential reading for bereavement researchers and clinicians alike and can provide a basis for new research developments, as well as therapeutic frameworks.

In Chapter 9, Jacobs presents a proposal for differential diagnoses of the complications of bereavement based on diagnostic criteria for normal and pathologic grief (Raphael 1989) and severe grief. He explores the relationship of posttraumatic stress disorder to pathologic grief and the differential diagnosis of depressive bereavement phenomenology and major depressions, as well as generalized anxiety disorder and panic disorder.

Building on these conceptualizations and data, and exemplified by rich case studies from his own research and clinical experience, Jacobs goes on to delineate frameworks for treatment and prevention. These are based on what is understood of pathogenesis in physiological, social, and psychological frameworks, as well as the adaptations of recovery, and what has been learned from effective and proven treatments. As Jacobs demonstrates, because data are limited, constructs for therapy need to build on and integrate psychological, behavioral, physiological, pharmacological and social parameters that may contribute differentially to recovery, at different stages, and with different pathologies and different individuals.

As a basis for treatment goals, Jacobs outlines the potential contribution of different therapies: pharmacological therapies for complications of major depression and anxiety disorders; psychotherapeutic therapies for psychoeducational, behavioral, and psychodynamic components to deal with the fear, helplessness, and loss; and mutual support to assist with adaptation to the new social reality. These approaches need to be synthesized and integrated for individual needs, and the overall approach should be one of conservatism. Chapter 11 provides one of the most succinct and clinically sound distillations of therapeutic wisdom for the management of bereavement and its pathologies yet available.

In Chapter 12, Jacobs considers the place of pharmacological agents in the treatment of complications of bereavement, emphasizing that there is no suggestion that they be used for normal bereavements. Nevertheless, the role of these agents has probably been neglected, especially for bereaved individuals who develop anxiety or depressive syndromes where their suffering and ill health may be indirectly prolonged or their capacity for psychotherapeutic working through and use of mutual support would be inhibited without such interventions.

Jacobs also reviews psychotherapeutic interventions. The models he proposes emphasize an individualized approach that incorporates psychodynamic understandings of the individual and his or her development, experience, and present context and reaction. Psychoeducation about the tasks of grief is seen as the cornerstone of therapy, with recognition of the processes of remembering and the continuing relationship with the lost person, issues of anger and forgiving, the significance of past losses, and transference.

In Chatper 14, Jacobs carefully explores the contributions of support groups to recovery and delineates the importance of their role in social adaptations. The need for interaction between mutual support and professional care systems is emphasized and links with earlier recognition of the failure of such an integrative approach in which support groups may present an antiprofessional approach. The contributions that both systems can make to prevention, treatment, and rehabilitation with respect to pathologic grief and bereavement complications need to be fully recognized.

Jacobs draws together the work of a number of researchers and his own experience to provide an overview of the opportunities for prevention and the value of this model for bereavement generally and with respect to other stressful live experiences. Education and crisis intervention contribute to primary prevention, as may early treatment of depression contribute to secondary prevention and later on mutual support to tertiary prevention with its framework for social rehabilitation. Further, it should be noted that some support groups also operate to provide crisis intervention and primary prevention.

In concluding, Jacobs reviews the significant findings presented in this valuable work and draws attention to the dialogue between clinical practice and clinical science, which must, in the end, serve the human needs of the patients. Jacobs has done a great service to clinical science in the rich research he has drawn together: both the comprehensive contributions of other scientists and his own thoughtful and systematic studies, which have brought substantial new insights and integration of earlier models. Clinical practice is clearly married to clinical science in this work; each chapter reveals the richness of the author's clinical experience, the depth of this clinical wisdom, and his capacity to integrate this with his clinically based research.

This is, in all, a thoughtful and integrating book. It will be essential as a baseline for researchers and clinicians alike. It will challenge many accepted wisdoms and will, I hope, stimulate those who read it to a more critical appraisal of their understanding of response to loss and the central place of attachment, separation, and loss in the evolution of human psychopathology and illness. It is the most comprehensive work to date on the topic of pathologic grief and stands as a testament to the work of Jacobs and his research team. Perhaps more than anything, it would have brought great pleasure to John Bowlby on whose theoretical conceptualizations it rests and whose wisdom it validates. Attachment, separation, and loss are central to human existence, and the understanding of the normalities and pathologies is critical to effective and human care.

Beverley Raphael, M.D., F.R.A.N.Z.C.P., M.B.B.S., F.R.C.Psych.
Fellow, Australian Academy of Social Science
Corresponding Fellow, American Psychiatric Association
Professor and Chairperson, Department of Psychiatry
University of Queensland, Queensland, Australia

References

Averill J: Grief: its nature and significance. Psychol Bull 70:721–748, 1968
Bowlby J: Attachment and Loss, Vol 1: Attachment. New York, Basic Books, 1969
Bowlby J: Attachment and Loss, Vol 2: Separation. New York, Basic Books, 1973
Bowlby J: Attachment and Loss, Vol 3: Loss, Sadness and Depression. New York, Basic Books, 1980
Freud S: Mourning and melancholia (1917), in The Standard Edition of the Complete Psychological Works of Sigmund Freud, Vol 14. Translated and edited by Strachey J. London, Hogarth Press, 1953, pp 243–258
Parkes CM: Bereavement: Studies of Grief In Adult Life. London, Tavistock, 1972
Raphael B: Diagnostic criteria for bereavement reactions. Paper presented at the International Symposium on Pathologic Bereavement, Seattle, WA, May 1989

CHAPTER 1

Introduction

The experience of bereavement offers one of the best opportunities for understanding psychological distress or psychiatric syndromes in the context of environmental contingencies. Bereavement is a naturally occurring, universal experience that serves as a prototype for understanding the pathogenesis of and interventions for the stress-related disorders that are associated with bereavement. An individual's efforts to cope with the changes caused by bereavement can be viewed as attempts to adapt to the new environment shaped by the loss. Maladaptations can occur that stall the process of spontaneous recovery from grief; these maladaptations are recognizable as complications of the process and require skilled help. Treatment is most effective when it considers the specific context of the clinical problems.

The following case example illustrates the development of a depressive syndrome late in the course of bereavement; Ms. A's major depression seemed to follow a period of delayed and then severe grief—a pattern characteristic of pathologic grief. Her clinical complications were associated with impairment in social and occupational functioning.

Ms. A's intense style of attachment, which included a vicarious enjoyment of her attentiveness to others, was manifested in her resourceful caring for her children; however, her level of attachment became a source of difficulty following first the traumatic, untimely death of her favorite son and then the death of her mother. The losses created a need for her to find a new way to cope. Also the cumulative stress of the two losses contributed to her psychological burden. Subsequent to her son's and mother's deaths, Ms. A perceived the environment as threatening and unpredictable. The first anniversary of her son's death loomed as a nemesis. Although she was reluctant to seek help, in the judgment of the referring clinicians, her family, and the evaluating psychiatrist, she required professional intervention.

Case 1

Ms. A, a proud 42-year-old woman, presented for evaluation of problems that arose during acute bereavement. Ten months previously her 24-year-old son, her first child, had died from a fulminating viral illness of uncertain etiology after a short illness of 1 week. Three months later, her 63-year-old mother succumbed to pancreatic cancer. Ms. A's chief complaint was, "I still can't believe it; it is such a shock." She kept her appointment for a psychiatric evaluation because her children felt that she needed help. In addition, the members and staff of a bereavement, mutual support group at a hospice that had cared for her mother urged her to get professional attention. Otherwise, she would not have come on her own.

Ms. A described a depressive syndrome including depressed mood, frequent crying episodes, feelings of uselessness, irritability, difficulty concentrating, weight gain of 15 pounds over 6 months, a difficulty falling asleep often lasting 4 to 5 hours, and anergia. She denied suicidal ideation and manifested neither psychomotor retardation nor delusional thinking. She reported conflict with her husband over her inability to fulfill family roles. In addition, she noted impairment in her performance at work as a departmental manager of a large retail store. She had no personal history of depressive episodes or other mental disorders and denied a family history of depression or anxiety disorders.

At the time of her son's death, Ms. A did not grieve but rather redoubled her efforts to care for her deteriorating mother whose illness had been diagnosed before Ms. A's son became ill. When her mother died, the full force of grief "hit" her and she could "not stop crying." At this point, she had symptoms of both grief and depression. She yearned intensely for the return of her recently deceased son and mother. It was like "a part of me was gone." The intensity of her grief was reflected in her fear that the sorrow over her losses would drive her crazy. The depressive symptoms began shortly after the death of her mother and became progressively worse. She felt helpless. She neither knew what to do for herself nor how to help her surviving children who had also been deeply hurt by the deaths. Her action-oriented style of coping, which had proven successful in surmounting not only the accidental death of her first husband but also severe poverty, did not serve her well in the present circumstances. Her sense of efficacy and pride as a dutiful daughter, as well as a resourceful mother, was lost. She viewed the world as unpredictable (if not hostile), desolate, and lacking in meaningful social structure. After her two most recent losses, it was understandable how she might have developed such an outlook.

Unfortunately, Ms. A's experience with bereavement is not unique. Although it is true that most bereaved individuals recover over time from a loss without serious difficulty, approximately 20% may develop clinical complications for which they need help (see Chapter 3).

The Vicissitudes of Clinical Attention to Pathologic Grief

Over the past 20 years, the complications of bereavement have not received adequate clinical attention given their frequency, the suffering they cause for bereaved individuals, and the important lessons their study provides for understanding certain types of psychopathology. Competing ideas for conceptualizing the complications of bereavement have not been resolved either to establish the superiority of one approach or to create a synthesis of approaches. Therefore, clinicians lack clear guidance for recognizing and treating complications during acute bereavement. Yet bereaved patients continue to present themselves for help and impress on practitioners the need to clarify the nature of these disorders.

Two theoretical and nosological traditions have been developed in the 20th century to conceptualize the complications of bereavement. One has its origins in psychoanalytic psychiatry and denotes the complications as pathologic grief (Freud 1917; Lindeman 1944). The other originates in descriptive psychiatry and applies standard diagnostic criteria for depression or anxiety disorders to symptoms that occur in the period of bereavement (DSM-III-R; American Psychiatric Association 1987). Until recently, no one has addressed the relationship between these two schools of thought, leaving uncertain the best approach for a clinical nosology (Kim and Jacobs 1991). Even recent, influential studies of bereavement document the occurrence of complications and then, paradoxically, avoid the implications for clinical practice (Bornstein et al. 1973; Parkes and

Weiss 1983). This curious omission is made on the assumption that the complications are self-limited or stems from a concern about the stigmatization that occurs if a psychiatric diagnosis is made. The net result is an unsettled field of inquiry, confusion about how to define the complications to set them apart from normal grief, and uncertainty about the need for and methods of treatment.

Purpose of This Book

The main purpose of this book is to address the state of ambiguity that exists about the psychiatric complications of bereavement. I have developed in it the idea that such complications are common outcomes that require professional attention. Unrecognized and untreated, these complications become chronic and disabling.

The complications of bereavement include pathologic grief, depressions, anxiety disorders, and sometimes posttraumatic stress disorders. Although, when compared with psychotic disorders, these disorders are less severe and chronically disabling, they are among the more common disorders seen in outpatient psychiatric practice (Lazare 1979) and on psychiatric consultation services (DeVaul et al. 1979). They are sufficiently disabling to interfere with family roles and effective functioning. They limit the formation of meaningful new friendships. They undermine work performance through compromised motivation, and they destroy the survivor's opportunities to enjoy leisure time. More than 800,000 men and women in the United States suffer the loss of their spouse every year (Osterweis et al. 1984) (this figure does not include the bereaved parents and children of those spouses). As many as one-fifth of the bereaved spouses are at risk for bereavement's complications (see Chapter 3). To ignore the importance of these disorders to those afflicted with them or to neglect their occurrence in clinical practice is shutting our eyes to a significant problem.

In developing a clinical perspective on bereavement, it is reasonable to weigh the risk of disability from the complications of bereavement against the risks of stigmatization incurred when an individual is identified as having a psychiatric problem and needing the help of a mental health professional. In my experience, this is an issue that arises immediately in any discussion of the clinical complications of bereavement, not only among laypersons, where the debate is usually fervent, but also among professionals. I believe the benefits of treatment outweigh the risk of stigmatization, and I hope this book satisfies the reader that this conclusion is justified.

With our current treatments, which are limited in specificity and effectiveness (see Chapters 12, 13, and 14), there is a need not only to search for new and more effective means of helping but also to construct multidimensional approaches to patient care that are consistent with the complex nature of the problems of bereaved individuals with complications (see Chapter 11). Complex models of treatment include self-help, mutual support groups. Although self-help efforts avoid the stigmatization associated with psychiatric treatment, they are not powerful enough when applied without professional intervention to prevent the disability associated with clinical complications (see Chapters 11 and 14). The role of the mental health professional as advisor and consultant to mutual support groups needs to be clearly conceptualized to avoid conflict with self-help efforts, foster collaboration, and justify the risk of stigmatization (see Chapter 14).

Using data from five studies of bereavement in adult life completed over 11 years, my colleagues and I have published several papers that have addressed specific aspects of the experience of losing a marital partner. In contrast to the analytic and compartmentalized approach taken in these papers, in this book I synthesize the multiple perspectives on bereavement provided by these studies (mainly Chapters 2 through 9). In addition, our observations are placed in the context of other modern studies on the nature of bereavement. Although our studies focused primarily on bereavement in middle-aged and older adults, the observations from them apply to young adults and children as well.

In addition to the clinical and epidemiological studies in which I have participated, I have also served as a psychiatric consultant for patients with clinical complications of bereavement. This book provides an opportunity to review and integrate these less systematic clinical experiences. The discussion of treatment is placed in the framework of other published reports on treating the complications of bereavement and the general treatment literature. Thus several issues that arise in treatment are discussed in Chapters 10 through 15. Insofar as this subspecialized clinical experience is a relatively unique one that other colleagues have not obtained, I hope that this part of the book is useful to clinicians and ultimately the patients who consult them during bereavement.

This book is directed to mental health specialists. A secondary audience is primary care physicians who have an interest in loss and bereavement and who are familiar enough with psychiatric terminology and practice to follow the discussion. Primary care physicians may see many if not most of bereaved patients. It has been well documented that acutely bereaved individuals use medical services more often than their nonbereaved counterparts as a reflection of their reduced sense of well-being and the multiple ailments that acute grief comprises (Jacobs and Ostfeld 1978; Klerman and Izen 1977). A substantial minority of these patients have syndromes reflecting complications of bereavement that require interventions that go beyond nonspecific symptomatic treatment and support. If this book contributes to better recognition and treatment of these complications by both family practitioners and mental health professionals, it will have fulfilled an ambitious goal.

Adaptation: A Loosely Developed Model

In this book I focus on pathologic grief, depressions, anxiety disorders, and, to a lesser extent, posttraumatic stress disorders and substance abuse that occur after a loss. These problems are conceptualized as disorders of adaptation or maladaptations. The best argument for the use of an adaptive model is provided by considering the role of trauma in shaping the emotional response to a traumatic loss. (Trauma and the elements of an adaptive model are taken up in more detail in Chapter 5.)

Although it is not my primary purpose to develop a complete, comprehensive model for viewing the complications of bereavement, I do believe it is useful to identify clearly a theoretical framework within which to study these complications. A model serves to identify and characterize the elements of the problems involved in understanding the complications of bereavement. Using an adaptive model is well within the medical tradition of thinking about disease. This model is most frequently encountered in attempts to understand illness from a public health (Dubos 1965) or psychiatric (Hartman 1958; Menninger 1963; Vaillant 1977) perspective. The conceptualization of the complications of bereavement in this book draws on both traditions. Adaptation is a paradigm that emphasizes the relationship between the environment and the individual who lives in it. It is primarily these features of an adaptive model that recommend it for use in thinking about the clinical complications of bereavement.

The choice of an adaptive model also has two major implications for treatment, which are developed throughout this book. One is the need to address during evaluation not only the symptoms and functional disturbance of patients with clinical complications of bereavement but also the nature and circumstances of the loss. This theme is introduced in Chapter 5 and is further discussed in Chapters 9 and 11. Another ramification of an adaptive model is the need for skillful, multidimensional, integrated treatment. In Chapter 11, I introduce the value of integrated treatment. Then, the main modalities of treatment are reviewed in Chapters 12 through 14. In Chapter 16, the conclusion, I return to this idea by emphasizing the need for well-trained, experienced clinicians capable of providing multiple modalities of treatment for the clinical complications of bereavement.

Organization of This Book

In each of the chapters, I address a major question about bereavement as a stressful experience and the stress-related disorders that can result from it. Chapter 2 is an examination of the concept of pathologic grief. Contemporary efforts to develop diagnostic criteria for pathologic grief are introduced here and then discussed in more detail in Chapter 9. In Chapter 3, I discuss the rates of complications for the purpose of establishing that a substantial minority of acutely bereaved individuals are at risk for pathologic grief, major depressions, or anxiety disorders. Alcohol and substance abuse are also considered in this chapter, although the evidence for their place in the spectrum of clinical complications of bereavement is far from definitive. In Chapter 4, I consider the relationship among pathologic grief, major depressions, and anxiety disorders of bereavement by examining the overlap in their occurrence, the epidemiological similarities among them, and their biological resemblances.

In Chapter 5, I develop the concept of an adaptive model for the purpose of understanding the origin and nature of pathologic grief. Traumatic losses are used to illustrate that characteristics of some losses, which are considered the environmental vectors of clinical complications, are important determinants of the nature of grief and its potential complications. In Chapter 5, I also set the stage for the next two chapters on social networks and coping. Important aspects of the social environment, which is changed by the loss and to which the bereaved individual must adjust, are introduced in Chapter 6. Both conscious and unconscious coping, or efforts of the bereaved individual to adapt to the altered environment, are the topic of Chapter 7. To round out an overview that includes both environmental and personal risk factors, in Chapter 8, I provide a review of personal characteristics that may make a bereaved individual susceptible to developing clinical complications. Biological aspects of bereavement are also reviewed in Chapter 8. In Chapter 9, the differential diagnosis of the complications of bereavement is discussed.

With Chapter 10, the book switches gears to begin to consider treatment. In this chapter, I review a framework for thinking about treatment by reviewing current hypotheses about pathogenetic mechanisms. Furthermore, in Chapter 10 I consider a number of systematic or controlled studies of treatment interventions during bereavement. We will find that the scientific basis for treatment of the complications of bereavement is still limited; therefore, the nature of the discussion changes at this point in the book. In subsequent chapters, the presentation relies more on clinical experience and anecdotal illustrations than on basic or clinical science or randomized controlled trials.

The goals of treatment and the integration of multiple treatment modalities are addressed in Chapter 11, in which I emphasize the value of integrated treatment and discuss the separate modalities of intervention. Chapter 12 is a review of the psychopharmacological treatment of the clinical complications of bereavement. Chapter 13 is devoted to a discussion of issues in the psychotherapy of bereaved patients.

Both psychopharmacological and psychotherapeutic modalities of treatment ought to be integrated into rehabilitative and self-help efforts. Therefore, in Chapter 14, mutual support interventions and the role of the professional in self-help organizations are examined. Mutual support interventions have been developed out of the crucible of preventive psychiatry, for which bereavement and its clinical complications have served as an important model over the years.

To round out the discussion of treatment, a preventive perspective on interventions for bereaved individuals is discussed in Chapter 15. Prevention serves as one type of concept for integrating the various approaches to helping bereaved individuals that supplements the discussion in Chapter 11. In Chapter 16, I conclude with a brief overview and synthesis.

Attachment in a Broader Perspective

As a social animal species, humans bond together and run the risks of separation and loss with their consequent distress that we call *grief*. Contemporary research into the nature of bereavement provides the insight that much of human behavior, such as that reflected in grief when a separation occurs, is motivated by the need to establish social membership, above and beyond the instinctual drives to procreate or protect oneself (Bowlby 1969, 1973, 1980; Parkes 1972). One psychiatrist interested in brain development suggested that the phylogenetic appearance of the neocortex occurred when primates first began to develop an "isolation call" for the purpose of reuniting with the mother when a separation befell a child (Maclean 1982). Thus the incredibly complex patterns of behavior that we understand in primarily psychological and social terms conceivably began to be laid down in the anatomy and physiology of the brain. Therefore, it is appropriate that the neuroanatomy and neurochemistry of attachment behavior is now a topic of tremendous interest to biological and social scientists. A recently edited volume summarizes the efforts of contemporary neuroscientists to understand how the brain is organized to perform these social tasks (Reite and Field 1985). A wide range of other contemporary investigators and clinicians are also actively involved in elucidating the psychosocial aspects of attachment and loss (Parkes 1972; Raphael 1983).

Men and women attach, fall in love, have children, separate and depart, grieve, recover, and reattach. In this book, I concentrate on the separation, loss, and grief, rather than the joys, of attachment. This telescopic view is adopted for the purpose of understanding the curious pain of separations and, indeed, the occasions when losses lead to serious psychiatric complications calling for professional intervention. This focus is not intended to undervalue the gratification of attachment nor to suggest that separation and loss are exclusively painful and destructive. On the contrary, bereavement is usually a natural and normal experience of life that, although a cause of heartache and familial disruption, heals spontaneously and often leads to personal growth and sometimes creativity (Calhoun and Tedeschi 1989–1990; Pollock 1978).

References

American Psychiatric Association: Diagnostic and Statistical Manual of Mental Disorders, 3rd Edition, Revised. Washington, DC, American Psychiatric Association, 1987

Bornstein PE, Clayton PJ, Halikas JA, et al: The depression of widowhood after thirteen months. Br J Psychiatry 122:561–566, 1973

Bowlby J: Attachment and Loss, Vol 1: Attachment. New York, Basic Books, 1969

Bowlby J: Attachment and Loss, Vol 2: Separation. New York, Basic Books, 1973

Bowlby J: Attachment and Loss, Vol 3: Loss, Sadness, and Depression. New York, Basic Books, 1980

Calhoun LG, Tedeschi RG: Positive aspects of life's problems: recollections of grief. Omega 20:265–272, 1989–1990

DeVaul RA, Zisook S, Faschingbauer TR: Clinical aspects of grief and bereavement. Prim Care 6:391–402, 1979

Dubos R: Man Adapting. New Haven, CT, Yale University Press, 1965

Freud S: Mourning and melancholia (1917), in The Standard Edition of the Complete Psychological Works of Sigmund Freud, Vol 14. Translated and edited by Strachey J. London, Hogarth Press, 1953, pp 243–258

Hartman H: Ego Psychology and the Problem of Adaptation. New York, International Universities Press, 1958

Jacobs SC, Ostfeld AM: The effect of illness and death of one family member on other family members. National Institute on Aging Document, Bethesda, MD, September 14, 1978

Kim K, Jacobs SC: Pathologic grief and its relationship to other psychiatric disorders. J Affect Disord 21:257–263, 1991

Klerman GL, Izen JE: The effects of bereavement and grief on physical health and general well being. Adv Psychosom Med 9:63–88, 1977

Lazare A: Unresolved grief, in Outpatient Psychiatry: Diagnosis and Treatment. Edited by Lazare A. Baltimore, Williams & Wilkins, 1979, pp 498–512

Lindeman E: Symptomatology and management of acute grief. Am J Psychiatry 101:141–148, 1944

Maclean PD: Evolutionary brain roots of family, play, and the isolation call: the Adolf Meyer Lecture. Presented at the Annual Meeting of the American Psychiatric Association, Toronto, Canada, May 18, 1982

Menninger K: The Vital Balance. New York, Viking Press, 1963

Osterweis M, Solomon F, Green M (eds): Bereavement: Reactions, Consequences and Care. Washington, DC, National Academy Press, 1984

Parkes CM: Bereavement: Studies of Grief in Adult Life. New York, International Universities Press, 1972

Parkes CM, Weiss RS: Recovery From Bereavement. New York, Basic Books, 1983
Pollock GH: Process and affect: mourning and grief. Int J Psychoanal 59:255–276, 1978
Raphael B: The Anatomy of Bereavement. New York, Basic Books, 1983
Reite M, Field T (eds): The Psychobiology of Attachment and Separation. New York, Academic Press, 1985
Vaillant GE: Adaptation to Life. Boston, MA, Little, Brown, 1977

CHAPTER 2

Pathologic Grief

Two basic questions are addressed in this chapter: What is the nature of pathologic grief? and How do we define it? The chapter begins with a discussion of normal grief to set the stage for understanding the concept of pathologic grief. The historical development of the concept of pathologic grief is also briefly reviewed. Next, a contemporary set of diagnostic criteria developed by Raphael (1989) for the purpose of defining pathologic grief is introduced. Finally, the conclusion is a general discussion of the nature of the clinical complications of bereavement.

Normal Grief

To understand pathologic variants of grief, it is essential to begin with a knowledge of normal grief. This is necessary because the syndromes of pathologic grief, with one exception, do not differ qualitatively from those of normal grief. Rather, the syndromes of pathologic grief are basically dysfunctional departures from a tolerable intensity of separation distress or deviations in the duration of such distress. In this sense, syndromes of pathologic grief are functional disorders in which normal attachment behavior and physiology, which are evoked by a loss, become aberrant. The one exception is the syndrome of absent grief in which separation distress is not present in someone who has suffered a meaningful loss. The rationale for including absent grief among the subtypes of pathologic grief is the most complicated of all, depending on cross-cultural studies, ethological studies, and an evolutionary argument. It is developed in more detail below.

Over the past 20 years, renewed attention has been given to the biological substrate of grief; this attention, perhaps, stems from the modern view that attachment behavior is a manifestation of the fundamental motivational system in the brain. Though we still have only sketchy knowledge in this area, the information from studies of primates and other social animals suggests that the prefrontal cortex, the amygdala, and the limbic system, as well as estrogen, oxytocin, and peptidergic transmitter systems are involved in attachment behavior (Reite and Field 1985). Also attempts to conceptualize the pathophysiology of major depressions and anxiety disorders may be directly applicable to efforts to understand bereavement (Ehlers et al. 1988; Gold et al. 1988a, 1988b; Klein 1980; see Chapter 10).

Despite these advances, we currently understand normal grief in humans in primarily psychological terms. The manifestations of grief are manifold and include emotional numbness, disbelief, intrusive images of death, yearning for the lost individual, preoccupations with the deceased, sighing, crying, dreams, illusions and hallucinations of the deceased individual, seeking out of places and things associated with the deceased individual, anger, protest over one's fate, sadness, anxiety, despair, insomnia, anorexia, fatigue, lethargy, guilt, loss of interest in usual activities, and disorganization of behavior patterns that used to involve the deceased individual (Table 2–1). This long itemization calls for some organizing principle to facilitate our understanding of these manifestations. Currently, in my judgment, attachment theory provides the most useful theoretical model for organizing this multiplicity of symptoms.

Separation Distress

Insofar as it is only observed in the circumstances of a separation or loss, separation anxiety is the type of emotional distress that appears to be most specifically related to loss. In the psychiatric literature, *separation anxiety* has been used to denote not only the normal separation distress of a child separated from his or her mother during the developmental phase of separation-individuation, but also a type of disorder in children. Bowlby and Parkes have also used this term to characterize one dimension of the psychological distress caused by child and adult bereavement (Bowlby 1973, 1980; Bowlby and Parkes 1970; Parkes 1972). It is this meaning that is intended in the present discussion. (It is worth noting that there are good reasons to suspect that these various manifestations of separation anxiety are related; however, this is an unresolved empirical and theoretical question.) Raphael (1983) introduced the term *separation pain or distress* to denote the same phenomena of adult bereavement described by Parkes and Bowlby. To avoid confusion in the meaning of the term *separation anxiety*, I will adopt the term *separation distress* for subsequent discussion.

According to the definition offered by Parkes and Bowlby, the *separation distress* of adult bereavement includes yearning for the lost individual; preoccupations focused on the deceased; crying; sighing; a perceptual set for

Table 2–1. Manifestations and symptoms of grief

Dimensions	Symptom groups	Manifestations and symptoms
Separation distress (anxiety)	Pangs	Yearning
		Preoccupations
		Sighing
		Crying
	Searching	Illusions
		Dreams
		Hallucinations
		Searching
	Protest	Anger
		Protest
	Anxious mood	Anxiety/arousal
		Panic
Mourning process	Depressive mood	Sadness
		Nostalgia
		Despair
	Neurovegetative symptoms	Insomnia
		Anorexia
		Fatigue
		Lethargy
		Loss of interests
	Nonspecific	Somatic symptoms
		Aimless behavior
Traumatic distress	Avoidance	Numbness
		Disbelief
	Intrusion	Horrific images
		Nightmares
Recovery		Coping behavior

the lost individual, including dreams, tactile or visual illusions, and frank hallucinations in some cases; and searching for the individual who is lost, such as seeking out places and things identified with the deceased (Table 2–1). Typically, the yearning and preoccupations coincide with a particular distressing emotional state. This state of mind is intrusive, episodic, and limited to brief periods of 20–30 minutes. This is the *pang of grief* described by Lindeman (1944). It may occur and subside spontaneously, particularly in the early stages of grief when separation distress is most intense, or it may be brought on by reminders of the individual who has died or as the bereaved individual searches unwittingly for what is lost.

Building on Lindeman's description of the pang of grief, Bowlby and Parkes recognized the searching component to separation distress, thus providing a more complete understanding of bereavement. Presumably, searching is a function of a primitive motivational system that has evolved in humans and other animals for the purpose of reestablishing intimate bonds that are broken. The evolutionary advantage of this searching function is most readily appreciated when the threat to the survival of an infant or child separated from the parents is considered. The need to search for the lost individual is typically expressed in unconscious, nonverbal behavior. Searching ordinarily culminates in acute separation distress when the search is fruitless and frustrating, as in the circumstances of a death. Ultimately, a repeatedly fruitless search is abandoned, the irrevocability of a loss is accepted emotionally and cognitively, and the emotional distress subsides. The bereaved individual begins to remember the dead individual in new and different ways, adjusts to a new status and changed roles, and slowly recovers. This part of grief is denoted as a mourning process during which the bond to the deceased individual is relinquished as the bereaved individual repeatedly reviews the lost relationship with sad, nostalgic, sometimes angry, sometimes guilty feelings (Freud 1917; Raphael 1983). The mourning stage has many depressive features, including sorrowful mood, dysphoria, despair, and neurovegetative symptoms.

Other Dimensions of Psychological Distress in Grief

Attachment theory recognizes multiple dimensions of psychological distress that are related to each other and yet evolved independently over time (Jacobs et al. 1987; Shuchter 1986) (Table 2–1; Figure 2–1). For example, separation distress is a dimension of psychological distress that appears to be specific to loss. It typically occurs early in grief and includes the pangs of grief and searching behavior. In addition, there may be a traumatic dimension of distress involving intrusive and avoidant components. For example, the initial emotional numbness that typically occurs after a sudden loss may well reflect the avoidance associated with traumatic distress; in this case, the distress would be caused by the loss, which resulted in injury to the individual's sense of well-being and assumptions about living in a safe, predictable world. Also there is a mourning-depressive dimension of psychological distress that typically reaches peak intensity later than separation distress. Perhaps the most important dimension, which is also the least well understood, is the recovery process in which the intensity of psychological distress subsides and the bereaved individual, often alone as a survivor, copes with the cognitive and behavioral tasks of adjusting to the status of being no longer a parent or spouse.

These dimensions of distress are represented in Figure 2–1, which portrays an idealized version of how they evolve over time. Implicit in this

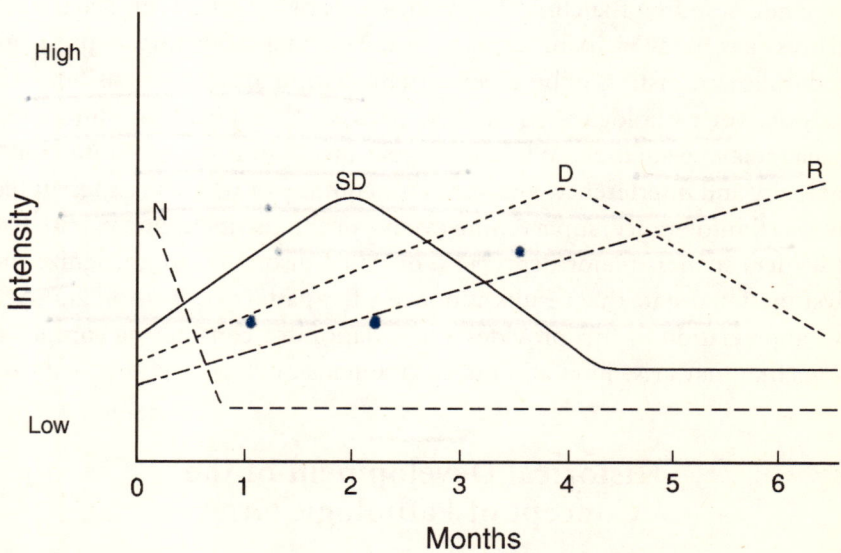

Figure 2–1. Diagram of the dimensions of grief. N = numbness, disbelief; SD = separation distress; D = depression, mourning; R = recovery.

representation is the idea that elements of each dimension of distress can be seen at many points in time. Still, in particular periods, one type of distress predominates. In this sense, it is meaningful to think about phases of grief, a commonly advocated perspective. For instance, the earliest phase of response is typically dominated by emotional numbing and disbelief, particularly in the circumstances of a sudden, unexpected loss. Separation distress dominates the next phase of grief, and mourning-depressive phenomena the following phase. When reference is made to the normal progression of grief—for instance, in the criteria for pathologic grief that are discussed below—it is this phasic evolution that is meant. Although it is sometimes instructive to conceptualize the manifestations of grief in this manner, it is important to emphasize that the idea that grief unfolds inexorably in regular phases is an oversimplification of the highly complex, personal waxing and waning of the emotional process. For this reason, it is more realistic and accurate to adopt a concept of multiple dimensions of distress that evolve independently. On the other hand, a cornerstone of the concept of recovery is the idea that grief progresses through phases to recovery and thus, in this broader sense, is a process, not a state.

Finally, a knowledge of grief in dimensional terms creates a foundation for understanding the clinical complications of bereavement. Separation distress has many vicissitudes, as does the normal mourning, depression, and traumatic distress of bereavement. In relation to each dimension, maladaptive (or pathologic) syndromes can occur that must be monitored in a diagnostic evaluation. When grief goes awry because of its intolerable intensity and interference with social functioning or when it is interrupted by social intolerance, supervening events, or illness (including psychiatric disorders such as major depression or panic disorder), we recognize the dysfunctional state that results as one of a few patterns of pathologic grief. An appreciation of this provides a foundation for considering complications that may arise in relation to each dimension.

Historical Development of the Concept of Pathologic Grief

No empirical studies of criteria for the diagnosis of pathologic grief have been completed, and no definitive consensus criteria have been developed by clinicians yet. Nevertheless, the idea that there are maladaptive consequences of bereavement for some vulnerable individuals is a time-honored concept that can be traced over the last 4 centuries (Jackson 1986). A historical perspective reveals that a distinction is repeatedly drawn between normal human sorrow and depressive illness. An additional historical theme that emerges is that bereavement can cause morbid depressions.

Early 20th Century—Freud and Deutsch

Freud. In the 20th century, Freud first contributed to the concept of pathologic grief with his formulation of the distinction between mourning and melancholia (Freud 1917). For him, the distinguishing features of *mourning* were painful dejection, cessation of interest in the outside world, loss of the capacity to love, and inhibition of activity. In his view, *melancholia* was distinguished from mourning by a disturbance of self-esteem that occurred after a loss when several psychological factors converge. When the relationship to the deceased individual was narcissistic and ambivalent, when attributes of the lost individual were psychologically introjected, and when anger at the deceased for abandoning the survivor was turned against the self, the bereaved individual became depressed.

This psychodynamic mechanism is the underlying process of *pathologic mourning*, according to Freud, who was the first to use this term. Based on this mechanism, Freud introduced the idea that the nature of the relationship with another individual is a crucial determinant of the survivor's adjustment to a loss. A developmentally immature attachment places the survivor at risk for melancholia. Latent in this concept is the idea that grief is one form of attachment behavior and, for some, it may be a disturbance of homeostasis evoked by the loss of another individual. Subsequently, Freud's concept became a recurrent theme as other aspects of the personal relationship to the deceased individual became implicated as risk factors for pathologic grief by Bowlby, Parkes, and Horowitz (see below).

Deutsch. Deutsch (1937) was the first to suggest that absent grief was a variant of pathologic grief. She presented four cases of pathologic grief in which the typical response to a loss was absent. Instead, the expression of grief was given some other form such as neurotic symptoms or narcissistic, schizoid character traits. Her conclusions were based on psychoanalytic theory and psychodynamic formulations; since her findings, other perspectives have supported her conclusion. Cross-cultural studies, although methodologically limited, have documented that, with only rare exceptions, grief is universal after meaningful losses. Furthermore, experience establishes that the apparent absence of grief will give way to active expression of separation distress in an environment, often psychotherapeutic, that supports and encourages it. Finally, ethological studies of other species of social animals have demonstrated that the human response to a loss is not unique in the animal kingdom. In fact, there is a close resemblance among reactions to loss across several species of social animals. This finding suggests that grief, as we know it in humans, is a basic biological and organismic response to a loss. If this is true, it is reasonable to ask if it serves a basic, biological purpose and confers evolutionary advantage. This argument has been put forward as an explanation of its pervasive presence among higher, social animal species. In this context, the absence of grief requires an explanation.

Mid 20th Century—Lindeman, Adler, Bowlby, and Parkes

Lindeman. Writing in 1944 about those who were caught in the Coconut Grove fire seen in emergency treatment at the Massachusetts General Hospital, Lindeman provided the first detailed description of the manifestations of grief (Lindeman 1944). His portrayal included symptoms of somatic distress, preoccupation with the image of the deceased, guilt, hostile reactions, and loss of patterns of conduct. Included in his thinking was the concept of the pang of grief, by which he meant the episodic, intrusive, intense, time-limited distress over the loss. Sometimes it is precipitated by unexpected reminders, and at other times it occurs spontaneously.

Lindeman introduced a typology of morbid grief reactions that broadened the scope of pathologic patterns of grief beyond depressive symptoms and absent grief. In addition to delayed grief, which Lindeman proposed as one main variation of morbid grief, he itemized nine clinical presentations of distorted grief, the other main variation of morbid grief in his typology. These were 1) overactivity without a sense of loss (i.e., absent grief), 2) the acquisition of symptoms belonging to the last illness of the deceased, 3) a recognized medical illness, 4) alterations in relationships to friends and relatives, 5) furious hostility against specific individuals, 6) schizophreniform symptoms ("wooden and formal" affectivity and conduct) reflecting an internal struggle with hostility, 7) a lasting loss of patterns of social interaction, 8) self-destructive social and economic behavior, and 9) agitated depression. According to Lindeman, without therapeutic intervention distorted grief becomes unresolved, prolonged grief.

Adler. At about the same time, Adler (1943) reported on her clinical observations of those who lived through the Coconut Grove fire seen for emergency care at Boston City Hospital. She was the first to relate the neuropsychiatric complications of the disaster not only to the losses but also, more importantly in her view, to the trauma. She characterized the complications of bereavement as anxiety neuroses or "general nervousness," including symptomatology similar to posttraumatic mental disorders. With the exception of Anderson (1949) in England, who also emphasized the symptoms of anxiety as part of pathologic grief, these ideas were largely ignored in thinking about the complications of bereavement until Horowitz reintroduced them in the 1970s. Adler's ideas served as a temporarily neglected counterpoint to Lindeman's description of the survivors of the Coconut Grove fire and illustrated how two perspectives of the same event can develop independently (Rynearson 1987). The relationship between these two views and their integration for the purpose of understanding traumatic losses is a topic of current interest.

Bowlby and Parkes. In the late 1950s and early 1960s, Bowlby and Parkes offered the next major insights into the nature of grief and its pathologic variants (Bowlby 1969; Parkes 1959). Parkes, working independently, discovered Darwin's treatise *The Expression of the Emotions in Man and Animals* (1872) and brought it to the attention of Bowlby, who was a student of Darwin. They were both interested in Darwin's description of loss reactions in animals because they felt it was relevant to understanding human grief. Both Parkes and Bowlby concluded that searching behavior was an integral part of the human response to a loss, as it was in other animal species. Acutely bereaved individuals seek out places and possessions of the deceased individual and maintain a perceptual set for that individual, reflected in illusory experiences and dreams as if they are searching for the deceased individual for the purpose of reuniting. Bowlby and Parkes defined the psychological distress of bereavement in terms of separation anxiety, which included both the pangs of grief and searching behavior. They were the first to reason that separation anxiety was a basic human response to a loss, independent of sexual and self-protective drives, and that it served evolutionary goals by promoting survival in social animals.

Early in his work, Bowlby considered four variants of pathologic grief within a psychodynamic framework. These were described in terms of the following psychodynamic mechanisms:

- Repressed yearning for the lost individual
- Self-reproach as an aspect of a desire to recover the lost individual
- Care of vicarious figures onto whom yearning and anger at the lost individual are projected
- Denial that the object is permanently lost

These psychodynamic mechanisms are associated with multiple clinical syndromes, including depressions (Bowlby 1963). Bowlby subsequently revised his thinking to include two main variants of disordered mourning: 1) chronic mourning, including severe and prolonged emotional response, and 2) a picture of persistent anger and self-reproach associated with depression in the prolonged absence of conscious sorrow—in other words, absent grief (Bowlby 1980).

Late 20th Century—Bowlby, Parkes, Horowitz, and Clayton

Bowlby. Bowlby's later formulation of the nature of pathologic grief is based in cognitive theory (Bowlby 1980). According to this view, cognitive biases about attachment figures, among other predisposing personality traits (e.g., the disposition to form anxious attachments) or childhood experiences (e.g., partial or intermittent rejection by parents), cause chronic or absent grief. The cognitive biases are reflections of internal representational models of attachment figures both from childhood experiences with parents and from adult experiences with spouses. They consist of ideas such as the conviction that attachment figures are above criticism and the self is less worthy. Connected with these biases are additional notions that attachment figures are grudging in their affection and the self is justified in demanding attention. A death in the family activates attachment behavior in the survivor that can be maladaptive and recognized as pathologic grief. A poor outcome occurs if the pathogenetic cognitive biases are not counterbalanced by other positive factors that influence outcome. In a sense, the relationship to the deceased had held these cognitive biases in check. This latter concept was explicitly developed at about the same time by Horowitz (Horowitz et al. 1980).

Parkes. Parkes offered a different formulation of pathologic grief that was more firmly anchored in his own direct observational studies. He classified untoward bereavement reactions into three categories:

- *Inhibited grief:* by which he meant that the reaction to a loss was absent or minimal in the nature of a forme fruste of grief
- *Delayed grief:* in which there was an inhibited response followed by a typical or prolonged reaction
- *Chronic grief:* characterized not only by prolongation but also by intense and exaggerated separation distress (Parkes 1965)

This typology seems familiar because of its relationship to concepts introduced previously by others. It became the cornerstone of contemporary attempts to develop descriptive criteria for diagnosis of pathologic grief.

Subsequently, Parkes and Weiss (1983) developed yet another typology that introduced both characteristics of the death and characteristics of the relationship to the deceased individual as part of the description of the clinical syndrome. This typology preserved a recognizable relationship to the variants of pathologic grief that Parkes earlier described and included the following:

- *Unanticipated grief:* such as is found in the circumstances of acute illness and death, characterized by denial of the loss and feelings of self-reproach and despair
- *Conflicted grief:* a syndrome that resembles delayed or absent grief and occurs when the relationship was ambivalent
- *Chronic grief:* characterized by prolonged, severe yearning, such as is found when the relationship was dependent as a result of long-term, antecedent insecurity about interpersonal relationships of the bereaved individual

Horowitz. In the 1970s, Horowitz wrote about the complications of bereavement from a cognitive perspective that incorporated traumatic distress as a main component of the emotional response (Horowitz 1976). In so doing, he integrated the idea of emotional trauma with the knowledge of separation distress. Coincident with Faschingbauer and colleagues, who developed the Texas Inventory of Grief (Faschingbauer et al. 1977), Horowitz was one of the first to operationalize his concept into an assessment form—the Impact of Event Scale (Horowitz et al. 1979). Although he usefully emphasized the important theme of trauma in many types of losses, Horowitz tended to confound trauma with loss. He seemed to assume that all losses are traumatic, which is, perhaps, a theoretical and clinical bias that stems from his use of treated samples. More recent studies suggest that traumatic distress and separation anxiety are independent but linked dimensions of the psychological distress caused by traumatic losses. Accordingly, they have different natural histories and treatment needs (Nader et al. 1990; Pynoos et al. 1987a, 1987b; Raphael 1983). This is an issue of great current interest that needs to be addressed by systematic study.

Horowitz made another contribution to knowledge about pathologic grief with his characterization of the nature of relationships that predispose an individual to maladaptive behavior when a loss occurs (Horowitz et al. 1980). He saw pathologic grief as the intensification or unusual prolongation of ego states found in normal grief. These maladaptive ego states are caused by the reemergence of self-images and role-relationship models that were held in check by the relationship to the deceased individual. These ego states are the product of preexisting mental schemata in the cognitive functioning of the survivor. The ego states are of two main types: 1) frighteningly sad ego states and 2) enraged and deflated ego states. Implicit in Horowitz's formulation is the idea that certain types of character structure with borderline and narcissistic traits underlie these sad, raging, and deflated ego states caused by a loss. Ordinarily, the maladaptive self-images and role relationships are played out in the clinical relationship.

Clayton. Approximately coincident with the work of Horowitz, Clayton began to publish the results of her studies on the risk of major depressions during acute bereavement in widows and widowers (Bornstein et al. 1973; Clayton 1990). She reprised the theme introduced by Freud about the emergence of depressions during bereavement. She and her colleagues systematically observed the symptoms of depression using structured assessments in carefully conducted studies. From her study, Clayton documented that 45% of acutely bereaved spouses will develop depressive syndromes sometime during the first year of bereavement (Bornstein et al. 1973). Most of these depressions are transient and subside spontaneously. However, this was not true for 17% of her sample, who essentially remained depressed throughout the whole first year of bereavement.

Clayton also traced the evolution of the symptoms over the first year into a clinical picture that appears more similar to melancholic depressions (Clayton and Darvish 1979). In this work, Clayton reemphasized a theme about depression in pathologic grief that had lain dormant for many years. She quantified the importance of unremitting, major depressions as a complication of bereavement and reactivated the question about the relationship between normal mourning and depressive illness.

Recent studies. In a similar vein, resuming the theme introduced by Adler that the complications of bereavement are characterized by symptoms of anxiety and anxiety neuroses, recent studies have begun to document the risk of anxiety disorders during acute bereavement (Jacobs 1987; Jacobs et al. 1990; Zisook et al. 1990). These anxiety syndromes include panic disorder and generalized anxiety disorder. Both of these disorders have some relationship to major depressions during acute bereavement, particularly generalized anxiety disorder, yet both also occur independently, particularly panic disorder (Jacobs et al. 1990). A similar pattern exists for the relationship of these two anxiety disorders to pathologic grief (Kim and Jacobs 1991). The question that remains to be resolved empirically is how this additional perspective on the complications of grief can be integrated into the earlier observations on depression, pathologic grief, and posttraumatic distress, and how, indeed, all these perspectives might be integrated into an overarching concept of pathologic grief.

These recent studies round out modern attempts to study the nature of the complications of bereavement and to define pathologic grief as an entity. This historical review indicates that pathologic grief is best understood in relationship to normal grief and serves to introduce concepts and criteria that define the nature of pathologic grief.

Through the review (see Table 2–2), we come across descriptions of pathologic grief characterized by

1. *Delayed or absent grief:* The absence of conscious or observable separation distress
2. *Severe grief:* Separation distress, anxious symptoms, or depressive symptoms of unusual severity
3. *Chronic grief:* Prolonged duration of grief usually associated with delayed or severe grief as early harbingers of difficulty
4. *Distorted grief:* Inhibited patterns of grief involving the absence of a typical response and associated with one or more of several phenomena, including a) somatic symptoms, b) identification symptoms, c) overt hostility, d) affective blunting related to underlying hostility, e) self-reproach, and f) self-destructive, overactive, socially withdrawn, or vicarious caregiving behavior

In addition, we find reports of traumatic distress with intrusive and avoidant components as well as posttraumatic syndromes when the loss is traumatic. Finally, we encounter observations on depressive syndromes and anxiety syndromes.

The development of diagnostic criteria for pathologic grief must try to incorporate these observations. In a crude theoretical framework, the maladaptive vicissitudes of separation distress and anxious symptoms can be viewed in relationship to normal separation distress; the depressive symp-

Table 2–2. Summary of the historical development of the concept of pathologic grief

---

I. Absence of separation distress (delayed or absent grief)
II. Severe separation distress, anxiety, and depressive symptoms
III. Prolonged separation distress (chronic grief, associated with absence of separation distress and with severe separation distress, anxiety, and depressive symptoms)
IV. Inhibited (distorted) grief
    a. Somatic symptoms
    b. Identification symptoms
    c. Overt hostility
    d. Affective blunting (underlying anger)
    e. Self-reproach
    f. Behaviors: self-destructive, hyperactive, social withdrawal, and vicarious caregiving
V. Traumatic distress and posttraumatic stress syndromes
VI. Depressive syndromes
VII. Anxiety syndromes

toms in relationship to the mourning process; absent or inhibited syndromes in relationship to the initial, mild dissociative manifestations of numbness and disbelief; and posttraumatic symptomatology in relationship to traumatic distress.

Diagnostic Criteria for Pathologic Grief: An Introduction

A recent development in the understanding of pathologic grief is the contemporary effort by Raphael to establish consensus criteria for its diagnosis (Raphael 1989). The criteria are introduced here for the purpose of providing a concrete example of the meaning of pathologic grief and the nature of this disorder. The criteria are presented in more detail and discussed in Chapter 9 when the differential diagnosis of the clinical complications of bereavement is considered.

Stemming from the nosology proposed by Parkes (see above), the consensus criteria include three variants of pathologic grief:

1. Delayed or absent grief
2. Inhibited grief
3. Chronic grief

The variants of the disorder have a sketchily charted relationship to each other. The criteria for diagnosis are based on unusually severe or prolonged manifestations of grief, or, on the other hand, inhibited manifestations of normal grief. They incorporate symptoms of separation distress, depression, and autonomic arousal. The criteria also assume a normal progression of grief over time; that is, no unusual delay or extension of grief and a typical sequence of emotional numbness, separation distress, mourning-depressive symptoms, and recovery.

In *delayed grief*, the typical manifestations of separation—the pangs of grief and searching phenomena—and the progressive emotional evolution of grief are delayed for more than 2 weeks after a loss. If the absence of grief becomes prolonged, it is recognized as absent grief. The diagnosis of *inhibited grief* refers to attenuation of the typical manifestations of grief in circumstances where one would expect it and provides for the various symptomatic and behavioral manifestations of distorted grief noted above. Delayed and inhibited grief both have the potential to become chronic disturbances. In *chronic grief*, the typical manifestations of separation anxiety are intense and do not diminish throughout the first year of bereavement and beyond. The grief does not progress normally. In addition, anger over the loss, guilt involving the deceased individual, and depressive symptoms are prominent in chronic grief. These consensus criteria define three variants of a disorder that first appear in the early stages of bereavement and have the potential for becoming chronic.

Based on a review of the consensus criteria, it appears that the manifestations of separation distress are the heart of grief and the core phenomena for diagnosing pathologic grief; this idea is not new. Indeed, many clinicians have had the same impression as did Parkes, who once noted in commenting on his clinical experience that "intense separation anxiety and strong but only partially successful attempts to avoid grieving were evident in all the forms of atypical grief" (Parkes 1972, p. 112). This statement not only tells us something about the nature of pathologic grief, it also implies that it may be possible to simplify the criteria for its diagnosis by focusing on the manifestations of separation distress. For example, it is the absence of separation distress that is the central issue in the syndrome of inhibited grief. It is also true that distorted manifestations of grief and major depression can be observed; however, they are secondary, associated phenomena.

To test the clinical impression that the diagnosis of pathologic grief hinges on the manifestations of separation distress, we (Kim and Jacobs 1991) applied a simplified diagnostic system in a study that focused on symptoms of separation distress as diagnostic criteria. Although this was a small study and needs expansion or confirmation, it did highlight several important issues about the nature of pathologic grief. Four variants of pathologic grief were defined: delayed, absent, severe, and prolonged syndromes. In this study, we found one individual who had delayed grief that became severe and prolonged and another person who had absent grief with multiple somatic complaints. The remaining 14 individuals with pathologic grief had prolonged grief. Four of them met criteria for prolonged grief as a single variant of pathologic grief. The remaining 10 of these 14 met criteria for both severe grief and then prolonged grief as the bereavement evolved over time. Usually, prolonged or chronic grief is appreciated at the first or second anniversary of the death. It was not necessary to introduce into the study the idea of "normal progression" of grief, which is predicated on the notion of sequential phases of grief, except with reference to delayed or prolonged grief and the still poorly understood processes that lead to recovery.

Our study also showed that the symptomatic manifestations of distorted grief can be subsumed under the categories of delayed, absent, or chronic grief. The diagnostic category of inhibited grief was not used in the study because of the difficulty in defining it, although there was one case of absent grief in which it was hard to determine retrospectively if separation distress was absent or severely attenuated.

Another finding of this study was that the presence of severe grief (a variant of pathologic grief marked by separation distress that is overwhelming or that interferes with social functioning) could be an early indication that the bereaved individual's grief would become prolonged. All of the 11 individuals with severe grief also met criteria for chronic grief. Coincidentally, all but one of the bereaved individuals with severe grief met criteria for major depression. The observation that severe grief is a variant of pathologic grief is supported by the empirical evidence from research testing the traditional assumption that intense emotional catharsis early in grief leads to good resolution (Parkes and Weiss 1983; Vachon et al. 1982; Zisook and Shuchter 1991). As a caveat, it is important to note that our small study (Kim and Jacobs 1991) was a retrospective study and does not lead to the conclusion that all individuals with severe grief will develop prolonged grief or major depression.

By including severe grief as a syndrome of pathologic grief in our study, we were successful in identifying 16 cases of pathologic grief in our study sample. This was not the whole story of clinical complications, however. Basing the diagnosis of pathologic grief primarily on the manifestations of separation distress did not cover the full range of clinical complications that can occur during acute bereavement (Jacobs et al. 1989, 1990). Although it is true that considerable overlap exists among syndromes of pathologic grief and other psychiatric syndromes, such as major depressions and anxiety disorders, the absence of complete overlap is also notable (Kim and Jacobs 1991). In our small study, 1 out of 5 cases of panic disorder (20%), 4 out of 13 cases of generalized anxiety disorder (31%), and 3 out of 18 cases of major depression (17%) did not meet criteria for any of the variants of pathologic grief. Posttraumatic stress disorder was not included in the study, and its relationship to pathologic grief is uncharted. Therefore, there is a need to provide for the possibility of a range of psychiatric disorders during acute bereavement independent of the diagnosis of pathologic grief. This is true not only because these disorders may occur independently, but also because these psychiatric diagnoses have implications for pharmacological treatments (see Chapters 10–13) that have not been established for pathologic grief. A convention such as "grief complicated by major depression" (or whatever psychopathologic entity is identified, including anxiety disorders and posttraumatic stress disorders) solves this problem.

There was an implicit assumption when we began our clinical study, true in general of clinical practice, that the symptomatic disturbance that delineated pathologic grief was also associated with some impairment in psychosocial functioning. When patients seek treatment, it is ordinarily because their symptomatology is subjectively overwhelming or because it interferes with their family, occupational, and social functioning. A structured assessment of psychosocial functioning was not part of the methodology of this small study, and we could only give consideration to it on an ad hoc basis. In the absence of systematic data, the correlation between symptoms and psychosocial functioning can only be illustrated in the case examples that are used throughout this book. However, it is important for future studies to check the assumption of a close correlation between symptomatology and functioning in clinical practice with bereaved patients and to test it in systematic studies of the pathologic grief syndromes. The degree of functional impairment is a useful dimension for distinguishing between normal grief and the symptomatic disturbance of a clinical complication. The concept of pathologic grief as an adaptive disorder on a continuum with normal grief reinforces the need for this type of judgment about functional impairment. (In Chapter 9, I return to a discussion of functional impairment as a dimension of psychopathology that is useful in differential diagnosis.)

Despite some of the limitations that have been discussed above, the nosology for pathologic grief proposed by Raphael (1989) provides a useful cornerstone for studying this phenomena. This descriptive approach is preferable to the recent nosology proposed by Parkes and Weiss (1983) that incorporates characteristics of both the death and the relationship to the deceased individual into the criteria for diagnosis. The characteristics of the death are an important environmental variable that are discussed more in Chapter 5. Until this variable is clarified as a risk factor, it is sensible to treat it as if it is independent of the outcome. The same argument can be made for characteristics of the relationship to the deceased individual, a type of diagnostic criterion that derives from a functional approach to the diagnosis of psychopathology. Qualities of the relationship to the deceased individual are discussed more in Chapter 8 on personal risk factors. Coping strategies, another type of personal and functional variable that can indicate how bereaved persons adapt to a loss and predict the outcome of coping, are discussed in Chapter 7. In general, it is worth emphasizing that one reason for a typology of pathologic grief that uses symptoms of separation distress as the essential criteria is to avoid a priori assumptions about the relationship among pathologic grief, major depression, anxiety disorders, and posttraumatic disorders. More cross-sectional and longitudinal research is needed to clarify the questions of comorbidity and sequential relationships among the syndromes.

Pathologic Grief as an Ecologically Specific Disorder

One final implication of this discussion for understanding the nature of pathologic grief, which is suggested by most of the available evidence, is that the clinical complications observed during acute bereavement are ecologically specific in that they are related both to the environmental vector of a death and to the resulting environmental absence created by the loss. The symptoms of separation distress that the loss provokes in the bereaved survivor occur and intermingle with the symptoms of depression and anxiety (Kim and Jacobs 1991). To the extent that separation distress is central to and essential for the definition of the disorder, pathologic grief is like an adult variety of separation anxiety disorder in children. Though this concept ought to be tested in systematic studies, the idea that the clinical complications of grief are ecologically specific is probably not a controversial claim when thinking about pathologic grief as a syndrome.

The idea that most of the major depressions and anxiety disorders of bereavement occur in this same context is more debatable. It can be argued that these disorders of bereavement are no different than the garden variety depressions and anxiety disorders seen in psychiatric clinics and that they occur in bereaved individuals who are predisposed to them. Yet approximately 60%–70% of bereaved individuals who develop major depressions and anxiety disorders do not have a personal or family history of a similar disorder. It has not been shown unequivocally that personal and family histories are risk factors for the occurrence of the psychopathology in bereavement (Jacobs et al. 1989, 1990; see also Chapter 8). The data on this question are not uniform, and new studies may require revision of the conclusions that I am proposing. In the meantime, the evidence suggests that it is useful to consider all the clinical complications of bereavement as *pathologic grief* in the broadest, conceptual sense. Within this framework, the anxious depressions of bereavement are a type of ecologically specific affective disorder (Kim and Jacobs 1991).

An ecological model of psychopathology contains important hypotheses about the major depressions and anxiety disorders of bereavement. Are they environmentally determined disorders? To what extent does a personal vulnerability to psychiatric disorders influence the risk of occurrence? Are these environmentally contingent disorders different symptomatically and physiologically from other similar clinical syndromes seen in our clinics? Are there different treatments that are effective for these disorders? and so on. The model of psychiatric disorders that bereavement and its complications provide permits the investigation of these fascinating questions.

Case Examples of Pathologic Grief

Ms. A, the woman presented in Chapter 1 who lost both her oldest son and her mother in a 3-month period, is a typical example of delayed grief over the death of her son. The emergence of separation distress was retarded for 3 months as she was obligated to care for her dying mother. In this case, the emotional burden of caring for her dying mother appeared to interfere with the expression of grief for her son. When her grief emerged, the separation distress was intense and protracted. The bereavement overload (Kastenbaum 1969) from the two losses contributed to the severe intensity and potential prolongation of her grief. Subsequently, she developed a major depressive syndrome that interfered with her ability to fulfill her roles within the family and at work. Without treatment intervention, the course of her grief promised to become prolonged. Case 2 provides another example of pathologic grief:

Case 2

Ms. B was a 59-year-old businesswoman whose husband died unexpectedly and suddenly from a cardiac arrhythmia secondary to a pulmonary embolus. From the room adjoining the one in which her apparently healthy husband was working, Ms. B heard a thud and had a premonition that something was dreadfully wrong. When, within seconds she found him unconscious, she "knew immediately that he was dead," and she "had no hope." It was "just he and me" facing his death, "the sudden transition from life to death in 3 minutes." Ms. B called an emergency number, and within minutes an ambulance was there. Her husband was taken to a local emergency room where he never regained consciousness.

Ms. B's close-knit family of adult children and their spouses rallied around, as did the neighbors among whom the family was well known. Initially swept up in the funeral arrangements, she carried herself through the first several weeks with poise and reserve. She stoically faced and made the best of two major holidays within 2 months after the death.

I first saw Ms. B about 2½ months after her husband's death when her separation distress, which was strong though not yet disruptive of function, was intensifying. There were moments when the distress was so intense she felt "like crawling out of my skin." She worried that it would get worse and wondered "how much I can take." In addition, she needed to periodically review the intellectual dissonance caused by her husband's sudden death. This was associated with a different type of distress that she described as "a stabbing injury" and a "shock." She knew that her husband was dead and gone; still, she could not believe it. She also had several depressive symptoms that did not meet enough criteria for a diagnosis of major depression. On the other hand, she importuned me for some sort of treatment to relieve the intensity of her distress. She was already using diazepam intermittently as prescribed by her family doctor, and it did not relieve the symptoms. She wondered about the use of antidepressants.

The intensity of her grief continued unabated and within a month she developed more depressive symptoms that now did meet sufficient criteria for major depression. She began to wonder if she would be able to keep going and get herself to work every morning. I encouraged her to ride out this period with psychotherapeutic support but without the use of antidepressants. This was done with the understanding that if the symptoms did not begin to subside by 4 months after the loss, I would recommend antidepressant drug treatment. Within another 2 weeks she began to report nighttime panic attacks and the fear that she would "lose my mind." She described how she felt "angry and cheated" by her husband's death; however, this anger was not directed at anyone in particular. On the verge of starting antidepressant drugs, she appeared for the next appointment reporting that she had experienced a few good days after a recent nighttime panic attack. This pattern of improvement continued for 3 months while she remained in weekly psychotherapy. With the end of the school year and an imminent summer vacation, she ended therapy with the conviction that she could manage on her own.

Ms. B had no history of psychiatric disorders. On the other hand, she believed that her father, who had divorced her mother and left the family when Ms. B was 7, had been depressed in his later years, and one of her siblings had been hospitalized multiple times for major depressions and substance abuse.

Ms. B appeared for treatment again a month after the first anniversary of her husband's death. This time she presented with a full-blown depressive syndrome and persistently intense separation distress. The holidays had been very difficult for her. She was progressively symptomatic and ruminative about a winter vacation, a long-standing family tradition that would require her to leave home, the current locus of most feelings of closeness that she preserved for her husband. She had always been fearful of leaving home and had depended on her husband's support to cope with leaving. Also the vacation would require her to play an active role as a single parent for her children and their families. Her family role since the death of her husband had become a painful reminder of her husband's absence. She no longer had a sense of security and safety as part of a stable community to which she and her husband had belonged. The anniversary of her husband's death and the winter vacation served to uncover her unresolved, unremitting grief.

Ms. B abandoned the idea of the vacation trip after careful consideration. She was treated with desipramine unsuccessfully because the drug precipitated a pharmacological panic attack and had to be discontinued. Nevertheless, she made a slow recovery in psychotherapy over 5 months and again left treatment at the beginning of the summer vacation.

Ms. B returned to treatment for a third time at the time of the second anniversary of her husband's death with the same symptomatic picture of major depression and intense separation distress as after the first anniversary. The salient difference for her, when she compared this with earlier episodes, was her current preoccupation with "accepting the permanence of being unmarried and coping with the insecurity of no longer being a member of a protective community." In psychotherapy, it became clear that there were still painful reminders of her husband's absence on the occasion of births of grandchildren and on the marriage of one of her children. At these times, her separation distress continued to be intense. For the first time she reviewed in detail the circumstances of her husband's death and how traumatic it had been for her. She still differentiated the pain of the trauma (like an injury) from that of the separation distress with which she now "felt more comfortable." Though she knew her husband was permanently gone, she still could not "accept" this fact. Because of a recurrent depressive syndrome she was started on nortriptyline, which caused essentially the same adverse reaction that desipramine had the year before. She described her condition as a state of alarm and panic over the depressive symptoms with the fear that she would lose control and need hospitalization. Again the medicine was discontinued after a short, inadequate trial. She remained in psychotherapy another 5 months during which she expressed her separation distress and traumatic distress much more openly. She said that she no longer felt that she had to prove herself by mastering it promptly. She was prepared to accept her unmarried status and handle the consequences of her loss as they came up over the course of her life. She made improvements, despite another failed trial of antidepressant medicine, and again left treatment at the time of an imminent vacation.

Cases 1 and 2 illustrate the utility of separation distress as the essential criterion for recognizing pathologic grief. Both women had delayed grief followed by intense separation distress that felt overwhelming. This pattern was a harbinger of a prolonged course of grief. Both women had depressive episodes that were closely associated with the pattern of pathologic grief and that had potential implications for treatment with antidepressants, but which were not essential for diagnosis of pathologic grief. Case 2 illustrates a psychological progression from emotional numbness to separation distress and then to depressive symptoms, but this progression was not essential for the recognition of pathologic grief except for a delay in the emergence of separation distress. Case 2 also exhibits a prominent traumatic dimension to the patient's distress that persisted in parallel with her separation distress. It appeared to be an independent dimension of distress, and it may have contributed to the prolongation of her grief. (This interplay between separation distress and traumatic distress is a topic of current interest and is discussed in more detail in Chapter 5.) In both Case 1 and Case 2, the clinical complications of bereavement appeared to be ecologically specific in the sense that they stemmed from the loss as a "vector of disease," an idea to be developed more in Chapter 5 on an adaptive model.

Conclusions

Pathologic grief is a concept that has solid historical roots reaching back centuries and that has drawn considerable attention in the 20th century. It can be best understood in relationship to normal grief. In the broadest sense, pathologic grief is a concept that denotes a group of affective disturbances that have a specific relationship to bereavement. There are variations in the symptomatic picture of pathologic grief that can be recognized as one of a few pathologic grief syndromes on the one hand, or as major depressions and anxiety disorders in association with bereavement on the other. The vicissitudes of separation distress are central to virtually all the clinical syndromes. Given our contemporary state of knowledge, it seems that we are on the threshold of the development of diagnostic criteria that will facilitate recognition of pathologic grief syndromes. Criteria that serve this purpose are discussed in more detail in Chapter 9. But first, there is a question about whether it is worth all the trouble to develop special criteria for the diagnosis of pathologic grief. In Chapter 3, I review data that provide an appreciation of the magnitude of the clinical problems that we understand as pathologic grief.

References

Adler A: Neuropsychiatric complications in victims of Boston's Coconut Grove disaster. JAMA 123:1098–1101, 1943

Anderson C: Aspects of pathological grief and mourning. Int J Psychoanal 30:48–55, 1949

Bornstein PE, Clayton PJ, Halikas JA, et al: The depression of widowhood after thirteen months. Br J Psychiatry 122:561–566, 1973
Bowlby J: Pathological mourning and childhood mourning. J Am Psychoanal Assoc 11:500–541, 1963
Bowlby J: Attachment and Loss, Vol 1: Attachment. New York, Basic Books, 1969
Bowlby J: Attachment and Loss, Vol 2: Separation. New York, Basic Books, 1973
Bowlby J: Attachment and Loss, Vol 3: Loss, Sadness and Depression. New York, Basic Books, 1980
Bowlby J, Parkes CM: Separation and loss, in The International Yearbook for Child Psychiatry and Allied Disciplines, Vol 1: The Child and His Family. New York, Wiley, 1970
Clayton PJ: Bereavement and depression. J Clin Psychiatry 51:34–38, 1990
Clayton PJ, Darvish HS: Course of depressive symptoms following the stress of bereavement, in Stress and Mental Disorder. Edited by Barrett JE, Rose RM, Klerman GL. New York, Raven, 1979, pp 121–136
Darwin C: The Expression of the Emotions in Man and Animals. London, John Murray, 1872
Deutsch H: Absence of grief. Psychoanal Q 6:12–22, 1937
Ehlers CL, Frank E, Kupfer DJ: Social zeitgebers and biological rhythms. Arch Gen Psychiatry 45:948–952, 1988
Faschingbauer TR, Devaul R, Zisook S: Development of the Texas Inventory of Grief. Am J Psychiatry 134:696–698, 1977
Freud S: Mourning and melancholia (1917), in The Standard Edition of the Complete Psychological Works of Sigmund Freud, Vol 14. Translated and edited by Strachey J. London, Hogarth Press, 1953, pp 243–258
Gold PW, Goodwin FK, Chrousos GP: Clinical and biochemical manifestations of depression: relation to the neurobiology of stress. Part I. N Engl J Med 319:348–352, 1988a
Gold PW, Goodwin FK, Chrousos GP: Clinical and biochemical manifestations of depression: relation to the neurobiology of stress. Part II. N Engl J Med 319:413–420, 1988b
Horowitz MJ: Stress Response Syndromes. New York, Jason Aronson, 1976
Horowitz MJ, Wilner N, Alvarez W: Impact of Event Scale: a measure of subjective stress. Psychosom Med 41:209–218, 1979
Horowitz MJ, Wilner N, Marmar C, et al: Pathological grief and the activation of latent self-images. Am J Psychiatry 137:1157–1162, 1980
Jackson SW: Melancholia and Depression From Hippocratic Times to Modern Times. New Haven, Yale University Press, 1986
Jacobs SC: Bereavement and anxiety disorders, in Grief and Bereavement in Contemporary Society, Vol I. Edited by Chigier E. London, Freund Publishing House, 1987, pp 212–220
Jacobs SC, Kosten TR, Kasl SV, et al: Attachment theory and multiple dimensions of grief. Omega 18:41–52, 1987
Jacobs SC, Hansen FF, Berkman L, et al: Depressions of bereavement. Compr Psychiatry 30:218–224, 1989
Jacobs SC, Hansen FF, Kasl SV, et al: Anxiety disorders during acute bereavement: risk and risk factors. J Clin Psychiatry 51:269–274, 1990
Kastenbaum R: Death and bereavement in later life, in Death and Bereavement. Edited by Kutcher A. Springfield, IL, Charles C Thomas, 1969, pp 28–54
Kim K, Jacobs SC: Pathologic grief and its relationship to other psychiatric disorders. J Affect Disord 21:257–263, 1991

Klein DF: Anxiety reconceptualized. Compr Psychiatry 21:411–427, 1980

Lindeman EL: Symptomatology and management of acute grief. Am J Psychiatry 101:141–148, 1944

Nader K, Pynoos RS, Fairbanks L, et al: Childhood PTSD reactions one year after a sniper attack. Am J Psychiatry 147:1526–1530, 1990

Parkes CM: Morbid Grief Reactions: A Review of the Literature. Dissertation for DPM, University of London, 1959

Parkes CM: Bereavement and mental illness, Part 2: a classification of bereavement reactions. Br J Med Psychol 38:13–26, 1965

Parkes CM: Bereavement: Studies of Grief in Adult Life. New York, International Universities Press, 1972

Parkes CM, Weiss RS: Recovery From Bereavement. New York, Basic Books, 1983

Pynoos RS, Frederick C, Nader K, et al: Life threat and posttraumatic stress in school-age children. Arch Gen Psychiatry 44:1057–1063, 1987a

Pynoos RS, Nader K, Frederick C, et al: Grief reactions in school-age children following a sniper attack at school. Isr J Psychiatry Relat Sci 24:53–63, 1987b

Raphael B: The Anatomy of Bereavement. New York, Basic Books, 1983

Raphael B: Diagnostic criteria for bereavement reactions. Paper presented at the International Symposium on Pathologic Bereavement, Seattle, WA, May 1989

Reite M, Field T (eds): The Psychobiology of Attachment and Separation. New York, Academic Press, 1985

Rynearson EK: Psychotherapy of pathologic grief. Psychiatr Clin North Am 10:487–499, 1987

Shuchter SR: Dimensions of Grief: Adjusting to the Death of a Spouse. San Francisco, CA, Jossey-Bass, 1986

Vachon MLS, Rogers J, Lyall WA, et al: Predictors and correlates of adaptation to conjugal bereavement. Am J Psychiatry 139:998–1002, 1982

Zisook S, Shuchter SR: Depression through the first year after the death of a spouse. Am J Psychiatry 148:1346–1352, 1991

Zisook S, Schneider D, Shuchter SR: Anxiety and bereavement. Psychiatr Med 8:83–96, 1990

CHAPTER 3

Defining the Range and Magnitude of the Clinical Complications of Bereavement

Appreciation of the psychiatric complications of bereavement has declined over the past 20 years. The diminished status for this important group of disorders is a product of several developments. One such development is the reluctance in American society to accept the possibility that psychiatric disorders complicate the normal process of grief. Undoubtedly, the stigmatization associated with having a problem that is identified as *psychiatric* contributes to this hesitant attitude.

Beyond stigmatization, this reluctance to recognize the psychiatric complications of bereavement is also a function of a growing "consumer" movement against medical expertise and authority. Within this movement, professional competence is questioned, the risk of undesirable side effects of treatment is highlighted, and self-help is advocated as a counterpoint. (The many merits of self-help are taken up in more detail during the discussion of treatment. That is not the point here.) This consumer challenge to the effectiveness of professional interventions during acute bereavement not only undermines the importance of a professional perspective, it also erodes an appreciation of the clinical complications with which a professional is prepared to help. This state of affairs affects not only laypeople but also clinicians. It leaves clinicians with a conceptual problem: do clinical complications occur and what professional interventions are helpful?

Another reason for the decline of clinical attention to the complications of bereavement stems from the eclipse of psychoanalysis and emotional crisis theory by biological psychiatry. This historical change creates a second conceptual problem that augments the professional incertitude mentioned above. The concept of *pathologic mourning* first appeared in the early part of the 20th century as part of an essay by Freud (1917) about the relationship between mourning and melancholia. In the 1940s and 1950s, Lindeman (1944), still working within the psychoanalytic tradition, further developed this view of grief. Caplan (1964), in collaboration with Lindeman, applied the principles about emotional response to a loss—learned from the study of bereavement—to the more general problem of emotional crisis. Crisis intervention techniques were developed to minimize the risk of complications during acute emotional crises. They were applied as preventive interventions designed to minimize the rate of occurrence of complications (primary prevention) or to reduce the severity and duration of an episode of illness once it had occurred (secondary prevention).

With the rise of interest in biological psychiatry, this earlier psychoanalytic perspective on the complications of bereavement was overshadowed in American psychiatry by an emphasis on the careful description and diagnosis of depressions and other psychiatric syndromes. This descriptive approach, which attempts to be atheoretical with regard to etiology, as opposed to psychoanalytic theory, is reflected in the current nosology of American psychiatry embodied in the *Diagnostic and Statistical Manual of Mental Disorders,* 3rd Edition, Revised (DSM-III-R; American Psychiatric Association 1987).

The net result of these competing and unresolved traditions of conceptualizing the complications of bereavement is the scant amount of material in DSM-III-R on the clinical problems of bereavement. This is reflected in the V code for uncomplicated bereavement, which briefly acknowledges that complications occur and should be diagnosed, in most cases, as depressions. Despite one notable effort to conceptualize the relationship between pathologic grief and psychiatric disorders (Parkes and Weiss 1983), the absence of standardized descriptive criteria for pathologic grief has prevented comparison of the psychoanalytic and descriptive tradition of defining the complications of bereavement. As a consequence, no one has offered an integration of the two competing nosologies. Indecision prevails therefore about how best to conceptualize the complications of bereavement. The ambiguity about the nature and the scope of the complications of bereavement leaves the clinician and his or her potential patients in a state of limbo about professional tasks in caring for the acutely bereaved individual in need.

Given the lack of consensus concerning clinical complications of bereavement, it would seem useful to examine the significance of these complications as a medical and public health problem. What is the scope and magnitude of the clinical complications of bereavement according to current evidence?

Rates of Complications

Epidemiological Studies

An examination of epidemiological data is a logical starting place for clarifying these questions. Unfortunately, few epidemiological studies have specifically addressed the question of the magnitude of clinical complications of bereavement.

According to the original reports of the Epidemiologic Catchment Area (ECA) study in the United States, the rate of major depressions within 1 year of bereavement ranged from 0.1% in St. Louis to 0.3% in New Haven (Myers et al. 1984). In absolute terms, this was considered to be infrequent, although no information on relative risks among bereaved individuals was provided. When we (Bruce et al. 1990) examined the relative risk of major depression or dysthymia during acute bereavement in the New Haven sample of the ECA study, which was the only site that included an elderly oversample, the odds ratios were quite high. They ranged from 22 for major depression to 32 for dysthymia when corrected for sex, age, and household size. Thirty-one percent of the bereaved individuals in the New Haven ECA sample developed a major depressive syndrome at some time in the first year of bereavement. Another 31% met criteria for dysthymia. The high relative risk for depression found in the ECA study is consistent with Blazer et al.'s findings (1987) in their epidemiological study of late-life depression in which the only sociodemographic factor that was significantly related to depression was widowhood. This relationship between a loss and depression among the elderly was also found in a large series of hospitalized, depressed patients (Conwell et al. 1989). The sum of these studies, in which the investigators used diagnostic approaches to assess major depression, suggests that bereavement is an important cause of depressive complications, despite the conclusion of the ECA study that the absolute size of the problem was small.

Clinical Studies on Various Outcomes of Bereavement

With the exception of epidemiological studies that use dimensional measures of depression rather than diagnostic methodologies (which are discussed below), the above review exhausts the epidemiological literature on bereavement and clinical complications. Therefore, to a large extent, we are left with the task of drawing conclusions about the nature and breadth of the clinical problems associated with bereavement from smaller, clinical studies. The authors of many of these studies did not carefully document the relationship of the sample to the population from which the participants were drawn. The consequence of this omission was to leave us skeptical about the denominators on which the rates of occurrence were based as well as dubious about the question of how representative the findings were. In addition, the definition of the clinical complications of bereavement varied from study to study, and this affected the estimate of rates. Furthermore, the period of risk varied somewhat among studies, thereby affecting the magnitude of the rate observed. All these problems make it hard to reach definite conclusions. Nevertheless, with these limitations, what do these studies tell us? In short, these studies impress one with the magnitude of the rate of complications of bereavement (Table 3–1). Estimates of the rate of complications range from 4% to 39% for bereaved spouses, depending on the way the complication is defined.

Pathologic grief. When the clinical complications were defined as *pathologic grief*, the estimates of occurrence among adults ranged from 14% to 34% (Dimond et al. 1987; Lazare 1979; Maddison 1968; Parkes 1970; Parkes and Weiss 1983; Vachon et al. 1982; Zisook and DeVaul 1983; Zisook et al. 1985). Using poor adjustment after a loss as a criterion for defining a poor outcome, Silverman and Worden (1992; see also Worden

1991) studied children who had lost a parent. They found that 18% of the children had poor outcomes at 13 months after the loss and 20% had poor outcomes at 25 months. This placed these children in the same range of risk for poor outcome as adults. The absence of standardized criteria for pathologic grief accounts in part for the wide range of the estimates. Despite this handicap, in studies of larger samples, investigators tended to find rates at the higher end of the spectrum summarized in Table 3–1 (32.1%, Maddison and Viola 1968; 33.8%, Parkes and Weiss 1983; 26%, Vachon et al. 1982), suggesting that a mid-range estimate is true.

Depression. When *major depression* was used as the criterion of poor outcome of bereavement, the estimates of clinical complications ranged from 4% to 31% for bereaved spouses (Bornstein et al. 1973; Bruce et al. 1990; Carey 1979–1980; Clayton et al. 1968; Jacobs et al. 1989; Lund et al. 1985–1986; Richards and McCallum 1979; Zisook and Shuchter 1991; Zisook 1991). Although most of these assessments were done 1 year after the loss, two included data from 2 years of follow-up (Lund et al. 1985–1986; Zisook 1991). The first modern study (Clayton et al. 1968) on this question established the low end of the range (4%) for depressions 1 year after bereavement. In later studies (Bornstein et al. 1973; Bruce et al. 1990; Carey 1979–1980; Jacobs et al. 1989; Lund et al. 1985–1986; Richards and McCallum 1979; Zisook and Shuchter 1991; Zisook 1991) of larger samples, researchers established a range between 16% and 31%. Therefore, it is probably the higher end of the total range of estimates of the risk of major depression that is true. At 2-year follow-up, the rate was 18% in one sample (Lund et al. 1985–1986) and 14% in another (Zisook 1991). If we assume that the rate of major depressions in bereaved individuals 1 year

Table 3–1. Risk of clinical complications 1 year after a loss

Type of outcome	Percentage
Any disorder	4–39
Pathologic grief	14–34
Major depression	4–31
Panic disorder	13
Generalized anxiety disorder	39

after a loss is about 20%, then the rate of depression among bereaved individuals exceeds the 2.2% 1-month prevalence rate of depression in the general population (Regier et al. 1988) ninefold.

Weller et al. (1991) reported on the rates of depression in bereaved children. Thirty-seven percent of the children, ranging in age from 5 to 12 years (average = 9 years), met DSM-III-R criteria for major depression. The children in this small sample ($N = 38$) were interviewed an average of 2 months after the loss of a parent. This is the only study in which data on depressed children have been reported and the investigators' assessment in the study occurred early in the course of bereavement. If the rate of depression in this study proves true in subsequent surveys, the rate of depression in bereaved children is consistent with the rates observed in adults during the first 2 months after their loss. This is interesting as far as it goes. Unfortunately, it is the unremitting depressions of bereavement that are significant for our purposes in estimating rates of clinical complications, rather than the mostly transient, depressive symptoms that are ubiquitous early in bereavement (Jacobs and Lieberman 1987; see also Chapter 9). We will have to wait for follow-up from the Weller et al. study (1991) to know the course of these depressive symptoms in children.

Anxiety disorders. If *anxiety disorders* are used to define the complications, the only estimate available also indicates a manifold increase in risk during acute bereavement. In a study completed in New Haven, we (Jacobs et al. 1990) interviewed 102 bereaved spouses at either 6 or 12 months after bereavement to evaluate the risk of anxiety disorders. In the subgroup interviewed 6 months after a loss ($n = 48$), 6.3% reported panic disorder and 22.9% reported generalized anxiety disorder. In the subgroup interviewed 13 months after the loss ($n = 54$), 13% reported panic disorder and 38.9% reported generalized anxiety disorder. (Concerning the methodology of this study, it should be noted that the rates of generalized anxiety disorder may have been inflated by the absence from the diagnostic procedures of the hierarchical rule used in DSM-III-R for excluding generalized anxiety disorder when major depression is present. For example, 83% of survivors with a major depression also reported an anxiety disorder, most often generalized anxiety disorder and less frequently panic disorder. Conversely, 56% of the acutely bereaved spouses who had an anxiety disorder also reported a concomitant major depression. Hence, much overlap exists.) Additional studies are needed to corroborate these observations and to clarify the nature and risk of anxiety disorders following bereavement. The finding of the our study (Jacobs et al. 1990) promises to be confirmed because it is consistent with the clinical literature on the precipitants of panic disorder and perhaps other anxiety disorders.

Conclusions from clinical studies. These rates of complications for pathologic grief, major depression, and anxiety disorders cannot simply be totaled to obtain a single rate because there is evidence of considerable overlap among the different definitions of the complications (Kim and Jacobs 1991; Jacobs et al. 1989, 1990). Nor is it reasonable to simply average the rates, given the differences in definition, the differences in methodology, and the absence of complete overlap. (These issues are given more consideration in Chapter 4.) Nevertheless, the estimates tend to center around 20%, if not higher, which is the crude rate of complications of acute bereavement cited by many clinicians.

Problems With Data From These Studies

Before accepting the conclusion that the rate of complications during bereavement is roughly 20%, it is sensible to question whether there is any evidence that would refute this conclusion. First, with regard to pathologic grief and the anxiety disorders of bereavement, there are not enough data, either clinical or epidemiological, to raise doubts about this conclusion; however, it would be desirable to confirm it in larger study samples. Second, with regard to major depression as an outcome of bereavement, certain epidemiological studies have found mixed results. Contrary to the conclusions of one epidemiological study (Blazer et al. 1987) that used a diagnostic approach in identifying cases of depression following bereavement, the authors of three epidemiological studies (Harlow et al. 1991; Hays 1991; Murrell and Himmelfarb 1989) using a dimensional measure of depression concluded that the depressive symptoms of bereavement were not clinically significant.

Investigators in the latter three studies used the Center for Epidemiologic Studies Depression Scale (CES-D; Radloff 1977). This self-report measure has proven to be sensitive over time for assessing the emotional distress of bereavement in contrast to a dimensional measure of anxiety

(Hays 1991). In these three studies, patients' depressive symptoms intensified during the first 6 months of bereavement, with patients roughly doubling their baseline scores and reaching a range of moderately severe depression. Their symptoms then attenuated in average number and severity back to control levels by 1 year after a loss. Based on this type of observation, Murrell and Himmelfarb (1989) concluded that "bereavement in particular, and life events in general, would appear to have quite limited etiologic importance for depressive symptoms in older adults" (p. 172).

Age and sex variations among studies. On the face of it, these observations of depression in elderly samples are not consistent with the idea that a substantial minority of acutely bereaved individuals suffer from persistent, major depressive syndromes. The explanation for the discrepancy between studies in which diagnostic case identification is used and studies in which dimensional assessments are used is not clear at present. A partial explanation may be related to the age of the sample studied. For example, if younger bereaved individuals run a higher risk of major depressions during bereavement (Carey 197–1980; Zisook and Shuchter 1991), depression will be less likely to be observed in the middle-aged and elderly individuals studied by investigators using dimensional measures (Harlow et al. 1991; Hays 1991; Murrell and Himmelfarb 1989).

Furthermore, age and sex variation in the rates of depression may exist among elderly people themselves. In analyses of data from the New Haven site of the Established Populations for Epidemiologic Studies of the Elderly (EPESE; Cornoni-Huntley et al. 1986), we (C. F. Mendes de Leon, S. V. Kasl, S. C. Jacobs, unpublished data, December 1992) found that widowed women between the ages of 65 and 74 in the second and third years of bereavement were significantly more likely ($P < .05$) to have high levels of depressive symptoms than were nonwidowed women. Like the studies discussed above, the EPESE study used the CES-D as a dimensional measure. The scores on the CES-D were in a range (average score = 13) in which many of the widows exceeded the CES-D cutoff of 16 for identifying cases of major depression. Thus this observation raises the possibility that a subgroup of bereaved individuals with major depressions can be obscured by the group averages from a large heterogeneous sample. The depressions will be appreciated only if an age and sex interaction is considered.

Methodological variations among studies. The explanation for the variation in rates of depression among studies may be methodological also. For example, when attrition over 25 months of follow-up was examined in a sample of 440 middle-aged and elderly bereaved spouses in New Haven, it was found that those who dropped out (34%) were significantly more likely to be depressed (Hays 1991). Obviously, selective attrition like this reduces the likelihood of finding persistent depressions after bereavement, which is the clinical phenomenon of central interest (Jacobs and Lieberman 1987; see also Chapter 9).

When we appreciated that the CES-D was not identifying a high rate of depression at 13 and 25 months of follow-up (Hays 1991), we (Jacobs et al. 1989) proceeded to do a small study of major depressions that occurred during acute bereavement, using both dimensional and diagnostic assessments. We found that, using a cutoff score of 16 for identifying bereaved individuals with major depression, the CES-D had a high level of sensitivity and specificity. We therefore concluded that the CES-D, with its standardized cutoff score, had proven to be a satisfactory screening instrument for major depression during bereavement. Certainly, the false negative rate of 7% did not explain the discrepancy between diagnostic case identification and dimensional assessments. In our small study (Jacobs et al. 1989), however, the CES-D was administered to young and middle-aged adults by a specially trained interviewer who was widowed herself and who had extensive experience doing interviews with bereaved spouses. In the other studies (Harlow et al. 1991; Hays 1991; Murrell and Himmelfarb 1989), the CES-D was one measure among many used by less specifically trained interviewers and not linked to a second stage clinical examination.

Significance of Rates of Occurrence

Although a systematic study is needed to clarify the differences between studies in which diagnostic assessments were used and studies in which dimensional assessments were used, it appears that the incongruities may be explained by selective dropout from samples during follow-up, the use of different types of assessment, and age or sex differences in the samples. Keeping in mind the caution that our current understanding needs to be verified in controlled studies of large samples using both types of measures of depression, it appears that it is reasonable to affirm the conclusion that the proportion of acutely bereaved individuals who develop clinical complications is about one-fifth.

Twenty percent is a substantial rate of clinical complications of bereavement. Considering that more than 800,000 spouses are widowed each year in the United States, let alone bereaved parents and siblings, a 20% rate of complications indicates that many bereaved individuals are in need of some type of help at some point during the first year of bereavement. By public health standards, this is a significant problem. Furthermore, although the complications of bereavement may not be as symptomatically severe and disabling as other psychiatric disorders, such as schizophrenia, they account for as many as 15% of admissions to ambulatory care (Lazare 1979) and 20% of requests for psychiatric consultations from medical and surgical services in the general hospital (DeVaul et al. 1979). This is a substantial clinical problem to which we ought to pay attention.

The following case example illustrates the presentation of symptoms during acute bereavement that meet criteria for major depression, panic disorder, and generalized anxiety syndrome. The clinical follow-up indicated that the patient's grief was prolonged, thereby qualifying her for a diagnosis of pathologic grief (see Chapters 2 and 9). Furthermore, her problems were compounded by alcohol abuse. Case 3 illustrates the overlap in the occurrence of these differently defined outcomes that can be observed in many patients.

Case 3

Ms. C was a 49-year-old saleswoman whose husband had died at age 45 from acute leukemia 6 months earlier. She was identified via a routine screening of death certificates with follow-up telephone calls to determine if the bereaved family members were having trouble with their grief. On diagnostic screening she met criteria for nonmelancholic, major depression. She reported sadness, loss of interest in her usual activities, weight loss, insomnia, fatigue, mild psychomotor agitation, difficulty concentrating, feelings of guilt and worthlessness, and practically constant preoccupation with death and dying. She also met criteria for panic disorder, including limited symptoms of avoidance, and virtually all the DSM-III-R criteria for generalized anxiety disorder, characterized in her case by extreme arousal and hypervigilance. Finally, she met criteria for severe, unremitting pathologic grief manifested in intense separation distress.

At first, Ms. C was unable to provide a precise chronological order for the onset of symptoms, saying that they all began immediately after her husband's death. After further thought, she stated that perhaps her difficulty started with the depressive symptoms. Her symptoms included chest pain similar to the predominant pain that her husband suffered in the terminal phase of his illness. She had been evaluated repeatedly by her family doctor, and the chest pain was thought to be an identification symptom secondary to the stress of bereavement. Now, 6 months after the loss of her husband, all her symptoms were getting worse. She had a long-standing phobia of snakes and was apprehensive about a psychiatric interview for fear that I would negligently mention the word *snake* and throw her into a panic. I viewed this fear as an indication not only of her insecurity with strange people but also of the marginal control that she felt over her feelings.

Ms. C had been married multiple times. Her last husband had also been her first husband; she had married him at age 19 and then divorced him at age 21. He had been her childhood sweetheart. She quickly married her second husband after her divorce. When she was 26, her second husband (age 36) died from a pulmonary embolism after an operation for kidney cancer for which she had given consent. She felt guilty about having made the decision for the operative procedure and became "extremely" depressed for a year without seeking treatment. Instead, she began to drink heavily. She pulled out of this drinking pattern after a few years and "learned to be independent." After another failed marriage, she then remarried her first husband. When her mother died 2 years before the interview, she became "depressed" again for about a year. She denied the excessive use of alcohol at that time.

At the time of the interview, she smelled slightly of alcohol and had a noticeable tremor. She was tearful and depressed. She was professionally dressed, handsomely groomed, and engaging. At the same time, she was quite apprehensive and skeptical about the potential for treatment interventions to help her. Her family doctor confirmed my impression that she was depressed and believed that antidepressants would be helpful. He also confirmed a past history of alcohol abuse, as well as alcohol use to varying degrees in the 6 months since the death of her husband.

Ms. C agreed to a treatment trial of the antidepressant desipramine and then took it only 1 day during the first week. She acknowledged to me that she had been drinking. On her second visit, she renewed her commitment to use the medicine and returned the next week with complaints about multiple side effects but no benefits. The medicine was changed to nortriptyline. She canceled all subsequent appointments and presumably never tried the second medicine. Her family doctor had the impression that she was drinking and continued to be very symptomatic, as if the alcohol abuse were prolonging and extending the grief.

It is clinical experience with this type of patients that provides incentive for considering alcohol abuse as a clinical complication, an issue that I now consider.

Alcohol Use and Abuse

As if the clinical picture were not already complex enough, another perspective on the nature of the complications of bereavement is provided by considering the risk of alcohol abuse following a loss. Although the data on alcohol abuse are quite limited, this is a complication that most clinicians have encountered in their practices. In addition, the association between depression and alcoholism (Mendelson et al. 1986; Ross et al. 1988) and between anxiety disorders and alcoholism (Quitkin et al. 1972) supports a hypothesis about alcohol abuse as a complication of bereavement. Clinical experiences with patients like Ms. C in Case 3 (and others, summarized in Chapter 7) are very persuasive and demand attention.

Aside from clinical anecdotes, there has been limited systematic study of alcohol abuse during acute bereavement. What has been done so far does not provide supportive evidence for the idea that alcohol abuse is a complication of bereavement that afflicts the average bereaved individual. Although one study (Zisook et al. 1990) found that some bereaved individuals reduce consumption of alcoholic beverages during bereavement, several studies have found that, on average, acutely bereaved individuals consume more alcohol (Clayton and Darvish 1979; Maddison and Walker 1967; Parkes 1970; Parkes and Brown 1972; Thompson et al. 1984; Zisook et al. 1990), particularly acutely bereaved men (Byrne and Raphael 1991; Mor et al. 1986). On the other hand, the difference in alcohol consumption between bereaved and control subjects in controlled studies is either statistically nonsignificant (Kasl et al. 1987) or the change in consumption over the first year is not clinically impressive (1.8 to 2.2 drinks per day) despite the fact that it is statistically significant ($P < .05$) (Zisook et al. 1990). One exception to this conclusion is the finding of Byrne and Raphael (1991) in their study of elderly Australian widowers who reported drinking in excess of nationally recommended safe limits for men (four standard measures of alcohol per day) 6 weeks after the death of their spouse by comparison with married control subjects.

When bereaved individuals are followed longitudinally, those with a past history of drinking consume a greater volume when they do drink, but they do not drink more frequently (Zisook et al. 1990). Findings from longitudinal studies indicate little evidence of an increased incidence of drinking as a result of bereavement (i.e., that bereaved individuals begin to drink for the first time during acute bereavement) (Kasl et al. 1987; Valanis et al. 1987; Zisook et al. 1990) with the possible exception of one study (Clayton and Darvish 1979).

The studies above concentrated on differences between bereaved and nonbereaved groups or changes in groups over time. Missing from these studies has been a systematic examination of the interaction between bereavement on the one hand and a predisposition to the abuse of alcoholic beverages on the other (reflected in a positive personal and possibly family history). The object would be to see if patients seen in clinical practice come from the bereaved subgroup predisposed to alcohol use. If we put together clinical anecdotes and the data from systematic studies, it appears that some acutely bereaved individuals who already have the habit of drinking alcoholic beverages increase their consumption during bereavement. It is conceivable that those individuals who already are alcohol drinkers are at high risk of losing control during acute bereavement.

This type of history is illustrated in the case of Ms. C, above. In her particular case, the history of onset of alcohol abuse appeared subsequent to the death of her second husband. In this way, the etiology could be traced back to the environmental circumstances of a previous bereavement. Curiously, she did not relapse into alcohol abuse at the time of death of her mother, to whom she was closely attached, but the problem did emerge again after her the loss of her second husband.

Based on the facts of Case 3, I suggest that the relationship between bereavement and alcohol abuse is complex. It varies over time, and although bereaved individuals who already have drinking habits may be at risk, it does not occur inevitably even among potentially predisposed individuals. (Ms. C's case was part of a clinical series of 16 patients with pathologic grief [Kim and Jacobs 1991]. Ms. C was one of 2 [12.5%] patients—the other being a widower—who had a personal history of alcohol abuse and who were diagnosed with current alcohol abuse. Although these numbers are very small, the 12.5% rate of alcohol abuse in our sample is more than four times the 1-month prevalence rate of alcohol abuse-dependence [2.8%] in the general, adult population [Regier et al. 1988].)

Alcohol use versus alcohol abuse. Another methodological problem that must be addressed in understanding the problem of alcohol consumption during bereavement is the difference between alcohol use and alcohol abuse. Three studies (Parkes and Brown 1972; Valanis et al. 1987; Zisook et al. 1990), two of them rather small, documented increased consumption of alcohol by both widows and widowers during acute bereavement and found an absence of self-reported "problems" with the use of alcoholic beverages. The findings from these studies suggest that alcohol abuse is not a complication of bereavement; however, it must be noted that the only reporting mechanism used in these studies was self-reporting, a method that is notoriously unreliable, with a bias toward underestimating the extent of the problem.

On the other hand, one longitudinal study (Clayton and Darvish 1979) of the course of symptoms and health-related behaviors in acutely bereaved spouses indicated that 50% of widowers, particularly young widowers, drank at least 16 ounces of alcohol per week 1 year after the death of their wife. This is a substantial level of consumption. The preliminary report of a study in Australia (Byrne and Raphael 1991) has indicated that elderly widowers in the early stages of bereavement also drink potentially dangerous amounts of alcohol, exceeding nationally recommended safe limits. The long-term consequences of this level of consumption are unclear until follow-up is completed for this sample. Still, it is reasonable to wonder if this level of consumption, even if it does not meet criteria for alcohol abuse, interferes with the natural process of grief by prolonging it, an issue raised in Case 3.

Hypnotic and Sedative Drug Use

Another potential complication of bereavement is prolonged hypnotic and sedative drug use and the development of dependence on them. The use of these pharmacological agents during acute bereavement is well documented (Maddison and Walker 1967; Parkes 1970; Thompson et al. 1984; Wiener et al. 1975). Usage of sedatives is characterized by an early peak in consumption in the first or second month after a loss, with twice as many people taking them during this stage of their bereavement than the general population rate of 10% (Clayton and Darvish 1979; Wiener et al. 1975; Zisook et al. 1990). Usage falls off by the seventh month or by 1 year unless the bereaved individual has a major depression (Clayton and Darvish 1979; Zisook et al. 1990).

It is possible that usage of benzodiazepines after a loss risks a poor outcome of the bereavement. This important issue has been raised by clinical anecdotes about the potential for benzodiazepines to interfere with the normal resolution of grief, resulting in *frozen grief* (e.g., see discussion by Marmar in Rynearson et al. 1990). Presumably, pharmacotherapy with benzodiazepines interferes with the capacity to psychologically work through the loss in psychotherapy, and the patient does not progress through the experience of grief to recovery. Nevertheless, there are several reasons for clinicians to be cautious about accepting such assumptions without testing them. These assumptions might simply be an extension of long-standing biases by therapists about the use of drugs in psychotherapy.

In addition, some clinicians speculate that carefully prescribed benzodiazepines may prevent depressions in stressful circumstances, which places their use in an entirely different context. Moreover, in an informal survey of psychopharmacologists who have experience in treating bereaved individuals that I have done, no one could remember an example of this. Other explanations for a delay in the working through of grief come readily to mind. For example, the phenomenon of frozen grief may be true only for patients who are in treatment because of severe grief or other clinical complications in the first place and therefore selected for prolonged (or "frozen") grief.

With respect to abuse of antianxiety drugs, only one study can be found in the literature in which the investigators looked at benzodiazepine abuse associated with bereavement (Hamlin and Hammersley 1988). In this study, one-fifth of 111 patients referred to a drug abuse program for withdrawal from dependence on benzodiazepines had been prescribed the medicine during bereavement. It was not clear from this report whether the use or abuse of the benzodiazepines preceded the bereavement (i.e., whether these were incipient cases or the exacerbation of preexisting problems with benzodiazepine abuse). Nevertheless, the findings of this study raise an important issue for the research agenda regarding the potential complications of bereavement. Presently, although it is wise to be concerned about the abuse of such drugs, it is not justified to conclude that benzodiazepine abuse is an unequivocal complication of bereavement.

Conclusions

For the time being, we will have to suspend judgment about alcohol and drug abuse as clinical complications of bereavement. The data about pathologic grief, major depressions, and anxiety disorders, although in varying stages of development (depending on the disorder), are more convincing on the whole. Yet even without a firm conclusion about substance abuse and despite the methodological problems involved in defining the clinical complications of bereavement, the sheer number of people suffering from pathologic grief, major depression, or anxiety disorders following a loss is impressive enough to encourage a commitment to understanding these disorders better and consideration of the most effective treatments for them.

One of the obstacles to better understanding the clinical complications of bereavement springs from the varying approaches that are used to define them. Competing nosological traditions for understanding the clinical complications of bereavement confuse the picture, and the lack of structured criteria for diagnosing pathologic grief prevents study of the overlap between pathologic grief, major depression, and anxiety disorders. The development of criteria for the diagnosis of pathologic grief is a methodological step that will make it possible to examine the relationship among the various syndromes in systematic studies. The development of diagnostic criteria therefore serves not only a clinical but also a research agenda.

References

American Psychiatric Association: Diagnostic and Statistical Manual of Mental Disorders, 3rd Edition, Revised. Washington, DC, American Psychiatric Association, 1987

Blazer D, Hughes DC, George LK: The epidemiology of depression in an elderly community population. Gerontologist 27:281–287, 1987

Bornstein PE, Clayton PJ, Halikas JA, et al: The depression of widowhood after thirteen months. Br J Psychiatry 122:561–566, 1973

Bruce ML, Kim K, Leaf PJ, et al: Depressive episodes and dysphoria resulting from conjugal bereavement in a prospective community sample. Am J Psychiatry 147:608–611, 1990

Byrne G, Raphael B: The impact of recent spousal bereavement on the mental health of elderly Australian men. Paper presented at the Third International Conference on Grief and Bereavement in Contemporary Society, Sydney, Australia, June 30–July 4, 1991

Caplan G: Principles of Preventive Psychiatry. New York, Basic Books, 1964

Carey RG: Weathering widowhood: problems and adjustment of the widowed during the first year. Omega 10:163–178, 1979–1980

Clayton PJ, Darvish HS: Course of depressive symptoms following the stress of bereavement, in Stress and Mental Disorder. Edited by Barrett JE, Rose RM, Klerman GL. New York, Raven, 1979, pp 121–136

Clayton PJ, Desmarais L, Winokur G: A study of normal bereavement. Am J Psychiatry 125:168–178, 1968

Conwell Y, Nelson JC, Kim K, et al: Elderly patients admitted to the psychiatric unit of a general hospital. J Am Geriatr Soc 37:35–41, 1989

Cornoni-Huntley J, Brock DB, Ostfel AM, et al (eds): Established Populations for Epidemiologic Studies of the Elderly: Resource Data Book (NIA, USDHHS PHS, NIH; NIH Pulbication No 86-2443). Bethesda, MD, National Institutes of Health, 1986

DeVaul RA, Zisook S, Faschingbauer TR: Clinical aspects of grief and bereavement. Prim Care 6:391-402, 1979

Dimond M, Lund DA, Caserta MS: The role of social support in the first two years of bereavement in an elderly sample. Gerontologist 27:599–604, 1987

Freud S: Mourning and melancholia (1917), in The Standard Edition of the Complete Psychological Works of Sigmund Freud, Vol 14. Translated and edited by Strachey J. London, Hogarth Press, 1953, pp 243–258

Hamlin M, Hammersley D: Benzodiazepines following bereavement. Paper presented at the International Conference on Grief and Bereavement in Contemporary Society, London, July 1988

Harlow SD, Goldberg EL, Comstock GW: A longitudinal study of the prevalence of depressive symptomatology in elderly widowed and married women. Arch Gen Psychiatry 48:1065–1068, 1991

Hays JC: Psychological distress, social environment, and seeking social support following conjugal bereavement. PhD Dissertation, Yale University School of Epidemiology and Public Health, 1991

Jacobs SC, Hansen FF, Berkman L, et al: Depressions of bereavement. Compr Psychiatry 30:218–224, 1989

Jacobs SC, Hansen FF, Kasl SV, et al: Anxiety disorders during acute bereavement: risk and risk factors. J Clin Psychiatry 51:269–274, 1990

Jacobs S, Lieberman P: Bereavement and depression, in Presentations of Depression. Edited by Cameron OG. New York, Wiley International, 1987, pp 169–184

Kasl SV, Ostfeld AM, Berkman LF, et al: Stress and alcohol consumption: the role of selected social and environmental factors, in Stress and Addiction. Edited by Gottheil E, Druley KA, Pashko S, et al. New York, Brunner/Mazel, 1987, pp 40–60

Kim K, Jacobs SC: Pathologic grief and its relationship to other psychiatric disorders. J Affect Disord 21:257–263, 1991

Lazare A: Unresolved grief, in Outpatient Psychiatry: Diagnosis and Treatment. Edited by Lazare A. Baltimore, Williams & Wilkins, 1979, pp 498–512

Lindeman E: Symptomatology and management of acute grief. Am J Psychiatry 101:141–148, 1944

Lund DA, Dimond MF, Caserta MS, et al: Identifying elderly with coping difficulties after two years of bereavement. Omega 16:213–224, 1985–1986

Maddison D, Viola A: The health of widows in the year following bereavement. J Psychosom Res 12:297–306, 1968

Maddison DC, Walker WL: Factors affecting the outcome of conjugal bereavement. Br J Psychiatry 113:1057–1068m 1967

Mendelson JH, Babor TF, Mello NK, et al: Alcoholism and prevalence of medical and psychiatric disorders. J Stud Alcohol 47:361–366, 1986

Mor B, McHorney C, Sherwood S: Secondary morbidity among the recently bereaved. Am J Psychiatry 143:158–163, 1986

Murrell SA, Himmelfarb S: Effects of attachment bereavement and pre-event conditions on subsequent depressive symptoms in older adults. Psychol Aging 4:166–172, 1989

Myers JK, Weissman MM, Tischler GL, et al: Six-month prevalence of psychiatric disorders in three communities. Arch Gen Psychiatry 41:959–967, 1984

Parkes CM: The first year of bereavement. A longitudinal study of the reaction of London widows to the death of their husbands. Psychiatry 33:444–467, 1970

Parkes CM, Brown RJ: Health after bereavement: a controlled study of young widows and widowers. Psychosom Med 34:449–461, 1972

Parkes CM, Weiss RS: Recovery From Bereavement. New York, Basic Books, 1983

Quitkin FM, Rifkin A, Kaplan D, et al: Phobic anxiety syndrome complicated by drug dependence and addiction. Arch Gen Psychiatry 27:159–162, 1972

Radloff LS: The CES-D Scale: A self-report depression scale for research in the general population. Applied Psychological Measurement 1:385–401, 1977

Regier DA, Boyd JH, Burke JD, et al: One month prevalence of mental disorders in the United States. Arch Gen Psychiatry 45:977–988, 1988

Richards JG, McCallum J: Bereavement in the elderly. N Z Med J 89:201–204, 1979

Ross HE, Glaser FB, Germanson T: The prevalence of psychiatric disorders in patients with alcohol and other drug problems. Arch Gen Psychiatry 45:1023–1031, 1988

Rynearson EK, Jacobs SC, Marmar CR: Pathologic grief. Psychiatric Update 10:1–9, 1990

Silverman PR, Worden JW: Children's reactions in the early months after the death of a parent. Am J Orthopsychiatry 61:93–104, 1992

Thompson L, Breckenridge J, Gallagher D, et al: Effects of bereavement on self-perceptions of physical health in elderly widows and widowers. J Gerontol 39:309–314, 1984

Vachon MLS, Sheldon AR, Lancee WJ, et al: Correlates of enduring distress patterns following bereavement: social network, life situation, and personality. Psychol Med 12:783–788, 1982

Valanis B, Yeaworth RC, Mullis MR: Alcohol use among bereaved and non-bereaved older persons. Journal of Gerontological Nursing 13:26–32, 1987

Weller RA, Weller EB, Fristad MA, et al: Depression in recently bereaved prepubertal children. Am J Psychiatry 148:1536–1540, 1991

Wiener A, Gerber I, Battin D, et al: The process and phenomenology of bereavement, in Bereavement: Its Psychosocial Aspects. Edited by Schoenberg B, Gerber I. New York, Columbia University Press, 1975, pp 53–65

Worden JW: Bereaved children one year after loss. Paper presented at the Third International Conference on Grief and Bereavement in Contemporary Society, Sydney, Australia, June 30–July 4, 1991

Zisook S: Diagnostic and treatment considerations in depression associated with late life bereavement. Paper presented at the NIH Consensus Development Conference on the Diagnosis and Treatment of Depression in Late Life, Bethesda, MD, November 4–6, 1991

Zisook S, DeVaul RA: Grief, unresolved grief, and depression. Psychosomatics 24:247–256, 1983

Zisook S, Shuchter SR: Depression through the first year after the death of a spouse. Am J Psychiatry 148:1346–1352, 1991

Zisook S, Shuchter S, Schuckit M: Factors in the persistence of unresolved grief among psychiatric outpatients. Psychosomatics 26:497–503, 1985

Zisook S, Shuchter SR, Mulvihill M: Alcohol, cigarette, and medication use during the first year of widowhood. Psychiatric Annals 20:318–326, 1990

CHAPTER 4

Relationship Among the Clinical Complications of Bereavement

Several strategies are available for examining the relationship among pathologic grief, depressions of bereavement, and anxiety disorders of bereavement. In this chapter, three strategies are developed that have been widely used in modern psychiatry to determine the relationship of disorders to each other (Guze 1970).

First, I review a descriptive study to examine the congruence of these three syndromes. Comorbidity would suggest a relationship among them, although conceivably they could all occur independently. In conjunction with this first strategy, longitudinal observations are presented. If the syndromes are coincident or occur in a regular chronological sequence, then a relationship between them would be suggested. Next, I use epidemiological studies to compare the epidemiological profiles of each syndrome to determine if they share the same risk factors and ecology. This strategy typically is limited to family studies to determine if the syndromes occur in consanguine individuals more frequently than in unrelated individuals. If a familial pattern for two or more syndromes is discerned, a common diathesis toward and relationship among the disorders would be suggested. Finally, I review neurobiological studies of bereaved individuals to determine if the syndromes are a function of the same pathophysiological mechanisms, in which case they might be considered to be related. I consider this type of data because response to pharmacological treatment is often used as a biological "probe." Based on the assumption that psychotropic drugs have known modes of action and provide information on the nature of the underlying pathophysiology, a comparison of pharmacological interventions for the syndromes in question would suggest a relationship among the syndromes if they respond to the same treatment.

Congruence of the Syndromes

The absence of standardized, descriptive criteria for pathologic grief has limited not only the study of this particular syndrome but also the comparison of it with major depressions and anxiety disorders. Investigators in two studies (Jacobs et al. 1987a; Zisook and DeVaul 1983) reported moderately high correlations among dimensional measures of unresolved grief, depression, and anxiety. These findings were based on the number and severity of symptoms reported by the bereaved patients. In these studies, the investigators were able to document the concurrence of symptoms of each syndrome, but could neither determine if the scope, intensity, and duration of the symptoms were adequate to meet DSM-III-R (American Psychiatric Association 1987) criteria for the syndromes of pathologic grief, major depressive disorder, and anxiety disorders nor establish comorbidity of the syndromes.

To explore the comorbidity of these syndromes, we (Kim and Jacobs 1991) defined criteria for the diagnosis of pathologic grief and used them in a clinical study of 25 widows and widowers. These bereaved patients had been referred for evaluation by a research assistant because of suspected complications in their grieving process. The criteria (similar to those introduced in Chapter 2 and discussed in Chapter 9) delineated four syndromes: delayed, absent, severe, and chronic grief. This nosology depended on the presence (or absence), the severity, and the duration of the manifestations of separation distress as defined by Bowlby and Parkes (Bowlby 1973, 1980; Parkes 1972; see also Chapter 2). These symptoms included crying, sighing, pining and searching for the deceased, preoccupation with thoughts of the deceased, and functioning with a perceptual set for the deceased.

The results of this small study (Kim and Jacobs 1991) revealed considerable congruence in the occurrence of these syndromes (Table 4–1). Sixteen of the 25 patients studied met criteria for one of the four syndromes of pathologic grief. Eighteen of the 25 were diagnosed with major depressive disorder. Only 1 patient with pathologic grief did not have a depressive syndrome. Three patients with a depression did not have pathologic grief. These results showed a high degree of overlap for pathologic grief and depression. At the same time, it is important to note that about 15% of the bereaved patients with persistent depressions during bereavement did not meet criteria for pathologic grief in our sample. They would have been missed if only criteria for pathologic grief were applied when identifying clinical complications of a loss.

When this study began, we were not concerned with the occurrence of anxiety disorders as we had not yet completed a study showing that bereaved individuals are at high risk for this type of disorder also. As soon as we appreciated the importance of anxiety disorders (Jacobs et al. 1990), we included them as diagnoses in our procedures (Kim and Jacobs 1991). Unfortunately, as a result of this delay, diagnoses for anxiety disorders were

Table 4–1. Cross-tabulations of bereaved persons with or without pathologic grief by presence or absence of panic disorder, generalized anxiety disorder, and depression

Psychiatric disorder	Pathologic grief				Total
	With		Without		
	n	(%)	n	(%)	
Panic disorder					
Present	4	(36)	1	(17)	5
Absent	7	(64)	5	(83)	12
Total	11		6		17
Generalized anxiety disorder					
Present	9	(82)	4	(67)	13
Absent	2	(18)	2	(33)	4
Total	11		6		17
Depression					
Present	15	(94)[a]	3	(33)	18
Absent	1	(6)	6	(67)	7
Total	16		9		25

[a] $P < .001$.
Source. Kim and Jacobs 1991.

obtained on only 17 of the 25 bereaved patients in this study. Of these 17, 11 met criteria for pathologic grief and 5 met criteria for panic disorder. Seven of the 11 patients diagnosed with pathologic grief did not meet criteria for panic disorder. Only one of the 5 who met the criteria for panic disorder did not have pathologic grief. Thus in this subgroup of our sample, almost two-thirds (7 of 11) of the bereaved patients diagnosed with pathologic grief would have been missed if only criteria for panic disorder were used to identify clinical complications of the loss.

Thirteen of the 17 participants in this reduced sample were diagnosed as having generalized anxiety disorder. As noted above, 11 of these met criteria for pathologic grief. Two patients with pathologic grief did not have generalized anxiety disorder. Four with generalized anxiety disorder did not have pathologic grief. Hence, the incidence of generalized anxiety disorder occurring concurrently with pathologic grief was lower than that for major depression and higher than that for panic disorder. The findings regarding generalized anxiety disorder were similar to those regarding depression when criteria for pathologic grief alone were used; about one-third (4 of 13) of the bereaved patients were not correctly diagnosed with a clinical complication.

This study, which needs replication and, ultimately, confirmation using a longitudinal design, serves as important background for the task of defining criteria for identifying the complications of bereavement. The absence of complete congruence among pathologic grief and the syndromes of depression and anxiety disorders is one reason that it is important to develop criteria for pathologic grief that are based on the manifestations of separation distress. This approach avoids a priori assumptions about a hierarchy or causal relationships among the clinical complications of bereavement as we currently understand them. Thus a diagnosis of pathologic grief defined in this manner could identify clinical complications that otherwise would be missed and would have the virtue of referring the clinical problem to the environmental stressor that precipitated it.

Furthermore, the definition of criteria for pathologic grief in terms of separation distress would avoid assumptions about the congruence of occurrence of the syndromes. Is the congruence a reflection of comorbidity when two maladaptive processes converge in the same individual, or does the congruence indicate that the different syndromes are different aspects of an identical process? Asked another way, is the occurrence of the various syndromes cumulative or is it a function of severity or specific aspects of the experience of loss such as trauma (see Chapter 5)? If the syndromes overlap, is the overlap completely coincidental or are the syndromes different phases in an evolving process? Cross-sectional, descriptive studies of the type described above cannot answer this type of question; what is needed are longitudinal follow-up, epidemiological surveys, and neurobiological studies.

Longitudinal Studies of the Complications of Bereavement

Longitudinal studies of the evolution of pathologic grief, major depressions, and anxiety disorders over the first year of bereavement have the potential to provide an important perspective on the relationship of these syndromes to one another. If the occurrence of two syndromes follows a regular chronological sequence, it may be suggested that those two syndromes reflect a common pathologic process. Sometimes retrospective reconstructions of the history of illness must substitute for longitudinal observations because of the prohibitive cost of the latter. The use of this type of strategy was illustrated in the recent controversy over the nature of panic disorder with agoraphobia in which the primacy and uniqueness of panic anxiety in the etiology of the disorder was debated (Brier et al. 1986; Lelliot et al. 1989).

With regard to bereavement, Parkes (1970) made the clinical observation, based in part on his small longitudinal study of 22 London widows, that delayed grief is associated with depressions that occur later in the first year of bereavement. Our (Kim and Jacobs 1991) retrospective reconstruction of the natural history of the clinical complications in our small sample (described above) confirmed this association of major depression with delayed grief in the two participants who reported having delayed grief. In addition, in our study we noted that panic disorder was associated exclusively with a severe separation anxiety syndrome, but we were unable to determine the sequence of this relationship.

Other than these limited observations, no longitudinal studies have addressed the question of natural history using psychiatric diagnoses. Although longitudinal studies using dimensional measures of depressive and anxious mood have been reported (Gallagher et al. 1982; Harlow et al. 1991; Hays 1991; Vachon et al. 1982), the data from these studies are limited insofar as the measures simply count the number of symptoms without documenting the occurrence of clinically significant syndromes. Thus aside from the suggestion that depressions late in the first year of bereavement may be an evolutionary phase in the course of delayed grief (a hypothesis that is consistent with the nature of separation in animal studies), the scant evidence from studies of the natural history of the clinical complications of bereavement does not help us much in forming a conclusion about the relationship among the syndromes.

Epidemiological Profiles of the Syndromes

Another strategy for examining the relationship among pathologic grief, major depressions of bereavement, and anxiety disorders of bereavement is to compare the epidemiological profile for each syndrome. An epidemiological profile consists of sociodemographic characteristics of and risk factors associated with a particular syndrome. If the profiles for two syndromes are quite different, the syndromes may be independent. If the profiles are similar, the idea of a close relationship between the two syndromes is reinforced, whether this idea presupposes that there is a common etiology for two separate pathologic processes or that the two apparently different pathologic processes are just two phases in the evolution of the same disease. This type of strategy has been used to help clarify the distinction between unipolar and bipolar depressions (Perris 1966). In addition, this strategy has been used to establish the similarity of unipolar depressions to the presence of depressive symptoms, which may be diagnostically subthreshold, measured by dimensional scales (Boyd and Weissman 1981). In general, this type of strategy has been used to identify diseases that share the same ecology, thereby identifying potential environmental factors, as well as physiological mechanisms, that are important in the etiology of a particular disease (Cassel 1976).

The data on sociodemographic variables and risk factors for the three syndromes that occur as complications of bereavement, obtained from three clinical epidemiological studies (Jacobs et al. 1989, 1990; Kim and Jacobs 1991), are summarized in Table 4–2. Also summarized in Table 4–2 is the information obtained from a review of the bereavement literature for each variable we studied. This information is included to place our particular findings in the context of other studies. The way in which these two sets of data are presented allows us to emphasize the large gaps that exist in our knowledge about the epidemiology of the clinical complications of bereavement.

Table 4–2. Sociodemographic characteristics and risk factors for complications of bereavement

	Complications			
Variables	Pathologic grief ($n = 25$)	Major depression ($n = 111$)	Panic disorder ($n = 102$)	Generalized anxiety disorder ($n = 102$)
Female gender	NS	+	NS	+[a]
Literature review	+	+/–	x	x
Younger age	NS	NS	NS	+
Literature review	+	+	x	x
Education	NS	NS	NS	NS
Literature review	x	x	x	x
Unemployment	NS	+	NS	NS
Literature review	+	x	x	x
Living alone	x	NS	NS	NS
Literature review	x	+	x	x
Major depressions, personal history	NS	NS	NS	+
Literature review	x	+/–	x	x
Major depressions, family history	NS	NS	NS	NS
Literature review	x	x	x	x
Anxiety disorders, personal history	NS	x	+	+
Literature review	x	x	x	x
Anxiety disorders, family history	NS	x	+[b]	+
Literature review				
Sudden Death	+	NS	x	x
Literature review	+	x	x	x

Note. NS = findings not significant; + = positive findings; +/– = both positive and negative findings; x = no data available.
[a]$P < .07$.
[b]$P < .06$.
Source. Jacobs et al. 1989, 1990; Kim and Jacobs 1991.

The juxtaposition of our data with that from other bereavement literature also points out contradictions between the two sets of data. For example, our negative findings (Kim and Jacobs 1991) were inconsistent with the findings of another study (Zisook and DeVaul 1983) in which women, younger individuals, and unemployed individuals were observed to be at a higher risk for pathologic grief (see Table 4–2). In fact, the findings regarding widows from one of our earlier studies that used dimensional measures (Jacobs et al. 1987a), contradicted our findings in a later study that used diagnostic measures (Kim and Jacobs 1991). The perspective offered by the literature review suggests more congruence of epidemiological profiles among the different syndromes than that indicated by our own data. On the other hand, when discrepancies between our data and other studies arise, it indicates that the evidence is mixed on the particular variable. The bereavement literature may also provide mixed evidence, as is indicated in Table 4–2.

An examination of the data in Table 4–2 that originated from our studies (Jacobs et al. 1989, 1990; Kim and Jacobs 1991) suggests that pathologic grief, major depressions of bereavement, and the anxiety disorders of bereavement have rather different epidemiological profiles. For example, the only variable significantly associated ($P < .05$) with pathologic grief is sudden death. (It should be noted that the number of participants in this particular study [Kim and Jacobs 1991] was quite small [$N = 25$].) With regard to major depression, we observed that women and unemployed people are at a higher risk than other bereaved individuals for developing complications (Jacobs et al. 1989). The suddenness of death was not a risk factor for depression. For panic disorder, the risk factors were a personal and family history of anxiety disorder. Generalized anxiety disorder presented yet a different pattern, with women, younger individuals, bereaved people with a personal history of major depression, and bereaved people with a personal and family history of anxiety disorders at higher risk than others. There was no evidence for a consanguineous pattern of occurrence for any of the complications of bereavement. These different profiles suggest that the different syndromes may be related to separate etiological processes and ecologies. However, when the evidence from the other studies is used to supplement our own data, the apparent discrepancies in risk factors among the syndromes are reduced.

Overall, the clearest impression we receive from looking at Table 4–2 is of the number of gaps in our knowledge (noted by the x's), which indicates the limits of our information on several aspects of these syndromes. The absence of data restricts the power of the strategy used in Table 4–2 for judging the relationship among the clinical complications of bereavement.

Neurobiological Comparisons

The rationale for making biological comparisons among the forms of psychopathology that are identified as clinical complications of bereavement stems from theoretical perspectives on the biomedical nature of bereavement and its complications. For example, as one of the latest in a series of such formulations (Engel 1961; Kaufman and Rosenblum 1967), Klein (1980) speculated that the biological control mechanisms that underlie protest-separation anxiety in bereaved individuals are the same as those underlying panic disorder. Similarly, he conjectured that the despair and withdrawal phase of bereavement may share the same biological, regulatory substrate with clinical depression. According to this view, thresholds in the regulatory systems that are abnormally lowered as a result of genetic or developmental factors can facilitate panic attacks on the one hand or major depressions on the other, particularly in stressful circumstances. Based on this rationale, there is good reason to look for similarities in the biology of pathologic grief, major depressions, and anxiety disorders.

Although animal models of separation and loss have been widely developed, thus providing preclinical data on physiological mechanisms and allowing the refinement of theories of biological mechanisms in humans, little has been done to study the physiology of normal and complicated bereavement in humans. The exceptions to this rule are a small number studies of neuroendocrine function (Das and Berrios 1984; Hofer et al. 1972a, 1972b; Jacobs et al. 1985, 1986a, 1986b, 1987b; Kosten et al. 1984a, 1984b; Shuchter et al. 1986), a small number of studies on immune function (Irwin and Weiner 1987; Irwin et al. 1987; Schleifer et al. 1983, 1984), and a recent study of sleep physiology (Reynolds et al. 1992).

Neuroendocrine function. In our series of studies conducted on bereaved spouses (Jacobs et al. 1986a, 1986b, 1987b; Kosten et al. 1984a, 1984b), we used a comparison group of spouses who were faced with a potential loss. Our observations were consistent with the conclusion in the extensive literature on stress that bereavement evokes a response from those endocrine systems that are identified as stress-responsive systems. Bereavement as a stressor did not appear to be more severe or unique in terms of endocrine physiology than did threatened loss. Furthermore, a state of high physiological arousal was not found in everyone who was bereaved; instead, physiological arousal was a function of the type, degree, and course over time of the psychological distress caused by the loss.

Some similarities between bereavement and both depression and anxiety emerged from the studies above. Several observations—such as evidence for increased adrenocortical activity, evidence for elevated adrenal medullary and sympathetic activity, the suggestion that the prolactin system may be activated, and the finding that growth hormone dynamics were altered in some bereaved subjects—were consistent with observations made in some depressed patients, as well as in some patients with panic disorder. These physiological changes in bereaved individuals were not associated directly and simply with scores on depression or general anxiety instruments but rather were a function of multiple variables including age, separation anxiety, and perhaps defensiveness (at least in the case of growth hormone) in complicated interactions. (These studies are reviewed in more detail in Chapter 8.)

Immune function. Immune function is another area on which biological studies of bereavement have begun to concentrate during the past 15 years (Bartrop et al. 1977; Schleifer et al. 1983). In these studies, the investigators observed both suppressed lymphocyte responses to mitogen stimulation (Bartrop et al. 1977; Schleifer et al. 1983) and defective natural killer cell activity in acutely bereaved patients (Irwin and Weiner 1987; Irwin et al. 1987). Alterations in T cell subpopulations, with a loss of T suppressor/cytotoxic cells, have also been observed in bereaved women who reported depressive symptoms (Irwin and Weiner 1987). In studies that differentiate between depression and separation distress, the immune changes appear to be mediated by depressive states (Calabrese et al. 1987; Schleifer et al. 1984). Thus the evidence from this line of investigation suggests there are common biological mechanisms between bereavement and depression, but an independent role for separation distress or pathologic grief as the psychological correlate of an immune disturbance is questionable.

Sleep physiology. The study of sleep physiology is another area of inquiry into the biology of bereavement. In a recent study, Reynolds et al. (1992) demonstrated that the changes in sleep physiology observed in patients with major depression are also observed in bereaved, depressed patients but not in bereaved patients who have no depression. These changes included lower sleep efficiency, more early morning awakening, shorter rapid-eye-movement (REM) latency, greater percentage of REM sleep, and lower rates of delta wave generation in the first non-REM period. The changes were associated with the depressive aspects of bereavement and not with separation distress unless depression was also present, suggesting in this case that the underlying anatomical and physiological substrates of separation distress are independent from that of depression.

Pharmacological responses. When psychiatric disorders are treated pharmacologically, the pharmacological agents are often used as probes for elucidating the underlying physiology of the disorder. This strategy is also potentially useful in understanding the relationship among the clinical complications of bereavement. Only two studies have focused on the pharmacological treatment of the clinical complications of bereavement (Jacobs et al. 1987c; Pasternak et al. 1991), both of which were small, open trials. When we (Jacobs et al. 1987c) did an open trial of desipramine treatment for major depressions of bereavement, we found that 8 of 10 bereaved, depressed participants responded to the treatment. Curiously, although the depressive symptoms improved, the symptoms of separation distress did not, suggesting that the biological substrates for these two syndromes are different. In an open trial of nortriptyline, Pasternak et al. (1991) observed the same distinction in the treatment of depression and separation distress. This observation requires more systematic testing because it is based on a limited amount of data. It conflicts with other anecdotal reports of the positive response of separation distress to tricyclic antidepressants (Shuchter 1982). It is also contrary to the finding in one placebo-controlled clinical trial in which imipramine was used to treat separation anxiety disorder of childhood (Gittelman and Klein 1971). However, in another placebo-controlled trial in which clomipramine was used to treat school phobia in children (Berney et al. 1981), 80% of whom have separation anxiety disorder, the authors found that the drug had no advantage over placebo. If tricyclics do act selectively, having an effect on depressive symptoms but not on the symptoms of separation distress, this suggests that the underlying physiology is distinct for each type of symptomatology.

Summary of neurobiological similarities. If the clinical complications of bereavement, pathologic grief, depression, and anxiety disorder share the same neurobiological substrates and mechanisms, it is reasonable to conclude that a relationship exists among them. If no similarity exists, the various complications may be quite separate. It is evident from the discussion above that our knowledge of the neurobiology of separation and loss in humans is still quite rudimentary, and it is premature to reach definitive conclusions about biological similarities between pathologic grief, depression, and anxiety disorders that are identified as complications of bereavement. Most of the evidence points to a distinction between separation distress, which is the essential manifestation of pathologic grief, and depression. On the other hand, there appears to be an increasing amount of evidence that depressions of bereavement are similar to clinical depressions not associated with bereavement, reflected in neuroendocrine function, immune physiology, sleep physiology, and patient response to tricyclic antidepressants.

For the purpose of conceptualizing these findings and future work, it is useful to remember the framework suggested by Parkes (1972) that some aspects of the physiological response to a loss are nonspecific to bereavement and other components are specific to bereavement. By nonspecific responses, he meant

1. The central nervous system arousal and the physiological alarm reactions (documented by Cannon [1929]) that characterize the response to all stresses and that are also at play in bereavement
2. Depressive reactions and the physiology of depression in the sense that they obviously occur in many different circumstances
3. The biology of the bereaved individual's predispositions and manner of coping with the loss insofar as they are traits that are brought to many situations

Knowledge in this area is growing in small increments. Specific aspects of the physiological response to a loss are directly related to the unique experience of a bereavement, such as in separation distress; as Parkes noted in 1972, little is known about these aspects. This is still the case 20 years later as the biological study of separation and loss in humans is still in its infancy.

Conclusions

To the extent that the strategies used in this chapter converge in providing evidence for a relationship among the syndromes that have been defined as clinical complications of bereavement, there is reason to have a greater conviction that these syndromes are different aspects of a single process. The strongest evidence for a relationship comes from the small descriptive study (Kim and Jacobs 1991) that established the coincidence of pathologic grief, major depression, and anxiety disorders during acute bereavement. The longitudinal data suggest a relationship between pathologic grief and major depression. The epidemiological data are not convincing in part because studies of these data are too few. The neurobiological data for humans are also quite limited and the findings in these studies are mixed.

In my review of the papers that have attempted the same kind of analysis done in this chapter, I found only one other report relevant to the syndromes that I am defining as complications of bereavement. This was an article on the relationship between separation anxiety and panic disorder with agoraphobia in adults (Gittelman and Klein 1984). The authors of that study concluded that a relationship between separation anxiety and panic disorder is probable in women based on the course, family histories, and response to treatment of the two types of symptomatology. This is a tangential line of evidence germane to the analysis done here; the Gittelman and Klein article (1984) was itself based on a very small number of studies and, as is usually the case, included mixed evidence. Under the circumstances, it seems that the wisest course is to reserve judgment about the relationship among pathologic grief, major depressions of bereavement, and anxiety disorders of bereavement until further study has been conducted on the relevant issues that are outlined in this chapter.

Having attempted to define pathologic grief by reviewing the historical development of the concept and considering the variety of clinical complications that are identified as a consequence of bereavement (Chapter 2), having examined the magnitude of the clinical problems associated with bereavement (Chapter 3), and having considered their relationship to each other (Chapter 4), in Chapter 5 I discuss a public health and psychiatric model that is recommended for understanding the nature of these clinical complications.

References

American Psychiatric Association: Diagnostic and Statistical Manual of Mental Disorders, 3rd Edition, Revised. Washington, DC, American Psychiatric Association, 1987

Bartrop RW, Luckhurst E, Lazarus L, et al: Depressed lymphocyte function after bereavement. Lancet 1:834–836, 1977

Berney T, Kolvin I, Bhate S, et al: School phobia: a therapeutic trial with clomipramine and short-term outcome. Br J Psychiatry 138:110–118, 1981

Bowlby J: Attachments and Loss, Vol 2, Separation. New York, Basic Books, 1973

Bowlby J: Attachments and Loss, Vol 3, Loss, Sadness and Depression. New York, Basic Books, 1980

Boyd JH, Wiessman MM: Epidemiology of affective disorders. Arch Gen Psychiatry 38:1039–1046, 1981

Brier A, Charney DS, Heninger GR: Agoraphobia with panic attacks. Arch Gen Psychiatry 43:1029–1036, 1986

Calabrese JR, Kling MA, Gold PW: Alterations in immunocompetence during stress, bereavement, and depression: focus on neuroendocrine regulation. Am J Psychiatry 144:1123–1134, 1987

Cannon WB: Bodily Changes in Pain, Hunger, Fear, and Rage. New York, Appleton and Company, 1929

Cassel J: The contribution of the social environment to host resistance. Am J Psychiatry 104:107–123, 1976

Das M, Berrios GE: Dexamethasone suppression test in acute grief. Acta Psychiatr Scand 70:278–281, 1984

Engel GL: Is grief a disease? a challenge for medical research. Psychosom Med 23:18–22, 1961

Gallagher DE, Breckenridge JN, Thompson LW, et al: Effects of bereavement on mental health of elderly widows and widowers. J Gerontol 38:565–571, 1982

Gittelman R, Klein DF: Controlled imipramine treatment of school children. Arch Gen Psychiatry 25:204–211, 1971

Gittelman R, Klein DF: Relationship between separation anxiety and panic and agoraphobic disorders. Psychopathology 17:56–65, 1984

Guze SB: The role of follow up studies: their contribution to diagnostic classification as applied to hysteria. Seminars in Psychiatry 2:392–402, 1970

Harlow SD, Goldberg EL, Comstock GW: A longitudinal study of the prevalence of depressive symptomatology in elderly widowed and married women. Arch Gen Psychiatry 48:1065–1068, 1991

Hays JC: Psychological distress, social environment, and seeking social support following conjugal bereavement. Ph.D. Dissertation, Yale University, 1991

Hofer M, Wolff C, Friedman S, et al: A psychoendocrine study of bereavement, part I: 17-hydroxycorticosteroid excretion rates of parents following death of their children from leukemia. Psychosom Med 34:481–491, 1972a

Hofer M, Wolff C, Friedman S, et al: A psychoendocrine study of bereavement, part II: observations on the process of mourning in relation to adrenocortical function. Psychosom Med 34:492–504, 1972b

Irwin MR, Weiner H: Depressive symptoms and immune function during bereavement, in Biopsychosocial Aspects of Bereavement. Edited by Zisook S. Washington DC, American Psychiatric Press, 1987, pp 159–174

Irwin MR, Daniels M, Bloom ET, et al: Life events, depressive symptoms, and immune function. Am J Psychiatry 144:437–441, 1987

Jacobs SC, Mason JW, Kosten TR, et al: Acute bereavement, threatened loss, ego defenses, and adrenocortical function. Psychother Psychosom 44:151–159, 1985

Jacobs SC, Brown SA, Mason JW, et al: Psychological distress, depression, and prolactin response in stressed persons. Journal of Human Stress 12:113-118, 1986a

Jacobs SC, Mason JW, Kosten TR, et al: Bereavement and catecholamines. J Psychosom Res 30:489–496, 1986b

Jacobs SC, Schaefer CA, Ostfeld AM, et al: The first anniversary of bereavement. Isr J Psychiatry Relat Sci 24:77–85, 1987a

Jacobs SC, Mason J, Kosten T, et al: Urinary free cortisol and separation anxiety early in the course of bereavement and threatened loss. Biol Psychiatry 22:148–152, 1987b

Jacobs SC, Nelson JC, Zisook S: Treating depressions of bereavement with antidepressants: a pilot study. Psychiatr Clin North Am 10:501–510, 1987c

Jacobs SC, Hansen FF, Berkman L, et al: Depressions of bereavement. Compr Psychiatry 30:218–224, 1989

Jacobs SC, Hansen FF, Kasl SV, et al: Anxiety disorders during acute bereavement: risk and risk factors. J Clin Psychiatry 51:269–274, 1990

Kaufman IC, Rosenblum LA: The reaction to separation in infant monkeys: anaclitic depression and conservation-withdrawal. Psychosom Med 29:648–675, 1967

Kim K, Jacobs SC: Pathologic grief and its relationship to other psychiatric disorders. J Affect Disord 21:257–263, 1991

Klein DF: Anxiety reconceptualized. Compr Psychiatry 21:411–427, 1980

Kosten TR, Jacobs SC, Mason JW, et al: Psychological correlates of growth hormone response to stress. Psychosom Med 46:49–58, 1984a

Kosten TR, Jacobs SC, Mason JW, et al: The DST in depression during bereavement. J Nerv Ment Dis 172:359–360, 1984b

Lelliot P, Marks I, Tobena A: Onset of panic disorder with agoraphobia. Arch Gen Psychiatry 46:1000–1004, 1989

Parkes CM: The first year of bereavement. A longitudinal study of the reaction of London widows to the death of their husbands. Psychiatry 33:444–467, 1970

Parkes CM: Bereavement: Studies of Grief in Adult Life. New York, International Universities Press, 1972

Pasternak RE, Reynolds CF, Schlernitzauer M, et al: Acute open-trial nortriptyline therapy of bereavement-related depression in late life. J Clin Psychiatry 52:307–310, 1991

Perris C: A study of bipolar (manic depressive) and unipolar recurrent depressive psychoses. Acta Psychiatr Scand 42(suppl):9–194, 1966

Reynolds CF, Hoch CC, Buysse DJ, et al: Electroencephalographic sleep in spousal bereavement and bereavement related depression of late life. Biol Psychiatry 31:69–82, 1992

Schleifer SJ, Keller SE, Camerino M, et al: Suppression of lymphocyte stimulation following bereavement. JAMA 259:374–377, 1983

Schleifer SJ, Keller SE, Stein M: Stress effects on immunity. Psychiatr J Univ Ott 10:126–130, 1984

Shuchter SR: Antidepressant treatment of grief reactions. Paper presented at the annual meeting of the American Psychiatric Association, Toronto, Canada, May 15–21, 1982

Shuchter SR, Zisook S, Kirkorowicz C, et al: The dexamethasone suppression test in acute grief. Am J Psychiatry 143:879–881, 1986

Vachon MLS, Sheldon AR, Lancee WJ, et al: Correlates of enduring distress patterns following bereavement: social network, life situation and personality. Psychol Med 12:783–788, 1982

Zisook S, DeVaul RA: Grief, unresolved grief, and depression. Psychosomatics 24:247–256, 1983

CHAPTER 5

An Adaptive Model

A clear choice of a conceptual model is useful in that it provides a theoretical framework that functions as a map to guide our thinking. A model can help identify and characterize the elements of the problem to be solved. In this chapter, I develop the thesis that an adaptive model is optimal for understanding the clinical complications of bereavement.

By using an adaptive model, investigators can consider 1) the agents of disease, 2) the afflicted individual, and 3) the environment in which the individual lives and becomes ill (Figure 5–1). It is a model that is part of public health medicine, as well as the psychiatric tradition of thought. This model emphasizes the environment, which promises to be an essential element in understanding the complications of bereavement, whether those complications are identified as pathologic grief, major depressions, or anxiety disorders. In fact, central to contemporary thinking about the complications of bereavement is the relationship of the complications to environmental determinants, such as the nature of the death (Stroebe et al. 1988) or the availability of social resources before and after a death occurs (Vachon and Stylianos 1988; also see Chapter 6). Because it prompts the clinician to consider all the environmental factors that may contribute to the etiology of the complications of treatment, an adaptive model is worthwhile not only for heuristic purposes but also for the clinician who is responsible for evaluating and caring for patients in need of help.

An adaptive model also encourages a clinician to consider the patient's process of adaptation to the challenges caused by the loss. A traditional approach to understanding the adaption challenge of a loss is to define the tasks of grief, based an our understanding of the process derived from experience with bereaved patients who have clinical complications. This approach is useful not only for the bereaved individual but also for the grief counselor (Worden 1982). Another approach to understanding adaptation is to study successful, as well as unsuccessful, coping behaviors of acutely bereaved individuals in the community. Optimally, these studies focus on the active efforts of the bereaved individuals to adjust to their new environment rather than dwelling exclusively on their presumed defects that make them vulnerable to a disorder. Investigations such as these can provide clues to the natural processes of recovery from grief, about which we currently know rather little. (Coping issues are discussed later in Chapter 7 in a review of studies of both conscious and unconscious coping, their relationship to each other, and their relationship to the outcome of bereavement.)

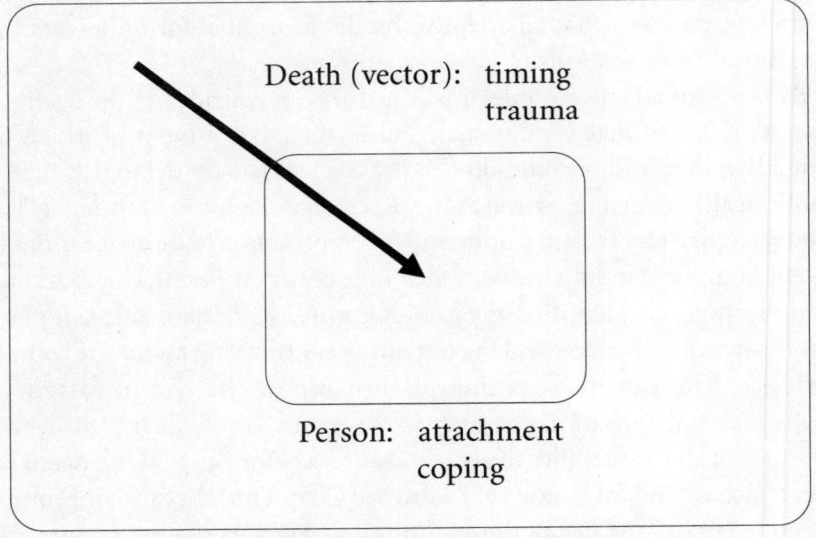

Death (vector): timing
trauma

Person: attachment
coping

Environment: social supports
stress overload

Figure 5–1. Diagram of an adaptive model applied to bereavement. Also indicated are the variations applicable to each element in the model (i.e., death varies in its timing and degree of trauma; the individual varies in his or her attachment to the deceased individual and methods of coping with the death; the individual's environment varies according to the social supports it holds and stress overload experienced by the bereaved individual).

An Adaptive Model

Several theoretical models have been proposed for understanding the nature of normal grief and the clinical complications of bereavement. These include psychoanalytic theory (Freud 1917; Lindeman 1944), attachment theory (Bowlby 1969), traumatic stress theory (Horowitz et al. 1980), and social transition theory (Parkes 1971; Silverman 1986). Each of these models offers a useful perspective on the experience of grief; however, none of them places adequate emphasis on the environment and its role in shaping the response to a loss. For example, attachment theory focuses on the environment primarily as a source of characteristics stemming from psychosocial development that affect the form of bereavement, yet it does so to the relative exclusion of the immediate environment as an important context for understanding an individual's grief. Social transition theory also offers a social perspective on the roles, status, and rituals of change; however it does not focus sufficiently on the characteristics of the death. Moreover, it practically ignores the relationship between the environment and the individual with all of his or her intrapsychic, personal, or biological attributes (Silverman 1986).

An adaptive model provides more adequately for the environment and the individual striving within it. This model of disease is not a new one in thinking about health and illness. In fact, not only is it a well-developed conceptual approach to understanding the occurrence, course, and interventions for diseases in a public health perspective (Dubos 1965), it is also a theoretical approach with a long history in American psychiatry (Hartman 1958; Menninger 1963; Meyer 1957; Vaillant 1977). Crisis theory, which derived from studies of bereavement as well as from studies of other life events, is closely related to an adaptive model (Caplan 1964). In the field of bereavement research, the *deficit model* developed by Stroebe and Stroebe (1987), which originates from social psychology and stress theory, is a close approximation of an adaptive model. The Leiden Bereavement Study (Cleiren 1991) was the only other bereavement project to explicitly choose the concept of adaptation as a basis for thinking about the bereaved patient's adjustment to a loss, choosing this model for essentially the same reasons that I have (i.e., an adaptive model of disease is well suited to the study of the complications of bereavement because it characterizes important aspects of the environment and the bereaved individual's active efforts to cope).

Definition of an Adaptive Model

The concept of an adaptive model requires some explication because many clinicians may be unfamiliar with it, despite its currency in public health medicine and psychoanalytic writings. An adaptive model takes into account not only essential environmental, contextual elements (e.g., social supports that influence an individual's response to a challenge), but also the environmental agent (e.g., a death) of disease or disorder, as well as personal strengths and vulnerabilities that determine if a disease state will occur (Henderson 1988; Susser 1981). It provides a broad enough umbrella to encompass the major insights of attachment theory, traumatic stress theory, psychoanalytic theory, and social transition theory into a perspective that allows clinicians to consider the major elements of the clinical problems when they see patients with complications of bereavement. By incorporating environmental variables into the clinical equation, this model helps to complete our understanding of an afflicted individual's reaction to bereavement.

Adaptation is a concept in medicine and psychiatry that provides an important conceptual foundation for defining health. Dubos (1965), who was interested in understanding diseases as forms of failed adaptation, formulated the definition of health in the following terms:

> I shall take the view that the man of flesh, bone, and illusions will always experience unexpected difficulties as he tries to adapt to the real world, which is often hostile to him. In this light, positive health is not even a concept of the ideal to be striven for hopefully. Rather it is only a mirage, because man in the real world must face the physical, biological, and social forces of his environment, which are forever changing, usually in an unpredictable manner, and frequently with dangerous consequences for him as an individual and for the human species in general. In the picturesque words of an English public health officer, "Man and his species are in perpetual struggle—with microbes, with incompatible mothers-in-law, with drunken car-drivers, and with cosmic rays from Outer Space.... The 'positiveness' of health does not lie in the state, but in the struggle—the effort to reach a goal which in its perfection is unattainable."

An Adaptive Model

In the framework created by Dubos, health was understood as the ability to function or, in other words, the ability to adapt to the environment in which we live. According to Dubos, the concept of perfect health is an elusive chimera toward which we may strive as an ideal but which is always transforming as we face new environmental challenges. Illness or disease is a consequence of maladaptation. Thus diseases of maladaptation are best understood as the result of the interaction between people and their environment, not as an isolated defective state of the individual. If we adopt an adaptive framework for understanding bereavement, the model specifies three components that we went to investigate: the individual, the environment, and vectors (or agents) of disease that provoke new states of adaptation (Henderson 1988; Susser 1981) (Figure 5–1).

The Course of Bereavement as Understood Through the Adaptive Model

In an adaptive model, the death of an intimate is a necessary but not sufficient cause of the clinical complications (or diseases) of bereavement. A loss, originating in the social environment and conceived of as a vector of potential disease, evokes grief in the survivor and, at the same time, causes a fundamental change in the environment. The changed environment is characterized by the irrevocable absence of the deceased individual and the empty situations caused by the loss. As was illustrated in the case example of Ms. A (see Chapter 1), the survivor is repeatedly confronted with these changes, which evoke grief, feelings of insecurity, loss of meaning, and aimlessness of many daily tasks that used to be oriented toward the deceased individual.

Bereaved individuals adapt to the new social environment to establish a homeostatic and ecological equilibrium (a new state of adaptation) that is favorable for their survival. In more concrete terms, the survivor searches for a place in life that is meaningful, secure, productive, and enjoyable and that includes involvement with others. The problems posed by a loss change over time and require varying, creative solutions. In a temporal perspective, adaptation is a dynamic intrapsychic and ecological process with interactions among the cause of illness with its specific features, the bereaved individual with his or her strengths and vulnerabilities, and the environment with its resources and scarcities. For example, a sudden death may increase a survivor's chances of developing clinical complications of bereavement; however, this is most likely in those individuals who perceive they have no ability to control their own lives, an attitude that in itself carries a high risk of complications, which can then be compounded by a sparse social network (Vachon and Stylianos 1988; Vachon et al. 1982).

New assumptions about themselves and the world emerge out of the bereaved individuals' efforts over time to solve the problems confronting them. Attachment behavior that may have been adaptive before the loss in a particular environment can become maladaptive afterwards, not only because the biological and emotional responses to a death can be overwhelmingly severe but also because the changed environment requires new solutions. In the case of the bereaved mother, Ms. A (see Chapter 1), her recovery hinged on acknowledging that she was not managing well as she approached the first anniversary of her son's death. In psychotherapy she adopted a few main strategies for coping with her double loss. Learning about grief and its natural history gave her a growing sense of mastery and confidence in the healing that would occur over time. Using her new knowledge to set an example and teach her surviving children about their grief and how to surmount it became a means of coping that was closely related to the role she had assumed earlier in her life of steering the family through major crises. Implicitly, she accepted her new role as the matriarch of the family after her mother's death. Finally, she made use of a mutual support network provided by the hospice where her mother had died to recognize that she had a problem and to seek professional help.

Clinicians perceive maladaptations to losses as depressions, anxiety disorders, and pathologic grief. All the complications of bereavement are most usefully viewed as variants of pathologic grief because this concept preserves an adaptive perspective in which the clinically salient characteristics of the individual, the environment, and the death can be defined. This view also leads to the identification of depressive or anxiety syndromes specifically linked to loss and grief. It defines the social ecology of an otherwise unrelated group of disorders (i.e., pathologic grief, major depressions, and anxiety disorders). In a sense, this view identifies a separation anxiety disorder in adults that probably occurs most often but not exclusively in the circumstances of bereavement and that probably has some relationship to separation anxiety disorder of childhood. By emphasizing the social environment and the grieving tasks derived from it, such as the need to adjust to the status of being widowed, it partially resolves the controversy over how long grief endures. For example, the shorter time course of recovery from separation distress on the average will lead to a different conclusion about when grief is completed than the more prolonged time course of social adjustment. Finally, the use of an adaptive model sets the stage for the most effective professional help by providing a framework for multidimensional treatment including pharmacological, psychotherapeutic, and social interventions, as well as their integration into an individual treatment plan (see Chapters 10–14).

Characteristics of Death and Their Effect on Responses to Loss

Only 20 years ago, when the concept of recent life event schedules was being developed, the death of a family member was appreciated as a human stressor of the greatest magnitude (Holmes and Rahe 1968). Little attention was paid to the circumstances or characteristics of the death as determinants of the bereaved individual's response. This omission occurred in a society in which denial of death seemed to be a deeply running undercurrent (Becker 1973), similar in a superficial way to the avoidance of public discussions about sexual life by people living in Victorian England (Gorer 1965). As a result of this denial of death, frantic efforts to prolong life distort the natural process of taking leave of family, friends, and places. Not until the hospice movement confronted members of society with this prevailing tendency to turn away from issues of death and dying were people forced to pause and reconsider death. Similarly, avoidance of the idea of death interferes with a close examination of the characteristics of a death as a risk factor for the bereaved individual. It is reasonable to assume that the circumstances of a death are critical factors that shape the form and content of the emotional responses of the survivors. Furthermore, the nature of the death promises to be an important risk factor for complications (Ball 1977; Cleiren 1991; Kim and Jacobs 1991; Lehman et al. 1987; Lundin 1984a; Parkes and Weiss 1983; Sanders 1989), although this is still a controversial question (Bornstein et al. 1973; Breckenridge et al. 1986; Heyman and Gianturco 1973; Lundin 1984b; Maddison and Walker 1967) for research to resolve. An adaptive model facilitates the recognition of clinically salient aspects of the death—the provocative agent of the disorders of bereavement—by explicitly acknowledging these as an essential part of the theoretical model.

In the literature on bereavement, several approaches to characterizing death have been used to understand the bereaved individual's response. These include the distinction between deaths that are timely or untimely, sudden or anticipated, caused by acute illness or chronic illness, and traumatic or nontraumatic. It is the untimely, unanticipated deaths from acute illness or trauma that usually create a higher risk of complications during bereavement. However, investigators have noted exceptions to this rule (Breckenridge et al. 1986; Heyman and Gianturco 1973; Sanders 1989), particularly among the elderly, for whom chronic illnesses before a death are associated with more difficult bereavement.

Traumatic Deaths

Traumatic losses illustrate how the circumstances of a death are a determinant of the survivor's emotional response. As a consequence of the Vietnam War, American psychiatric attention was once again focused on the traumatic disorders of returning war veterans. This renewed interest in traumatic symptomatology extended into many areas, including the realization that many deaths in American society result from traumatic causes. Trauma may not be the leading cause of mortality in the United States, but traumatic deaths are not unusual in our society. Annually, trauma causes 8% of the deaths in the United States, and is the leading cause of death for people in the United States under age 30 (U.S. Bureau of the Census 1985). As a consequence, traumatic losses are very frequent among young surviving spouses and families.

With regard to the survivors of a loss, a distinction can be made between deaths from natural causes and deaths from unnatural causes (e.g., disasters, accidents, suicides, and homicides). The form and meaning of unnatural dying strongly shapes the bereavement of the survivor. It does so by introducing themes of violence, victimization, and volition (i.e., the choice of death over life, as in the case of suicide) (Rynearson 1987). A traumatic death leaves many bereaved survivors horrified by the grotesqueness of the end of life and terrified by a sense of vulnerability caused by exposure to a life-threatening experience. Traumatic deaths create the vehement emotions (Van der Kolk and Van der Hart 1989) felt by some bereaved survivors of traumatic losses who endure in a resulting environment that is not only desolate but also dangerous. The emotional turmoil is expressed in frightening perceptions, hypervigilance, heightened startle reactions, feelings of helplessness, and insecurity (Horowitz 1986). The circumstances of the death are life-threatening to the survivor in their ugliness, their brutality, and, in the case of suicide, their rejection of life. The death evokes psychologically self-protective reactions such as denial, dissociation of reality from consciousness, and avoidance of consequences. This is expressed in emotional numbing, disbelief, and failure to cognitively integrate the death into the bereaved individual's world view (Horowitz 1986). Disorganization of behavior patterns occurs as the meaning of many ordinary tasks of life is lost. These reactions to a traumatic loss are associated with severe grief (Cleiren 1991). They may lead to prolonged emotional distress for years after a loss (Lehman et al. 1987), as well as to a higher risk for major depressions, anxiety disorders, and posttraumatic stress disorder than does nontraumatic bereavement (Shore et al. 1986), although the evidence is mixed (Cleiren 1991; Lundin 1984b). Thus traumatic processes can interfere with the typical evolution of grief and interrupt its spontaneous resolution.

Separation Distress and Traumatic Distress

There is preliminary evidence (Nader et al. 1990; Pynoos et al. 1987) that traumatic losses introduce a separate and distinct dimension of emotional distress into bereavement, resulting from the survivor's perception of a dangerous environment; this is known as *traumatic distress*. If this theory is confirmed, it buttresses the importance of considering the traumatic aspects of deaths and their implications for bereaved individuals. For example, investigators in a study of children who were exposed to a terrorist shooting of their schoolmates observed that separation distress and traumatic distress were indeed two separate dimensions of emotional distress secondary to a traumatic loss (Nader et al. 1990; Pynoos et al. 1987). One type of distress was characterized by fear, horror, vulnerability, and disintegration of cognitive assumptions; this type of distress was related primarily to self-protective motivation. The other type of distress was characterized by longing, loneliness, searching, and sorrow; this was related to the motivation to attach and remain bonded to others. Conceivably, these distinctions could be extended into diagnostic criteria that are developed to identify complications of trauma and bereavement. In the case of traumatic distress, the criteria would be based on traumatic theory; in the case of separation distress, they would be based on attachment theory.

In their study of recent life events, Finlay-Jones and Brown (1981) advanced the analogous argument that specific qualities of an experience have a relationship to specific qualities of the subsequent emotional distress. They distinguished between fear-provoking life events that are associated with a risk for anxiety disorders and loss-related life events that are associated with a risk for depressions. This intriguing pattern requires confirmation.

In emphasizing the distinction between traumatic distress and separation distress, the similarities that exist between these types of distress should not be ignored. Notably, both emotional processes are characterized by episodes of intrusion of thoughts, images, and feelings into consciousness, on the one hand, and avoidance of event-specific cognition and emotion when the distress is excessive, on the other hand. Also both processes may be associated with secondary somatic, depressive, or anxious symptoms that add to the appearance, if not the reality, of their being similar rather than different. One interesting task of future clinical research will be to test the similarities and differences between these type of distresses.

Degree of exposure. Just as it is useful to consider exposure to an exogenous toxin or microbial agent of disease, there is evidence that it is also helpful to estimate the degree of exposure to trauma in judging the risk of clinical complications after disastrous events. Estimations of the magnitude of the traumatic event, the directness of exposure, and the extent of involvement in the traumatic event are all elements of the degree of exposure that are now beginning to receive attention with regard to both adults and children (Pynoos et al. 1987; Shore et al. 1986; Smith et al. 1990; Terr 1983). Estimates of the intensity of exposure to traumatic experiences are now recommended for use in predicting who should receive early intervention (Pynoos and Nader 1990). This is another example of how an adaptive model, which serves to clarify the role of the environment in the origin of illness, fosters a better understanding of clinical problems. The following example of a bereaved father whose daughter was brutally murdered illustrates the consequences of a traumatic loss:

Case 4

Mr. D was a 45-year-old businessman whose 22-year-old daughter was assaulted and murdered by a stranger who was high on drugs. This occurred in a downtown parking lot at the end of the work day as she was about to return home. This traumatic loss occurred 1 year before Mr. D came to the clinic, stating that he was concerned about becoming dependent on lorazepam and that he wished to have a psychiatric evaluation of his "confusion." He said that he was suffering from intense grief over the loss. His grief was compounded by anger at the failure of the judicial system to bring the alleged murderer to justice promptly and efficiently. He was tortured with the images of his daughter's death that flooded him repeatedly and left him feeling helpless, violated, and revengeful. Over repeated meetings it was my impression that the traumatic replay of the death overshadowed his grief over the loss.

During the first year of bereavement, Mr. D reported mild intermittent depressive symptoms, and for the month prior to his evaluation he described a major depressive syndrome. This included depressed mood and crying, a complete disruption of his sleep pattern (difficulty falling asleep, sleep continuity disturbance, early morning awakening), chronic fatigue, poor concentration, loss of interest in athletic and social activities, anhedonia (including reduced sexual drive), guilt over not being a better father (including the feeling that he had failed his deceased daughter), occasional suicidal ideation, and conspicuous worsening of his mood in the early mornings when he would become agitated to the point of feeling like screaming. At these moments he would ruminate about death. When Mr. D described his "confusion," he referred to the intermingling of his grief and deeply felt need for revenge against his daughter's assailant as if his anger was interrupting and interfering with his grief, thereby preventing him from accepting the loss and working through it. He feared that he would lose control and do something crazy.

Mr. D's family was concerned about his violent fantasies toward the murderer, whose defense attorney was postponing the trial through judgments of incompetency to stand trial, thus signaling the likelihood of an insanity defense when the case did come to trial. Mr. D maintained a self-image of his role in the family as a resourceful father, and the circumstances sorely taxed that image. Managing his family's part in the trial of his daughter's assailant was the central aim of his life. He was constantly frustrated and left feeling helpless by the postponements. He did not know what to do. All Mr. D's assumptions about safety and justice in American society were overturned. Instead of feeling comfortable in his environment he seemed on edge and felt a need to prowl. His wife was very supportive. She seemed to be less intensely disturbed by the loss and appeared to be resolving her grief at a faster pace than he was. Mr. D believed that she was frustrated by his lack of sexual interest in her.

Mr. D attended a mutual support group, but did not find it helpful, in part because it stimulated feelings that were very intense and hard to control. He left the meetings feeling worse and concerned that he would become like the other chronically bitter and aggressive people, as he perceived them, who attended the meetings. He was started on desipramine (75 mg/day) and experienced relief of his insomnia within 1 week. Over the next 3 weeks, he reported continued improvement in concentration, mood, and resiliency to stresses at work and a growing feeling of being under control. As these changes emerged he appeared to be freer to discuss his grief, his intense yearning and searching for his daughter (leaving the light on at night as if she would return home), and his murderous rage at his daughter's assailant without fear of losing control of his feelings and actions. He continued to improve despite going through a court hearing 18 months after the murder, the type of event that used to emotionally derail him. At this point, Mr. D stopped his treatment, complaining that the desipramine caused a sensation of dryness in his mouth and stating that he was now confident that he could manage on his own.

The court hearings dragged on, the trial was repeatedly postponed, and, after 3 months, because of his frustration, anger, and stress, Mr. D reentered treatment with a depressive relapse. This was yet another example of how the traumatic aspects of the loss prolonged the emotional complications. Because use of desipramine again relieved his symptoms, Mr. D decided that he would continue its use until the trial occurred. More than 2 years after his daughter's death, the trial still had not been scheduled. In the meantime, Mr. D made use of psychotherapy to understand the nature of his grief, the interaction of his grief with traumatic distress, and the limitations of his ability to control or change the situation faced by him and his family. On the other hand, he also took considerable initiative to prod the judicial system into action on a judgment about his daughter's murderer.

Mr. D's experience illustrates the interplay between loss and trauma, separation distress and traumatic distress, and an empty social environment and a threatening, hostile, untrustworthy environment. Although he was not directly exposed to the traumatic event, for him his daughter's death was unequivocally traumatic. Traumatic distress was an intense recurrent theme in the course of his grief that seemed to interfere with the resolution of his separation distress. His basic assumptions about himself and his family's life in a safe, predictable, and just world were violently shaken. He found little solace in his social environment, which failed to understand his uniquely horrible loss and his desire for revenge. In these ways, the nature of his daughter's death fundamentally altered the quality of his environment and the course of his emotional response to the loss. An adaptive model that incorporates an environmental component into thinking about the clinical complications of bereavement thus facilitates our understanding of salient aspects of Mr. D's experience that might otherwise be given short shrift or even neglected.

Sudden, Unexpected Deaths

The bereaved survivor of an unnatural, traumatic death is unprepared for the loss that is usually sudden and unexpected, as well as premature. The survivor of a sudden, unexpected loss from natural causes, such as an acute heart attack, is equally unprepared for the loss, particularly if the death occurs at a young age. In this sense, lessons learned from traumatic losses offer a perspective on the emotional consequences of deaths that are not conspicuously traumatic in nature. These include not only deaths from acute illness, for which there is a lack of preparation, but also deaths from chronic, disfiguring, painful diseases that horrify the survivors and break down their usual denial or other defenses used to cope with death.

The relationship of premature, unexpected, and calamitous deaths to trauma and the importance of this for clinical work was appreciated by Weisman (1973); however, it is the traumatic stress literature that has driven the message home. The findings of Schut et al. (1991) buttress the contention of a relationship between the consequences of traumatic and untimely deaths. These authors studied 128 bereaved adults whose family members had died from multiple causes (cardiac disease and cancer were the major causes of death; unnatural, traumatic causes were rare) and found evidence of intrusive and avoidant, traumatic symptoms in 60%–80% of the sample. (The rate of traumatic symptomatology depended on when the participants were observed at four points in time over the first 25 months of bereavement.) Posttraumatic stress syndromes were observed in 20%–31%; 9% met criteria for posttraumatic stress disorder on all four assessments during the first 25 months of bereavement. (Death by unnatural, traumatic causes was not associated with the posttraumatic stress syndrome.) The traumatic symptomatology was significantly associated with not having anticipated the loss and not having taken leave of the individual who had died. This is an important study in that it searched systematically for traumatic symptoms in a sample of bereaved individuals who were not selected because of a presumed traumatic loss and found impressive levels of traumatic symptomatology.

Other investigators have observed that sudden deaths cause higher rates of maladjustment to the loss (Carey 1977; Lundin 1984a; Parkes and Weiss 1983). Furthermore, in another study, Cleiren (1991) found that intrusion and avoidance (measured by the Impact of Event Scale [Horowitz et al. 1979]) was just as intense among those who had experienced deaths of family members from long-term illness as among those who had experienced death of family members through traffic fatalities. Needless to say, one implication of the findings from these studies, if they are confirmed, is that the DSM-III-R criteria (American Psychiatric Association 1987) for posttraumatic stress disorder that exclude "normal bereavement" from the spectrum of traumatic experiences need to be revised.

The traumatic dimension of bereavement from a sudden death was illustrated in the case example of Ms. B, whose husband had died suddenly from a pulmonary embolus (see Chapter 2). Her exposure to the sudden death was direct and intense although the death of her husband was less inherently traumatic than that of Mr. D's daughter. Traumatic distress was latent in Ms. B's grief and eventually became explicit on her third return for help. The loss precipitated a massive challenge to her assumptions about her life and her world that left her insecure and frightened about the future. For example, she took great pride in her family and its cohesiveness, particularly in the light of the divorce of her parents when she was young. She had counted on an intimate and enjoyable retirement with her husband. The sudden loss of her presumably healthy husband left her unprepared for the loneliness of living unmarried, the role of serving as a single parent for her adult children, and the absence of membership in a protective social milieu. Her adjustment to the status of being widowed followed an independent course over time by comparison with the course of the separation distress. The social adjustment to her new and more threatening social environment appeared to take longer and still was incomplete when she left therapy the third time. In her case, she had excellent social supports not only in her family but also in the friends who formed a well-developed social network that survived intact after the loss and mitigated the traumatic aspects of the loss.

Conclusions

In this chapter, I have introduced an adaptive model for understanding the nature of the complications of bereavement. The concept of an adaptive model includes the idea that the force or agent of disease emanates out of the environment, impinges on the individual, changes both the individual and his or her environment in the process, and requires active, creative, and reactive efforts from the individual in interaction with the environment to cope with the change. The occurrence of a traumatic death illustrates many of these issues. The case examples given illustrate the importance of understanding the characteristics of the death in determining the bereaved individual's response to the loss. Traumatic aspects of the death and the degree of exposure to the trauma not only shape the bereaved individual's response, as reflected in traumatic distress, but also influence that individual's vulnerability to clinical complications through prolonging the grief.

The lessons learned from studying traumatic deaths, which are an extreme but not uncommon example, can be applied to sudden, unexpected deaths from other causes. Once the courses of separation distress, traumatic distress, and eventually social adjustment to widowhood (see Chapter 6) are separated out, it becomes clearer that each may follow a different schedule of resolution, an observation that in turn can help us to clarify the controversy over when grief is completed. In other words, the question of when grief is completed can only be addressed in reference to a specific type of distress or task. This is an important issue in nosology and clinical practice that I return to in Chapter 6. Finally, emphasis on a bereaved individual's interaction with either a desolate or a frightening environment or both places greater accent on the different means that an individual uses to cope with the problems caused by different types of loss (this topic is taken up in more detail in Chapter 7 on adaptation).

References

American Psychiatric Association: Diagnostic and Statistical Manual of Mental Disorders, 3rd Edition, Revised. Washington, DC, American Psychiatric Association, 1987
Ball JF: Widow's grief: the impact of age and mode of death. Omega 7:307–333, 1977
Becker E: The Denial of Death. New York, Free Press, 1973
Bornstein PE, Clayton PJ, Halikas JA, et al: The depression of widowhood after thirteen months. Br J Psychiatry 122:561–566, 1973
Bowlby J: Attachment and Loss, Vol 1: Attachment. New York, Basic Books, 1969
Breckenridge JN, Gallagher D, Thompson LW, et al: Characteristic depressive symptoms of bereaved elders. J Gerontol 41:163–168, 1986
Caplan G: Principles of Preventive Psychiatry. New York, Basic Books, 1964
Carey RG: The widowed: a year later. Journal of Counseling Psychology 24:125–131, 1977
Cleiren MPHD: Adaptation After Bereavement. Leiden, Holland, DSWO Press, 1991
Dubos R: Man Adapting. New Haven, CT, Yale University Press, 1965
Finlay-Jones R, Brown G: Types of stressful life events and the onset of anxiety and depressive disorders. Psychol Med 11:803–815, 1981
Freud S: Mourning and melancholia (1917), in The Standard Edition of the Complete Psychological Works of Sigmund Freud, Vol 14. Translated and edited by Strachey J. London, Hogarth Press, 1953, pp 243–258
Gorer G: Death, Grief, and Mourning in Contemporary Britain. London, Cresset Press, 1965
Hartman H: Ego Psychology and the Problem of Adaptation. New York, International Universities Press, 1958
Henderson AS: An Introduction to Social Psychiatry. New York, Oxford University Press, 1988
Heyman DK, Gianturco DT: Long term adaptation by the elderly to bereavement. J Gerontol 28:259–262, 1973
Holmes TH, Rahe RH: The Social Readjustment Rating Scale. J Psychosom Res 11:213–218, 1968
Horowitz MJ: Stress response syndromes: a review of posttraumatic and adjustment disorders. Hosp Community Psychiatry 37:241–249, 1986
Horowitz MJ, Wilner N, Alvarez W: Impact of Event Scale: a measure of subjective stress. Psychosom Med 41:209–218, 1979
Horowitz MJ, Wilner N, Marmar C, et al: Pathological grief and the activation of latent self-images. Am J Psychiatry 137:1157–1162, 1980
Kim K, Jacobs SC: Pathologic grief and its relationship to other psychiatric disorders. J Affect Disord 21:257–263, 1991

Lehman DR, Wortman CB, Williams AF: Long term effects of losing a spouse or child in a motor vehicle accident. Journal of Personal and Social Psychiatry 52:218–231, 1987

Lindeman E: Symptomatology and management of acute grief. Am J Psychiatry 101:141–148, 1944

Lundin T: Morbidity following sudden and unexpected bereavement. Br J Psychiatry 144:84–88, 1984a

Lundin T: Long term outcome of bereavement. Br J Psychiatry 145:414–428, 1984b

Maddison DC, Walker WL: Factors affecting the outcome of conjugal bereavement. Br J Psychiatry 113:1057–1067, 1967

Menninger K: The Vital Balance. New York, Viking Press, 1963

Meyer A: Psychobiology: A Science of Man. Springfield, IL, Charles C Thomas, 1957

Nader K, Pynoos RS, Fairbanks L, et al: Childhood PTSD reactions one year after a sniper attack. Am J Psychiatry 147:1526–1530, 1990

Parkes CM: Psychosocial transitions: a field for study. Soc Sci Med 5:101–105, 1971

Parkes CM, Weiss RS: Recovery From Bereavement. New York, Basic Books, 1983

Pynoos RS, Nader RS: Children's exposure to violence and traumatic death. Psychiatric Annals 20:334–344, 1990

Pynoos RS, Frederick C, Nader K, et al: Life threat and posttraumatic stress in school age children. Arch Gen Psychiatry 44:1057–1063, 1987

Rynearson EK: Psychological adjustment to unnatural dying, in Biopsychosocial Aspects of Bereavement. Edited by Zisook S. Washington, DC, American Psychiatric Press, 1987, pp 77–93

Sanders CM: Grief: The Mourning After. New York, John Wiley, 1989

Schut HAW, de Keijser J, van den Bout J: Incidence and prevalence of post-traumatic symptomatology in conjugally bereaved (abstract). Presented at the Third International Conference on Grief and Bereavement in Contemporary Society. Sydney, Australia, June 30-July 4, 1991

Shore JM, Tatum EL, Vollmer WM: Psychiatric reactions to disaster. Am J Psychiatry 143:590–595, 1986

Silverman P: Widow to Widow. New York, Springer, 1986

Smith EM, North CS, McCool RE, et al: Acute post disaster psychiatric disorders: identification of persons at risk. Am J Psychiatry 147:202–206, 1990

Stroebe W, Stroebe MS: Bereavement and Health. New York, Cambridge University Press, 1987

Stroebe W, Stroebe MS, Domittner G: Individual and situational differences in recovery from bereavement: a risk group identified. Journal of Social Issues 44:143–158, 1988

Susser M: The epidemiology of life stress. Psychol Med 11:1–8, 1981

Terr LC: Chowchilla revisited: the effects of psychic trauma four years after a school bus kidnapping. Am J Psychiatry 140:12–21, 1983

Vachon MLS, Stylianos SK: The role of social support in bereavement. Journal of Social Issues 44:175–190, 1988

U.S. Bureau of the Census: Statistical Abstract of the United States Bureau of the Census. Washington, DC, U.S. Government Printing Office, 1985

Vachon MLS, Sheldon AR, Lancee WJ, et al: Correlates of enduring distress patterns following bereavement: social network, life situation, and personality. Psychol Med 12:783–788, 1982

Vaillant GE: Adaptation to Life. Boston, MA, Little, Brown, 1977

Van der Kolk BA, Van der Hart O: Pierre Janet and the breakdown of adaptation in psychological trauma. Am J Psychiatry 146:1530–1540, 1989

Weisman A: Coping with untimely death. Psychiatry 36:366–377, 1973

Worden JW: Grief Counseling and Grief Therapy: A Handbook for the Mental Health Practitioner. New York, Springer, 1982

CHAPTER 6

Social Networks and Supports

The fundamental concept developed in this chapter is that the death of an intimate not only acts as a vector of disease, but also drastically alters the survivor's social environment. After a death occurs, the survivor must adapt to the desolation caused by the loss. The individual who has died is absent for breakfast, does not return from work at the usual time, or is not at home when the survivor returns from work; the house is empty. These *empty situations* (Horowitz 1990) repeatedly remind the survivor of the absence that typically evoked the painful pangs of grief in the early stages of bereavement. Later in bereavement, the simple fact that the bereaved individual has to learn and practice new skills serves as a reminder of what has been lost. Thus while a death is the vector of grief and its associated disorders, the desolate environment created by a death is part and parcel of the consequences of a loss. In this sense, elements of the social environment are potential risk factors that must be accounted for in understanding the vicissitudes of clinical complications of bereavement. Within an adaptive model for understanding bereavement, the personal responses of bereaved individuals, including their means of coping with the loss, can only be understood in this social context.

However desolate the environment is, it is also a potential source of support. Family, friends, and intimates can fundamentally affect the survivor's health by reducing his or her social isolation and discontent (Lopata 1973), moderating the unhealthy consequences of stress (Cassel 1976; Cobb 1976), and reducing the risk of mortality (Berkman 1985;

Berkman and Syme 1979). Therefore, a study of the social environment can provide clues, just as the study of personal coping promises to do (see Chapter 7), to the processes and resources necessary for healing and recovery. The social aspects of bereavement need to be better understood.

A formal evaluation of the bereaved individual's social support network is often at the core of self-help efforts and ought to be part of every clinical assessment. Knowledge of the social environment provides direction for social interventions that are clinically useful in treating patients. Furthermore, knowledge of the social processes that are a part of bereavement furnishes a foundation on which a professional may base his or her role as consultant and collaborator with self-help groups for newly bereaved individuals.

In this chapter, I also introduce the treatment and rehabilitative tasks that are discussed as part of mutual support programs, including the coordination of professional and self-help services, in Chapter 14.

Concepts of Social Support and a Social Network

Social support is a multidimensional process characterized by a structure and organization (Vachon and Stylianos 1988; see Figure 6–1). It is a product of an individual's social network.

A *social network* can be large or small in the size of its membership (Walker et al. 1977). It can be dense or dilute in the sense that many of the members know each other or do not. It contains various sources of support such as family, confidants, friends, and community services. It serves a variety of functions including the provision of companionship, a sense of belonging, feelings of value, and social comparisons for the purpose of self-evaluation (Vachon and Stylianos 1988).

The social support that a social network provides comprises several components: emotional support through participation in activities that sustain self-esteem, appraisal support that provides a cybernetic control on behavior through the comments and critiques of others, informational support that facilitates the understanding and cognitive processing of the stressful experience, and instrumental support in the form of a helping hand or financial assistance (Vachon and Stylianos 1988). For analytical purposes, the goal of social supports will be viewed as providing both a social framework and the resources needed by the bereaved individual to adjust to the death of a family member or intimate friend.

Stress Within the Social Network

Not only the surviving individual but also the social environment is changed by a death. For example, the social environment of the widow or widower includes married couples, met as friends in adult life, who have common interests, a certain socioeconomic status, and set patterns of social activities (Bankoff 1983; Lopata 1973). This part of the social network often does not know how to help the newly bereaved individual. Married friends experience discomfort in the intense emotional situations that

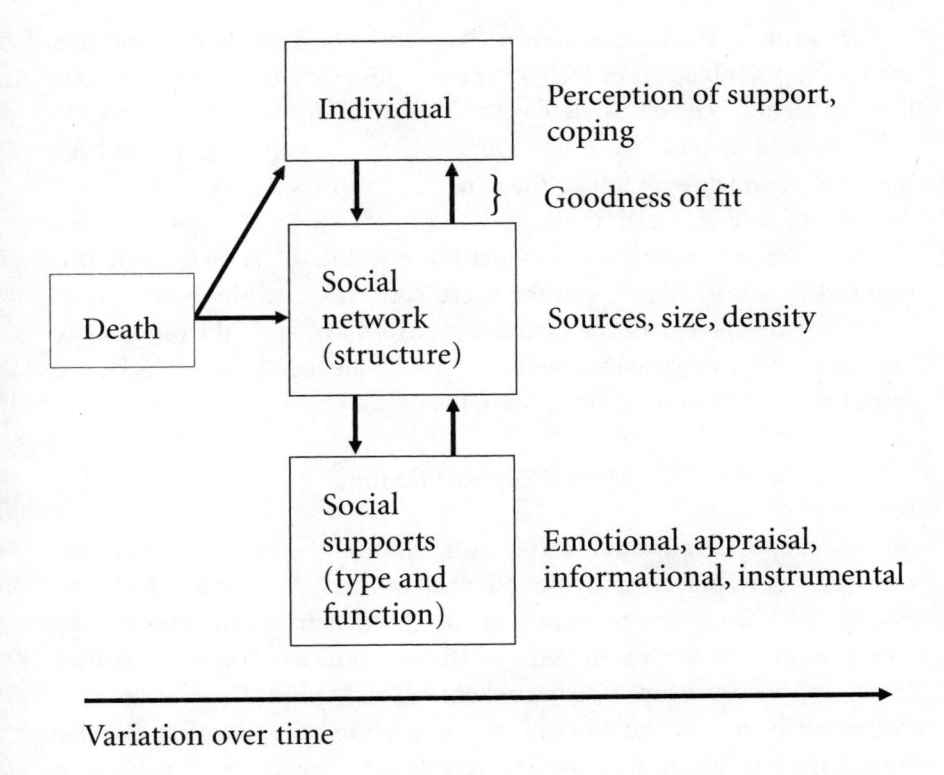

```
                    ┌────────────┐
                    │ Individual │      Perception of support,
                    └────────────┘      coping
                         ↓↑      } Goodness of fit
┌───────┐          ┌────────────┐
│       │──────→   │  Social    │
│ Death │          │  network   │      Sources, size, density
│       │      ↗   │ (structure)│
└───────┘          └────────────┘
                         ↓↑
                    ┌────────────┐
                    │  Social    │
                    │  supports  │      Emotional, appraisal,
                    │ (type and  │      informational, instrumental
                    │  function) │
                    └────────────┘
```

──────────────────────────────────────→

Variation over time

Figure 6–1. The bereaved individual and the social environment.

occur with the survivor subsequent to their loss. Friends may also become frustrated in efforts to help for a variety of reasons related to the interaction between acutely bereaved people and those who try to comfort them. As a result, they sometimes set unrealistic agendas for the acutely bereaved individual's recovery. As part of an integrated social system, the married friends of a surviving spouse cannot change or adapt easily to the loss of socioeconomic status that sometimes occurs (Lopata 1973). Widows, in particular, are subjected to stigmatization (Lopata 1973). Even more pointedly, according to many stories that I have heard from widows, bereaved women feel that, as an unattached female, they are perceived as a threat to the integrity of other pairs. Other researchers have noted the same thing (Yalom and Vinogradov 1988). The net result of these various processes is the exclusion of the bereaved friend from the social circle. The widow or widower is subtly ostracized and feels like a "fifth wheel" (Lopata 1973).

Furthermore, if the social network happens to be dense in the sense that many of its members know each other and were intimate with the deceased individual, it may be devastated by the loss itself. This has been referred to as *network stress* (Eckenrode and Gore 1981). The surviving family, each member of which may follow their own trajectory of grief, is the prime example of a dense social unit.

Therefore, not only the individual but also the social environment is changed by a loss. Changes in the social context caused by bereavement add to the complexity of the dynamic system that shapes the outcome of the bereavement experience. We cannot ignore the social environment and must try to arrive at some understanding of it.

Mutual Support Groups

Mutual support groups play a role in facilitating the process of bereavement for many, but certainly not all, acutely bereaved individuals. In the case of death from natural causes, the need for such involvement may be seen as more elective than imperative. In the instance of traumatic deaths, the survivors' experience is so overwhelming and unique that most people cannot easily understand it or aid the survivors in dealing with it. For this reason, the regular social networks available to survivors are more likely to fall short in providing adequate social supports. In this case, self-help services for those who have been victimized by crime probably should be seen as one of the formal, societal institutions that help individuals cope with the stress. Sometimes, bereaved survivors of a traumatic loss are so overcome by feelings of anger, grief, traumatic distress, and depressive symptoms that they are unable to enter a mutual support group for fear of losing control. They often need a sequence of professional help—providing for alleviation of their symptoms and a greater sense of self-control—followed by mutual support to experience relief. This need for two-pronged support was illustrated in the case of Mr. D, who was presented in Chapter 5 as an example of traumatic loss and distress.

Stage of Bereavement and the Type of Social Support Needed

As if the theoretical model for understanding social supports was not complicated enough, it is also necessary to introduce a dimension of time. There is evidence that the needs of the acutely bereaved individual change over time (Bankoff 1983; Walker et al. 1977). Typically, immediately following the death, the acutely bereaved individual turns for support to family and close friends. This provides the foundation for coming to terms with the loss and weathering the most intense emotional distress. Later, however, when the task becomes one of learning and adjusting to new roles and responsibilities, new friends and self-help groups become essential. At this stage, old friends and family may even encumber the process of recovery if they are reluctant to give up old assumptions about the bereaved individual and time-honored relationships.

Social Supports as Moderating or Mediating Factors

The place of social supports in a theoretical model for understanding stress and the bereaved individual's adaptation to it is unclear, particularly with respect to depression as a clinical complication (Aneshensel and Stone 1982). A case can be made for understanding social support networks as moderating variables of stress (Cobb 1976), that is, preexisting aspects of the environment that have an interactive effect with a loss on the occurrence of an outcome, such as major depression. This effect of social supports on mental health will only be appreciated when an individual is under stress and the social network must be called into action. Otherwise, the effect will not be evident (Monroe et al. 1986). A case can also be made for understanding social supports as mediating variables, which means that they are part of the mechanisms of pathogenesis. An example of this is the effect of emotional support on self-esteem; the absence of adequate support, among other factors, and the consequent reduction in self-esteem would elevate the risk of depressive states (Bibring 1953). Probably, a case can be made for both points of view of how to fit social supports into a comprehensive adaptive model: moderating and mediating (Aneshensel and Stone 1982). An example from clinical practice illustrates the importance of social networks to recovery from bereavement:

Case 5

Ms. E was a 63-year-old widowed clerk in a discount store whose husband had died from colon cancer after an extended illness. She presented for evaluation shortly following the seventh anniversary of his death. She stated that after her husband's death, every June and December (June 1 being the anniversary of her husband's death and Christmas being the most difficult holiday for her to face in his absence) she would experience a cyclical pattern of multiple somatic symptoms associated with a major depressive syndrome, which lasted several weeks. There was nothing in her history such as euphoria, expansiveness in the summer, or sensitivity to light to suggest bipolar disorder or a seasonal affective disorder. She easily met criteria for recurrent, unipolar depression when she was acutely ill. What was striking about the clinical history was her repetitive, relatively complete recovery within a few months after each occurrence of the depressive syndrome, providing a relatively asymptomatic period until the next recurrence. This was not typical of the natural history of unipolar depressions, which are ordinarily characterized by increasingly prolonged recurrent depressive episodes and increasingly reduced intercurrent asymptomatic periods with each recurrence.

Ms. E had a personal history of an untreated major depressive episode at age 39, 2 years after her mother had died. The somatic symptoms of her current depression included urinary symptoms, irritable gastrointestinal symptoms, and labyrinthitis, as well as multiple other ailments, such as pain in the corns of her feet. Although it was difficult to reconstruct the history of her husband's illness, Ms. E's somatic symptoms vaguely resembled his terminal symptomatology, which would be consistent with the idea of the symptoms being identification symptoms.

Ms. E had fallen out with her church when a new parish priest who had arrived 2 years earlier advised her that she would just have to accept her suffering. He implied that it was God's will. She was also estranged from her children, all of whom were in one difficulty or another. Two of her sons were substance abusers, another had been implicated in a murder, and her daughter, her youngest child, to whom she had turned for support, was preparing to leave home, in part, it sounded, to escape the responsibility of caring for her mother. According to Ms. E, the children blamed her for the death of their father because she had approved surgery that, according to her children, "had exposed the cancer to the air and caused it to spread." They were also intolerant of her prolonged difficulty in accepting his death without appreciating the cyclical quality of it.

Ms. E had a passive, dependent personality style that led her to lean heavily on her children for help, particularly her daughter. The pervasiveness of Ms. E's complaints about others' failures to support her suggested a systematic perception of nonsupportiveness, reflective more of subjective problems, rooted in anger over the loss, than of problems within her social network. She lacked confidence in her own ability to master the problems she faced and was resigned to recurrences of the highly symptomatic state and impaired functioning that characterized her acute illnesses in June and December. Although there was a masochistic quality to this acceptance, she did not manifest profound or pervasive feelings of guilt or other evidence of a disturbance of self-esteem.

Treatment of Ms. E focused on the tasks of bereavement (see Chapter 5) and psychoeducation about the nature of grief and her particular clinical complications. True to the cyclical course of her illness, her depressive symptoms abated during the 3 weeks after her first appointment. She was referred to a mutual support group that was professionally supervised. She found the mutual support group to be extremely supportive and helpful. Although follow-up was not prolonged, her reaction to the subsequent Christmas holidays was greatly attenuated.

Because of her estrangement from her church and family, Ms. E perceived her social environment as nonsupportive. Although it was hard to judge where the primary problem was (i.e., with the widow or with her family), it was easy to appreciate a poorness of fit between her perceived need for support and her social environment. This case example also illustrates the frequency with which many patients present for treatment at the time of anniversaries and the occurrence of "identification" symptoms in bereaved patients (topics that are discussed in Chapter 13 on the psychotherapy of the clinical complications of bereavement).

One case example such as this one, however convincing in its own right, does not prove the importance of social supports in the adaptation of bereaved people to a loss. To evaluate the effect the social environment has on adaptation to bereavement, it is necessary to turn to empirical studies of the question for scientific evidence.

Review of Studies on Social Networks and Social Supports

Clinical research on the role of social supports in mediating the adaptation to a loss is surprisingly sparse, in contrast to the amount of theoretical attention and clinical speculation that the topic receives. On the other hand, it is important to remember that the concept of social support as an important mediating process is relatively new, having emerged only in the late 1970s. With this perspective, the amount of work that has been done to investigate this important question in such a short time is more impressive.

Longitudinal Studies

In a review of the literature, it is difficult to find evidence that objective characteristics of the social network, such as the number of close friends or the number of actual contacts an individual makes with others per week, have any long-term effects on the adaptation to bereavement. Four longitudinal studies (Dimond et al. 1987; Hays 1991; Stroebe and Stroebe 1987; Vachon et al. 1982) provided data on outcome for longer than 2 months.

In Vachon et al.'s study (1982), the only variable that was associated with persistent distress (i.e., unresolved grief) was a perceived deficit in social supports measured 2 years after the loss. However, perceived nonsupportiveness could just as easily have been a subjective trait of the bereaved individual as an attribute of the environment. Hence this is not a convincing finding about the social environment. Characteristics of the antecedent social environment have no predictive relationship or association with the outcome of bereavement according to this study.

In the three other studies (Dimond et al. 1987; Hays 1991; Stroebe and Stroebe 1987), there was some evidence that the social environment, including perception of support, affected emotional distress shortly after a loss for up to 2 months. Thereafter, social networks and social supports no longer had an effect. In one of these studies (Dimond et al. 1987), the measure used to judge effectiveness of the social network was a composite score made up of the perception of closeness to network members and the opportunity to express oneself, as well as the number of contacts, frequency of confidences, and the amount of mutual helping within the network. In other words, this was a composite index of personal perception and objective characteristics of the social environment. The more frequently the elderly bereaved individuals reported these characteristics and the more positive their perception, the less likely they were to be depressed 2 months after a loss. This effect disappeared at 6-, 12-, 18-, and 24-month follow-up. Other objective characteristics, such as network size, strength, and density, had no relationship to depression or self-reported health at 2 months or later for a period up to 2 years.

In another longitudinal study of widows and widowers in Tübingen, Germany, Stroebe and Stroebe (1987) found that the size of the social network had no buffering effect on depressive and somatic symptoms of bereavement for 2 years of follow-up. This is the second study (in addition to Vachon et al. 1982) that failed to affirm the role of objective characteristics of social supports, as opposed to perceived supportiveness (see below), in predicting the adjustment to a loss over time.

In an analysis of 101 widows and widowers (Hays 1991) (from a study done by my colleagues and me [A. M. Ostfeld, S. C. Jacobs, S. V. Kasl: The Effect of Spousal Illness and Death in Older Families in New Haven, July 1991]), only the density of the social network (i.e., the number of individuals in the network who knew each other) was associated with outcome at 13- and 25-month follow-up after bereavement. Acutely bereaved spouses whose social networks were less dense at the outset of bereavement subsequently made more new friends during the first year of the loss. In turn, making new friends was associated with less emotional distress at 13 and 25 months of bereavement. This was the only observation that we made that was consistent with the hypothesis well established in the literature about the value of social contacts outside the family later in the course of bereavement (Bankoff 1983; Walker et al. 1977).

Although the New Haven, Connecticut, study had other findings about the relationship of social networks to concurrent psychological distress, none was related to outcome. For example, women who depended on their husband for social arrangements before his death were more distressed 1 month after the loss. There was no evidence, however, that they fared more poorly than others after the first month (Hays 1991). As widows, they started out with a constricted social network and made more new friends, particularly widowed friends, by 1 year. At 6-, 13-, and 25-month follow-up, the relationship of social dependency to depressive mood and separation distress no longer held. Furthermore, in this study, structural aspects of the social environment—such as the size of the social network, the number of close relationships with family and friends (confidants), and the number of visual contacts with intimates per week—had no relationship to measures of depression, anxiety, or unresolved grief at any time during follow-up. The New Haven study, then, is the third study that, with one exception, provided meager evidence on the role of social resources in affecting the outcome of bereavement.

Cross-Sectional Studies

In the absence of more longitudinal data, it is worthwhile examining the evidence from cross-sectional studies with the proviso that the direction of the relationship between variables is always uncertain when an association is found. For example, in post hoc analyses of cross-sectional data at 2 months of follow-up, Sanders (1979–1980) found that a group of bereaved individuals who attended church often and interacted more frequently with family grieved less intensely, were less angry, and were less pessimistic than a comparison group who did not attend church regularly and who were isolated from their family. An obvious question to ask about such cross-sectional data is whether the emotional distress interfered with social involvement or the social isolation aggravated the emotional distress. Furthermore, the consequences of social isolation 2 months after bereavement for long-term adaptation to the loss were unknown.

In another study, Bankoff (1983) compared the social support characteristics and needs of a group of widows who were bereaved 18 months or less with a group of widows who were bereaved for more than 18 months (range = 19 to 35 months). Bankoff's interesting comparison showed that overall crisis support made no difference for the psychological adjustment of the recently bereaved widows and very little difference for the widows who were bereaved longer. Based on these findings, Bankoff documented that different components and sources of social support were associated with the psychological well-being of the widows, depending on their stage of bereavement. The more recently bereaved widows, who presumably were still experiencing significant emotional distress, profited from emotional support, particularly from parents and other bereaved friends. The widows who were bereaved longer and presumably faced more social readjustment tasks, benefited from not only emotional support but also frequent social and intimate contacts. The latter group also took advantage of support from multiple sources consisting of parents and widowed friends as well as children, married friends, and neighbors. Although useful as evidence for the idea that bereaved individuals need different types of support at different times during the course of bereavement, findings from a cross-sectional study like this one cannot be conclusive without a single cohort being followed over time.

In another study, Mendes de Leon and colleagues (C. F. Mendes de Leon, S. V. Kasl, S. C. Jacobs, unpublished data, December 1991) performed cross-sectional analyses on data from the Established Populations for Epidemiologic Studies of the Elderly (EPESE; Cornoni-Huntley et al. 1986) in New Haven and found that high levels of instrumental support in the form of bringing in meals or providing resources and emotional support were associated with low depression scores in elderly widowers who were bereaved for more than 1 year. Conversely, elderly widowers with poor supports who were bereaved for 2 to 3 years reported levels of depression that were higher than those for both widowers with good supports who were bereaved for 2–3 years and widowers with poor supports who were bereaved for 1 year or less. Elderly widowers who were bereaved for less than 1 year reported moderate levels of depression that were comparable to depression in widowers with good supports. Thus elderly widowers with low levels of instrumental and emotional support appeared to have persistently higher levels of depressive symptoms, suggesting that the availability of social supports could protect them from unremitting depression. Again the caveat must be given that cross-sectional information like this cannot conclusively address the question of whether the characteristics of the social environment affect long-term adaptation to a loss.

Perceived Nonsupportiveness

Investigators in two early, related studies in Boston (Maddison and Walker 1967) and Sydney, Australia (Maddison and Viola 1968), introduced the bereaved individual's perception of nonsupportiveness as a characteristic that was associated with poor scores on measures of general health status 13 months after bereavement. In their major study of social supports, Vachon et al. (1982) confirmed the observation that a perceived deficit in social supports was associated with persistent psychological distress 2 years after bereavement. In another study of individuals whose partners or close friends had died from complications due to acquired immunodeficiency syndrome (AIDS), Lennon et al. (1990) found a similar relationship. Those survivors who perceived that the emotional and instrumental support they had received during the terminal illness had been inadequate grieved more intensely than their counterparts, who had a favorable attitude toward their social supports. Availability of support was not related to the intensity of grief in this study. Although the findings from these studies (Lennon et al. 1990; Maddison and Walker 1967; Maddison and Viola 1968; Vachon et al. 1982) indicated that a perceived deficit in social support was associated with poor psychological and health status after a loss, only one of these studies (Vachon et al. 1982) was longitudinal, and none established the perception of such a deficit as a predictor of outcome.

Three longitudinal studies (Hays 1991; Stroebe and Stroebe 1987; Vachon et al. 1982) failed to demonstrate that perceptions of the social environment have any relationship to outcome of bereavement. In Vachon et al.'s study (1982), perceived deficits were not predictive of outcome but rather were associated cross-sectionally with persistently high levels of emotional distress at 25 months after a loss. This association can be a product of the unresolved grief as easily as its cause. In Stroebe and Stroebe's study (1987), the bereaved individual's perception of various types of social support as well as the people in the social network had no relationship to depressive somatic symptoms 1 year after a loss. In analyses of data from a study of bereavement in New Haven (Hays 1991), perceived deficits in the social environment were associated cross-sectionally with lower levels of separation distress and depressive symptoms 2 months after the death of a spouse, but they had no relationship to outcome at 6, 13, and 25 months after bereavement. Therefore, the evidence on the role of perception of deficits in the social environment in shaping the bereaved individual's adaptation to a loss is mixed. The fact that the longitudinal studies have failed to demonstrate a predictive relationship calls into question the importance of perceived deficits of the social environment as a determinant of the outcome of bereavement.

Assuming for the moment that perceived nonsupportiveness will prove to be an important variable that predicts outcome, a fundamental question still remains about the nature of this observation. Is the perception of support a personality variable (i.e., a tendency to see things a certain way) or an environmental variable (i.e., a real deficiency in social resources) (O'Connor and Brown 1984)? In attempting to resolve this question, it soon becomes clear that it is virtually impossible to differentiate between the characteristics of the social environment and personal characteristics that affect the perception of supportiveness unless a special experiment designed to assess both types of characteristics systematically is done. These conditions are seldom met. Investigators in one study (Henderson et al. 1981) of social isolation and the occurrence of neurotic disorders in the circumstances of stress argued that personality factors governed the state of loneliness ("anophelia") of the neurotically depressed and anxious patients who were studied. The authors concluded that it was the individual's attitude, through the perception of the quality of the social supports, that was associated with neurotic disorders. In their prospective study of elderly people in the community, Grant et al. (1988) found that those individuals who had high depression scores reported having less emotionally satisfying and consistent support from relatives than those who had low depression scores, thereby indicating that it was this personal, depressed state rather than a characteristic of the social environment that determined the perception of nonsupportiveness.

In the New Haven study, Hays (1991) examined the relationship among social networks, social supports, and perceived supportiveness in a study of 101 middle-aged and elderly, widowed individuals who were followed for 25 months after bereavement. In this sample, those bereaved individuals who perceived their social networks to be supportive were middle-aged, were likely to talk to other bereaved individuals, had close family and friends, and were likely to have frequent face-to-face contacts with their friends and family during the first 6 months of bereavement. They tended to be women, although this factor did not meet statistical significance ($P < .05$). Consistent with the study mentioned above (Grant et al. 1988), these bereaved individuals were significantly less depressed ($P < .05$) and were less likely to report a history of dysthymia, which would reflect chronic depressive symptoms or a depressive personality style, than were bereaved individuals who perceived their social networks as nonsupportive. Thus perception of social supportiveness was a function of personal characteristics (e.g., age, sex, the presence of depression, and a history of dysthymia), interactive variables (e.g., the frequency with which these individuals talked to other bereaved people and the number of face-to-face contacts they had), and characteristics of the social environment (e.g., the availability of a large social network). Perception of support was not solely a product of either personal or social characteristics, although the balance weighed more heavily on the side of the personal characteristics.

This pattern of findings is consistent with the idea suggested by Vachon and Stylianos (1988) that perceived supportiveness is a function of a good fit between the bereaved individuals's needs and the supportiveness of the social environment. As a way of conceptualizing this interaction, Vachon introduced the notion of *goodness of fit* between the amount, source, and quality of social supports and the unique needs of the bereaved individual (see Figure 6–1). Some bereaved individuals will not be happy with the supports provided them even if the efforts of the family and social network are perfection itself. This hypothetical example provides a perspective on the goodness of fit that primarily emphasizes an individual's personality. Other bereaved individuals will be left in isolation and destitution, never having a chance by objective standards, which would primarily suggest a deficit in the social environment. Until more studies have been completed to settle the polarity between the person and the social environment empirically, it is probably reasonable and useful to conclude that both personality and social environment (i.e., the goodness of fit) contribute to an individual's perception of supportiveness. In a majority of cases, there is some of both, and the clinician can often help in making small adjustments that improve the fit between the social environment and the bereaved individual's needs, with potentially far-reaching benefit for the newly bereaved individual.

Relationship Between Social Environment and Personal Means of Coping

It is logical to expect that the way a bereaved individual copes with a loss will depend not only on his or her personal coping style (see Chapter 7) but also on the social resources available to him or her (Stroebe and Stroebe 1987). Reciprocally, the way that people cope will have an effect on the social support they receive. For example, in their study of middle-aged community residents coping with a variety of stressors, Dunkel-Schetter et al. (1987) found that the individual's way of coping was strongly associated with all types of social support received. The investigators found that problem-focused coping and coping by seeking social support, in comparison with emotion-focused coping, were related to a wide range of social support (e.g., information, direct aid, and emotional support). Confrontational coping and coping by exerting self-control were associated more selectively with informational support but not with other types of support. Coping by distancing oneself from the problem was associated with significantly less informational support than other forms of coping. Other personal factors, such as self-esteem, religious beliefs, and personal values, were weakly associated with the social support received by the individual.

In the New Haven study, Hays (1991) examined the relationship between the social environment and problem-focused coping reflected in actively seeking social supports as an example of coping directly related to the availability of social resources. Widows and widowers who were privately religious and who had frequent direct face-to-face contacts with their close family and friends were likely to cope by seeking social supports. They also were likely to perceive their social supports as positive and helpful. Therefore, seeking social support as a personal coping strategy was associated with the availability of direct social contacts within the bereaved individual's social network and his or her perception that the social contacts were helpful. However, regarding these data, our study was merely descriptive, and could not say anything about the direction of these relationships. It is possible that religiousness and direct social contacts evoke choices among coping strategies that include seeking social support, not to mention the perception that this is helpful or that seeking social support creates a certain type of social environment. Despite the limitations of the cross-sectional data, we can begin to appreciate the interdependence of coping and social resources.

Psychosocial Transitions: Sociological Versus Medical Perspectives

To understand the adaptive tasks of the acutely bereaved individual in relationship to the social environment, we need to have a means for conceptualizing the process of social change caused by bereavement that is parallel and complementary to that used for conceptualizing the process of personal change that occurs after a loss. In the latter case, we use the ideas of psychological distress and psychiatric disorders. These are often characterized as elements of a medical model that do more harm than good by ignoring the nature of the experience as a psychosocial transition (Silverman 1986). Yet medicine at its best incorporates an understanding of the individual into an environmental context through a comprehensive model. The most recent version of this model in psychiatry has been the biopsychosocial model (Engel 1977, 1980). Traditionally, it has been public health medicine and psychoanalytic psychiatry, which use the concept of adaptation, that have led the rest of medical practice in this regard (see Chapter 5).

To help psychiatrists and other mental health workers understand the adaptation of the bereaved individual to the social environment, several concepts from sociology are useful (Lopata 1973). Using the concepts of identity, status, and role, we can begin to develop an alternative perspective on the experience of the bereaved individual. The status of the acutely bereaved individual changes in many respects. In the case of a bereaved spouse, widows and widowers must slowly come to terms with the fact that they are no longer married. Also they may abruptly become a single parent for a growing family. Depending on the finances of the family and who is employed, there may be a decline in socioeconomic status. As the changes in status become apparent and the previous division of labor is no longer possible, the widowed individual must learn new roles in the family or the workplace for the purpose of carrying on independently. Recovery involves a cognitive process of accepting these new statuses and mastering the new roles. The implications for the individual's self-concept and social identity, as well as his or her assumption about the world, must be integrated into a new, assumptive world view (Parkes 1971). Ordinarily, recovery involves a small series of progressive transitions in pursuit of these tasks. For the widow, Silverman has described this as the change from wife to widow to woman on her own (Silverman 1986).

These are useful theoretical concepts that have not been developed and operationalized into easily used measures so that they may be tested empirically. Nevertheless, the basic principle that there are social processes in the adjustment to bereavement serves a very useful purpose and may well help us resolve the dispute about the duration of bereavement. As was pointed out in Susser's review (1981) of the epidemiological studies of the mortality of bereavement, we must examine not only the acute effects of a loss but also the prolonged effects of the change in status for the survivor if we are to understand the total process of bereavement, as well as its medical implications. For instance, some of the mortality attributed to bereavement, such as cardiovascular disease in widowers, appears to occur in close proximity to the loss. Some of the risk of mortality appears to be much more enduring, such as the risk of suicide, which may extend for several years (MacMahon and Pugh 1965). Cardiovascular mortality may be associated with the acute effects of bereavement, such as emotional and physiological arousal, and suicide with the longer-term effects of change in status.

Most psychiatric writers, who tend to be interested in emotions and their vicissitudes, have focused on the course of the psychological distress of bereavement over time and have concluded that the peak of distress is over, on average, by 4–6 months after a loss (Windholz et al. 1985). Other writers with a primary interest in the social processes of bereavement have concluded that bereavement extends much further in time (Barrett and Schneweis 1980; Silverman 1986). In truth, both points of view are probably accurate for the respective processes with which they are concerned. Sociologists have something to learn about the vicissitudes of separation distress and its complications, which would be useful for their understanding of the acute effects of bereavement. Physicians have something to learn about loneliness, a psychosocial analog for separation distress (Weiss 1987), which would illuminate much about bereaved individuals' adjustment to their new status associated with a loss.

The acute psychological distress of bereavement begins to attenuate on average sometime during the first year of bereavement, and if attention is confined only to this part of bereavement, it leads to the conclusion that bereavement is completed. On the other hand, the adjustment to the new status of widowhood begins slowly. To take widows and widowers as an example, social adjustment commences only after the bereaved individual can accept the idea that "I am widowed." As a process in its own right, this adjustment builds up toward the end of the first year of bereavement and may extend over several years. In this sense, bereavement is certainly not over at the end of the first year and may not ever end (Silverman 1986), although certainly the major psychosocial transitions have to be traversed within the first few years if bereaved individuals are going to get on with their lives. Clinical experience indicates that both perspectives on the course of bereavement are useful for the clinician and the patient when clinical complications occur. An empirical test of this assumption, probably through clinical trials of specifically designed interventions related to each, is needed.

These two perspectives on the process of bereavement not only serve to clarify an apparent controversy over the duration of grief, but also complement each other in another important way. Narrow medical tradition focuses on the definition and recognition of clinical problems and, at its worst, ignores the individual and the environment in which disease occurs. A psychosocial perspective focuses on social processes and has no effective means of conceptualizing personal, clinical problems or complications when they occur. In this tradition, at its worst, it is almost as if neither personal problems nor biological disturbances exist. Consistent with such an assumption, skilled intervention, especially medical intervention, is rarely if ever recognized as necessary. One of my purposes in this book is to argue that both points of view contribute to the total picture of bereavement and its complications and that to ignore one or the other is an exercise in telescopic vision.

Case Examples

Ms. A (presented in Chapter 1) is a good example of someone who had a truly excellent social network, superb social supports, and who perceived her supports very positively. This conclusion was repeatedly confirmed over the 3 years that I intermittently treated her. Still, she needed help with her separation distress and profited from learning the distinction between the natural history of separation distress and the natural history of the social adjustment to a loss. As she progressively worked through the problems posed by the death of her husband, she repeatedly fell back on her attentive, considerate adult children, her friends from work, and her ongoing friendships with couples, which were preserved despite her no longer being married. Eventually, she turned her attention to the social adjustment made necessary by her husband's death, but only after feeling she had more mastery over her separation distress. This is a case, then, in which a single-minded perspective on bereavement as a psychosocial transition would have been practically useless. Rather, in Ms. A's case, it was initially useful to focus on the nature and evolution of separation distress and the problems it caused for her and then proceed on the assumption that her social network was reasonably adequate. (This treatment issue is taken up later in Chapter 13.)

In contrast, the case of Ms. E (presented above) is an example of a bereaved individual for whom a focus on the psychosocial transition of bereavement and entrance into a mutual support group was the main thrust of helping her. Mr. D, the father of the daughter who had been brutally murdered, would have potentially received benefit from both focuses. Still, during the period of my involvement with him, he was never ready to return to the mutual support group that he unsuccessfully tried to attend shortly after the first anniversary of his daughter's death. Exposure to the discussion in the group evoked feelings that were too unpleasant and intense for him to manage successfully on his own, even with the support of the group.

Conclusions

If we choose to view the clinical complications of bereavement in the framework of an adaptive model, attention to social supports for the grieving individual and to the psychosocial transitions of bereavement provides an essential perspective. In the last 10 years, there has been a growing empirical basis for understanding the role of social networks and supports in the efforts of the individual to cope with the stress of a loss. Evidence for the role of social supports in affecting the outcome of bereavement is mixed and still not very convincing. Yet given the relatively short period of time that the social environment of bereavement has been under investigation, it is premature to conclude anything definitively about the importance of the social supports in shaping the response to a loss.

There has been little or no progress in empirically understanding psychosocial transitions. Rather, there is a tendency to rework previous theoretical concepts without venturing into a scientific testing of the ideas. The concept of psychosocial transitions is clinically useful and deserves continuing attention. While we are waiting for answers from clinical and epidemiological research on the concept of social transition and the role of the social environment in the recovery from bereavement, it is better to eschew sterile theoretical arguments about which point of view—a medical or a psychosocial one—gives us the truth about bereavement. Both make useful contributions to understanding the bereaved individual's experience; in some cases one view will be more important, and in other cases, the other.

A basic tenet of an adaptive model is that the individual strives to adapt to a particular environment. In this chapter I emphasize that not only the individual but also the environment is altered by a loss. In our attempt to understand maladaptation to a loss it is just as important to understand the nature and effects of inimical environments that prejudice the outcome of adaptation as it is to understand personal vulnerability. We are just beginning to understand and characterize the social environment in the ways that I have discussed in this chapter. There are other aspects of the environment, such as the social disorganization that accompanies traumatic disasters, that have yet to be considered and studied systematically (Erikson 1976). For the time being, surveying our present state of knowledge, it is my impression that we are more advanced in our understanding of personal vulnerability and the personal, psychological changes caused by a loss than in our understanding of social changes. For this reason, in Chapter 9 I emphasize conceptualizing pathologic grief in personal, symptomatic terms. It is possible to assume this point of view and also reserve judgment about what environments are threatening or helpful until more research addresses the issue as an open question. In thinking about how personality affects adaptation to bereavement (see Chapters 8 and 9), I enunciate a parallel argument for the sake of remaining open-minded about personality factors until we have more insight based on evidence for a decision.

Regardless of the state of evidence about the social environment, mutual support groups, which have developed in part on the basis of the theoretical interest in social networks and social supports (Caplan 1964), have emerged as a major type of intervention for the acutely bereaved individual. As clinicians, we need to understand the mechanisms of mutual support interventions and how to integrate them into the care of bereaved patients. (This topic is taken up in Chapter 14.)

References

Aneshensel CS, Stone JD: Stress and depression: a test of the buffering model of social support. Arch Gen Psychiatry 39:1392–1396, 1982

Bankoff EA: Social support and adaptation to widowhood. Journal of Marriage and the Family 10:827–839, 1983

Barrett CJ, Schneweis KM: An empirical search for stages of widowhood. Omega 11:97–105, 1980

Berkman L: The relationship of social networks and support to morbidity and mortality, in Social Support and Health. Edited by Cohen S, Syme SL. New York, Academic Press, 1985

Berkman LF, Syme SL: Social networks, host resistance, and mortality: a nine year follow-up of Alameda County residents. Am J Epidemiol 109:186–204, 1979

Bibring E: The mechanism of depression, in Affective Disorders. Edited by Greenacre A. New York, International Universities Press, 1953, pp 151–181

Caplan G: Principles of Preventive Psychiatry. New York, Basic Books, 1964

Cassel J: The contribution of the social environment to host resistance. Am J Psychiatry 104:107–123, 1976

Cobb S: Social support as a moderator of life stress. Psychosom Med 38:300–314, 1976

Cornoni-Huntley J, Brock DB, Ostfeld AM, et al (eds): Established Populations for Epidemiologic Studies of the Elderly: Resource Data Book (NIA, USDHHS, PHS, NIH, NIH Pulbication No 86-2443, 1986). Bethesda, MD, National Institutes of Health, 1986

Dimond M, Lund DA, Caserta MS: The role of social support in the first two years of bereavement in an elderly sample. Gerontologist 27:599–604, 1987

Dunkel-Schetter C, Folkman S, Lazarus RS: Correlates of social support receipt. J Pers Soc Psychol 53:71–80, 1987

Eckenrode J, Gore S: Stress events and social supports: the significance of context, in Social Networks and Social Support. Edited by Gottlieb B. Beverly Hills, CA, Sage, 1981, pp 43–68

Engel GL: The need for a new medical model: a challenge for biomedicine. Science 196:129–136, 1977

Engel GL: The clinical application of the biopsychosocial model. Am J Psychiatry 137:535–544, 1980

Erikson KT: Loss of communality at Buffalo Creek. Am J Psychiatry 133:302–305, 1976

Grant I, Patterson TL, Yager J: Social supports in relation to physical health and symptoms of depression in the elderly. Am J Psychiatry 145:1254–1258, 1988

Hays JC: Psychological distress, social environment, and seeking social support following conjugal bereavement. PhD dissertation, Yale University, School of Epidemiology and Public Health, 1991

Henderson S, Byrne DG, Duncan-Jones P: Neurosis and the Social Environment. New York, Academic Press, 1981

Horowitz MJ: A model of mourning: change in schemas of self and other. J Am Psychoanal Assoc 38:297–324, 1990

Lennon MC, Martin JL, Dean L: The influence of social support on AIDS-related grief reaction among gay men. Soc Sci Med 31:477–484, 1990

Lopata HZ: Widowhood in an American City. Cambridge, MA, Schenkman Publishing, 1973

MacMahon,B, Pugh TF: Suicide in the widowed. Am J Epidemiol 81:23–31, 1965

Maddison DC, Viola A: The health of widows in the year following bereavement. J Psychosom Res 12:297–306, 1968

Maddison DC, Walker WL: Factors affecting the outcome of conjugal bereavement. Br J Psychiatry 113:1057–1067, 1967

Monroe SM, Bromet EJ, Connell MM, et al: Social support, life events, and depressive symptoms: a one year prospective study. J Consult Clin Psychol 54:424–431, 1986

O'Connor P, Brown GW: Supportive relationships: fact or fancy? Journal of Social and Personal Relationships 1:159–175, 1984

Parkes CM: Psychosocial transitions: a field for study. Soc Sci Med 5:101–115, 1971

Sanders CM: A comparison of adult bereavement in the death of a spouse, child, and parent. Omega 10:303–322, 1979–1980

Silverman P: Widow to Widow. New York, Springer, 1986

Stroebe W, Stroebe MS: Bereavement and Health. New York, Cambridge University Press, 1987

Susser M: Widowhood: a situational life stress or a stressful life event? Am J Public Health 71:793–795, 1981

Vachon MLS, Stylianos SK: The role of social support in bereavement. Journal of Social Issues 44:175–190, 1988

Vachon MLS, Sheldon AR, Lancee WJ, et al: Correlates of enduring distress patterns following bereavement: social network, life situation and personality. Psychol Med 12:783–788, 1982

Walker KN, MacBride A, Vachon MLS: Social support networks and the crisis of bereavement. Soc Sci Med 2:35–41, 1977

Weiss RS: Recovery from bereavement: findings and issues, in Preventing Mental Disorders: Research Perspectives. Edited by Steinberg JA, Silverman MM. Rockville, MD, US Department of Health and Human Services, Public Health Service, ADAMHA, 1987, pp 108–121

Windholz MJ, Marmar CR, Horowitz MJ: A review of the research on conjugal bereavement: impact on health and efficacy of intervention. Compr Psychiatry 26:433–437, 1985

Yalom ID, Vinogradov S: Bereavement groups: techniques and themes. Int J Group Psychother 38:410–446, 1988

CHAPTER 7

Adaptation to a Loss

In this chapter, I focus on the reactive and creative efforts of the bereaved individual to adjust to a desolate environment. The bereaved individual adapts to the new social environment for the purpose of establishing a homeostatic and ecological equilibrium (i.e., a new state of adaptation). The new equilibrium provides gratification, support, fulfillment, and enjoyment, as well as new challenges. The problems and opportunities posed by a loss change over time and require varying, creative solutions. The bereaved individual copes with a multiplicity of intellectual, emotional, and behavioral techniques.

I develop two principal perspectives on coping: one on conscious coping, which typically denotes a problem-solving orientation, and the other on unconscious coping, which implies a more defensive function. (However, on close examination, we will see that both views of coping have problem-oriented and defensive qualities.) I explore both types of coping in relationship to each other and also in relation to neuroendocrine function as an index of physiological arousal. Also both types of coping will be used to predict the bereaved individual's success or failure in adapting to a loss, judged by scores on depression, anxiety, and separation distress scales and the occurrence of hospitalizations and death.

In stress reduction programs, it is practically axiomatic that it is not the stress that is ubiquitous, but rather how an individual copes with it that determines the outcome of a stressful experience. There are many analogous assumptions about coping made in clinical practice. Few of these assumptions have been systematically tested in research. For instance, we assume that mature coping, coping that effectively modulates emotion, problem-oriented coping, and active coping are more desirable than immature, neurotic, ineffective, emotion-focused, and passive coping. Indeed, there are some studies that provide a basis for these clinical biases, which I review below. The true picture, however, is much more complicated. Without an appreciation of the complexity of the process of coping, there is a tendency to apply oversimplified formulas and theoretical assumptions to bereaved individuals who are doing their best to cope. Treatment based on these assumptions risks doing more harm than good. Hence there is a need for more empirical studies of coping during bereavement. My colleagues and I have carried out a few studies on coping that illustrate many of the issues in this area; these are summarized below.

It is important to understand coping for many other reasons. Coping is a functional aspect of temperament, or character, which is relatively enduring. A better understanding of maladaptive coping will provide a functional perspective on psychopathology to complement the more static, descriptive criteria that were introduced in Chapter 2 and that are elaborated on in Chapter 9 on differential diagnosis. The development of dynamic criteria for characterizing the psychopathology of bereavement is consistent with the idea that the clinical complications of bereavement are disorders of adaptation, a major thesis of this book.

Another, more important motive for studying coping is that it is reasonable to expect that a knowledge of coping will provide an understanding of the natural processes of recovery from the pain, disability, and suffering of bereavement. This view emphasizes the proactive and creative aspects of coping rather than dwelling exclusively on presumed defects of the afflicted individuals, thus making them more vulnerable to complications. It is the recovery process that we understand the least, as I noted in Chapter 2, and an understanding of coping promises insight into it. By understanding spontaneous recovery better, we will have a firmer foundation for the treatment interventions that we can apply to bereaved individuals who develop clinical complications.

Understanding Coping

As an introduction to the rather complicated concepts of coping discussed in this chapter, I begin with a case example. Case 6 introduces basic concepts about coping that are discussed below in the review of the literature and summary of empirical studies. Some readers may prefer to start with the review section and then read the case example. The widower's coping style in Case 6 is representative of the pattern of coping that distinguished acutely bereaved spouses from a nonbereaved comparison group (Jacobs et al. 1991).

Case 6

Dr. F was a 69-year-old retired veterinarian whose wife died from lung cancer after an illness of 9 months. He was identified for participation in our study of bereavement when his wife was admitted to a general hospital with terminal illness. Two months after her death, during an interview with a psychiatrist, Dr. F still could not believe that it had happened. He reported that life had been "horrible" since her death and that he was still doing poorly. He felt that her death was unfair and he resented the loss. He was very lonely; his loneliness was compounded by the death of his pet dog 2 days after his wife's death. He described painful pangs of grief when he was reminded of his wife's absence, particularly in the mornings when he was accustomed to her greeting him when he descended the stairs for breakfast. He visited the cemetery daily where he "talked" to her. In these "dialogues" he sometimes asked for help and sometimes "kidded her," as he was accustomed to doing when she was alive. At these times, he felt closer to her and was comforted by the feeling of her presence.

Dr. F's score on a depression scale—the Center for Epidemiologic Studies Depression Scale (CES-D; Radloff 1977), was moderately high at 24. He reported sad mood, crying, insomnia, anorexia, impaired concentration, intermittently feeling like he had failed his wife, intermittent fatigue, and intermittent anergia. In short, he met criteria for a major depressive syndrome. However, he denied irritability, suicidal ideation, and any symptoms of anxiety.

Dr. F had no individual or family history of depression or anxiety disorders. He smoked more than two packs of cigarettes per day and usually had two cocktails per evening. He acknowledged that he was a heavy drinker and that sometimes this was a problem. However, he had never been treated for alcohol dependence, and he felt his drinking was under control at present. He related a history of coronary artery disease and a previous heart attack.

Dr. F described his wife in idealized terms and repeatedly characterized their relationship as "special." In fact, it sounded as if he had had a happy marriage. He said that he spent a lot of time "looking back" at their relationship. He regretted that he had not been more compassionate and caring, especially during his wife's final illness. On the other hand, he reported many pleasant reminiscences of his marriage. He still enjoyed working part-time (2 days per week) for another veterinarian, which he had done since retirement from his own practice 5 years earlier. He said that his adult children and their spouses had been very considerate and helpful since the death of his wife. He did not appear to have any other social contacts.

On a self-report, Ways of Coping measure (Lazarus and Folkman 1984), Dr. F scored high on coping by fantasy-escape, seeking social support, and self-blame. He scored moderately high on problem-focused planning and philosophical acceptance. He scored low on suppression of thoughts and feeling related to the loss. (This self-reported profile was typical of those coping strategies that distinguished bereaved individuals 2 months after their loss from nonbereaved individuals who had been threatened with loss [Jacobs et al. 1991]). These results meant that Dr. F was coping with his severe separation distress by trying to avoid, deny, and escape from it by fantasizing, daydreaming, and drinking to make himself feel better. He was not trying to suppress his reaction through plunging himself into his work or other activities. To help cope with the loss, he was relying heavily on his adult children for emotional and instrumental support. He regretted some omissions of care and compassion during the final illness of his wife and during their marriage, but there was no clinical evidence of a pervasive disturbance of self-esteem. He was not particularly philosophical about the loss; rather he resented it and had not actively planned how he was going to manage with it.

In contrast, nonbereaved individuals in the study from which Dr. F is drawn, whose spouses had been hospitalized with severe illness and had recovered, characteristically faced the stress of life-threatening illness with high scores on coping by philosophical acceptance and suppression (Jacobs et al. 1991). These coping styles denoted a positivist philosophical attitude. This attitude was characterized by the conviction that these individuals could draw from past experience in coping with the illness of their spouse and trust in the idea that time would heal the problem. In addition, they actively tried to get their mind off the problem, worked to divert themselves, and in general did what they could to not let the life-threatening illness of their spouse and their feelings about it get to them.

In his formulation, the psychiatrist who completed an interview with Dr. F emphasized Dr. F's use of the ego defenses of idealization, suppression, sublimation, and undoing. These are mostly mature and neurotic ego defenses. Dr. F's score on neurotic ego defenses was average, and his score on immature ego defenses was low. On the whole, Dr. F's profile of ego defenses seemed promising. On the other hand, his score on ego defensive work was moderately high, indicating that his ego functioning was significantly invested in managing internal conflict. In his discussion of the interview, the psychiatrist underlined his impression of Dr. F's efforts to avoid the pain of grief, consistent for the most part with the impression given by the Ways of Coping profile about fantasy and escape. He concluded that the interview had been very stressful insofar as during it Dr. F had been confronted with his loss, often resulting in his crying and being unable to express himself in words. The psychiatrist felt that Dr. F had considerable psychological work to do to come to terms with his loss. He speculated that Dr. F would experience difficulty ahead in adjusting. He wondered if Dr. F were the type of individual to find a replacement for his wife as a way of never fully coming to terms with his loss.

The psychiatrist's prognosis and Dr. F's score on self-reported fantasy-escape as a coping style, which had negative implications for long-term adaptation, proved true for Dr. F when he was followed up 13 months after the death of his wife. At that time, Dr. F still had severe depressive symptoms (score on CES-D = 23), qualifying him by use of standard cutoff scores for a diagnosis of major depression. He also had severe separation distress (score = 21) (Jacobs et al. 1987), indicating unresolved grief. He was hospitalized once during the first year of bereavement for coronary disease and was now asymptomatic. His self-rated health at 1 year was "good," indicating an obvious discrepancy between his evaluation and ours. This was consistent with a suppressive coping style at 13 months, which became modal for bereaved individuals later in bereavement (Jacobs et al. 1991).

Over the next year, there was considerable improvement. By 25 months, Dr. F's scores on the depression scale had returned to normal (CES-D = 7), and he reported minimal separation distress. He was not hospitalized during the second year of bereavement. At 2 years, he rated his own health as "very good;" 2½ years after his wife's death, Dr. F died of a myocardial infarction.

The case of Dr. F illustrates the type of coping that distinguishes coping with bereavement from coping with severe illness in a spouse. In addition, it depicts some aspects of the profile of coping that were associated with poor outcome in our statistical analyses of a group of bereaved individuals (see below). According to our longitudinal analyses, Dr. F's profile of coping scores had mixed implications for the resolution of emotional distress

1 year later. His moderately high scores on problem-focused planning and on self-blame augured well for him. However, his score on fantasy-escape predicted poor outcome. It is counterintuitive that the mature ego defenses in Dr. F were associated with a style of conscious coping that was not particularly successful in promoting successful adaptation. Yet in our studies (see below), we found this same coping style was typical of bereaved individuals in the early stages of grief, a time during bereavement that is characterized by severe emotional distress.

The pattern of coping that predicted good outcome in a group of bereaved individuals is discussed in more detail in regard to the next case example and the empirical analyses that follow it. The concepts and descriptions of coping that are introduced in this first case example are discussed in the next two sections.

Coping: Ego Defenses

One perspective on coping comes from ego psychology, which has been the basis for a long tradition of clinical descriptions, theoretical formulations, and, more recently, empirical studies of adaptation (A. Freud 1937; Hartman 1958; Menninger 1963; Vaillant 1977). The concept of ego defenses stems from Anna Freud who defined them as "the ways and means by which the ego wards off unpleasure and anxiety, and exercises control over impulsive behavior, affects and instinctive urges" (A. Freud 1937, p. 32). In a well-known example of this theoretical tradition, Vaillant (1977) defined coping in terms of ego defenses. Ego defenses are unconscious ego functions that are characteristic for an individual and that mediate one's response to a stressor—not only internal threats, as indicated in the definition above, but also external threats (Vaillant 1977). Ego defenses serve the purpose of maintaining psychological homeostasis by modulating affect within tolerable limits, pacing oneself through the cognitive adjustment to changes in the self and the outside world, and managing emotional conflict (Table 7–1).

In their well-known study of parents of leukemic children, Wolff et al. (1964a, 1964b) demonstrated that ego defenses modulated emotional arousal and adrenocortical function in the circumstances of stress. These investigators were working within the theoretical framework of ego psychology, using ego defenses as the way of describing coping. However, when these same parents were followed up after the death of their children, the observation that ego defensive effectiveness in modulating emotion was related to adrenocortical function was not confirmed (Hofer et al. 1972a, 1972b).

Ego defenses can be conceptualized in many ways, including not only their adequacy or effectiveness in regulating emotional arousal (Katz et al. 1970; Wolff et al. 1964a, 1964b) but also their developmental maturity (i.e., whether they are mature, neurotic, or immature) (Vaillant 1977; see Table 7–1). Mature and effective ego defenses were found to be more adaptive than were neurotic and immature ego defenses throughout life in a longitudinal study (Vaillant 1977) of university-educated and working class adult men. In a large ($N = 863$), cross-sectional study of Australian suburbanites, Andrews et al. (1978) supported this conclusion with their finding that immature coping was associated with psychological impairment. However, in cross-sectional studies, it is impossible to know which phenomenon comes first, the immature ego defenses or the poor adjustment.

More recently, with the development of structured, self-report measures of ego defenses, it has been shown that patients with anxiety disorders score lower on mature ego defenses and higher on neurotic and immature ego defenses than either a control group or a group of family practice patients (Pollock and Andrews 1989). Also specific patterns of ego defenses were identified for each anxiety disorder, including panic disor-

Table 7–1. Ways of coping and ego defenses

	Ways of coping	Ego defenses
Definition	Conscious cognitive and behavioral efforts	Unconscious ego defenses
Purpose	Management of stressful demands	Psychological homeostasis
Elements	Specific coping strategies	Specific ego defenses
Conceptual dimensions	Problem focused Emotion focused Active/passive	Mature Neurotic Immature Effectiveness in modulating emotion
Personality functioning	Coping styles Flexibility Complexity	Character style Maturity

der with agoraphobia, social phobia, and obsessive-compulsive disorder, although not for the ego defenses traditionally associated with these disorders in psychoanalytic theory (Pollock and Andrews 1989). In the only study of bereavement using self-report methodology (Byrne and Raphael 1991), bereaved individuals with major depressive episodes were comparable to nondepressed bereaved control subjects in their self-reports of mature ego defenses but were more likely to report neurotic and immature ego defenses such as projection, undoing, and somatization.

Conscious Coping Styles

In the past 20 years, the concept of coping has been significantly developed by cognitive psychologists (Coelho et al. 1974; Hamburg and Adams 1967; Lazarus and Folkman 1984; Moos 1976). Cognitive psychologists have worked in parallel with ego psychologists for the most part, as I know of no reports that have compared these two types of coping. This work has provided another perspective on coping. The definition of coping developed by Lazarus and Folkman (1984) is the "constantly changing cognitive and behavioral efforts to manage specific external and/or internal demands that are appraised as taxing or exceeding the resources of the individual" (p. 141). In this framework, coping is seen as an active or passive mediating process that an individual engages in to manage a challenging situation that is perceived as potentially overwhelming. This type of coping takes place on a conscious and reportable or observable level (see Table 7–1). Recently, a Ways of Coping measure has become available that provides an assessment of coping defined in these terms (Folkman and Lazarus 1980). It also characterizes the different styles of coping so that they can be categorized as problem focused or emotion focused, active or passive, and so on.

According to a review of the literature on coping, multiple factors determine the style of coping that is used to manage a particular stressful situation. These include the nature of the situation itself (e.g., marital, occupational) (Lazarus and Folkman 1984; McCrae 1982, 1984; Pearlin and Schooler 1978), the individual's cognitive appraisal of the significance of the situation (Lazarus and Folkman 1984), gender differences (Folkman et al. 1986b; Vingerhoets and Van Heck 1990), and variation in personality function. Central to this field of research is the idea that different situations call for different coping strategies (Lazarus and Folkman 1984) and that complex, flexible styles of coping are optimal for successful adaptation (Ilfeld 1980; Lazarus and Folkman 1984; Pearlin and Schooler 1978).

The idea that bereavement evokes and requires special coping strategies that are less active, less problem focused, and more emotion focused than other coping strategies is a common stereotype in the bereavement literature. This perspective has been supported by the findings of some studies. For example, in a study of multiple stressors (Billings and Moos 1981), participants who reported a death as a recent life event also reported less active and less problem-focused coping than participants who reported illness or interpersonal events as recent life events. In another study, McCrae (1984) found similar results, that is, that faith, fatalism, and expression of emotions were more often reported in the elderly participants as coping strategies after a loss, whereas rational action, positive thinking, and other active coping strategies were reported in the face of other challenges. In another study (Clark et al. 1986), widowers reported that active coping, social supports, and social involvement were most effective for them in coping with bereavement. Thus the empirical evidence on the nature of adaptive coping to bereavement is mixed; also, none of these studies was longitudinal or controlled.

Few longitudinal studies of coping are available in the stress literature (Folkman and Lazarus 1980; Stone and Neale 1984a, 1984b). None has reported on the style of coping as a predictor of subsequent psychological distress or psychiatric status after a stressful event. On the other hand, several cross-sectional studies have addressed the association between coping and psychological distress. In some studies (Billings and Moos 1981; Felton and Revenson 1984; Gass and Chang 1989; Vitaliano et al. 1987), problem-focused coping was associated with reduced levels of depressive symptoms and anxiety symptoms, as well as with good psychosocial functioning. However, Pearlin and Schooler (1978) found no relationship between problem-focused coping and depression. Other investigators (Andrews et al. 1978; Billings and Moos 1981; Felton and Revenson 1984; Gass and Chang 1989; Holahan and Moos 1982; Hovanitz 1986; Miller et al. 1985; Vitaliano et al. 1987) have associated other coping strategies with high levels of depressive symptoms, anxiety, somatic symptoms, and psychological impairment. These strategies included emotion-focused coping (unless it is for affective regulation as opposed to emotional discharge; Billings and Moos 1981), immature coping, self-blame, substance abuse, passive coping, wishful thinking, avoidant coping, and, in one case (Vitaliano et al. 1987), coping by seeking social supports. These observations serve as a background for working hypotheses about what coping styles predict psychological distress, depression, and anxiety as outcomes in longitudinal studies of bereavement.

Empirical Studies of Coping During Bereavement

We have completed three studies (Jacobs et al. 1991; Kim et al. 1991; Schaefer et al. 1988) that examined the pattern of coping in bereaved spouses, explored the relationship between conscious and unconscious coping, and tested which style of coping, if any, is predictive of successful resolution of grief with the least consequences for health. Using the Ways of Coping measure of Lazarus and Folkman (1984), we clinically assessed ego defenses according to a procedure developed by Katz et al. (1970) and another by Vaillant (1977).

In one study of 494 participants, we (Schaefer et al. 1988) compared acutely bereaved spouses with married men and women whose spouses either were severely ill or had only minor ailments. We found that the bereaved individuals coped more by escaping into fantasy, seeking social support, and blaming themselves than did the nonbereaved spouses. The bereaved spouses were less inclined to cope by use of suppression-activity substitution and philosophical acceptance than were the nonbereaved spouses. With the exception of seeking emotional support, which has both problem-focused and emotion-focused qualities, these observations matched those of other studies that emphasized the value of emotion-focused coping during bereavement.

It is important to emphasize that, in this study (Schaefer et al. 1988), we described coping strategies only for the acute stages of bereavement. Over the first year of bereavement, the pattern of coping among the bereaved individuals changed. This evolution of coping included increased copy by making changes and suppression-activity substitution, on the one hand, and decreased coping by seeking social supports and progressively decreased coping by philosophical acceptance on the other. The trend as bereavement progressed was toward the greater and exclusive use of emotion-focused coping and coping that was associated with denial and avoidance of the loss. These changes occurred coincident with a reduction, on average, in the intensity of emotional distress. This profile of coping over time distinguished the average, bereaved individual from the nonbereaved comparison groups, but it was not the pattern of coping that was associated with good outcome (see the next example). This discrepancy points out a crucial distinction between what is modal and perhaps effective in dealing with intense emotional distress immediately after a loss and what is effective over time.

In another study, we (Kim et al. 1991) looked for differences in ego defensive functioning between 43 bereaved spouses and 24 nonbereaved, married individuals whose spouses had been admitted to the hospital with a serious illness. (We used this smaller sample [$n = 67$] because we completed clinical ratings of ego defenses only on that reduced number.) This sample was also used for exploring the relationship between self-reported, conscious coping and unconscious, ego-defensive style coping, as well as for searching for associations between different coping strategies and neuroendocrine function. We observed no pattern of ego defenses (ego-defensive effectiveness in modulating affect, ego-defensive work, or ego-defensive maturity) that distinguished bereaved individuals from the nonbereaved control subjects.

Conscious and Unconscious Coping

In our study, we (Kim et al. 1991) found that unconscious coping defined in terms of ego defenses had little relationship to conscious styles of coping either between the bereaved or the nonbereaved participants. Given the different theoretical backgrounds of the two traditions for conceptualizing coping that were developed in parallel rather than in concert with each other, perhaps this observation is not surprising. Nevertheless, we originally thought that it was not unreasonable to expect that problem-focused coping, which is considered to be more realistic and goal oriented than emotion-focused coping, would be associated with more mature ego defenses. As another working hypothesis, we also suspected that coping found to be predictive of poor outcome might be associated with immature ego defenses. Furthermore, we wondered if ego defenses that were effective in modulating affect would have special relationships to specific styles of emotion-focused coping. Perhaps in the circumstances of bereavement such conventional assumptions do not hold. If nothing else, our observations have emphasized the need to investigate these issues empirically and avoid assumptions of the kind that not only guided our hypotheses but also might slip inadvertently into clinical work.

Coping and Neuroendocrine Function

In our study, we (Kim et al. 1991) found that high scores on neurotic ego defenses were associated with lower amounts of change in serum cortisol levels during a stressful interview. This relationship was interesting to us; we began to form a string of associations from neurotic ego defenses through adrenocortical function to depression (see the discussion of the prediction of outcome below). However, it is important to note that the use of neurotic ego defenses appeared to suppress serum cortisol response. This inverse relationship is not consistent with a simple hypothesis of adrenocortical activation associated with depression, unless this observation reflects the bereaved individual's successful efforts to suppress an overactive hypothalamic-pituitary-adrenocortical system that subsequently breaks through the suppression.

High scores on coping by suppression-activity substitution were associated with low baseline serum cortisol levels before the stressful interview. This was a potentially interesting finding that was consistent with previous observations that individuals under stress who suppress their emotional experience have low levels of adrenocortical activity (Wolff et al. 1964a, 1964b; Hofer et al. 1972a, 1972b). Unfortunately, the methodology used in our study for assessing baseline serum cortisol levels undermined confidence in our observation. Because the study was conducted in the community, we chose a time for the study (between 11:00 A.M. and 2:00 P.M.) that would minimize the effect of diurnal variation in serum cortisol. Also we controlled for variation in the time of sampling in our analyses. Nevertheless, we did not achieve the same degree of control that is obtained in a hospital or laboratory, leading to some skepticism about whether these initial serum cortisol levels were truly baseline.

Coping by making a change (or distancing oneself from the experience) was associated with high adrenocortical activity, reflected in 24-hour urinary free cortisol output 2 months after bereavement. The intense use of this same style of coping predicted lower scores on separation distress or unresolved grief at 13 months (see below). We knew from the analysis of Schaefer et al. (1988), which was performed on a larger sample, that coping by making a change was associated with high scores on psychological distress, the type of measure that has been shown consistently over the years to be associated with adrenocortical activation. This did not prove to be the case in our small sample of 67 in the neuroendocrine study (Kim et al. 1991). Thus coping by making a change and substituting activities appeared to be independently related to high adrenocortical activity. It was not the emotional arousal but rather the means of coping with it that provided the key to physiological arousal. This conclusion is consistent with the basic concept of Wolff et al. (1964a, 1964b) in their study of parents with children who had leukemia in which the authors determined that ego defenses were essential moderators of the physiological response in stressful situations. No other relationships were observed among coping variables and neuroendocrine function in our study.

Another Example of Coping With Bereavement

It is interesting that the style of coping that bereaved spouses typically used to adapt to a loss 1 to 2 months into bereavement, in contrast to married individuals coping with a gravely ill spouse after 2 months of illness, was not the same as the coping strategies that predicted successful adaptation over the long term. This distinction can only be appreciated when longitudinal follow-up is included in the design of a study. The next case example illustrates the pattern of coping that was associated with good mental health outcomes. We measured outcome in our study (Jacobs et al. 1991) at follow-ups 13 and 25 months after the death of the spouse. Statistical analyses of coping styles that were related to outcome follow the case example.

Case 7

Mr. G, a 62-year-old contractor, was initially identified by screening admissions to a general hospital to identify critically ill, married patients. The spouses of the patients were invited to take part in a longitudinal, epidemiological study.

At the time of the psychiatric interview, Mr. G was living alone in his own home following the death of his wife from metastatic cancer 2 months earlier. They had been married for 36 years and had no children. Aside from mild hypertension, his wife had not been ill until 6 months before her death. Watching her die had horrified Mr. G, yet he was fundamentally gratified by the quality of the medical care his wife had received. At the time of the interview he stated that it was "still hard to conceive that she is not here." He was experiencing intense separation distress, which had been worse immediately after her loss and which had attenuated just slightly over the 2 months of bereavement. The loneliness of his life weighed heavily on him, and he commented on it repeatedly. His wife, in the absence of children, had "babied" him, and now she was gone. He was preoccupied by the question of who would care for him. He made a point of how much it meant to him that his wife's relatives had cared for him over the first holiday (Thanksgiving) after her death. He had no symptoms of depression and he did not meet criteria for any anxiety disorders. Mr. G acknowledged drinking at least a few cocktails every night, but denied any problem drinking. He anticipated retirement from his work as a contractor and expected to fill his time with involvement in a local, amateur theater, which gave him much gratification.

In the interview with a psychiatrist, which focused on the loss of his wife, Mr. G was uncomfortable and repeatedly exhibited a nervous laugh. Aspects of the interview were worrisome to the psychiatrist. Mr. G once made a conspicuous slip of the tongue, substituting the word "bleakly" for "briefly"; this confirmed the psychiatrist's growing impression of how Mr. G viewed his situation. In general, it was the interviewer's impression that Mr. G was avoiding the expression of feeling and that the parapraxis was a glimpse into his underlying emotional state. Also in response to a query about the intensity of his separation distress, Mr. G flippantly replied, "I haven't thought about cutting my throat." Finally, at the end of the interview, without much time left to discuss it, Mr. G said "I don't think I'm going to drink too much." It was the psychiatrist's impression that Mr. G left much anger about his situation unexpressed and perhaps only dimly perceived this anger.

On the coping scales, Mr. G scored high on problem-focused planning and coping by making a change (or distancing himself from the stressor). He scored low on coping by fantasy-escape. This pattern of coping shortly after the death of his wife denoted an approach characterized by making a plan of action, taking one step at a time, and concentrating on the next step. In addition, Mr. G tried to cope with the stress by pacing himself and rest-ing, trying new interests, and making changes in himself. He did not report any efforts to avoid, deny, or escape the implications of the loss. (In the statistical analyses summarized in the next section, this pattern of scores on the coping scales was associated with low levels of depression and separation distress—a measure of unresolved grief—1 year later.)

In the formulation of the psychiatrist, this widower's basic character style was thought to be obsessional. He was rated high on the ego defenses of rationalization, displacement, isolation of affect, idealization (of his deceased wife), mastery, sublimation, and suppression. This ego defensive pattern was fairly neurotic and, according to conventional clinical wisdom, augured poorly for Mr. G's spontaneous recovery from the distress of bereavement. His rating score on neurotic ego defenses was moderately high, predicting a high risk for major depression. His score on defensive work was low, indicating relatively autonomous ego functioning and also predicting a high risk for depression. Thus the two assessments of coping—one self-reported as summarized in the preceding paragraph and the other a clinical rating of ego defensive functioning—provided mixed implications for the outcome of his bereavement.

On follow-up, Mr. G denied symptoms of depression at 1 and 2 years. His self-rated health was "very good" at 1 year after bereavement and "excellent" at 2 years. He was not hospitalized at any time during the first 2 years of bereavement. All was not well, however. When the same psychiatrist who did the original psychiatric interview met with him once again 2 years after the death of his wife, he recognized heavy drinking in Mr. G that had not been picked up in the structured research interview or by the fantasy-escape coping items in particular.

Four-and-a-half years after the death of his wife, Mr. G died at age 67 from a compound fracture of his upper arm according to the death certificate. The circumstances of his death were obscure.

The pattern of coping that Mr. G illustrated is representative of the coping strategies that predicted successful psychological adaptation in our group analyses (summarized in next section). Despite the evidence for good outcome after the loss, according to our structured assessments, it was also apparent that this widower drank excessively, at least as evidenced in the follow-up interview by the psychiatrist. It was clear to us that the first interview had been stressful for this man, and it is conceivable that his drinking was specifically related to the second interview and other stressful encounters. There was no evidence from our structured research assessments, including our self-report items on fantasy-escape, which had an item that referred to drinking, that this widower was abusing alcohol. His death occurred at age 67, 4½ years after the death of his wife, presumably as the result of an accident or fall. The death certificate was vague, and no family members would consent to clarify the issue.

It is curious in this case how the profile of self-reported coping at 2 months, which promised successful adaptation, was associated with a high rating on neurotic ego defenses and a low rating on ego defensive work, both of which predicted a high risk of depression. In Mr. G's case, at least, it appeared that the self-reported coping was operative, and we were left wondering if there was something atypical about the experience of a psychiatric interview for this widower that led to the misleading implications of the ratings of ego defenses.

Prediction of Outcome Using Coping Variables

In our studies, we completed two sets of analyses on outcome. One analysis (of the larger sample described above [$n = 494$]) used hospitalization for serious illness as the outcome criterion (Schaefer et al. 1988) and the other analysis (of the smaller sample [$n = 67$]) used measures of depression, anxiety, and unresolved grief as the outcome criteria (Jacobs et al. 1991; Kim et al. 1991). The pattern of coping that predicted good outcome varied for each outcome.

In the study by Schaefer et al. (1988), coping by philosophical acceptance and seeking social support predicted a significantly lower risk of hospitalization for serious illness over the first year of bereavement. Conversely, low philosophical acceptance and low seeking of social support—perhaps reflecting denial, avoidance, and inability to recognize the need for social support—predicted higher risk of hospitalization. With regard to mental health outcomes (Jacobs et al. 1991), high scores on coping by problem-focused planning predicted low scores on depression and separation distress at 13 months after bereavement. This was an indication that problem-focused planning played an important role in outcome, although it was not conspicuous in our assessment of average, typical coping after a loss (Kim et al. 1991). High scores on coping by making a change also predicted low scores on separation distress, suggesting that the bereaved individuals may have been pacing themselves through the experience.

Thus different coping strategies predicted successful adaptation, depending on the criterion of outcome used. In a broad sense, this finding supports the idea that flexible coping is more adaptive than rigid adherence to a single coping pattern to address all of one's needs. One further implication of the analyses of outcomes is that a single coping style may have positive, negative, and neutral implications for different outcomes, and individuals must find the right balance for their particular needs.

We (Jacobs et al. 1991) also found that high scores on self-blame predicted lower scores on separation distress (our measure of unresolved grief) 25 months after the death. However, there are a few reasons to be skeptical about this observation. One is that the effects of coping on outcome in general were consistently observed at 13 rather than 25 months. It appeared as if the effect of early coping dissipated or the effects of early coping were overdetermined by supervening events on outcome at 25 months. Also this observation about self-blame runs counter to clinical wisdom that a disturbance of self-esteem should be associated with a higher risk of distress and depression in particular. On the other hand, the scores on this style of coping may reflect the appropriate expression of a self-evaluative process, which is precipitated by a death, that is useful for bereaved individuals to go through. This may include consideration of omissions of care or survival guilt that is normal and adaptive. Those who do not or are unable to perform such an evaluation, perhaps because of a more profound disturbance of self-esteem, may be at greater risk for depression as an outcome. If this is the case, it suggests that our measure of self-blame assessed something different from our usual clinical concept of self-esteem.

The pattern of coping that predicted a successful adaptation using hospitalization as the criterion of outcome was different from the pattern of coping that predicted successful outcome using mental health indicators as the criteria of outcome. This variation between the two studies (Schaefer et al. 1988; Jacobs et al. 1991) is evidence of the need for flexible coping styles, that is, different coping styles for different problems. Our observation of the discrepancy between typical coping 2 months after a loss and the style of coping that predicted good outcome indirectly supports this conclusion also. Emotion-focused coping, which is more characteristic of the typical coping style that we observed 2 months after a loss, makes sense given that the emotional intensity of grief is greatest at that time. On the other hand, problem-focused coping was a characteristic of the coping style that predicted good outcome 1 year after bereavement and augured better for the long term.

These variations in the patterns of coping associated with bereavement suggest that a particular coping style may have both positive and negative implications for outcome, depending on the criterion for outcome, and that the individual must find the right balance for his or her particular needs. It is worth noting, for the purpose of emphasizing the need for further studies, that not all the evidence from our analyses supported the value of flexible coping. In our smaller study (Jacobs et al. 1991), a complex style of coping, reflected in a wide range of coping strategies, predicted a higher risk of depression at 13 months as assessed by CES-D depression scores. This observation ran counter to what we expected from the review of the literature, which suggested that complex coping was the most adaptive coping style. It may be that "complex" coping styles in our sample reflected the need of the acutely bereaved individual to enlist additional coping strategies because their initial, simpler, single coping strategies had failed to adequately manage the situation.

With regard to ego defenses and outcome in this same study (Jacobs et al. 1991), high scores on neurotic ego defenses predicted high depression scores 1 year after a loss, thus indicating that neurotic ego defenses, perhaps as a reflection of conflict during bereavement, were associated with poorer outcome. This observation makes clinical sense and is consistent with the observation that conflicted grief becomes prolonged and unresolved (Parkes and Weiss 1983). In this earlier study (Parkes and Weiss 1983), conflict was primarily defined as interpersonal in nature. After the death of a spouse occurred, however, it appeared the conflict became internalized and was related to the concept of intrapsychic, neurotic conflict.

The observation from our study (Jacobs et al. 1991) on the association between scores on neurotic ego defenses and poor outcome was also consistent with Byrne and Raphael's observation (1991) from their cross-sectional study of bereavement that higher self-ratings of neurotic and immature ego defenses were found among depressed, bereaved subjects by comparison with nondepressed, bereaved control subjects. Because of the longitudinal design of our study, we were able to conclude that neurotic ego defenses are a risk factor for depressive symptoms rather than a by-product of depression. Thus neurotic ego defenses were not only associated with physiological arousal, as noted above, but also with a higher risk of depression 1 year after a spousal death. Although the prediction of depression by neurotic ego-defensive functioning makes sense clinically, it is important to appreciate the point the mature ego defenses did not predict good outcome (Jacobs et al. 1991), an observation that would have bolstered our confidence in the construct validity of the role of neurotic ego defenses in determining poor outcome if it had been made.

The more ego functioning was associated with managing intrapsychic conflict in the acute stages of bereavement (we labeled this *defensive work*), the lower the risk of depression was 13 months later (Jacobs et al. 1991). This observation might seem to contradict the relationship of neurotic ego defenses to depression insofar as both variables are theoretically related to internal conflict. On the other hand, we know from our analyses that these two variables (i.e., neurotic ego defenses and defensive work) did not correlate in our sample (Jacobs et al. 1991). This indicated that there was no empirical relationship between the two variables in our sample. We also know from our analyses that ego defensive work was positively correlated with ego defensive effectiveness, that is, the effectiveness of ego defenses in modulating emotions. Thus it may be that our assessment of ego defensive work was an indication of the useful, psychological work done by the acutely bereaved individual to modulate his or her emotions early in the course of bereavement.

Tasks of Bereavement

Ten years ago, when the study of coping during bereavement began, there was an implicit assumption that bereavement created a sufficiently specific problem for the bereaved individual that it would be meaningful to ask in general how the individual coped. That point of view now seems naive. This is yet another example of how our understanding of bereavement has evolved over the past decade. Increasingly, it has become evident, although it probably should have been obvious at the outset, that the problems facing the acutely bereaved individual are multiple and complex. Both case examples in this chapter serve to illustrate how complicated the clinical issues are and how rudimentary our understanding of coping is.

Our contemporary definition of the tasks of bereavement reflects a synthesis of multiple efforts on the parts of many curious and concerned observers over the past 80 years to clarify the problems facing the bereaved individual. Modern clinical thinking about the tasks of bereavement stems from Sigmund Freud's concept of grief work (1917), which utilized psychoanalytic concepts. Essentially, for Freud, grief prolonged the psychological existence of the lost individual while the bereaved individual slowly gave up his or her emotional investment (i.e., *decathected*): "each single one of the memories and expectations in which the libido is bound to the object is brought up and hypercathected, and detachment of the libido is accomplished in respect of it" (S. Freud 1917, p. 245). Subsequently, several authors have redefined the meaning of grief work outside of the framework of psychoanalytic theory with the aim of making the definition more precise, specific, and concrete (Bowlby 1980; Lindeman 1944; Parkes 1971). In Worden's well-known formulation (1982), the tasks of mourning were defined as 1) withdrawal of emotional investment from the deceased individual and commitment to another relationship, 2) adjustment to the environment in which the deceased individual is missing, 3) acceptance of the reality of the loss, and 4) the need to experience the pain of the loss. Recent variations on this list of tasks have appeared that incorporate essentially the same content with an additional emphasis on 1) remembering the deceased spouse and 2) developing a new, integrated self-concept and world view (Shuchter 1986).

So far, our discussion of tasks should be reasonably familiar to the clinician and should seem manageable as a conceptual framework. However, the discussion of tasks to this point has remained on a psychosocial and largely theoretical level. It has not begun to identify the multitude of new roles and skills that the newly bereaved individual may have to learn in order to live independently rather than as one part of a dyadic, functional unit (Parkes 1971). I suspect that it is this practical challenge to the acutely bereaved individual that governs Silverman's choice (1986) of a learning model, in contrast to a medical model, for conceptualizing the tasks of bereavement. For each task that confronts the acutely bereaved individual, a particular type of coping may be suitable. As the tasks multiply, the need for a complex coping repertoire becomes self-evident. This perspective serves to correct oversimplified assumptions about the work of bereavement. For example, one idea that has been expressed in the coping literature is that bereavement calls primarily for emotion-focused coping, given that a death is final and irrevocable (McCrae 1984). Presumably, little in the way of instrumental efforts can be done to cope with death. Yet even a theoretical analysis undermines this premise, and, in fact, our empirical analyses of coping during acute bereavement (Jacobs et al. 1991) provide evidence on the value of instrumental coping in promoting good mental health outcomes. In addition, our studies have suggested that typical coping during the acute stages of bereavement, which may have been primarily aimed at managing the emotional distress characteristic of the early stages of grief, was not the same as the pattern of coping that was most useful for long-term adaptation. Hence the evidence suggests that there are different coping styles for different tasks during bereavement.

One prominent example of the emphasis on emotion-focused coping in the clinical realm is the concept of grief work used most often by grief counselors and therapists. Although *grief* was defined by Lindeman (1944) as "emancipation from the bondage to the deceased, readjustment to the environment in which the deceased is missing, and the formation of new relationships" (p. 143) and should be interpreted broadly, it is often taken primarily as a prescription for confronting the loss and dealing with the emotions of bereavement. To emphasize the emotional work of bereavement to the exclusion of cognitive and social tasks is an exercise in telescopic vision. This emphasis on emotional work is also misguided as a therapeutic strategy, particularly if it is taken as a rationale for encouraging emotional catharsis as a single-minded therapeutic goal rather than promoting equally useful cognitive work to seek meaning in the loss and to learn about new social roles (Stroebe and Stroebe 1987, 1990).

In a discussion of the tasks of bereavement, it becomes clear that it is virtually impossible to understand coping in an environmental vacuum (Parkes and Weiss 1983). When we describe coping, it is always essential to specify not only the task at hand but also the environmental resources available to the bereaved individual. (The latter issue is discussed in relation to the example of problem-focused coping in Chapter 6.)

Conclusions

Some of our analyses of coping during bereavement, summarized above, were longitudinal and provided assessments of mental health outcomes.

The analyses indicated that coping during bereavement is an active process that includes problem-focused, as well as emotion-focused, coping. These findings, which require confirmation in subsequent work, provide a start for empirically understanding how acutely bereaved individuals cope with a loss (or a threatened loss). Unfortunately, studies of coping during bereavement completed to date have mainly served to emphasize the complexity of coping. A largely untouched task that remains is to clarify the nature of coping during bereavement with the necessary degree of detail to be useful in clinical practice.

The observations of our studies were sometimes consistent with other investigations of coping and with clinical wisdom, sometimes contradictory, and at other times unrelated and novel. These discrepancies indicate the need to be professionally humble about the theoretical assumptions and clinical speculations that we make about successful and unsuccessful coping during bereavement. This is our best posture until our clinical assumptions, largely based on theory and inference, are empirically tested in systematic studies. In the absence of empirical findings from multiple social and cultural groups at different points in the process of adaptation to a loss and with regard to multiple, specific outcomes, we must remain skeptical of our assumptions and open-minded about various adaptations as solutions (Wortman and Silver 1989). Overconfidence in our current understanding of coping with bereavement based on general coping studies or general clinical theory runs the risk of mistaken efforts to help individuals cope with this natural experience about which we still have enormous amounts to learn. Without empirical data on bereaved samples, there is an unchecked potential for cultural chauvinism, professional solecism, and, most worrisome of all, blaming bereaved survivors as they do their best to cope with the stress of a loss. In the meantime, continued, careful observation of acutely bereaved individuals will teach us much about bereavement, natural healing processes, and psychopathology.

Although effective coping is most likely a part of the picture of successful adaptation to a loss and ineffective coping most likely figures into pathologic grief as a functional dimension of the disorder, our limited understanding at present does not allow us to specify these elements. The closest approximation that we can make at present will be introduced in Chapter 9 on differential diagnosis. In that chapter, I discuss the relationship between symptoms and social functioning, although, admittedly, social functioning is a distant cousin of coping. If symptoms interfere with social functioning, it is cause for increased clinical concern about the need for professional intervention. Similarly, if symptoms are associated with maladaptive coping, an important dimension of personal functioning, professional help may be indicated. Our knowledge of coping is so rudimentary at present that achievement of the goal of integration of a functional perspective into the definition of psychopathology is not imminent. Nevertheless, it is an objective to strive for in order to move beyond our predominantly static, descriptive criteria for diagnosis. A knowledge of maladaptive coping can enhance our understanding of pathologic grief as a functional disorder, or a disorder of adaptation.

Although there is much to learn about coping during bereavement, there is also much to be gained with such knowledge. An understanding of how acutely bereaved individuals successfully cope with a loss holds the potential for providing a greater appreciation of the natural history of healing and recovery from the emotional distress and social disruptions caused by a death. This knowledge can serve as a cornerstone for developing psychotherapeutic interventions to help bereaved individuals that go beyond the basic strategies of fostering expression of feelings, if there is avoidance of grief, and supporting mitigatory efforts of the individual to modulate the emotion, if the distress of grief is subjectively overwhelming. We need to interpret grief work in the broadest terms, including not only emotion-focused but also problem-focused coping, as well as strategies for the emotional, social, and cognitive tasks discussed above. Eventually, encouragement of specific coping strategies that are known to be adaptive for specific tasks holds the potential for greater impact. The clinical implications of our rudimentary knowledge of coping during bereavement, limited though they are at present, are picked up again in Chapter 9 on differential diagnosis and Chapter 13 on psychotherapy.

References

Andrews G, Tennant C Hewson D, et al: Life event stress, social support, coping style, and risk of psychological impairment. J Nerv Ment Disord 166:307–315, 1978

Billings AG, Moos RH: The role of coping responses and social resources in attenuating the stress of life events. J Behav Med 4:139–157, 1981

Bowlby J: Attachment and Loss, Vol 3: Loss, Sadness and Depression. New York, Basic Books, 1980
Byrne G, Raphael B: The impact of recent spousal bereavement on the mental health of elderly Australian men. Paper presented at the Third International Conference on Grief and Bereavement in Contemporary Society, Sydney, Australia, June 30–July 4, 1991
Clark PG, Siviski RW, Weiner R: Coping strategies of widowers in the first year. Family Relations 35:425–430, 1986
Coelho G, Hamburg D, Adams J (eds): Coping and Adaptation. New York, Basic Books, 1974
Felton BJ, Revenson TA: Coping with chronic illness: a study of illness controllability and the influence of coping strategies on psychological adjustment. J Consult Clin Psychol 52:343–353, 1984
Folkman S, Lazarus RS: An analysis of coping in a middle-aged community sample. J Health Soc Behav 21:219–239, 1980
Folkman S, Lazarus RS, Dunkel-Schetter C, et al: The dynamics of a stressful encounter: cognitive appraisal, coping, and encounter outcomes. J Pers Soc Psychol 50:992–1003, 1986
Freud A: Ego and the Mechanisms of Defense. London, Hogarth Press, 1937
Freud S: Mourning and melancholia (1917), in the Standard Edition of the Complete Psychological Works of Sigmund Freud, Vol 14. Translated and edited by Strachey J. London, Hogarth Press, 1953, pp 243–258
Gass KA, Chang AS: Appraisals of bereavement, coping, resources, and psychosocial health dysfunction in widows and widowers. Nurs Res 28:31–36, 1989
Hamburg DA, Adams JE: A perspective on coping behavior: seeking and utilizing information in major transitions. Arch Gen Psychiatry 17:277–284, 1967
Hartman H: Ego Psychology and the Problem of Adaptation. New York, International Universities Press, 1958
Hofer M, Wolff C, Friedman S, et al: A psychoendocrine study of bereavement, part 1: 17-hydroxycorticosteroid excretion rates of parents following death of their children from leukemia. Psychosom Med 34:481–491, 1972a
Hofer M, Wolff C, Friedman S, et al: A psychoendocrine study of bereavement, part 2: observations on the process of mourning in relation to adrenocortical function. Psychosom Med 34:492–504, 1972b
Holahan CJ, Moos RH: Social support and psychological distress: a longitudinal analysis. J Abnorm Psychol 90:365–370, 1982
Hovanitz CA: Life event stress and coping style as contributors to psychopathology. J Clin Psychol 42:34–41, 1986
Ilfeld FW: Coping styles of Chicago adults: description. Journal of Human Stress 1:2–10, 1980
Jacobs SC, Kosten TR, Kasl SV, et al: Attachment theory and multiple dimensions of grief. Omega 18:41–52, 1987
Jacobs S, Kim K, Schaefer C, et al: Conscious and unconscious coping under stress, part 2: relationship to one and two year outcomes after bereavement. Paper presented at the Third International Conference on Grief and Bereavement, Sydney, Australia, June 30–July 4, 1991
Katz J, Weiner H, Gallagher T, et al: Stress, distress, ego defenses and neuroendocrine response to impending breast biopsy. Arch Gen Psychiatry 23:131–142, 1970

Kim K, Jacobs S, Schaefer C, et al: Conscious and unconscious coping under stress, Part 1: relationship to each other and neuroendocrine function. Paper presented at the Third International Conference on Grief and Bereavement, Sydney, Australia, June 30–July 4, 1991

Lazarus RS, Folkman S: Stress, Appraisal, and Coping. New York, Springer, 1984

Lindeman E: Symptomatology and management of acute grief. Am J Psychiatry 101:141–148, 1944

McCrae RR: Age differences in the use of coping mechanisms. J Gerontol 37:454–460, 1982

McCrae RR: Situational determinants of coping responses: loss, threat, and challenge. J Pers Soc Psychol 46:919–928, 1984

Menninger K: The Vital Balance. New York: Viking Press, 1963

Miller PM, Surtees PG, Kreitman FRC, et al: Maladaptive coping reactions to stress: a study of illness inception. J Nerv Ment Dis 173:707–716, 1985

Moos RH (ed): Human Adaptation: Coping With Life Crises. Lexington, MA, Heath, 1976

Parkes CM: Psychosocial transitions: a field for study. Soc Sci Med 5:101–105, 1971

Parkes CM, Weiss RS: Recovery From Bereavement. New York, Basic Books, 1983

Pearlin LJ, Schooler C: The structure of coping. J Health Soc Behav 19:2–21, 1978

Pollock C, Andrews G: Defense styles associated with specific anxiety disorders. Am J Psychiatry 146:1500–1502, 1989

Radloff LS: The CES-D: a self-report depression scale for research in the general population. Applied Psychological Measurement 1:385–401, 1977

Schaefer C, Kasl S, Jacobs S, et al: Coping and hospitalization following bereavement. Paper presented at the Society for Epidemiologic Research, Vancouver, BC, Canada, June 15–18, 1988

Shuchter SR: Dimensions of Grief: Adjusting to the Death of a Spouse. San Francisco, CA, Jossey-Bass, 1986

Silverman P: Widow to Widow. New York, Springer, 1986

Stone AA, Neale JM: New measure of daily coping: development and preliminary results. J Pers Soc Psychol 46:892–906, 1984a

Stone AA, Neale JM: Effects of severe daily events on mood. J Pers Soc Psychol 46:137–144, 1984b

Stroebe W, Stroebe MS: Bereavement and Health. New York, Cambridge University Press, 1987

Stroebe M, Stroebe W: Does "grief work" work? a review and empirical investigation. Reports from the Psychological Institute, University of Tübingen, Number 31, 1990

Vaillant GE: Adaptation to Life. Boston, MA, Little, Brown, 1977

Vingerhoets A, Van Heck G: Gender and coping: their relationship to symptoms (abstract). Psychosom Med 52:239, 1990

Vitaliano PP, Maiuro RD, Russo J, et al: Raw versus relative scores in the assessment of coping strategies. J Behav Med 10:1–17, 1987

Wolff C, Friedman S, Hofer M, et al: Relationship between psychological defenses and mean urinary 17-hydroxycorticosteroid excretion rates, I: a predictive study of parents of fatally ill children. Psychosom Med 26:576–591, 1964a

Wolff C, Hofer M, Mason J: Relationship between psychological defenses and mean urinary 17-hydroxycorticosteroid excretion rates, II: methodologic and theoretical considerations. Psychosom Med 26:592–609, 1964b

Worden JW: Grief Counseling and Grief Therapy: A Handbook for the Mental Health Practitioner. New York, Springer, 1982

Wortman CB, Silver RC: The myths of coping with loss. J Consult Clin Psychol 57:349–357, 1989

CHAPTER 8

Personal Risk Factors for Complications

In this chapter, I address the interesting question of why some people appear to be vulnerable to the stress of bereavement and others do not. The environment, with its vectors of psychiatric disorders and its resources for recovery, is not the only character in the story about how the psychiatric complications of bereavement occur. Personal vulnerability must also be considered. An adaptive model of psychiatric disorders provides a framework for considering both sides of the equation: the environmental stressors and the personal diathesis. A stress-diathesis model has been used successfully in studies that show that the relationship between life events and depression is clarified if the individual's vulnerability to depression (defined by dependent and self-critical cognitive schemas), is known (Hammen et al. 1985, 1989). The success of the stress-diathesis model lends support to its use for our purposes. Therefore, in contrast to Chapters 5 and 6, which concern environmental issues, in this chapter I consider several personal characteristics that influence the development of psychiatric complications during bereavement. I extend here the discussion of personal characteristics begun in Chapter 7 on coping and adaptation.

Each of us is a unique individual with a unique personality and style of attachment that influence the manner in which we respond to separation and loss, not to mention the risk we run of clinical complications. In this chapter, I discuss the personal factors that are predisposing characteristics, such as age and gender, as well as characteristics that presumably are inherited, such as shyness. In addition, I review patterns of attachment behavior and personality traits that are either inherited or established in developmental experiences through early losses and privations; I also review how these patterns affect the manner in which we respond to a loss. Finally, I review personal vulnerabilities to clinical complications reflected in histories of psychiatric illness. These predisposing, personal characteristics shape how we adapt when a loss occurs (Bowlby 1980).

Our personal response to a loss is also determined by our biological characteristics. Rather little is known about biological functioning during bereavement, and the distinction between state and trait aspects of the biological reaction to a loss is rudimentary. Nevertheless, biological aspects of bereavement are an important component to understanding personal responses to loss and as such are also reviewed briefly in this chapter.

In the following sections, as the discussion shifts from study to study, the definition of the outcome of bereavement changes. In other words, the clinical outcome varies according to the particular risk factor—e.g., age, gender, personality trait, or biological characteristic—under discussion by the author of each study. In most cases, the clinical outcome is pathologic grief or depression, for which there is considerable overlap (as discussed in Chapter 4). This is the state of the art that characterizes current research in this field as there is no universal agreement yet on how to conceptualize outcome and the complications of bereavement.

Age and Gender

In Chapter 4, while considering the relationship among the several clinical syndromes that are recognized as complications of bereavement, I compared the risk factor profiles of sociodemographic characteristics, such as age and gender, and multiple other variables for each type of psychopathology. This comparison was summarized in Table 4–2 to determine the overlap, if any, among the different syndromes. Table 4–2 illustrates the gaps in our knowledge and, in some cases, the disagreement among studies about these risk factors. For age and gender, there was somewhat more consistency in findings that women and younger individuals are at greater risk for psychiatric complications of bereavement, particularly for major depressions and, to a lesser extent, for pathologic grief.

It is unclear why women are more likely to develop complications of bereavement. However, the higher risk among women of developing complications during bereavement is consistent with the higher risk among women in the general population for major depressions, anxiety disorders, and somatization disorders (Regier et al. 1988). For example, with regard to major depressions, it is recognized that there is a twofold higher risk of major depressions for women—presumably related to the stresses of child rearing and married life rather than to genetic or innate biological differences, such as the obvious hormonal differences between men and women (Merikangas et al. 1985; Weissman and Klerman 1977). The same psychosocial risk factors may hold true for the complications of bereavement, although in the case of widowhood it is the dissolution of the marriage that is in question.

In the circumstances of a loss, it is possible that women's attachments, not only to spouses but also to children and parents, differ from men's attachments, thereby predisposing women to a higher risk of complicated bereavement. This is a hypothesis that deserves consideration. For example, Jacobs et al. (1986a) documented differences in grief between widows and widowers; however, it is not obvious that these differences inherently carry a higher or lower risk. Alternatively, women may be exposed to a greater risk of environmental stresses, such as economic hardship and role strain, when a spouse dies. Thus both personal and environmental explanations are possible and may be additive. Until further research clarifies these questions, we must reserve judgment about the mechanisms.

The reasons that younger people appear to run a greater risk for the complications of bereavement are equally obscure if only empirical data are consulted. Inferential and theoretical perspectives on this phenomenon are also available. For example, it is conceivable that the nature of attachments and grief changes with age. There is no evidence that the grief of elderly people is attenuated in intensity, although it may differ from grief among younger bereaved individuals by virtue of reduced manifestations of emotional numbness and disbelief (Jacobs et al. 1986a). In fact, the observation of intense grief among elderly people runs counter to the sociological theory of disengagement, and presumably attenuated attachments, among elderly people (Cummings and Henry 1961). On the other hand, the evidence of greater, initial emotional shock among younger bereaved individuals—to the extent that this reflects a mild dissociative response to sudden, unexpected, untimely, and possibly traumatic losses—

may indicate an environmental factor as an explanation.

A recent study of traumatic experiences documented that 40% of young adults are exposed to traumatic events and 25% of these develop posttraumatic stress disorders subsequent to the exposure (Breslau et al. 1991). Seventeen percent of these traumatic experiences involve the sudden injury or death of family and close friends. Furthermore, the leading cause of death among young adults is accidents (see Chapter 5). Taken together, these data suggest that the occurrence of traumatic losses lies at the bottom of the higher rates of clinical complications of bereavement among young adults. Again, as was the case with gender, it appears that age differences are potentially related as much to environmental factors as to personal factors.

The Nature of Attachment

One of the time-honored factors that presumably affect the outcome of bereavement is the quality of the attachment to the deceased individual. This concept was introduced in Chapter 2 when historical views about pathologic grief were reviewed. In that discussion, three qualities of attachments—ambivalent feelings toward the deceased individual; insecure attachments; and latent, negative self-images and role models—were implicated in causing pathologic grief. It is important to note that, although these ideas about personality functioning may have considerable currency, they have not been systematically tested.

For example, Freud (1917) used the term *ambivalence* to describe interpersonal relationships that were considered problematic in the circumstances of rejection, separation, or loss. Ambivalent relationships are narcissistic and characterized by intense feelings of love and hate that are not integrated into a coherent mental representation of the other individual (Freud 1917). According to Freud's clinical observations, ambivalent relationships, through a psychological process of introjection, place the bereaved individual at greater risk of depressive illness as a consequence of the loss. However, this conclusion was challenged in subsequent psychoanalytic writings as clinical observers noted ambivalent qualities in most relationships in the circumstances of a loss. This revision in clinical observations led to the conclusion that ambivalence was not uniquely associated with narcissistic attachments and depressive reactions (Abraham 1949; Siggens 1966). Still, the hypothesis that ambivalent relationships are associated with a higher risk of complications after a loss has not been tested in a systematic controlled study, in part because the concept of ambivalence is so complicated that it has been difficult for psychosocial scientists to develop structured assessments of it.

In one study, Parkes and Weiss (1983) attempted to crudely approximate the idea of ambivalence by rating the self-reported degree of conflict in a marriage after the death of a spouse. They found that 38 bereaved spouses who reported high levels of marital conflict (conflict with the spouse in two or more areas of family functioning) had significantly worse outcomes 2 and 4 years after a loss than their counterparts who reported low conflict. The pattern of grief they observed in the high-conflict group was similar to the delayed grief syndrome introduced in Chapter 2 (and that discussed in Chapter 9 in the context of differential diagnoses). It is not clear to what extent the observations in this study were independent of illness in the family or socioeconomic status, factors that might also contribute to marital conflict. However, it should be emphasized that marital conflict is not the same as ambivalence (as defined above). Still, the observation from the Parkes and Weiss study suggests that the quality of the attachment may play a role in causing one type of pathologic grief.

Kinship

Another means for characterizing the nature of the attachment is to consider the kinship to the deceased individual. Attachment differs according to whether it is to a parent, a spouse, a homosexual partner, a child, or a sibling. The effect of this variation on the process and outcome of grief can be observed in studies designed to provide comparison groups according to kinship to the person who dies. However, relatively little has been done to examine the effect of this relatively easily managed variable on the process and outcome of bereavement (Osterweis et al. 1984).

In the only study that used mortality as an outcome, Rees and Lutkins (1967) found that the death of a spouse or a child was associated with significantly ($P < .05$) higher rates of death among the survivors compared to the death of a sibling or adult parents. Interestingly, though, the Rees and Lutkins study of mortality as an outcome establishes a pattern of higher risk for spouses and parents that holds true in studies that use psychological measures of the adjustment to bereavement.

One study (Sanders 1979–1980), using a thorough assessment of the emotional response to a loss, found that bereaved parents experience more intense grief—death anxiety, anger, guilt, somatic symptoms, and depression—than do bereaved spouses or bereaved children who had an elderly parent die. In addition, the duration of the parents' grief was prolonged, particularly among the mothers for whom it remained unresolved for several years. Moreover, the emotional distress of the mothers intensified after the second year of bereavement (Sanders 1989). In another study, Cleiren (1991) observed a similar pattern of severe separation distress, in addition to intense guilt, depression, and multiple somatic symptoms, that persisted beyond the first anniversary of the death of a child, which was more problematic for bereaved mothers than for bereaved fathers. The investigator found that parents were the most severely affected after the death of a family member, followed by the bereaved spouses, siblings, and adult children, although the intensity of grief was nearly as great among bereaved spouses as among bereaved parents. This observation was roughly similar to that in a study by Clayton et al. (1968) that compared the psychological manifestations of grief and outcomes in bereaved spouses to those in bereaved parents and found no differences. In Cleiren's study (1991), bereaved widowers were more severely affected than bereaved widows, and bereaved mothers were more severely affected than bereaved fathers, illustrating an important interaction between gender and type of loss.

Three studies have found an association between depressive symptoms during bereavement and kinship to the deceased individual. McHorney and Mor (1988) found that the odds of an individual who lost a spouse being depressed about 4 months after a loss were significantly higher ($P < .05$) than for bereaved individuals who lost parents, siblings, or more distant relatives. In a study by Murrell and Himmelfarb (1989), the death of a spouse, parent, or child—in contrast to the death of a sibling, grandchild, or good friend—was significantly associated with depression in the surviving family member within a year of the loss. In these studies, the meaning of the relationship to the deceased individual was interpreted in terms of consanguinity in the first case (McHorney and Mor 1988) or the degree of attachment in the second (Murrell and Himmelfarb 1989). Both concepts are a characterization of the nature of the attachment.

Cleiren's study (1991) confirmed the pattern of depression according to kinship in the first year of bereavement, finding that bereaved spouses and parents were significantly more depressed ($P < .05$) than were bereaved siblings and children 4 months after a death. When the sample was followed up at 14 months of bereavement, 15% of the bereaved spouses continued to experience severe depressive symptoms, whereas 31% of the bereaved parents were severely depressed, representing a slight increase over the 4-month rate. By this time, the bereaved, depressed parents also reported little hope of recovery.

On the whole, the death of a parent for adult children appears to be less distressing than the death of a child or spouse. Nevertheless, grief for an elderly parent has special qualities, such as an association with death anxiety as the adult child assumes the role of matriarch or patriarch of the family and enters the generation in which death is likely to occur next (Moss and Moss 1983–1984; Sanders 1979–1980). Also there is some evidence of an elevated risk of suicide in the 3 years after the loss of a mother among adult, unmarried sons with a history of a depressive disorder (Bunch et al. 1971). In addition, reports of clinical series of patients have documented that some adults seek help with their grief over the death of a parent (Horowitz et al. 1984). In contrast to these clinical observations, it should be noted that the rate of complications in one sample (Cleiren 1991), which was representative of the total population in the community of such bereaved individuals, was low in comparison with bereaved spouses, parents, and siblings.

One surprising finding in a Dutch study (Cleiren 1991) of the relationship between kinship and bereavement, not confirmed in other studies (McHorney and Mor 1988; Murrell and Himmelfarb 1989), is the observation that bereaved sisters are just as affected by the death of siblings as widows are by the death of a spouse. Bereaved sisters experienced intense feelings of grief, scored higher than widows on avoidance, were equally depressed, and had multiple somatic complaints (Cleiren 1991). Although they experienced improvement over the first year of bereavement, about one-third of the bereaved sisters, many of whom had a sibling die in a traffic accident, still felt helpless and reported a low sense of control over their lives 14 months after the loss. If this observation proves to be true in subsequent surveys, bereaved sisters may be one neglected subgroup within the field of bereavement research that warrants more study and perhaps specific intervention programs (Cleiren 1991).

A number of other studies are available on the bereavement of parents (Kennell et al. 1970; Levav et al. 1988; Miles 1985; Shanfield et al. 1984), children (Black 1979; Pynoos et al. 1987; Raphael 1983; Worden 1991), and adult children of older parents (Birtchnell 1970a, 1970b, 1970c; Horowitz et al. 1984; Malinak et al. 1979). However, these studies were not well controlled. In addition, baseline data on the measures of outcome were often absent in these studies. There have also been some studies of bereavement among the partners and intimate friends of people who have died from acquired immunodeficiency syndrome (AIDS) (Lennon et al. 1990; Martin 1988), but, again, conclusions about any unique characteristics of grief of this type, in which bereavement overload is more likely and the bereaved individuals may be infected or ill themselves, are hampered by the absence of control subjects.

Personality Traits

In this section, I review aspects of the personalities of bereaved individuals that have been implicated as risk factors in shaping the reaction or outcome of bereavement. Various approaches to understanding personality traits or personality style are feasible, such as our discussion of coping style and ego defenses in Chapter 6, which is taken up again below.

An intrinsic problem in most studies that include an assessment of personality is the absence of baseline data on the personality traits. Routinely, the assessment of personality traits takes place after a loss has already occurred. It is probably assumed, and it may be true, that personality traits are fairly stable during a stressful experience of this magnitude. But when the stressful experience results in a clinical complication, this assumption may be tenuous. For example, in their study of major depressions, Hirschfeld et al. (1989) suggested that episodes of depression can cause personality changes, such as increases in introversion, dependency, neurosis, and emotional lability. Therefore, the assumption that personality traits predate an acute disturbance, such as pathologic grief, should be tested. Until this is done, there is reason to be skeptical about claims that personality traits observed during or subsequent to an acute disturbance are preexisting, moderating variables. These claims may do nothing more than describe how bereaved individuals cope with a death (i.e., they may explain the process and course of grief rather than describe preexisting personality traits). (An example of using personality functioning to define the process of grief is provided in the section below titled "Personality Characteristics as Part of the Typology of Pathologic Grief.")

Only in the past 10 years have a few studies assessed the contribution of personality traits to the formation of attachments and the reaction to separation. Lund et al. (1985–1986) examined self-esteem of acutely bereaved elderly individuals using structured assessments and found that their self-esteem was no different from that of matched, nonbereaved controls. The assessment of self-esteem remained stable over 2 years in this study and did not vary as the process of grief evolved. In their study of widows in Toronto using the Cattell 16 Factor Personality Questionnaire, Vachon et al. (1982) found that women who were apprehensive, worrying, emotionally labile, and anxious were at risk for prolonged emotional distress after a loss. Women who were emotionally stable, mature, conscientious, traditional, and precise about social conventions had continuously low levels of distress throughout the first 2 years of acute bereavement. Using the Eysenck Personality Inventory, Stroebe and Stroebe (1987) found that bereaved individuals who scored high on neuroticism and low on a sense of internal control were at high risk for depression and somatic complaints, particularly in the circumstances of an unexpected loss. In their study, Raphael and Middleton (1990) confirmed the observation of neuroticism and anxious attachment as risk factors as well, although the methodology for personality assessment, presumably the Eysenck Personality Inventory, was not well described.

Finally, if perceived nonsupportiveness is considered a personality trait rather than a characteristic of the environment (see Chapter 6), it is yet another aspect of personality functioning that is relevant to behavior in bereavement (Maddison and Viola 1968; Maddison and Walker 1967). Nonsupportiveness is a variable that has been linked to poor outcome of bereavement, and its relationship to the other traits described here is potentially interesting.

One well-known clinical observation in psychopharmacology is that there is an increased occurrence of atypical depressive syndromes in rejection-sensitive adults who seek treatment (Quitkin et al. 1979). This observation may also hold true in understanding the personality traits that predispose an individual to the clinical complications of bereavement. Rejection sensitivity seems to be a prime risk factor for complications during bereavement, but it has never been operationalized in a systematic assessment. If this observation proves to be true, it would have implications not only for identifying high-risk individuals but also for treating depressions that might be observed with monoamine oxidase inhibitors (Quitkin et al. 1979).

The hodgepodge of observations on personality traits described above at first seems difficult to integrate into a coherent picture. Despite the heterogeneity, the picture that emerges from the review of this small body of literature is one of an anxious, worrying, introverted, neurotic individual for whom attachment may serve critical supportive functions and who is sensitive to losses, particularly if they are perceived as rejections. When a loss occurs to such an individual, he or she may be at a higher risk for poor adaptation and clinical complications. The idea that neurotic, anxious individuals are at risk for the affective syndromes of pathologic grief is consistent with the observed association between low emotional strength and resiliency and the risk of major depressions in a group of adults with one family member who had been diagnosed as having a major depression (Hirschfeld et al. 1989). Because the personality characteristics that predicted risk in the latter study did not have a well-established theoretical relationship to depression, the authors concluded that these characteristics served as nonspecific vulnerability factors for mental illness in general (Hirschfeld et al. 1989).

A fascinating question that has not been addressed is the relationship of personality traits in adults that are related to the process and outcome of bereavement to personality traits observed in children studied for their temperament and attachment behaviors. Three major types of child studies may suggest a reason to assume such a relationship: 1) studies of insecure attachment in children using the Ainsworth Strange Situation paradigm (Ainsworth 1970; Ainsworth et al. 1978), 2) studies of separation-individuation in toddlers and the relationship of arrests in this developmental process to borderline personality disorders in adulthood (Mahler et al. 1975), and 3) studies of shyness in children with its presumed relationship to panic disorders, agoraphobia, and neuroticism in adults (Kagan et al. 1988). No longitudinal studies have been completed to investigate this issue and conclusions about a direct relationship are speculative. Unfortunately, the longitudinal studies that are necessary will be very complicated and expensive; thus good scientific data for addressing this important question may not be available in the near future.

Personality Characteristics as Part of the Typology of Pathologic Grief

Investigators in two studies have incorporated personality characteristics into the typology of pathologic grief that was observed in their samples. In one study, Parkes and Weiss (1983) connected conflicted grief syndrome with bereaved spouses who had ambivalent or conflicted relationships and linked chronic grief syndrome with bereaved individuals who had dependent relationships. In a second study, using the Minnesota Multiphasic Personality Inventory (MMPI; Hathaway and McKinley 1943), Sanders (1989) observed a positive linkage between bereaved individuals, who had schizoid personalities and high depression scores, and pathologic grief. Sanders also noted that individuals with emotional tension, dysphoria, anxiety traits, oversensitivity, and a history of multiple family losses developed depression as a psychopathological outcome. This latter outcome was related to the "frighteningly sad" ego state that Horowitz et al. (1980) described as one vicissitude of pathologic grief.

In Sanders's study (1989), one sample group that had an optimistic outlook and used denial as a defense mechanism reported more somatic rather than psychological symptoms and had good outcomes. This group is reminiscent of the emotionally stable, mature group of Toronto widows described by Vachon et al. (1982). Curiously, this observation on optimism and denial contrasts with a previous study (Parkes 1970) that found that irritable widows reported more somatic symptoms than their less sensitive, yet distressed, counterparts.

Ego Functioning

Rather than focusing on descriptive diagnoses according to DSM-III (American Psychiatric Association 1980), psychodynamic psychiatry emphasizes the task of clarifying the psychological genetics of the clinical problem and the functional impairment of the patient (Alarcon 1984; Volkan 1972). In the clinical interview, the clinician focuses on the affective experience of the individual, the ego defenses that are used to modulate the affect, and the implications of these factors for unconscious motivation and personality functioning. This type of assessment can be used for understanding the "functional" disorders that are treated in this tradition of practice. As a general proposition, specific ego defenses, presumably as enduring traits, are associated with certain personality styles. For instance, people with obsessive personality styles predominantly make use of reaction formation, isolation of affect, and rationalization. Individuals with hysterical personality styles make use of repression and denial, and so on. In this framework, ego defenses offer another functional perspective on the personalities of bereaved individuals. The question is whether certain ego defenses carry a higher risk of poor outcome of bereavement and whether these ego defenses suggest a certain type of personality.

My colleagues and I tried to address these questions in the analyses that we completed of ego defenses (see Chapter 7). We did not find that any specific ego defense had a significant relationship to outcome (Jacobs et al. 1991). Thus it was impossible to extrapolate from specific ego defenses, or small groups of ego defenses, to personality styles and the outcome of bereavement. We did observe that widows and widowers with high scores on neurotic ego defenses 2 months after the death of a spouse were more likely to have high scores on depression scales 13 months after the loss (Jacobs et al. 1991; Kim et al. 1991). To the extent that neurotic ego defenses are associated with intrapsychic conflict, this suggests that internal conflict is related to depression as an outcome. This observation is roughly consistent with the conclusions above about neurotic personality traits being associated with pathologic grief, but is subject to the repeated caveat that the ego defensive assessments were not made prior to bereavement and, therefore, do not represent baseline functioning.

In the Jacobs et al. study (1991), high scores on defensive work, reflecting conflict-related ego defensive functioning, predicted low scores on depression later in follow-up. If high scores on both neurotic ego defenses and defensive work reflect internal conflict, this observation would appear contradictory to the findings discussed in the previous paragraph. However, my colleagues and I found that neurotic ego defensive scores and the rating of defensive work did not correlate with each other. Therefore, we speculated that the rating of defensive work, rather than serving as an index of internal conflict, may capture the bereaved individual's effort to modulate the intense emotions of the early stages of bereavement, which ultimately has a salutary effect on the evolution of the individual's grief.

Personality Diagnoses

Some authors have advanced the idea that most of what is understood as pathologic grief is nothing more than a reflection of preexisting personality disorders (Alarcon 1984; Middleton et al., in press). This is an important question that requires scientific investigation, which Middleton and colleagues have undertaken (Raphael and Middleton 1990). For example, it has been suggested that the characteristics of dependent personality disorder—such as the inability to function independently, the subordination to others, the passivity, and the sense of helplessness—resemble Bowlby's description (1980) of anxious attachment. Anxious attachment, in turn, has a direct relationship to the manifestations of pathologic grief (Middleton et al., in press).

As another example, the characteristics of avoidant personality disorder include sensitivity to rejection, approval seeking, and social isolation, all of which might easily complicate an individual's adaptation to loss and possibly be construed as pathologic grief (Middleton et al., in press). Bereavement may overwhelm an individual's restricted ability to cope and upset a marginal state of adaptation, thereby exacerbating a preexisting personality disorder. Indeed, one epidemiological study of the prevalence of borderline personality disorder in the community found that widowhood was associated with a severe impairment in personality functioning (Swartz et al. 1990). Because this study used prevalence data, it is impossible to know whether widowhood is associated with the inception of borderline personality disorder or with a prolonged duration of borderline disturbance in the circumstances of bereavement. The latter explanation seems more likely. In comparison, it seems unlikely that bereavement causes borderline disturbance given our understanding of this diagnostic entity as an enduring, developmental disorder. An association between widowhood and borderline personality disorder in other samples needs to be confirmed by additional studies before we can accept it unquestioningly.

The conceptual issues involved in investigating the role of personality in pathologic grief are complex. To critically examine the hypothesis that pathologic grief is an expression of personality disorders, it is useful to begin by comparing the diagnostic criteria for the personality disorders in question and the criteria for diagnosing the clinical complications of bereavement (these are also discussed in the Chapter 9). The results of such a comparison do not persuasively support this hypothesis. The enduring traits of dependent personality disorder are not the same as the specific, acute symptomatic criteria for pathologic grief.

Theoretical perspectives on personality disorders in general make the link between personality disorders and pathologic grief even more problematic. A personality disorder is, by its DSM-III-R (American Psychiatric Association 1987) definition, a chronic disorder, characterized by the presence of current as well as long-standing maladaptive traits that are presumably established in childhood experiences. If it is a chronic disease subject to acute exacerbations that periodically motivate the afflicted individual to seek help, then it is important to characterize the acute disturbance. This is analogous to any other chronic disease. For example, a loss for an individual with dependent personality disorder resembles a glucose overload for an individual with "brittle" diabetes mellitus. In either case, there is an aggravation or even a major crisis of the underlying disease state. For dependent personality disorder it is conceivably pathologic grief; for diabetes it is diabetic ketoacidosis. It is just as important to have criteria for recognizing the acute disturbance with its implications for treatment in the one case as in the other. In a recent discussion of the relationship between major depression and borderline personality disorder (Gunderson and Phillips 1991), these same distinctions (i.e., the symptomatic distinctions and the difference between a developmentally determined chronic disorder and an environmentally determined acute disorder) were used to differentiate the two disorders.

If an individual with a personality disorder develops one of the acute complications of bereavement, it seems reasonable to diagnose it as an Axis I disorder according to the system adopted in DSM-III-R. If a personality disorder coexists, it can be diagnosed on Axis II. In other words, the bereaved patient's problems can be addressed as a multiaxial disorder. The occurrence of the affective disturbances that we recognize as pathologic grief (Kim and Jacobs 1991) can be conceptualized as complications not only of the personality disorder (as DSM-III [American Psychiatric Association (1980)] does for all the personality disorders associated with major depression or other Axis I disorders) but also of the environmental vector of a loss. If nothing else, a multiaxial approach provides a conceptual framework for empirically examining the relationship between the two axes. Furthermore, a multiaxial approach provides a basis for thinking about not only psychodynamic approaches to treatment but also specific treatments for acute symptomatic disturbances.

In the early 1960s, when psychoanalytic thought held sway in clinical practice, American psychiatry addressed the issue under discussion here when it adopted crisis theory as a way of conceptualizing acute emotional crisis and strategies for brief treatment (Caplan 1964). It is probably no accident that the study of bereavement laid the foundation for crisis theory (Klein and Lindeman 1961). We are now wrestling with the same issues in the face of a decline of interest in crisis theory and a contemporary understanding of psychopathology reflected in DSM-III-R. It is also worth mentioning that the basic idea of an acute, maladaptive emotional crisis caused by bereavement in an individual with personality vulnerabilities is generically akin to Horowitz et al.'s model (1980) of pathologic grief in which enduring, latent maladaptive self-images and role models (i.e., personality traits) are held in check by an intimate relationship to another individual and then emerge as acute problems when that individual dies.

Personality Traits and Acute Symptomatology

The following example illustrates the relationship between personality traits and acute symptomatology:

Case 8

> Mr. H was a 47-year-old personnel director whose partner died from AIDS 9 months before he was referred for outpatient follow-up after a 3-month psychiatric hospitalization. On admittance, Mr. H complained "I've had a whole bunch of losses. . . . I hear my dead lover's voice telling me to jump off a tall building." His partner of 10 years had died after an illness of 6 months from bowel cancer. Largely motivated by the needs of Mr. H to do everything possible for his partner, the two men had searched frantically for a cure and commuted from city to city as they went from hospital to hospital on the East Coast. Care for the terminally ill partner, including multiple hospitalizations, exhausted their life savings of more than $200,000. When

his partner died, Mr. H reported that he experienced immediate, intense grief that became overwhelming within a month. It was then that he began to hear his partner's voice telling him to join him in death, and he had heard it every day since.

Two months after his partner's death, alone, out of money, and unable to continue his job, Mr. H returned home to his family in another state. He did this over their initial objections, which he perceived as a rejection. He was admitted to a psychiatric hospital for the first time 3 months after the loss because of persistent suicidal ideation and growing concern by his parents that he would act on his impulse to jump off a building, reflected in a command "hallucination" of his deceased partner's voice telling him to do this. He met criteria for a major depression, and because of the psychotic symptomatology, he was given the diagnosis of psychotic depression. During a period of ambulatory treatment in between this first and his next hospitalization, the diagnosis was changed to schizoaffective disorder. At the time of the second admission, Mr. H not only reported suicidal ideation in the form of auditory hallucinations but also depressed mood, feelings of worthlessness and hopelessness, shame over his deteriorated level of functioning, and loss of interest in his occupation and in the future. Later, he also experienced anergia, major weight gain associated with overeating, and sleep disturbances, including difficulty falling asleep, early morning awakening, and an irresistible urge to sleep during the day.

Mr. H was an only child in a comfortable family. He reported no traumatic experiences in early childhood. Lacking interest in athletics, he said he was distant from his father. He described his mother as reliable but withdrawn. He had few friends as he engaged in no social activities. He characterized himself as a bookworm. Reaching puberty at age 13, he discovered his homosexual preference and had a brief affair. Then, he "went through hell" for 3 years, in part on the assumption, prevalent at that time, that he had a disease. Typically, he coped with stress by plunging into his work; he called himself a "workaholic." Reacting against the homosexuality, at age 15 he became sexually active with a girl, which resulted in the girl becoming pregnant. Tragically, the teenage mother died in childbirth. The child was placed for adoption. Mr. H was "devastated . . . crushed" by the experience. Shortly afterward, escaping from the traumatic situation, he left for boarding school. From there he went to college and met his future lover who was his first and only significant partner. Slowly but surely, the relationship with his partner led to acceptance of his homosexuality and "raised his self-esteem immeasurably." At the same time, Mr. H's homosexuality caused estrangement from his family, and he never returned home again until after his partner's death.

Though his mother had been treated for a psychiatric disorder, it was impossible to get an idea of the nature of the illness. There was no other family psychiatric history. There was no personal history of psychiatric disorder before the death of his lover.

At the time of mental status examination, Mr. H presented as an overweight, sloppily dressed man who was eager to engage in the interview. He had an importuning quality. He acknowledged that the voice was not really experienced as coming from outside himself and rather "must be based on my feelings." In addition, he denied a wish to die and emphasized, rather, that he was "scared" and had lost his sense of self-worth. His affect varied from flat to being charged and volatile, during which time he appeared agitated. He appeared tired, and his mood was depressed. These was no thought disorder or bizarre, delusional, or pessimistic thought content. He was extremely articulate and his cognitive functioning was intact, including the capacity of abstract thinking.

During the second hospitalization, Mr. H was initially treated with fluoxetine without relief of his depressive symptoms. He was then switched to a combination of psychotropic drugs on which he was discharged. They included perphenazine 24 mg at bedtime, lithium carbonate 300 mg qid, tranylcypromine 10 mg bid, and diazepam 10 mg at bedtime. There was growing concern about his "dependence" on the diazepam. The tranylcypromine was chosen because of the atypical features of the major depression including hypersomnia, overeating and weight gain, severe anxiety, and apparent rejection sensitivity. During the hospitalization, he developed a reputation for exaggerating his symptoms, presumably for the purpose of secondary gain, specifically to extend his care in the hospital rather than be discharged. Although there was a decided histrionic quality, the hospital conservatively refrained from making a personality diagnosis because of the acute symptomatology.

I was asked to consult on his treatment because of my interest in the complications of bereavement and the hospital staff's anticipated difficulty in effecting a discharge from inpatient care. On my first examination of Mr. H in the hospital, I was impressed with two processes. One was severe separation distress (or pathologic grief) and the other was major depression. I viewed the agitation and auditory hallucinations as a severe manifestation of separation distress that coexisted in relationship to a depressive syndrome. In addition, Mr. H presented as an intensely importuning individual who readily accepted the opportunity to display and discuss his symptoms in a dramatic way. He struck me as similar to a patient described in a clinical case report who was diagnosed with pathologic grief and histrionic personality disorder for whom the personality disorder was viewed as the fundamental psychopathological process that was distorting the expression of grief (Alarcon 1984).

Mr. H was discharged to my care. His treatment is described in more detail in Chapters 12 and 13.

This patient not only had acute symptomatology of intense separation distress and depression, but also had a dependent, avoidant, and histrionic personality style that shaped his response to the loss of his partner. He met criteria for severe and prolonged separation distress (i.e., pathologic grief) and major depression as Axis I diagnoses (see Chapter 9). This symptomatology was, in part, a product of the trauma of the loss. I also believe that Mr. H's character traits and functioning fundamentally compromised his ability to cope with the loss of his lover. This was first reflected in the frenetic search for a cure. In Mr. H's case, the maladaptive coping style probably had its roots in his early psychosexual development and the teenage trauma of coming to terms with his homosexuality and the death of his girlfriend. Perhaps the best example of the destructive effect of his personality style on his treatment was the "psychotic" symptom of his lover's voice telling him to take his own life. Both the patient, who was suggestible and wanted to prove his suffering and need for care, and the staff, who were searching for some explanation for his symptomatology within a familiar conceptual framework, had their own reasons for construing the symptom as part of a psychotic illness. Their perspective was obviously different from the formulation that I made, which I believe was more useful. Finally, both Axis I and Axis II perspectives on the psychopathology had useful implications for treatment (see Chapters 11 and 12).

Personal and Family Histories

In clinical psychiatry we routinely make use of personal histories and family histories of psychiatric disorders to determine the likelihood of a patient having a particular disorder. These historical data presumably reflect an inherited vulnerability, although, in fact, genetic and early developmental influences cannot be separated out from each other without appropriate control subjects. For example, if any individual, irrespective of bereavement, has a history of major depression, there is indisputable evidence that he or she is at higher risk for recurrent major depression than another individual without such a history, whether the diathesis is genetic or developmental in origin. In this fashion, histories of psychiatric problems can be useful personal attributes for predicting the risk of acute clinical disorders. Curiously, this type of personal factor is not extensively represented in studies of the outcome of bereavement. The evidence is scanty and, in some cases, mixed depending on how the clinical complication is defined.

Several studies have examined the relationship of personal histories of depression to the risk of depression during bereavement. Positive personal and family histories of major depression are not uncommon in bereaved spouses (Bruce et al. 1990; Gallagher et al. 1983; Jacobs et al. 1989). Some studies have not found this type of history to be a risk factor for depression following bereavement (Bruce et al. 1990; Jacobs et al. 1989) whereas other studies have found that a personal history of depression increases the risk of depression about twofold (Richards and McCallum 1979; Zisook and Shuchter 1991). One study (Bornstein et al. 1973) reported a history of mental illness (including major affective disorder, alcoholism, hysteria, and undiagnosed psychiatric illness) as a risk factor for depression, yet the history of major affective illness itself did not emerge independently as a risk factor and was rare in the sample.

Only one study (Jacobs et al. 1990) has examined past histories as risk factors for anxiety disorders. In this study, a personal history of anxiety disorders or major depression and a family history of anxiety disorders were associated with a higher risk of panic disorder and generalized anxiety disorder.

Childhood Losses and Their Long-Term Consequences

Numerous studies have examined the relationship between childhood losses and the subsequent occurrence of psychopathology in adulthood.

Most of this literature addresses the risk of occurrence and the severity of major depression in adults after a childhood loss (Lloyd 1980), though other types of psychopathology are occasionally reported (see below). The question that is central to this literature is whether the developmental experience of a childhood separation or loss predisposes the individual to psychiatric illness as an adult (i.e., what are the long-term consequences of a death in the family?).

The preponderance of evidence on major depression indicates that the childhood loss of a parent by death increases depressive risk by a factor of two to three (Lloyd 1980). Still, association of a childhood loss with adult psychopathology does not necessarily imply causation. Based on considerable evidence, it can be argued that it is not the death of a parent in childhood itself that causes depression later in adulthood (Tennant 1988), but rather that it is the failure to provide substitutive nurturance in the circumstances of the loss of a parent that is associated with later risk of major depression. According to this point of view, the combination of a loss and inadequate attention to the child's needs appears to place the individual at higher risk for psychiatric complications in adulthood.

According to attachment theory (Bowlby 1980), the period of risk of major depression is highest in the circumstances of a loss during adult life. In this regard, my colleagues and I found that death of or separation from parents in childhood was not related to scores on depression, anxiety, separation distress, and demoralization scales as indices of outcome after 1 year of bereavement in widows and widowers (Jacobs et al. 1987b). In addition, self-reported, previous problems with the death of parents, siblings, or spouses in adult life were unrelated to outcome. This is the only study that has systematically assessed these variables in an acutely bereaved sample as opposed to in samples of patients who were being studied because of psychopathology irrespective of bereavement (Jacobs et al. 1987b). Although the findings of this study do not support the hypothesis that the risk of major depression during adult life is greatest during bereavement, this hypothesis deserves further testing.

In an important study, Kendler et al. (1992) differentiated between childhood loss of a parent by separation or death and estimated the risk of major depression, panic disorder, generalized anxiety disorder, phobia, and eating disorders in adult life among female twin pairs. A complex pattern of findings emerged from their study. The authors found that even if the childhood loss of a parent is directly and causally related to the risk of major depression in adult life, the contribution of this experience to a liability for major depression ranges from 1.5% to 5.1%, a rather small effect. This study showed that the childhood loss of a parent may be more strongly related to the occurrence of other types of psychopathology during adulthood. The authors found that parental separation, but not parental death, was associated with an increased risk for major depression and generalized anxiety disorder. Separation from either a mother or father in childhood also was associated with an increased risk of major depression and generalized anxiety disorder as an adult woman. Parental death and maternal, but not paternal, separation were associated with panic disorder. Parental death and not parental separation was associated with increased risk for phobia. Finally, parental loss of either kind was found to be unrelated to risk for eating disorder. If the results of this study are confirmed, it appears that the occurrence of anxiety disorders in adulthood is the most important consequence of childhood bereavement as a developmental experience for women. This study usefully shifts the focus from major depression as the only long-term psychopathological outcome. Also it illustrates that not all adult psychopathology, such as an eating disorder, has a relationship to the childhood loss of a parent and suggests that the observed associations for anxiety disorders and major depression are specific.

According to the findings of two studies (Barry et al. 1965; Birtchnell 1975), another long-term consequence of early loss may be the appearance of dependent personality traits in adulthood, assessed clinically or on the MMPI (Hathaway and McKinley 1989). Most other types of personality traits have not been associated with early losses. In one study (Barry et al. 1965), the loss of a mother before age 5 years was more significantly associated with dependency traits than was the loss of a mother after age 11 years. All 17 patients who were bereaved in childhood in another study (Birtchnell 1975) presented for psychiatric care with some sort of depressive symptomatology in association with dependent personality traits in adulthood. Most of them also had experienced a deprivation of maternal care after the deaths of their mother and had assumed responsibility as mother surrogates for younger family members. These patients may have experienced the onset of the depressive illness after adult bereavements, although the report of the study is vague about this. If so, these women may serve as examples of the relationship between personality disorder and depression as an acute clinical complication of bereavement, as discussed above.

Biological Aspects of Bereavement

Effects on neuroendocrine function. Little is known about the biological aspects of bereavement. For example, studies during acute bereavement and other stressful experiences indicate that adrenocortical activation occurs in some individuals but not in others (Hofer et al. 1972a, 1972b; Jacobs 1987; Jacobs et al. 1984). Elevated adrenocortical activity is a function not only of stress but also of age and gender (Jacobs 1987; Jacobs et al. 1984, 1987a). On the other hand, no evidence of loss of diurnal pattern has been reported in bereaved individuals.

Recent studies of the dexamethasone suppression test (DST) indicated that nonsuppression occurs in 10%–20% of acutely bereaved individuals (Das and Berrios 1984; Shuchter et al. 1986). In one study (Das and Berrios 1984), no measures of depression were used; in the other (Shuchter et al. 1986), nonsuppression was associated not with depression scores but rather with anxiety scores. A third study (Kosten et al. 1984a) reported normal results in bereaved people who met criteria for major depressive disorders 6 months after spousal loss. However, the post-DST serum cortisol levels of participants in this study were positively correlated with depression scores. Thus the more depressed widows and widowers had less serum cortisol suppression by dexamethasone. The limited implications of these observations for diagnosis of major depressions during bereavement are discussed in Chapter 9.

Knowledge of other neuroendocrine systems is even more circumscribed than that of adrenocortical function. The thyroid system has not been investigated during acute bereavement. Other systems have been examined in a preliminary way. For example, a study of growth hormone following spousal loss demonstrated a large daytime rise in growth hormone in those individuals who were anxious and used denial during a stressful interview in which the loss was reviewed (Kosten et al. 1984b). When the participant was highly defensive according to the Crowne-Marlowe Scale (Crowne and Marlowe 1964), the amount of anxiety associated with a growth hormone response during the interview was lower. The predictive value of a growth hormone rise for subsequent depression or pathologic grief is not clear, but growth hormone is normally not secreted during the daytime in adults and may indicate a high level of distress.

A study of prolactin (Jacobs et al. 1986b) showed a direct correlation between a rise in serum prolactin during the interview and the separation anxiety of grief among bereaved individuals with depressive symptoms. If this observation is confirmed, prolactin levels may serve in the future as an index of the degree of separation distress and thereby help to define pathologic grief. Lane et al.'s analysis (1987) of these data revealed that the rise in serum prolactin correlated with a measure of the cognitive complexity of the bereaved patient's mental representation of the deceased individual. The association was positive for widows and negative for widowers, thus revealing intriguing gender differences in prolactin response, attachment, and their interaction that are difficult to explain without further investigation. In unpublished analyses (S. C. Jacobs, C. Gardner, May 1985), we found that prolactin responders during the interview were disposed to affiliate and engaged in the interview process, whereas those who did not respond to prolactin reacted to the interview in a rehearsed, unengaged manner.

In another study, Jacobs et al. (1986c) observed that elevated urinary catecholamine output occurs in acute bereavement but is not associated with depression or anxiety scores. Given the absence of a correlation of catecholamine levels with depression and anxiety, it is hard to relate the findings of this study to the observation of higher secretion or higher levels of serum norepinephrine in depressed patients (Esler et al. 1982; Lake et al. 1982) and patients with panic disorder (Charney et al. 1987). It is conceivable that the stress of bereavement overrides the effects of depression or anxiety on catecholamine systems.

With the possible exception of serum growth hormone response in which the Crowne-Marlowe Scale was the measure of defensiveness (see above), no evidence from the series of studies discussed above supports the role of ego defenses as mediating psychological mechanisms for any of the endocrine systems that were monitored. Our observations contrasted with the findings from a study (Wolff et al. 1964a, 1964b) of parents of leukemic children in which ego defensive effectiveness was related to 17-hydroxycortisol excretion during the terminal illness of the child. On the other hand, our observations were consistent with follow-up findings

(Hofer et al. 1972a, 1972b) that, following the death of their children, that ego defenses of the same parents had no demonstrable relationship to adrenocortical activity, a fact about this well-known study of the 1960s that has been obscured by time.

In the first longitudinal study (Kim et al. 1990) that used neuroendocrine variables 2 months after bereavement to predict outcome at 13 and 25 months, the findings were limited by the small sample size of 43 bereaved participants. The criteria of outcome were indices of depression, anxiety, hopelessness, and separation distress and assessments of health status reflected in self-rated health questionnaires used in an interview, hospitalizations, and death. The investigators used a variety of serum and urinary measures of adrenocortical and adrenomedullary function because these neuroendocrine systems were considered to be sensitive to stress. None of the neuroendocrine measures predicted levels of depression, anxiety, separation distress, hospitalizations, or death at 13 and 25 months after the death of a spouse. Low 24-hour urinary free cortisol and high 24-hour urinary epinephrine predicted high levels of hopelessness at 13 and 25 months in multiple regression analyses. Although the clinical significance of these relationships was unclear, the urinary cortisol also inversely predicted self-rated health at 13 months, and the urinary epinephrine predicted the number of visits to the doctor during the second year of bereavement.

More follow-up and epidemiological studies need to incorporate biological assessments such as these into the theoretical model for investigating the nature of bereavement. Such studies should enhance our understanding of this important aspect of the personal response to a loss and clarify the relationship between biological and environmental factors that influence the outcome of the experience.

Effects on sleep. Recently, the first report on sleep physiology during bereavement has appeared (Reynolds et al. 1992). Elderly, bereaved patients with major depression were found to have significantly lower sleep efficiency, more early morning awakening, shorter rapid-eye-movement (REM) latency, greater REM sleep percentages, and lower rates of delta wave generation in the first non-REM period of sleep compared with patients with uncomplicated bereavement. These sleep changes resembled those of age-matched patients with unipolar depressions. The implications of these novel observations are still unclear. Whether these electroencephalographic (EEG) changes in sleep identify a group of bereaved individuals that would benefit from treatment to diminish the subsequent burden of psychiatric impairment is a question that remains to be determined in an early intervention study.

Effects on immunological function. The studies of bereaved spouses by Bartrop et al. (1977) and Schliefer et al. (1983) suggested that not only neuroendocrine systems but also immunological function can be disturbed as a result of the stress from a loss (Bartrop et al. 1977; Schleifer et al. 1983). These changes during bereavement now appear nonspecific. This conclusion is based on the fact that the changes observed in both T-lymphocyte response to in vitro mitogens and natural killer cell activity, originally considered to be associated with bereavement, are a function of the severity of depression and increasing age rather than bereavement itself (Irwin and Weiner 1987; Kronfol et al. 1986; Schleifer et al. 1984). Although high circulating cortisol levels will also inhibit immune competence as part of the general stress response, in at least three studies the immune changes that were observed were independent of neuroendocrine change (Bartrop et al. 1977; Irwin and Weiner 1987; Schleifer et al. 1983).

Conclusions

A central issue that is latent in the discussion in this chapter is the following question: To what degree are the psychiatric complications of bereavement related to preexisting, moderating personal factors and to what extent are they related to environmental factors? Personal characteristics such as age, gender, the loss of a parent during childhood, and, perhaps, the style of attachment contribute to the risk of developing psychiatric complications after a loss. Critical environmental variables (including the nature of the loss—whether it was traumatic or not—and the quality of the environment in which grief occurs—whether it is supportive or not) are also at play. The task of future research is to clarify the relative contributions of all these factors (Henderson 1988) in a model that considers not only the stressor but also the diathesis of the individual in a cogent environment context.

A related debate concerns the relative value of biological versus epidemiological research in understanding the nature of bereavement and its complications. Again, the task ahead is to integrate knowledge of the neurobiology of bereavement and its clinical complications into models for understanding the nature of these adaptive disorders and the relationship of personal physiology to environmental risk factors (Henderson 1988).

Often, we make inferences about the characteristics of attachment from our observations in clinical work of the reaction to separation or loss (Vaillant 1985). This is a pitfall that is inherent in retrospective designs for research on personal characteristics that are risk factors for the clinical complications of bereavement. Good baseline data are hard and expensive to obtain, and this methodological problem will probably continue to plague this area of inquiry. In the meantime, it is useful to distinguish between indisputable preexisting variables, such as kinship or consanguinity, and questionable preexisting variables, such as personality traits. As noted in the introduction to this chapter, the status of biological parameters is uncertain as well.

With regard to personality traits, there is reason for researchers to remain skeptical about conclusions concerning the relationship between the traits and the acute clinical complications associated with bereavement. This recommendation stems from the review above, which indicates that there is not enough evidence that the personality characteristics implicated in pathologic grief are truly preexisting and are not simply another dimension of the response to an adverse experience. It can be argued that the manifestations of pathologic grief are nothing but the accentuation of preexisting psychopathology (Middleton et al., in press). Another position is that personality traits are the overriding if not exclusive determinants of poor resolution (Sanders 1989). My thesis is that personality factors probably affect the risk of acute complications and probably influence the individual's expression of grief and its clinical complications (Horowitz 1976). A theoretical framework, such as an adaptive model, provides for both environmental and personality variables and thereby facilitates the empirical investigation of both types of factors. This type of model best serves the development of new knowledge in this area.

Several studies in the past 10 years have incorporated personality variables in their design as risk factors for pathologic grief. These studies provide results that are heterogeneous. One theme that emerges, which is roughly consistent with recent studies, indicates that individuals with neurotic, anxious personality traits are at higher risk for major depression. These observations require confirmation. To some extent, the limitations of our knowledge about personality traits are secondary to methodological problems.

When my colleagues and I began our studies of bereavement in 1979, the measures that were available for the assessment of personality were either inefficient in the time and space they required in a questionnaire or unrelated to prevailing clinical concepts of personality disorders. Under these circumstances, my colleagues and I decided not to include these measures in our studies, aside from the assessment of ego functioning described in Chapter 7. This was an omission in our attempt to develop a comprehensive model for understanding the clinical complications of bereavement. The measures mentioned in this chapter and Chapter 7 now provide methodological opportunities for addressing these important questions.

References

Abraham K: A short study of the development of the libido, in Selected Papers on Psychoanalysis. London, Hogarth Press, 1949

Ainsworth MD: Attachment, exploration, and separation illustrated by the behavior of one year olds in a strange situation. Child Dev 41:49–67, 1970

Ainsworth M, Blehar M, Waters E, et al: Patterns of Attachment: A Psychological Study of the Strange Situation. Hillsdale, NJ, Lawrence Erlbaum Associates, 1978

Alarcon RD: Personality disorder as a pathogenic factor in bereavement. J Nerv Ment Dis 172:45–47, 1984

American Psychiatric Association: Diagnostic and Statistical Manual of Mental Disorders, 3rd Edition. Washington, DC, American Psychiatric Association, 1980

American Psychiatric Association, Diagnostic and Statistical Manual of Mental Disorders, 3rd Edition, Revised. Washington, DC, American Psychiatric Association, 1987

Barry H, Lindeman E: Dependency in adult patients following early maternal bereavement. J Nerv Ment Dis 140:196–206, 1965

Bartrop RW, Lazarus L, Luckhurst E, et al: Depressed lymphocyte function after bereavement. Lancet 1:834–836, 1977

Birtchnell J: Recent parent death and mental illness. Br J Psychiatry 116:289–297, 1970a

Birtchnell J: Depression in relation to early and recent parent death. Br J Psychiatry 116:299–306, 1970b

Birtchnell J: The relationship between attempted suicide, depression, and parent death. Br J Psychiatry 116:307–313, 1970c

Birtchnell J: The personality characteristics of early bereaved psychiatric patients. Soc Psychiatry 10:97–103, 1975
Black D: The bereaved child. J Child Psychol Psychiatry 19:287–292, 1979
Bornstein PE, Clayton PJ, Halikas JA, et al: The depression of widowhood after thirteen months. Br J Psychiatry 122:561–566, 1973
Bowlby J: Attachment and Loss, Vol 3: Loss, Sadness and Depression. New York, Basic Books, 1980
Breslau N, Davis GC, Andreski P, et al: Traumatic events and posttraumatic stress disorder in an urban population of young adults. Arch Gen Psychiatry 48:216–222, 1991
Bruce ML, Kim K, Leaf PJ, et al: Depressive episodes and dysphoria resulting from conjugal bereavement in a prospective community sample. Am J Psychiatry 147:608–611, 1990
Bunch J, Barraclough BM, Nelson B, et al: Suicide following death of parents. Soc Psychiatry 6:193–199, 1971
Caplan G: Principles of Preventive Psychiatry. New York, Basic Books, 1964
Charney DS, Woods SW, Goodman WK, et al: Neurobiological mechanisms of panic anxiety: biochemical and behavioral correlates of yohimbine induced panic attacks. Am J Psychiatry 144:1030–1036, 1987
Clayton PJ, Desmarais L, Winokur G: A study of normal bereavement. Am J Psychiatry 125:168–178, 1968
Cleiren MPHD: Adaptation After Bereavement. Leiden, Holland, DSWO Press, 1991
Crowne DP, Marlowe D: The Approval Motive: Studies in Evaluation Dependence. New York, Wiley, 1964
Cummings E, Henry WE: Growing Old. New York, Basic Books, 1961
Das M, Berrios GE: Dexamethasone suppression test in acute grief. Acta Psychiatr Scand 70:278–281, 1984
Esler M, Turbott J, Schwarz R, et al: The peripheral kinetics of norepinephrine in depressive illness. Arch Gen Psychiatry 39:295–300, 1982
Freud S: Mourning and melancholia (1917), in the Standard Edition of the Complete Psychological Works of Sigmund Freud, Vol 14. Translated and edited by Strachey J. London, Hogarth Press, 1953, pp 243–258
Gallagher DE, Breckenridge JN, Thompson LW, et al: Effects of bereavement on indicators of mental health in elderly widows and widowers. J Gerontol 38:565–571, 1983
Gunderson JG, Phillips KA: A current view of the interface between borderline personality and depression. Am J Psychiatry 148:967–975, 1991
Hammen C, Marks T, Mayol A, et al: Depressive self-schemas, life stress, and vulnerability to depression. J Abnorm Psychol 94:308–319, 1985
Hammen C, Ellicott A, Gitlin M, et al: Sociotropy/autonomy and vulnerability to specific life events in patients with unipolar depression and bipolar disorders. J Abnorm Psychol 98:154–160, 1989
Hathaway SR, McKinley JC: Minnesota Multiphasic Personality Inventory. Minneapolis, MN, University of Minnesota, 1943
Henderson AS: An Introduction to Social Psychiatry. New York, Oxford University Press, 1988
Hirschfeld RMA, Klerman GL, Lavori P, et al: Premorbid personality assessments of first onset of major depression. Arch Gen Psychiatry, 46:345–350, 1989

Hofer M, Wolff C, Friedman S, et al: A psychoendocrine study of bereavement, part 1: 17-Hydroxycorticosteroid excretion rates of parents following death of their children from leukemia. Psychosom Med 34:481–491, 1972a

Hofer M, Wolff C, Friedman S, et al: A psychoendocrine study of bereavement, part 2: observations on the process of mourning in relation to adrenocortical function. Psychosom Med 34:492–504, 1972b

Horowitz MJ: Stress Response Syndromes. New York, Jason Aronson, 1976

Horowitz MJ, Wilner N, Marmar C, et al: Pathological grief and the activation of latent self-images. Am J Psychiatry 137:1157–1162, 1980

Horowitz MJ, Weiss DS, Kaltreider N, et al: Reactions to the death of a parent. J Nerv Ment Dis 172:383–392, 1984

Irwin MR, Weiner H: Depressive symptoms and immune function during bereavement, in Biopsychosocial Aspects of Bereavement. Edited by Zisook S. Washington, DC, American Psychiatric Press, 1987, pp 159–174

Jacobs SC: Psychoendocrine aspects of bereavement, in Biopsychosocial Aspects of Bereavement. Edited by Zisook S. Washington, DC, American Psychiatric Press, 1987, pp 141–155

Jacobs SC, Mason J, Kosten T, et al: Urinary free cortisol excretion in relation to age in acutely stressed persons with depressive symptoms. Psychosom Med 46:213–221, 1984

Jacobs SC, Kasl SV, Ostfeld AM, et al: The measurement of grief: age and sex variation. Br J Med Psychol 59:305–310, 1986a

Jacobs SC, Brown SA, Mason JW, et al: Psychological distress, depression, and prolactin response in stressed persons. Journal of Human Stress 12:113–118, 1986b

Jacobs SC, Mason JW, Kosten TR, et al: Bereavement and catecholamines. J Psychosom Res 30:489–496, 1986c

Jacobs SC, Mason J, Kosten T, et al: Urinary free cortisol and separation anxiety early in the course of bereavement and threatened loss. Biol Psychiatry 22:148–152, 1987a

Jacobs SC, Schaefer CA, Ostfeld AM, et al: The first anniversary of bereavement. Isr J Psychiatry Relat Sci 24:77–85, 1987b

Jacobs SC, Hansen FF, Berkman L, et al: Depressions of bereavement. Compr Psychiatry 30:218–224, 1989

Jacobs SC, Hansen FF, Kasl SV, et al: Anxiety disorders during acute bereavement: risk and risk factors. J Clin Psychiatry 51:269–274, 1990

Jacobs S, Kim K, Schaefer C, et al: Conscious and unconscious coping under stress, part 2: relationship to one and two year outcomes after bereavement. Paper presented at the Third International Conference on Grief and Bereavement, Sydney, Australia, June 30–July 4, 1991

Kagan J, Reznick JS, Snidman N: Biological bases of childhood shyness. Science 240:167–171, 1988

Kendler KS, Neale MC, Kessler RC, et al: Childhood parental loss and adult psychopathology in women. Arch Gen Psychiatry 49:109–116, 1992

Kennell JH, Slyter H, Klaus MH: The mourning response of parents to the death of a newborn infant. N Engl J Med 283:344–349, 1970

Kim K, Jacobs SC: Pathologic grief and its relationship to other psychiatric disorders. J Affect Disord 21:257–263, 1991

Kim K, Jacobs SC, Mason JW, et al: Conjugal bereavement: the relationship between neuroendocrine measures and long term outcome (abstract). Psychosom Med 52:241, 1990

Kim K, Jacobs S, Schaefer C, et al: Conscious and unconscious coping under stress, part 1: relationship to each other and neuroendocrine function. Paper presented at the Third International Conference on Grief and Bereavement, Sydney, Australia, June 30–July 4, 1991

Klein DC, Lindeman E: Preventive intervention in individual and family crisis situations, in Prevention of Mental Disorders in Children. Edited by Caplan G. New York, Basic Books, 1961, pp 283–306

Kosten TR, Jacobs SC, Mason JW, et al: The DST in depression during bereavement. J Nerv Ment Dis 172:359–360, 1984a

Kosten TR, Jacobs SC, Mason JW, et al: Psychological correlates of growth hormone response to stress. Psychosom Med 46:49–58, 1984b

Kronfol Z, House JD, Silva J, et al: Depression, urinary free cortisol excretion and lymphocyte function. Br J Psychiatry 148:70–73, 1986

Lake CR, Pickar D, Ziegler M, et al: High plasma norepinephrine levels in patients with major affective disorder. Am J Psychiatry 139:1315–1318, 1982

Lane RD, Jacobs SC, Mason JW, et al: Sex differences in prolactin change during mourning. J Psychosom Res 31:374–383, 1987

Lennon MC, Martin JL, Dean L: The influence of social support on AIDS-related grief reaction among gay men. Soc Sci Med 31:477–484, 1990

Levav I, Friedlander Y, Kark JD, et al: An epidemiologic study of mortality among bereaved parents. N Engl J Med 319:457–461, 1988

Lloyd C: Live events and depressive disorders reviewed. Arch Gen Psychiatry 37:529–535, 1980

Lund DA, Dimond MF, Caserta MS, et al: Identifying elderly with coping difficulties after two years of bereavement. Omega 16:213–224, 1985–1986

Maddison D, Viola A: The health of widows in the year following bereavement. J Psychosom Res 12:297–306, 1968

Maddison DC, Walker WL: Factors affecting the outcome of conjugal bereavement. Br J Psychiatry 113:1057–1067, 1967

Mahler MS, Pine F, Bergman A: The Psychological Birth of the Child. New York, Basic Books, 1975

Malinak DP, Hoyt MF, Patterson V: Adults' reaction to the death of a parent: a preliminary study. Am J Psychiatry 136:1152–1156, 1979

Martin JK: Psychological consequences of AIDS-related bereavement among gay men. J Consult Clin Psychol 56:856–862, 1988

McHorney CA, Mor V: Predictors of bereavement depression and its health services consequences. Med Care 26:882–893, 1988

Merikangas KR, Weissman MM, Pauls DL: Genetic factors in the sex ratio of major depression. Psychol Med 15:63–69, 1985

Middleton W, Raphael B, Martinek N, et al: Pathological grief reactions, in The Handbook of Bereavement. Edited by Stroebe MS, Stroebe W, Hansson RO. Cambridge, UK, Cambridge University Press (in press)

Miles MS: Emotional symptoms and physical health in bereaved parents. Nurs Res 34:76–81, 1985

Moss MS, Moss SZ: The impact of parental death on middle aged children. Omega 14:65–75, 1983–1984

Murrell SA, Himmelfarb S: Effects of attachment bereavement and pre-event conditions on subsequent depressive symptoms in older adults. Psychol Aging 4:166–172, 1989

Osterweis M, Solomon F, Green M (eds): Bereavement: Reactions, Consequences and Care. Washington, DC, National Academy Press, 1984

Parkes CM: The first year of bereavement. A longitudinal study of the reaction of London widows to the death of their husbands. Psychiatry 33:444–467, 1970

Parkes CM, Weiss RS: Recovery From Bereavement. New York, Basic Books, 1983

Pynoos RS, Nader K, Frederick C, et al: Grief reactions in school age children following a sniper attack at school. Isr J Psychiatry Relat Sci 24:90–98, 1987

Quitkin F, Rifkin A, Klein D: Monoamine oxidase inhibitors. Arch Gen Psychiatry 36:729–760, 1979

Raphael B: The Anatomy of Bereavement. New York, Basic Books, 1983

Raphael B, Middleton W: What is pathologic grief? Psychiatric Annals 20:304–307, 1990

Rees WD, Lutkins SG: Mortality of bereavement. BMJ 4:13–16, 1967

Regier DA, Boyd JH, Burke JD, et al: One month prevalence of mental disorders in the United States. Arch Gen Psychiatry 45:977–986, 1988

Reynolds CF, Hoch CC, Buysse DJ, et al: Electroencephalographic sleep in spousal bereavement and bereavement related depression of late life. Biol Psychiatry 31:69–82, 1992

Richards JG, McCallum J: Bereavement in the elderly. N Z Med J 89:201–204, 1979

Sanders CM: A comparison of adult bereavement in the death of a spouse, child, and parent. Omega 10:303–322, 1979–1980

Sanders CM: Grief: The Mourning After. New York, Wiley, 1989

Schleifer SJ, Keller SE, Camerino M, et al: Suppression of lymphocyte stimulation following bereavement. JAMA 259:374–377, 1983

Schleifer SJ, Keller SE, Stein M: Stress effects on immunity. Psychiatr J Univ Ott 10:126–130, 1984

Shanfield SB, Benjamin AH, Swain BJ: Parents' reactions to the death of an adult child from cancer. Am J Psychiatry 141:1092–1094, 1984

Shuchter SR, Zisook S, Kirkorowicz C: The dexamethasone suppression test in acute grief. Am J Psychiatry 143:879–881, 1986

Siggens LD: Mourning: a critical survey of the literature. Int J Psychoanal 47:14–25, 1966

Stroebe W, Stroebe MS: Bereavement and Health. New York, Cambridge University Press, 1987

Swartz M, Blazer D, George L, et al: Estimating the prevalence of borderline personality disorder in the community. Journal of Personality Disorders, 4:257–272, 1990

Tennant C: Parental loss in childhood. Arch Gen Psychiatry 45:1045–1050, 1988

Vachon MLS, Sheldon AR, Lancee WJ, et al: Correlates of enduring distress patterns following bereavement: social network, life situation, and personality. Psychol Med 12:783–788, 1982

Vaillant GE: Loss as a metaphor for attachment. Am J Psychoanal 45:59–67, 1985

Volkan V: The recognition and prevention of pathologic grief. Va Med Q 99:535–540, 1972

Weissman MM, Klerman GL: Sex differences and the epidemiology of depression. Arch Gen Psychiatry 34:98–111, 1977

Wolff C, Friedman S, Hofer M, et al: Relationship between psychological defenses and mean urinary 17-hydroxycorticosteroid excretion rates, I: a predictive study of parents of fatally ill children. Psychosom Med 26:576–591, 1964a

Wolff C, Hofer M, Mason J: Relationship between psychological defenses and mean urinary 17-hydroxycorticosteroid excretion rates, II: methodologic and theoretical considerations. Psychosom Med 26:592–609, 1964b

Worden JW: Bereaved children one year after loss. Paper presented at the Third International Conference on Grief and Bereavement in Contemporary Society, Sydney, Australia, June 29–July 4, 1991

Zisook S, Shuchter SR: Depression through the first year after the death of a spouse. Am J Psychiatry 148:1346–1352, 1991

CHAPTER 9

Differential Diagnosis of the Complications of Bereavement

When a patient presents with a problem that occurs in the context of bereavement, the central evaluative task for the clinician is to differentiate among normal patterns of grief, pathologic grief, and other psychiatric disorders. In Chapter 2, I introduced the concepts of normal and pathologic grief and provided a preliminary discussion of the nature of pathologic grief, as well as its potential diagnostic criteria. In this chapter, I discuss the recently proposed diagnostic criteria for pathologic grief in more detail for the purpose of making a clinical determination on the need for treatment. In addition, I consider the differential diagnosis between normal depressive mood changes and major depressive disorder, on the one hand, and normal apprehensions and anxiety disorders, on the other. I also discuss post-traumatic stress disorder (PTSD) briefly in relationship to pathologic grief.

The implication of a diagnosis of pathologic grief, major depression, anxiety disorder, or PTSD is the need for skilled professional or professionally supported intervention. In the instance of pathologic grief, the treatment signified by the diagnosis is primarily psychotherapy, although anecdotal evidence exists for some pharmacological treatments (see Chapters 10 and 13). When a diagnosis of major depression or an anxiety disorder is made, the implication is for both psychotherapy and pharmacotherapy (see Chapters 10 through 13). In the following discussion, the treatment implied by the diagnosis will be made explicit because this will facilitate the presentation of differential diagnosis when discussing single symptoms, subsyndromal symptom patterns, and nonsymptomatic criteria that assist in diagnosis. This is particularly true when discussing the differential diagnosis of depressive symptoms and major depressive syndromes that are ubiquitous during bereavement.

There are four types of criteria for differential diagnosis of complications of bereavement: symptomatic criteria, social and occupational functioning, personal and family historical data, and biological assessments.

Symptomatic Criteria

Normal Grief and Pathologic Grief

As noted in Chapter 2, a recent development in the understanding of pathologic grief is a contemporary effort to establish consensus, symptomatic criteria for its diagnosis (Raphael 1989). Before entering a discussion of these criteria, it is important to emphasize their provisional nature. Development of diagnostic criteria by a process of consensus, although essential, is only the beginning of the task of establishing empirically validated criteria. The criteria that are discussed have to be tested in studies for consistency in family histories, utility for prognosis, biological correlates, and concurrent validity with respect to functional impairment, disability, and risk for subsequent morbidity and mortality. Furthermore, we must strive to move beyond predominantly static, descriptive criteria to the integration of functional criteria for diagnosis into our nosology. This goal is consistent with an understanding of pathologic grief as a disorder of adaptation. Unfortunately, our knowledge of adaptive and, more to the point for our discussion here, maladaptive coping during bereavement is too rudimentary at present to suggest that this goal is imminent (see Chapter 7). In the meantime, the consensus criteria for pathologic grief provide a reasonable, contemporary working approach for recognizing this complication of bereavement.

With the caveat just noted, what are the consensus criteria for diagnosing pathologic grief? They are presented in their entirety in the Appendix. In short, the current version of the criteria includes four variants of pathologic grief: 1) delayed grief, 2) absent grief, 3) inhibited (or distorted) grief, and 4) chronic grief. Based on the discussion in Chapter 2, I am going to add the diagnosis of severe grief as a fifth variation for the purposes of this discussion. These criteria are based either on unusually severe or prolonged manifestations of grief or on delayed, absent, or inhibited manifestations of normal grief. They incorporate both symptoms of separation distress and depression as well as nonspecific symptoms such as somatic complaints. The criteria also assume a normal progression of grief over time. At a minimum, this means that there is no unusual delay or persistence of grief over time. More ambitiously, a normal progression signifies that a typical sequence ordinarily occurs starting with emotional numbness, then separation distress, then a mourning process associated with depressive symptoms, and finally a process of recovery (see Chapter 2).

Delayed and absent grief. In *delayed grief syndrome,* the pangs of grief and searching phenomena (i.e., the typical manifestations of separation distress [see the description under *Severe grief* below]) are delayed for more than 2 weeks after a loss. At the same time, three other variations of symptoms may be present: 1) severe emotional numbing and disbelief, 2) severe symptomatology of other types such as depressive symptoms and pain syndromes, or 3) virtually no other symptoms or signs of disturbance. Each of these variations tends to be associated with particular circumstances. For example, severe emotional numbing and disbelief is typically associated with traumatic or sudden, unexpected deaths (Parkes and Weiss 1983). After a traumatic loss, a full-blown posttraumatic stress syndrome may be present in the absence of normal grief, as if the traumatic aspects of the experience override the reaction to the loss. Alternatively, a preexisting or concurrent depressive syndrome may appear to interfere with the normal expression of grief. In some cases, there is no significant reaction of any kind to the loss, and the bereaved individual presents a picture of very circumscribed and superficial social relationships as if there were an avoidance of interpersonal commitments.

Whatever the variation and presumed etiological considerations, the central descriptive, diagnostic consideration in delayed grief syndrome is the delay in the onset of separation distress. This syndrome is differentiated from normal grief by means of the absence of the specific distress caused by a loss (i.e., separation distress) for an extended period of time at the beginning of bereavement. Pure examples of delayed grief are rarely observed in practice because bereaved individuals do not routinely consult psychiatrists at this early stage of grief. Emergency teams providing psychiatric services at disasters are probably the most likely to observe this phenomenon. More commonly in practice, a patient presents later in the course of bereavement and the delay in onset of grief is appreciated historically. By the time of presentation, the delay in the onset of grief is associated with either severe grief or chronic grief syndrome (Kim and Jacobs 1991) as well as major depression (Kim and Jacobs 1991; Parkes 1972). According to my clinical experience, this syndrome probably occurs in 10%–15% of the patients with pathologic grief. The proportion of bereaved patients with delayed grief syndrome probably depends on the number of individuals bereaved secondary to traumatic losses in the particular clinical series that is being discussed.

Absent grief syndrome is closely related descriptively to delayed grief and is diagnosed when grief is absent in circumstances in which the clinician would expect to find it (see the Appendix). The rationale for this syndrome of pathologic grief is developed in Chapter 2. Absent grief has the same basic variations as delayed grief, suggesting multiple etiological pathways. In descriptive terms, the relationship between delayed grief and absent grief seems simple and is defined by the potential for delayed grief to become absent grief if the delay is prolonged. The differentiation between delayed grief and absent grief depends in part on the time the patient presents for evaluation. If the patient presents early in the course of bereavement, it is more reasonable to refer to delayed grief than absent grief. If the patient presents later in the course of grief, certainly after the first anniversary and perhaps as early as 6 months after a loss, it is more appropriate to refer to absent grief. Absent grief is rare, occurring in about 5% of cases of pathologic grief in my experience.

Inhibited (or distorted) grief. The diagnosis of *inhibited grief* refers to the attenuation of the typical manifestations of grief (see the Appendix). Typically, the various symptomatic and behavioral manifestations of *distorted grief* are associated with this syndrome of pathologic grief. Separation distress appears secondary or even insignificant in comparison to the more nonspecific symptomatology of distorted grief.

The manifestations of distorted grief include somatic symptoms, "identification" symptoms, overt hostility, affective blunting related to underlying hostility, self-reproach, and self-destructive, overactive, socially withdrawn, or vicarious caregiving behavior. Depressive and anxious symptoms may be prominent and meet criteria for major depression or anxiety disorders or they may be subclinical. The nucleus of this syndrome is the inhibition of the typical manifestations of separation distress and the exaggeration of ancillary symptomatology characterized as *distorted*. It has a relationship to delayed grief and absent grief in the sense that they are all attenuated forms of the expression of normal grief. Inhibited grief is distinguished from normal grief by the diminution of typical separation distress. By extension, the normal evolution of the multiple dimensions of grief does not occur. Bereaved individuals with inhibited grief syndromes often present with distorted symptoms as chief complaints and often at the time of anniversaries. Ordinarily, by the time of the first anniversary, the history of an inhibited pattern of grief is associated with a chronic disturbance. It is hard to know what percentage of patients with pathologic grief present with an inhibited clinical picture as no one has systematically documented it. Lindeman's writing on pathologic grief implies that it is common; however, this syndrome probably accounts for only about 5%–10% of a large series of patients in my experience.

Severe grief. *Severe grief syndrome* is another pattern of pathologic grief that is gaining greater acceptance as a distinct diagnostic entity. In some ways, it is the easiest to define insofar as it is an exaggeration of the manifestations of normal separation distress. On the other hand, it can be the hardest to diagnose because it is distinguished from normal grief more by degree than by its qualities. Severe grief is characterized by the exaggerated expression of separation distress. This includes, in varying patterns, intense yearning for the lost individual, preoccupations focused on the deceased, crying, sighing, a perceptual set for the lost individual (including dreams, tactile or visual illusions, frank hallucinations in some cases), and searching for the individual who is lost such as seeking out places and things identified with the deceased (Table 2–1). The bereaved individual experiences this flood of distress as overwhelming and often fears that he or she will lose control or fall apart. The severe grief syndrome may begin early in bereavement, or it may occur after a period of delayed grief, as if the bereaved individual had been avoiding something that was expected to be turbulent and relentless. It is increasingly appreciated that the intense expression of grief early in the course of bereavement is associated with persistent distress (Hays 1991; Stroebe and Stroebe 1987; Vachon et al. 1982; Zisook and Shuchter 1991). The syndrome of severe grief probably carries a higher risk of depressive and anxiety disorders in association with it, certainly by the time it merges into chronic grief (Bornstein and Clayton 1972; Bornstein et al. 1973; Jacobs et al. 1987; Zisook and DeVaul 1983). It is hard to quote an estimate of how frequently this syndrome occurs as it has not been systematically looked for until recently. It is a common form of pathologic grief.

Chronic grief. In *chronic grief* the symptomatic manifestations of bereavement are intense and do not diminish, or diminish only slightly, throughout the first year of bereavement and beyond. In some cases, the separation distress or other symptoms become worse, often as the bereaved person approaches the first anniversary of the death. Also there is a failure of the normal progression of grief in the sense that the grief does not attenuate and acceptance of the loss is incomplete or impossible. Bereaved people with chronic grief continue to experience severe separation distress; in other cases, the "distorted" manifestations of bereavement predominate. These symptoms are usually associated with depressive syndromes. In essence, chronic grief is distinguished from normal grief by the unabated continuation of the clinical picture of acute grief. It is the most common variant of pathologic grief encountered in clinical practice.

Also although it may already have been strongly implied, it is worth noting that delayed grief, inhibited or distorted grief, and severe grief early in the course of bereavement are strongly associated with, and indeed presumably predictive of, chronic grief. If the clinician is seeing a patient for the first time 1 year of more after a loss, it may seem as if there are simply variations in the patterns of chronic grief: 1) delayed, chronic grief, 2) inhibited, chronic grief, and 3) severe, chronic grief. Alternatively, if the clinician is seeing the patient earlier in the course of bereavement, delayed, inhibited, or severe grief may be observed more in isolation. In this case, they are patterns of pathologic grief that the clinician looks for as early signals that the bereavement has gone awry. None of the pathologic grief syndromes are pure disorders, as the discussion above might suggest. Rather, aspects of each may be found in others. This discussion of the variations in pathologic grief is intended to characterize the predominant clinical picture. The criteria for the diagnosis of these five variations in pathologic grief (delayed, absent, inhibited, severe, and chronic) are summarized in Table 9–1.

When these diagnoses are made, there are several implications for treatment, the main one being the need for psychotherapy, including psychoeducation about the nature and vicissitudes of separation distress, that are discussed in the following chapters.

PTSD and Pathologic Grief

In the circumstances of a traumatic loss, traumatic distress may occur independently of grief (see Chapter 5). Furthermore, an individual who has experienced a traumatic loss is open to the risk of a PTSD. For diagnostic purposes, the criteria for PTSD in DSM-III-R (American Psychiatric Association 1987) are applicable in the circumstances of a traumatic loss.

Although no systematic, empirical studies have been done, it is interesting to consider the relationship between PTSD and pathologic grief. The most direct connection appears to be between PTSD and delayed grief. Delayed grief occurs typically in the circumstances of a sudden, unexpected loss. Many delayed grief syndromes are characterized by severe emotional numbing and disbelief, which are symptoms that are akin to the dissociative processes that occur in traumatic stress reactions. In addition, traumatic stress symptomatology is thought to interfere with the expression and recovery from grief. For these reasons, it is logical to wonder if a relationship between delayed grief and PTSD exists. In this framework, delayed grief without intrusive symptoms may be a forme fruste of PTSD. On the other hand, by definition, intrusive symptoms such as frightening images, hypervigilance, and autonomic arousal are usually not part of delayed grief syndrome. This is the clinical picture unless the absence of grief finally gives way to severe grief with intrusive symptomatology, which then coexists with the numbing and avoidant phenomena. In short, when the intrusive symptoms are absent, the delayed grief syndrome is not like typical PTSD.

Careful, matter-of-fact review by the clinician of the circumstances of the death and the patient's reactions to it are essential parts of the diagnostic evaluation for the purpose of clarifying whether the event was trau-

Table 9–1. Differential diagnosis of normal grief and pathologic grief

Criteria	Normal grief	Delayed/absent grief	Inhibited grief	Severe grief	Chronic grief
Onset of separation distress	Within 2 weeks	Delayed more than 2 weeks	Within 2 weeks	Immediate, sometimes delayed	Sometimes delayed
Numbness, disbelief	Transient, usually a few days	Severe, persistent, or absent	Transient	Severe or transient	Sometimes severe, persistent
Separation distress	Transient, peaks usually in 4–6 weeks	Absent	Attenuated, sometimes absent	Severe, fear of losing control	Sometimes severe
Distorted symptoms	Absent or minimal		Severe		Sometimes prominent
Depressive symptoms	Transient, peaks usually in 4–6 months	Sometimes severe	Sometimes severe		Usually severe
Anxiety symptoms	Transient		Sometimes severe	Usually severe	Sometimes severe
Evolution of grief or recovery	Acceptance, some improvement by 1 year	Prolonged	Prolonged	Prolonged	Prolonged
Psychiatric comorbidity	Rare	High risk of major depressive disorders	Some risk of major depressive disorders	High risk of major depressive disorders and anxiety disorders	High risk of major depressive disorders and anxiety disorders

matic for the patient. This part of the evaluation also allows the clinician to reconstruct the initial reaction to the loss, an opportunity that is otherwise lost. In some cases, a death is clearly accidental or the result of a disaster and there is a reasonable presumption of trauma. Even in these circumstances, the degree of exposure to the event remains an important question. In other instances, when the death is sudden and unexpected, the presumption of trauma is not as strong although still reasonable. In these cases, it is necessary to key off of the bereaved individual's reaction. When the bereaved individual is frightened and shocked and cannot face these issues immediately, or if there is apparent nonplussed or superficial avoidance of this discussion when the circumstances are manifestly grotesque and horrifying, this signals the need to monitor the patient for traumatic symptomatology if this is not already apparent in the clinical picture.

Fear of Losing Control

Fear of losing control is a nonspecific symptom of pathologic grief that usually signals that the separation distress is extremely severe, that traumatic aspects of the loss are latent, or that the bereaved individual is experiencing severe generalized anxiety or panic (Clayton et al. 1971). In some patients, this fear is associated with a coexisting major depression and seems to reflect a reduced tolerance for separation distress. The exact meaning of this fear of losing control requires elucidation through systematic study. In any event, if the patient reports a fear of losing control, it often crystallizes a clinician's conviction about a particular diagnosis; this symptom is also a useful indicator of the need for careful professional evaluation and probably intervention. The usefulness of psychotherapeutic interventions for addressing the fear of losing control is discussed in Chapter 13.

Anniversaries of the Death

Anniversaries of the loss are critical points in time for evaluation of the clinical complications of bereavement. Often patients will present for evaluation near the time of an anniversary because they have set this time as a deadline for improvement, they become disappointed, or they experience an aggravation of symptoms that typically occurs at this time. In this way, anniversaries serve as subtle, sometimes unconscious, markers in time or "clocks" by which patients evaluate themselves (Pollock 1970). Ordinarily, the exacerbation of symptoms on an anniversary or a major holiday is transient. It lasts only a few days and causes no prolonged interference with functioning (Jacobs et al. 1987). Observance of the anniversary is typically accomplished through a personal or socially accepted ritual such as attending religious services (Jacobs et al. 1987). This transient exacerbation of grief at the time of anniversaries should not be misconstrued as a chronic grief syndrome. When the worsening of symptoms at the time of an anniversary is prolonged more than a few days and when it interferes with social functioning, there is evidence that the symptomatic disturbance is associated with severe separation distress, depression, anxiety, and demoralization (Bornstein and Clayton 1972; Jacobs et al. 1987). Thus a careful evaluation of anniversary phenomena, particularly at the time of the first anniversary, is useful in making judgments about clinical complications. Sometimes the recurrent pattern of anniversary problems is misconstrued as cyclical, bipolar disease (Cavenar et al. 1977). The value of correct diagnosis and the organization of treatment around anniversaries are taken up in Chapter 13.

Normal Depressive Mood of Bereavement and Major Depression

The differential diagnosis of major depression from the normal depressive mood associated with the mourning process is more highly developed than that for pathologic and normal grief, although many empirical studies on important questions remain to be done. The symptomatic criteria that will be discussed are consistent with those identified in DSM-III-R (Table 9–2). A clear distinction between bereavement and depression is difficult to achieve because during the period of acute bereavement depressive syndromes are observed in up to 45% of bereaved individuals (Bornstein et al. 1973; Jacobs et al. 1989; Zisook and Shuchter 1991). Most of these depressive syndromes (about 80%) are transient and benign (i.e., they resolve spontaneously in 6 months or less). The others are persistent, psychologically and socially crippling, and require professional intervention. When these unremitting depressive syndromes are recognized, a diagnosis of major depression should be made.

Table 9–2. Differential diagnosis of the depression of uncomplicated bereavement and major depressive disorder superimposed on bereavement

Criteria	Depression of uncomplicated bereavement	Major depressive disorder, complicated bereavement
Symptomatic		
Self-esteem	Focused feeling of guilt; feeling useless; "the world is poor and empty"	Pervasive and unrealistic feeling of guilt; feeling worthless; "it's the ego itself that is poor and empty"
Psychomotor disturbance	Agitation is seen; retardation seldom, if ever	Agitation and retardation
Suicidal gestures	Rare, though risk is higher	Common
Hallucinations and delusions	Focused on deceased	Congruent with depression, pessimism, and poor self-esteem
Duration and timing of depressive symptoms	Early syndromes common, mostly transient; neurovegetative symptoms, usually transient	Persistent
Psychosocial stress	Loss	Persistent stress may be associated with depression
Social and occupational functioning	Transient, minor impairment	Impairment by time of consultation
Personal and family history		
Sex ratio	Equal in females and males?	Females greater than males
Personal history of depression	Common	Common
Family history of depression	Unknown	Common
Biological tests		
Loss of diurnal variation in cortisol secretion	Not reported	In some
Dexamethasone suppression test nonsuppression	10%–20% acutely	30%–50%
Abnormal TSH response to TRH	Unknown	25%
Catecholamines	Elevated acutely	Elevated in some
Sleep physiology	Reduced REM latency and sleep efficiency, early morning awakening	Reduced REM latency and sleep efficiency, early morning awakening

Note. TSH = thyroid-stimulating hormone; TRH = thyrotropin-releasing hormone; REM = rapid eye movement.

In most cases, the major depression is associated with pathologic grief, and both should be diagnosed as they have different implications for treatment. In a few cases, major depressions occur in the absence of pathologic grief, and a diagnosis of grief complicated by major depression should be made (Kim and Jacobs 1991). This is the principal reason for considering major depression as a separate diagnostic problem. In addition, a diagnosis of major depression holds significance for the use of antidepressant medication and certain types of psychotherapy as parts of treatment.

Follow-up studies of acutely bereaved individuals and supplementary studies of the nosology and symptomatology of depression have identified three specific symptoms of depression that are rarely seen during uncomplicated bereavement and that reinforce the diagnosis of major depression (Bornstein et al. 1973; Clayton et al. 1974; Nelson and Charney 1981; Parkes 1972). These are pervasive disturbance of self-esteem, marked psychomotor retardation (both of which are melancholic symptoms), and suicidal gestures.

A morbid disturbance of self-esteem is one feature distinguishing grief from depression that was originally recognized by Freud (1917) and has been confirmed in modern studies (Bornstein et al. 1973; Jacobs et al. 1989; Parkes 1972) and has been included in DSM-III-R (American Psychiatric Association 1987). Disturbed self-esteem is not simply regret about omissions during a terminal illness, but rather an inappropriate, obsessional guilt with an accompanying sense of personal failure and worthlessness. The presence of such pervasive, unrealistic guilt should strongly suggest a major depressive syndrome. With regard to other individual symptoms, the absence of psychomotor retardation and suicidal gestures in uncomplicated bereavement has been noted in observations by Clayton et al. (1974) and Bornstein et al. (1973). Although it is true that psychomotor retardation is rarely seen in the absence of major depression, this may be a methodological artifact associated with the study of elderly people who tend to exhibit agitated depression more frequently than younger individuals. Suicidal gestures, as opposed to simply thinking about death or passively wishing to be dead (which occurs frequently during acute bereavement), are also rare and speak for themselves with regard to the need to intervene even if they are not reinforcers of the diagnosis of major depression.

Investigators in two studies of the course of depressive symptoms during bereavement (Blanchard et al. 1976; Clayton and Darvish 1979) have reported that the persistence of depressed mood and neurovegetative symptoms beyond 1 year is unusual. According to these findings, the clinician should especially note these symptoms in making a judgment about the seriousness of a persistent depressive syndrome.

If an acutely bereaved patient presents with a major depressive syndrome, including psychotic features, the diagnosis of major depression and the decision to treat is obvious, with the caveat that normally occurring perceptual disturbances of bereavement include, in some cases, frank tactile, visual, and auditory hallucinations (Rees 1971). Also focused, unrealistic beliefs about a recent loss, such as disbelief about what has happened that is consciously recognized as cognitively dissonant, ought not to be misconstrued, along with concurrent depressive symptoms, as a psychotic depression.

The implication of melancholic symptoms for the diagnosis of major depression and intervention during acute bereavement is more ambiguous. Melancholia includes symptoms such as the loss of pleasure in activities, a distinct quality of mood, the worsening of mood in the morning, early morning insomnia, marked psychomotor changes, significant anorexia with weight loss, or inappropriate guilt. (Both psychomotor retardation and a disturbance of self-esteem were already identified above as symptoms that are rarely seen in uncomplicated bereavement.) On the other hand, there is no systematic evidence that a melancholic depressive syndrome that occurs early in bereavement will not spontaneously resolve as most early depressive syndromes do. As a precaution, if nothing else, these patients might be monitored more closely than usual.

One caution in adopting any single or subsyndromal set of symptoms as diagnostic criteria is to avoid the assumption that their absence means that an otherwise existent depressive syndrome is benign. Prolonged duration of a major depressive syndrome, overwhelming subjective distress, and severe impairment in social and occupational functioning (see below) even in the absence of these specific symptoms are still sufficient criteria to justify a diagnosis of major depression and subsequent professional intervention.

The evolution of depressive symptoms over time. A longitudinal perspective on the major depressions of bereavement indicates that the symptomatic pattern of the depressive syndromes evolves over time. Loss of interest in activities, self-depreciation, anger, and elevated alcohol use persist and become more prominent later in the course of the depression (Blanchard et al. 1976; Clayton and Darvish 1979). In other words, the clinical picture evolves away from a typical, reactive dysphoria toward that of endogenous depression as the individual presumably becomes less reactive to the environment and a disturbance of self-esteem grows in importance. The presence of substance abuse suggests that the afflicted individuals are "treating" themselves to correct a chronic affective disturbance, although the substance abuse may be contributing to the disorder also. If this pattern of symptoms emerges in the evolution of a depressive syndrome, it adds weight to the diagnosis of major depression.

The concept that a mild, reactive depression can evolve into a symptomatic pattern consistent with endogenous (or psychotic) depression has been established in longitudinal studies of neurotic depression (Akiskal et al. 1978). Although the concept therefore appears viable, it is also important to recognize that neither the situational depression of bereavement nor the population in which it occurs is the same as the neurotic depressions observed in psychiatric clinic populations.

Duration and timing of the depressive syndrome. It seems obvious that the longer a depressive syndrome persists, the more pressing the need for diagnosis and treatment. Yet no simple guidelines exist for judging when the duration of a depressive syndrome that occurs during bereavement should prompt intervention. Clinical experience and systematic studies (Bornstein et al. 1973; Jacobs et al. 1989; Zisook and Shuchter 1991) have indicated that most of the depressive syndromes of normal bereavement last several weeks. This period easily exceeds the DSM-III-R criterion for duration in the diagnosis of major depressions. In these circumstances, a working approach to making the diagnosis of major depression includes consideration of when in the course of grief the depression occurs. If a depressive syndrome lasts for several weeks early in the course of bereavement (i.e., in the first 6 months of bereavement), then the clinical signs and symptoms discussed here (psychosis, guilt, psychomotor retardation, severe impairment of function, and suicidality) are criteria to use in evaluating the need for intervention. Later in the course of bereavement (after 6 months or 1 year), the standard DSM-III-R criteria for a major depressive disorder, including depressed mood and neurovegetative symptoms as noted above, are relevant. As a rough guideline, the longer the bereavement is, the shorter the duration of a depressive syndrome that merits diagnosis and intervention is.

In general, it is the timing of a major depressive syndrome within the course of bereavement that has implications for diagnosis. Depressions that are observed late in the course of bereavement (e.g., those present 1 year after a loss) probably warrant diagnosis and intervention. This conclusion is based on consideration of their duration, the improbability of spontaneous resolution, and the evolution of symptoms to a nonreactive state. It appears that most of these bereaved, depressed patients also report depression starting very early after the loss. In fact, one of the strongest predictors of unremitting depression is the number of depressive symptoms that occur 1 month after a loss (Bornstein et al. 1973; Hays 1991; Zisook and Shuchter 1991). Thus depressions that are observed late in the course of the first year of bereavement usually manifest a prolonged or recurrent course and, on this basis, deserve to be diagnosed as major depressions and warrant treatment. It is likely that the major depressions of late onset (more than 6 months after the death) also have ominous clinical implications. This clinical impression needs to be confirmed in a systematic study.

Suicidal risk. Although suicidal gestures are unusual in clinical practice with bereaved patients, there is evidence of an elevated risk of suicidal gestures (Birtchnell 1970) and suicide following spousal and parental bereavement (Bock and Webber 1972; Bunch 1972; Bunch et al. 1971; MacMahon and Pugh 1965; Murphy et al. 1979; Stein and Susser 1969). The period of higher risk is during the first 3–5 years of bereavement (Birtchnell 1970; Bunch 1972; MacMahon and Pugh 1965). A salient point for clinicians is that patients who present for treatment during bereavement are at greater risk for suicidal gestures than bereaved individuals in the general population (Bunch 1972). Young widows (Stein and Susser 1969) and elderly widowers (Bock and Webber 1972; MacMahon and Pugh 1965) are also at higher risk than other bereaved individuals. Adult men who lose a mother may be a particularly vulnerable group (Bunch et al. 1971). A history of treatment for major depression or of suicidal gestures are additional risk factors for suicide during bereavement. Other criteria for judging the risk of suicide are the absence of social support from relatives during bereavement, being left to live alone after the loss, and alcohol abuse (Bunch 1972; Murphy et al. 1979). Patients who make suicidal gestures or commit suicide present with anxious or agitated depressions (Birtchnell 1970; Bunch 1972). This risk profile of suicidal behavior during bereavement overlaps considerably with criteria used in general psychiatric practice and can be supplemented with additional, established criteria for judging the risk of suicide such as medical comorbidity, a family history of suicide, pervasive despair, and evidence of a lethal plan. Although rare in occurrence, vigilance for the potential risk of suicide during bereavement is the wisest approach to the evaluation of depressed, bereaved patients.

Normal Apprehensions and Anxiety Disorders

Given the recent recognition of anxiety disorders as a potential clinical complication of bereavement, it is not surprising that not much has been done to consider the differential diagnosis of normal apprehensions of bereavement and anxiety disorders. Little is known of the specific, anxious symptoms that serve as red flags in differential diagnosis. In addition, little is known of the evolution of these symptoms over the course of the first few years of bereavement. It seems likely that the task of differential diagnosis will prove easier for panic disorder than for generalized anxiety disorder because the former is a better defined diagnostic entity (Brier et al. 1985).

In the meantime, the outline of the discussion of major depression serves as a useful model for conceptualizing the distinguishing features of clinically important panic disorder and generalized anxiety during bereavement. In particular, the discussion of the timing and duration of depressive syndromes probably creates a framework that is equally useful for judging anxiety syndromes. When an anxiety disorder is recognized in the absence of pathologic grief, the diagnosis of grief complicated by anxiety disorder should be made. Generalized anxiety disorder will most often be associated with pathologic grief, although not always, and panic disorder will tend to occur more independently (Kim and Jacobs 1991). If both pathologic grief and an anxiety disorder are recognized, both should be diagnosed because of their divergent implications for treatment.

Social and Occupational Functioning

When a patient presents requesting help because the stress of bereavement has become unbearably severe, the symptoms alone may be sufficient criteria for making a diagnosis and recommending professional intervention. If the patient is uncertain about the need for professional help and the form and duration of the psychopathological syndrome are marginal, other criteria besides symptoms become important determinants of a diagnosis and the need for psychiatric treatment. The most important supplementary criterion is change in social and occupational functioning. This part of the evaluation of the acutely bereaved individual is more dynamic and functional than the more static and descriptive criteria for the recognition of symptoms discussed above.

In practice, impairment in social and occupational functioning associated with the dysphoria of bereavement is often a determining criterion that affirms the diagnosis of psychopathology and the decision to intervene professionally. Impairment in social functioning as a criterion of psychopathology is supported not only by widespread clinical experience but also by a limited number of empirical studies (Blumenthal and Dielman 1975; Brown and Davidson 1978; Sturt 1981). The most notable investigation of the relationship between descriptive psychopathology and social functioning is the recent Rand study (Wells et al. 1989) in which the investigators documented that the functional impairment of major depressions exceeds the disability of coronary disease, rheumatoid arthritis, and several other chronic diseases. Longitudinal studies of coping support the idea that certain styles of coping are more successful than others for adaptive outcomes (Vaillant 1977; see Chapter 5). When psychopathological syndromes (e.g., pathologic grief, major depression, or an anxiety disorder) are severe and persistent enough to interfere with the individual's ability to manage the emotional and instrumental tasks posed by a loss, to take responsibility for self-care, or to fulfill parental or occupational roles, a diagnosis of a clinical complication is warranted. By extension, intervention is also indicated. As a variation on this theme, clinical experience suggests that depressive and anxiety syndromes can interfere with the expression of grief as a normal emotional process. Only after treatment does the grief emerge (see Chapter 12). These impairments in functioning may be perceived by the afflicted patient, others who encourage the bereaved individual to seek help, or both.

Although the conclusion that symptoms that interfere with social and occupational functioning ought to be diagnosed and treated appeals to common sense, it is important to emphasize that more systematic empirical research is needed to substantiate these propositions. When a patient is chronically ill or ill enough to be hospitalized, the physician reasonably assumes that symptomatology, among other factors, has interfered with role functioning. However, Dohrenwend et al. (1983) found that the association between symptoms and impairment in social functioning, particularly in cases identified in the community, was not as robust as expected. This is a scientific issue of special importance for the validation of pathologic grief as a diagnostic entity.

Personal and Family Historical Data

Systematic family studies of pathologic grief have not been completed. Therefore, it is hard to draw any conclusions about the value of personal and family histories of problematic reactions to a loss as diagnostic criteria. In their report of a small clinical series of cases, Paul and Grosser (1965) suggested that a failure to grieve can be passed down to succeeding generations, possibly influencing the occurrence of schizophrenia. The mechanism may involve an inherited diathesis to attach and separate in a certain way or the failure to learn to grieve during childhood development. This is an interesting concept that requires more systematic investigation, particularly with reference to psychopathology that is commonly associated with bereavement.

The evidence for a positive personal or family history of major depression as a risk factor for major depressions of bereavement is mixed (see Chapter 4). Until this issue is resolved by more controlled family studies, it is reasonable to maintain an elevated level of concern for an acutely bereaved patient who gives a personal or family history of depression because of the presumed vulnerability inherent in such a history. If the existence of such a vulnerability from a positive personal or family history is eventually established, the next important research issue is whether the vulnerability is hereditary or developmental.

In the only study of anxiety disorders of bereavement to address these questions (Jacobs et al. 1980), both personal history and family history of anxiety disorders were risk factors for panic disorder and generalized anxiety disorder during the first year of bereavement. Curiously, a personal history of major depression was also a risk factor for generalized anxiety disorder. These observations require confirmation in future studies. In general, when a diagnosis can be based on symptomatic and functional criteria, a positive history crystallizes conviction about a clinical problem and the need for at least careful monitoring if not actual intervention.

Biological Assessments

Findings from recent studies of acutely bereaved individuals (Das and Berrios 1984; Shuchter et al. 1986), in which the dexamethasone suppression test (DST) was used, indicated that nonsuppression occurs in 10%–20% of these patients. In another study, Kosten et al. (1984) reported normal results on the DST for bereaved individuals who met criteria for major depressive disorders 6 months after spousal loss. Thus not only is the evidence on the occurrence of nonsuppression mixed, the meaning of nonsuppression during acute bereavement is unclear (see Chapter 8). Even if adrenocortical function during bereavement was well understood, tests of neuroendocrine functioning for depression are neither specific enough nor sensitive enough to provide definitive biological criteria for judging the nature of the depressive syndromes that occur during acute bereavement (Amsterdam et al. 1982). The significance of these considerations for diagnosis is this: when nonsuppression is observed, the DST can help confirm a diagnostic impression of major depression during bereavement; however, normal suppression on the DST does not necessarily mean a depressive syndrome is transient and benign. Rather, the other criteria that have been discussed above must be applied in making a clinical judgment.

Diagnostic Dimensions Rather Than Categories

Having completed a discussion of the differential diagnosis of the complications of bereavement based on diagnostic categories, I want to briefly reconsider the psychopathology of bereavement in terms of symptomatic and functional dimensions. Several symptomatic, behavioral, and biological dimensions derived from clinical practice, including the four dimensions of grief portrayed in Figure 2–1, are outlined in Figure 9–1. Obviously, for clinical purposes, the dimensions that must be considered in evaluating patients have proliferated beyond the original sketch of the dimensions of grief in Figure 2–1. As I have emphasized before, the vicissitudes of separation distress remain, in my judgment, the core phenomena of psychopathology associated with bereavement. Yet, severe variation

		Spectrum	
None	Mild	Severe	Extreme

Separation distress
Fear, anxiety
Traumatic distress
Numbness, disbelief, dissociation
Depressive symptoms
Duration of severe symptoms
Impairment in social functioning
Disturbance of self-esteem
Depressive cognition (pessimism)
Hopelessness, demoralization
Suicidal ideation
Autonomic arousal
Psychomotor agitation
Psychomotor retardation
Dexamethasone suppression
Rapid eye movement disturbance
Insecurity of attachment
Perceived nonsupportiveness
Maladaptive coping style

Figure 9–1. Overview of a dimensional approach to clinical evaluation and treatment planning.

on each of the dimensions represented can be the basis for clinical intervention, and, when severity is high on multiple dimensions, the patient's need for help is obvious.

A dimensional model more accurately represents the continuum between normal and abnormal aspects of bereavement than a categorical, diagnostic system. It facilitates the description of patients by characterizing them on multiple dimensions rather that requiring that they fit into categorical, Procrustean niches, which does not seem appropriate for the nature of the psychopathology as I have conceptualized it. To take separation distress as an example, it is quantitative variation over time, rather than qualitative differences, that distinguishes severe grief syndrome or chronic grief in one patient from normal grief in another person. This example illustrates variation on one continuum.

The relationship among different dimensions is important also. For instance, I have suggested that many of the depressive syndromes of bereavement are associated with severe separation distress and symptoms of anxiety. In other words, they look like depressions with high arousal and sensitivity to separation from intimates, if not rejection sensitivity. However, this does not provide a complete picture of the depressive syndromes that can occur during bereavement. Less frequently, depressive syndromes occur in the absence of separation distress and appear to be anergic, anhedonic, and pessimistic. Other depressive syndromes are associated with severe suicidal ideation, and of course, some depressive syndromes are part of a traumatic disorder with varying degrees of dissociative phenomena, an issue that was emphasized in Chapter 5.

In addition to facilitating the description of patients, each of the dimensions used for evaluation are also associated more or less directly with treatment implications. For example, a severe depressive syndrome ought to be treated with antidepressants or specific psychotherapies for depression; suicidal ideation ought to be treated with measures to protect the patient and reduce the risk of a suicidal act, including, possibly, hospitalization; and impairment in social functioning ought to be treated with some combination of psychotherapy and a rehabilitative, mutual support intervention. Therefore, a dimensional approach for describing psychopathology contains concrete, useful implications for multidimensional treatment and, furthermore, fosters the consideration of thresholds for treatment on each of the dimensions. The rationale for various treatments and their integration into individualized treatment plans are discussed in the remaining chapters of this book.

Clinical Examples

Several of the clinical examples that I present in the other chapters illustrate the differential diagnosis of the clinical complications of bereavement. Case 1 (in Chapter 1) illustrated the development of a persistent depressive syndrome during bereavement that required psychotherapeutic treatment. Ms. A's depression followed a period of delayed and severe grief after the double loss of her son and her mother, which seemed to have an accumulative effect. This has been referred to as *bereavement overload* (Kastenbaum 1969). In addition, had it not been for the intervention, all indications were that Ms. A's grief would have been prolonged. Her symptomatic disturbance was associated with impairment in social and occupational functioning, reflected in her feeling useless as a mother and her impaired performance at work. This was easily perceived by her family, acquaintances, and the professional staff in the hospice who had cared for her mother, who all encouraged her to seek help.

Case 2 (see Chapter 2 in which the concept of pathologic grief is introduced) illustrated similar issues in addition to the concurrence of traumatic distress, presumably related to the sudden, unexpected death of Ms. B's husband. As a function of the severity of her distress, she feared she was losing control, a symptom that served as an index of the seriousness of her clinical problem.

Case 3 (in Chapter 3) was singular among the clinical examples in that Ms. C met diagnostic criteria for all the clinical complications of bereavement that have been identified: pathologic grief, chronic type; major depression; panic disorder; and generalized anxiety disorder, not to mention alcohol abuse.

Case 9 illustrates the delayed onset of grief in a woman who initially suppressed her feelings at the wish of her terminally ill husband. One year after his death, she experienced significant anniversary phenomena that signaled a prolonged course of grief. When she began to grieve, the intensity of the emotional response overwhelmed her. She feared losing her mind. This patient demonstrated not only symptoms of striking severity and chronic failure to adapt to the loss, but also a marked delay in the onset of grief. In short, her history was consistent with the diagnosis of delayed and severe, chronic grief. She eventually developed a depressive syndrome within the context of this pattern of pathologic bereavement. Interestingly enough, the patient herself distinguished between her feelings of grief and her depressive affect and discovered that the depressive syndrome prevented her from facing the loss and experiencing grief. Her depressive syndrome included frightening psychotic symptoms that could be understood within the framework of attachment theory (see Chapter 13 for discussion of this point).

Case 9

Ms. I, a 51-year-old widow, was referred for follow-up ambulatory treatment after hospitalization. When she presented for treatment, she stated that "I didn't realize that I was grieving for my dead husband, but I was." She had been admitted to the hospital 2 weeks earlier for a major depressive disorder that had begun approximately 2 years after the death of her fourth husband. She had been depressed for 5 months. Her symptoms included anxious and depressed mood, psychomotor agitation, poor concentration, severe insomnia with sleep continuity disturbance and early morning awakening, anorexia, weight loss of 35 pounds, aggravation of symptoms in the morning, anergia, loss of interest in her usual activities (including sexual intimacy with others), suicidal ruminations without a plan, the conviction that her husband's spirit would enter her and thus cause her death, and auditory hallucinations ("not really outside of me") of her deceased husband's voice and "his guide" commenting on her imminent death in 6 months.

Ms. I's husband of 14 years had died from cancer after a 1-year illness. On his insistence, because "it hurt him too much," they had never talked about his disease or the prospect of death. At his death, which was "a relief" to Ms. I, she felt "shocked and exhausted." She reported no feelings over the loss in the first year, except that she had "cried three times." The first episode of distress occurred 2 weeks after her husband's death when his ashes were returned to her. Although she denied anything notable about the first anniversary of his death, weight loss began in close association with it.

Twenty months after her husband's death, while on a Thanksgiving visit to her son in Hawaii, Ms. I became convinced that her husband had sent her a message during a family game with a Ouija™ board. Although confused by this experience at the time, in retrospect she viewed it as an expression of her intense yearning to have him back and hear his voice. The Christmas (her husband's favorite holiday) that followed at home was devastatingly lonely. She began to yearn intensely for her husband, to experience a strong sense of his presence, and "to talk with him in my head." As these manifestations of separation distress became increasingly intense, she became concerned that they were bizarre. She felt like she was losing her mind, was out of control, and stated that she "cannot sleep or eat, for fear that someone will put me away." This development roughly coincided with the exacerbation of acute depressive symptoms. As the depressive symptoms became more severe, the manifestations of separation distress diminished and disappeared. This led to a brief hospitalization without follow-up at the time of the second anniversary of her husband's death. The depression was temporarily relieved when her family doctor prescribed amitriptyline, which Ms. I discontinued herself shortly after discharge from the hospital.

Ms. I was readmitted to the hospital 7 months later, at which time little grief was noted and the symptoms of depression were prominent. The hospital staff observed that she was practically unable to face her loss although the unavoidable fact of her husband's death would repeatedly break through her denial and suppression. She distinguished between a depressed mood "that goes down to your toes," which she was experiencing at the present time, and a depressed mood that occurred in association with the intense manifestations of grief. A DST, done while the patient remained severely symptomatic, revealed a postdexamethasone serum cortisol of 3 µg/dl at 8:00 P.M.. Repeated serum cortisol levels done before administration of dexamethasone documented no adrenocortical hyperactivity or disturbance of the diurnal pattern.

Ms. I's current course of treatment was her first psychiatric treatment, even though she gave a history of prolonged dysphoria lasting at least 1 year after her first and second divorces. She described her mother as an unhappy individual who left the family when Ms. I was 6 years old. No other family history suggestive of mental disorder was obtained. The details of Ms. I's successful treatment with desipramine are picked up later in Chapter 12.

In all the cases just discussed, the depressive syndrome was stable and sufficiently durable in time to justify the diagnosis of major depression and intervention. The specific symptoms of morbid guilt, psychomotor retardation, and suicidal gestures were absent and did not help in diagnosis.

These patients were "false negatives" in this sense, and thus the other criteria for making the decision to intervene became essential.

A DST was done on Ms. I indicating normal suppression. A DST was not done in the workups of the other patients and therefore did not contribute to the diagnosis or the decision to intervene professionally. In all the cases, the indications for treatment were clinical and sufficient to justify a treatment intervention.

Conclusions

In this chapter I have reviewed five variations of pathologic grief: delayed grief, absent grief, inhibited grief, severe grief, and chronic grief (Table 9–1; see also, the Appendix). The definitions of these syndromes and the criteria for their diagnosis center on the manifestations of separation distress, although other criteria are useful also. It must be acknowledged that the empirical foundation for the various syndromes of pathologic grief is limited. It is derived from historical concepts (see Chapter 2) and clinical observations reflected in a recent survey of expert opinion (Middleton et al. 1991). I highlight the value of "a fear of losing control" as a nonspecific symptom to reinforce a potential diagnosis. In addition, I emphasize that the careful evaluation of anniversaries is an important strategy for judging the presence of clinical complications.

I have also presented several criteria (Table 9–2) and guidelines for the diagnosis of major depressions during bereavement. These are useful in judging when professional intervention is indicated. Criteria for the diagnosis of anxiety disorders of bereavement are not well developed and require future attention; however, the framework for thinking about depressions of bereavement will probably be useful in addressing anxiety disorders. In the circumstances of a traumatic loss, the possibility of PTSD must be considered using standard DSM-III-R criteria.

A careful diagnostic evaluation sets the stage for treatment of the clinical complications of bereavement. I discuss the theoretical and scientific basis for treatment of the complications of bereavement in Chapter 10 as an introduction to Chapters 11 through 14 on caring for bereaved individuals exhibiting these complications.

References

Akiskal HS, Bitak AH, Puzantian VR, et al: The nosological status of neurotic depression. Arch Gen Psychiatry 35:756–766, 1978

American Psychiatric Association. Diagnostic and Statistical Manual of Mental Disorders, 3rd Edition, Revised. Washington, DC, American Psychiatric Association, 1987

Amsterdam JD, Winokur A, Caroff SN, et al: The DST in outpatients with primary affective disorder and healthy control subjects. Am J Psychiatry 139:287–291, 1982

Birtchnell J: The relationship between attempted suicide, depression and parent death. Br J Psychiatry 116:307–313, 1970

Blanchard CG, Blanchard EB, Becker JV: The young widow: depressive symptomatology throughout the grief process. Psychiatry 39:394–399, 1976

Blumenthal M, Dielman T: Depressive symptomatology and role function in a general population. Arch Gen Psychiatry 32:985–991, 1975

Bock EW, Webber IL: Suicide among the elderly: isolating widowhood and mitigating alternatives. Journal of Marriage and the Family 8:24–31, 1972

Bornstein PE, Clayton PJ: The anniversary reaction. Diseases of the Nervous System 33:470–472, 1972

Bornstein PE, Clayton PJ, Halikas JA, et al: The depression of widowhood after thirteen months. Br J Psychiatry 122:561–566, 1973

Brier A, Charney D, Heninger G: The diagnostic validity of anxiety disorders and their relationships to depressive illness. Am J Psychiatry 142:789–797, 1985

Brown GW, Davidson S: Social class, psychiatric disorder of mother, and accidents to children. Lancet 1:378–380, 1978

Bunch J: Recent bereavement in relation to suicide. J Psychosom Res 16:361–366, 1972

Bunch J, Barraclough BM, Nelson B, et al: Suicide following death of parents. Soc Psychiatry 6:193–199, 1971

Cavenar JO, Nash JO, Maltbie AA: Anniversary reactions masquerading as manic depressive illness. Am J Psychiatry 134:1272–1276, 1977

Clayton PJ, Darvish HS: Course of depressive symptoms following the stress of bereavement, in Stress and Mental Disorder. Edited by Barrett JE, Rose RM, Klerman GL. New York, Raven, 1979, pp 121–136

Clayton PJ, Halikas JA, Maurice WL: The bereavement of the widowed. Diseases of the Nervous System 32:597–604, 1971

Clayton PJ, Herjanic M, Murphy GE, et al: Mourning and depression: their similarities and differences. Canadian Psychiatric Association Journal 19:309–313, 1974

Das M, Berrios GE: Dexamethasone suppression test in acute grief reaction. Acta Psychiatr Scand 70:278–281, 1984

Dohrenwend BS, Dohrenwend BP, Link B, et al: Social functioning of psychiatric patients in contrast with community cases in the general population. Arch Gen Psychiatry 40:1174–1182, 1983

Freud S: Mourning and melancholia (1917), in The Standard Edition of the Complete Psychological Works of Sigmund Freud, Vol 14. Edited and translated by Strachey J. London, Hogarth Press, 1953, pp 243–258

Hays JC: Psychological distress, social environment, and seeking social support following conjugal bereavement. PhD Dissertation, Yale University, School of Epidemiology and Public Health, 1991

Jacobs SC, Schaefer CA, Ostfeld AM, et al: The first anniversary of bereavement. Isr J Psychiatry Relat Sci 24:77–85, 1987

Jacobs SC, Hansen F, Berkman L, et al: Depressions of bereavement. Compr Psychiatry 30:218–224, 1989

Jacobs SC, Hansen FF, Kasl SV, et al: Anxiety disorders during acute bereavement: risk and risk factors. J Clin Psychaitry 51:269–274, 1990

Kastenbaum R: Death and bereavement in later life, in Death and Bereavement. Edited by Kutcher A. Springfield, IL, Charles C Thomas, 1969, pp 28–554

Kim K, Jacobs SC: Pathologic grief and its relationship to other psychiatric disorders. J Affect Disord 21:257–263, 1991

Kosten TR, Jacobs SC, Mason JW, et al: The DST in depression during bereavement. J Nerv Ment Dis 172:359–360, 1984

MacMahon B, Pugh TF: Suicide in the widowed. Am J Epidemiol 81:23–31, 1965

Middleton W, Moylan A, Raphael B, et al: An international perspective on bereavement related concepts. Paper presented at the Third International Conference on Grief and Bereavement in Contemporary Society, Sydney, Australia, June 29-July 4, 1991

Murphy GE, Armstrong MD, Hermele SL, et al: Suicide and alcoholism. Arch Gen Psychiatry 36:65–69, 1979

Nelson JC, Charney DS: The symptoms of major depressive illness. Am J Psychiatry 138:1–13, 1981

Parkes CM: Bereavement: Studies of Grief in Adult Life. New York, International Universities Press, 1972

Parkes CM, Weiss RS: Recovery From Bereavement. New York, Basic Books, 1983

Paul NL, Grosser GH: Operational mourning and its role in conjoint family therapy. Community Ment Health J 1:339–345, 1965

Pollock GH: Anniversary reactions, trauma, and mourning. Psychoanal Q 39:347–371, 1970

Raphael B: Diagnostic criteria for bereavement reactions. Paper presented at the International Symposium on Pathological Bereavement, Seattle, WA, May 4–5, 1989

Rees WD: The hallucinations of widowhood. BMJ 4:37–41, 1971

Shuchter SR, Zisook S, Kirkorowicz C, et al: The dexamethasone suppression test in acute grief. Am J Psychiatry 143:879–881, 1986

Stein Z, Susser M: Widowhood and mental illness. British Journal of Preventive and Social Medicine 23:106–110, 1969

Stroebe W, Stroebe MS: Bereavement and Health. New York, Cambridge University Press, 1987

Sturt E: Hierarchical patterns in the distribution of psychiatric symptoms. Psychol Med 11:783–794, 1981

Vachon MLS, Sheldon AR, Lancee WJ, et al: Correlates of enduring distress patterns following bereavement: social network, life situation, and personality. Psychol Med 12:783–788, 1982

Vaillant GE: Adaptation to Life. Boston, MA, Little, Brown, 1977

Wells KB, Stewart A, Hays RD, et al: The functioning and well being of depressed patients: results from the medical outcomes study. JAMA 262:914–919, 1989

Zisook S, DeVaul RA: Grief, unresolved grief, and depression. Psychosomatics 24:247–256, 1983

Zisook S, Shuchter SR: Depression through the first year after the death of a spouse. Am J Psychiatry 148:1346–1352, 1991

CHAPTER 10

Introduction to Treatment

Ideally, treatment is based on a knowledge of pathogenetic mechanisms. With a knowledge of these mechanisms and the specific treatments that interrupt them, the clinician can intervene in the etiological process of a disorder. When the knowledge of pathogenetic mechanisms is obscure, randomized, controlled clinical trials of specific treatment interventions provide an alternative empirical basis for treatment. In this chapter, I review both domains of knowledge with regard to the psychiatric complications of bereavement. As I reveal in this review, most of our concepts of pathogenesis are theoretical rather than empirical, although a growing empirical context makes our suppositions about etiology seem plausible and appealing.

Turning to controlled trials of treatments, we will find that there are none for psychotropic drugs and a quite limited number for psychotherapeutic interventions. The predominantly theoretical perspective on etiology and the limited empirical basis for specific treatments during bereavement are the two tenuous cornerstones of a scientific foundation for therapeutic interventions at present. While the scientific basis for treatment is limited in scope, it is an appropriate place to begin to conceptualize the tasks of treatment. Specific implications of this review for treatment interventions are interspersed throughout the discussion.

Pathophysiology and Mechanisms of Pathogenesis

Bereavement offers a unique opportunity in psychiatry to investigate mechanisms of pathogenesis. It is a powerful model for this purpose insofar as bereavement is associated with convincing psychopathology in a significant minority of bereaved individuals. As a secondary consideration, the status of being bereaved allows us to identify individuals who are at a high risk for developing complications and to follow them longitudinally. Both of these conditions hold to a reasonable degree.

The value of separation and loss as a model for understanding the pathogenesis of some clinical depressions and other diseases has been recognized for years (Adamson and Schmale 1965; Caplan 1964; Clayton et al. 1974; Engel 1961; Freud 1917; Schmale and Iker 1966). This interest continues into contemporary thinking about the genesis of psychiatric disorders. For example, although definitive data on pathogenesis are still lacking, separation and loss have been cited as potential stressors in models for understanding major depressions in three formulations in the past 6 years (Ehlers et al. 1988; Gold et al. 1988a, 1988b; Siever and Davis 1985).

The mechanisms of pathogenesis can be conceptualized on three levels: physiological, psychological and behavioral, and social processes (Jacobs and Douglas 1979). Undoubtedly, interrelationships exist among the different concepts of pathogenesis (Blois 1988; Engel 1977, 1980; Leigh and Reiser 1985), but these vertical connections are largely uncharted at present. Each type of mechanism seems to have its own natural history over time and is complex in its own right. For example, in the physiological realm, at least two types of processes appear relevant: 1) processes underlying the acute waves of distress that ordinarily last a period of minutes and 2) processes underlying a prolonged disturbance in homeostasis lasting weeks and months (Hofer 1984). As another example of the complexity within a particular conceptual framework, each of the psychological dimensions of grief seems to follow a relatively independent course over time. (Figure 2–1, on the dimensions of grief, illustrates this concept.)

The processes of recovery, about which we know even less than pathophysiology, also appear to follow different courses over time and may even be sequential. For instance, it appears that recovery from the painful, separation distress of bereavement, which usually diminishes by the first anniversary of the loss (Windholz et al. 1985), makes it easier to learn new roles and enter into new friendships, tasks of social adjustment that are extended over 2 or more years (Silverman 1986). Case 2 (in Chapter 2, on pathologic grief, and further discussed in Chapter 13, on psychotherapy) illustrates how prolonged, severe separation distress can interfere with the process of social adjustment.

In the discussion that follows, I attempt to convey the internal complexity of each mechanism of pathogenesis that is discussed. At the same time, the potential relationships among physiological, behavioral, or social processes will be pointed out when possible.

Physiological Mechanisms

Drawing on data from animal models, basic neuroscience research, and studies of individuals under stress, three physiological hypotheses for understanding major depressions have recently emerged. First, stress disrupts homeostasis of central nervous system (CNS) centers responsible for arousal. Second, there is dysregulation of norepinephrine neurotransmission in individuals who have a trait vulnerability such as alpha$_2$ receptor subsensitivity. And finally, homeostatic disturbance may occur secondary to interpersonal loss. All of these models can be applied to understanding the nature and potential mechanisms for major depressions as clinical complications of bereavement. All three types of pathophysiology include the potential for a compromised immunological competence (this is discussed below as another physiological disturbance associated with bereavement).

Disturbance of stress response systems. Based on studies of corticotropin-releasing hormone (CRH) and locus coeruleus–norepinephrine systems, some neuroscientists have proposed a contemporary stress hypothesis of depression (Gold et al. 1988a, 1988b). According to this formulation, depression occurs as a result of the failure of acute, adaptive physiological processes to respond normally to homeostatic regulation. CRH from the hypothalamus and the locus coeruleus–norepinephrine system in the midbrain are interconnected systems that serve as the main neurobiological effector systems for facilitating adaptation to environmental challenges. The systems are now strongly implicated in the generalized stress response described originally by Cannon and subsequently by Selye (cited in Gold et al. 1988a, 1988b). The acute physiological changes that occur during the general stress response are strikingly similar to the chronic physiological changes observed in melancholic depression (Gold et al. 1988b). With this similarity in mind, Gold argued that major depression is a complication of any severe stress, such as bereavement, that occurs in vulnerable individuals for whom an acute, generalized stress response has escaped from the usual cybernetic feedback loops that ordinarily prevent the consequences of prolonged or excessive activation of the locus coeruleus and the hypothalamus. One example of potential homeostatic failure is when glucocorticoids fail to dampen the CRH or locus coeruleus–norepinephrine systems in a normal negative feedback loop during stressful situations. This may happen as a result of defects in the biologic system. The defects may be created by inherited traits, such as a lower threshold to arousal (reflected behaviorally, for example, in shyness [Kagan et al. 1988]) or by previous and cumulative chronic stresses that have sensitized the critical limbic sites in the system.

Hence, a disturbance in the regulation of the stress response can lead to major depression, one of the common complications of bereavement. Variables related to both brain function and, equally important, environmental risks, such as a traumatic loss or bereavement overload observed in disasters or among survivors whose partners have died from acquired immunodeficiency syndrome (AIDS), define the vulnerability to the dysregulation of stress response. With regard to environmental variables, homeostatic mechanisms also may fail in those bereaved individuals for whom the loss becomes a chronic stress. Prolonged separation distress might reasonably be considered an index of the chronic stress of bereavement and therefore identify those bereaved individuals who are at risk for depression, if not already depressed, when the pathophysiological mechanism is of this type.

Nonsuppression on the dexamethasone suppression test (DST) would appear to be a useful index of physiological disturbance of the stress response during acute bereavement. Unfortunately, our small study of dexamethasone suppression (Kosten et al. 1984) did not identify any nonsuppressors; the only other patient from my clinical practice for whom a DST was done was a suppressor (see Case 9, in Chapter 9). On the other hand, it is worth noting that while there were no nonsuppressors in our study, the degree of suppression was inversely related to the level of depression (Kosten et al. 1984). It is conceivable that nonsuppressors identified in other studies (Das and Berrios 1984; Shuchter et al. 1986) may have been at risk for major depressions if they had been followed over the first year of bereavement. This type of longitudinal study is important to do as a test of this hypothesis.

Dysregulation of norepinephrine. A second physiological model for understanding the nature of both depressive and anxious disorders involves the dysregulation of norepinephrine systems (Siever and Davis 1985). This model gives a possible explanation for what happens at the neuronal synapse when prolonged stress disturbs physiological homeostasis.

Two animal models support this hypothesis about norepinephrine systems. One is learned helplessness in rats, which is associated with norepinephrine depletion (Weiss et al. 1970), and the other is separation-induced syndromes of "depression" in primates that appear to be a function of norepinephrine dysregulation (McKinney 1985, 1986; McKinney et al. 1984). Increases in noradrenergic activity in brain centers such as the locus coeruleus enhance orientation to the environment. Decreases in noradrenergic activity are associated with vegetative, conservative, and restorative functions. Sustained decreases may cause withdrawal from the environment of the type that has been observed in primates (McKinney 1985). Earlier investigators denoted this as conservation withdrawal in primates, which they thought was an essential phenomenon of separations (Kaufman and Rosenblum 1967). Clinicians have used the same concept to describe the reaction of patients seen in psychiatric consultation practice who suffered losses (Adamson and Schmale 1965; Engel 1962; Schmale and Iker 1966).

The dysregulation model is constructed in the following way. Dysphoric hyperarousal that occurs when an individual is confronted by threatening stimuli is mediated by norepinephrine activity. Anergic and vegetative symptoms, which occur when an individual is exhausted by excessive or unrelenting stimuli, are mediated by CNS depletion of the availability of norepinephrine as a transmitter. Some individuals are more vulnerable to this disturbance by virtue of biological traits such as alpha$_2$ receptor subsensitivity, which ordinarily acts as a brake on the norepinephrine system.

The exact pattern of norepinephrine dysregulation, including its associated symptomatology, varies among and within individuals, depending on the phase of adaptation to the stressor. Ultimately it is characterized by downregulation of central norepinephrine transmission when a depressive illness sets in. The disturbances of neurovegetative function, sleep, and affective response to the environment, which are a function of the downregulation, are the nucleus of the manifestations of depression. The same symptoms are also relevant to the clinical picture of anxiety disorders.

These two classes of disorders, and in many cases mixed depression and anxiety syndromes, are the most common clinical complications of bereavement. For this reason, the dysregulation hypothesis provides a plausible basis for understanding the pathophysiology and, perhaps, the pathogenesis of major depression and anxiety disorders in acutely bereaved individuals. The norepinephrine dysregulation hypothesis also has the potential to explain the relationship between depression and anxiety disorders that is observed in not only phenomenological but also familial, biological, and treatment-response studies.

Homeostatic disturbance secondary to an interpersonal loss. Another hypothesis about the pathogenesis of depressions is predicated on the evidence and insight that interpersonal relationships regulate homeostasis (Hofer 1984). In a series of studies, Hofer (1984) demonstrated the effect of separation from the mother on the physiology of rat pups. These studies set the stage for a theory of major depressions related to separation and loss in humans (Ehlers et al. 1988). According to Hofer (1984), maternal regulators of the rat pup's physiology are multiple and pervasive. For example, maternal body warmth increased activity levels in the rat pup while tactile as well as olfactory stimuli reduced it. Maternal body warmth also increased levels of norepinephrine and dopamine in the rat pup's brain. Maternal milk and tactile stimulation increased rapid-eye-movement (REM) sleep and reduced sleep arousals in the infant. These are a few examples of the multiple effects the mother had on the rat pup's physiology, leading to the conclusion that the mother is an important interpersonal regulator of the homeostasis of the pup.

Using this work on animals as background, in addition to more sketchy evidence of such effects in humans, clinicians have proposed a social *zeitgeber* ("time giver") theory of the etiology of depression (Ehlers et al. 1988). According to this hypothesis, separations or losses cause disruption of social rhythms that in turn disrupt biological rhythms, in particular sleep patterns (Ehlers et al. 1988). The state of acute grief, including its multiple somatic symptoms, is a function of the disorganization of normal biological rhythms of sleeping, eating, and hormonal regulation subsequent to the loss. The somatic symptoms are normal psychobiological responses to a disruption in social interactions and patterns that are usually self-limiting. In some bereaved individuals, who are vulnerable for a variety of reasons, the risk of depressive complications is higher as biological rhythms remain derailed and unsettled. The vulnerability can be related to a lowered threshold to rhythm disruption, long time constants for reentrainment, predisposition to perpetuation of psychological depressive processes, or phase-delay (instead of phase-advance) responses to reentrainment. The disturbances of biological rhythms that are characteristic of major depressive illness include decreased REM latency, dexamethasone nonsuppression, and loss of normal circadian patterns of cortisol and growth hormone secretion. Thus this hypothesis establishes a direct connection between a loss and major depression, one of the prominent manifestations of complicated bereavement, using disruption of the homeostatic mechanisms governing sleep as the basic pathway.

In their studies, Bartrop et al. (1977) and Schleifer et al. (1983) suggested that not only neuroendocrine systems but also immunological function can be disturbed as a result of the stress from a loss. These changes during bereavement now appear to be independent of neuroendocrine change, nonspecific to bereavement, and more related to depression than grief (Bartrop et al. 1977; Irwin and Weiner 1987; Kronfol et al. 1986; Schleifer et al. 1983, 1984; see Chapter 8). The relationship of these immune changes to the etiology of the depressions of bereavement is not clear. The limited speculation on the pathophysiology of psychiatric disorders involving immune system dysfunction is more developed for schizophrenia than major depression (DeLisi et al. 1985). Furthermore, the evidence is quite sketchy that other diseases that involve the immune system—such as infectious diseases, lymphoblastic diseases and other cancers, or autoimmune diseases like rheumatoid arthritis—are specifically related to bereavement (Ciocco 1940; Jacobs and Ostfeld 1977; Lindeman 1945; Paulley 1983; Ward 1976). Therefore the study of immunological function during bereavement, while an interesting area for potential future developments, has not yet led to new insights into the pathophysiology of disease.

One implication of this discussion of physiological mechanisms for treatment is that antidepressant medicines that affect norepinephrine systems can be used to treat the depressive and anxious complications of bereavement. In fact, the rationale for such pharmacological treatment is supported by studies of antidepressant usage in primates to prevent or alleviate the "depressive" states created in these animal models (McKinney

1985, 1986). In addition, two open trials have shown that treating the depressions of bereavement with antidepressant medicines can be successful (see discussion below).

I am not implying from this discussion that only pharmacological interventions should be used to treat depressions and anxiety disorders of bereavement. Behavioral interventions (such as stress management) and social interventions (such as mutual support groups) may have a direct effect on personal physiology as well. One fascinating, recent essay about psychotherapeutic treatment (Reite 1990) stems from physiological studies of animals and the concept of interpersonal regulators of homeostasis. Specifically, the author suggested that a fundamental function of the therapeutic relationship during acute bereavement is to help reestablish homeostatic equilibrium quite independent of other psychotherapeutic strategies that are used (Reite 1990). Essentially, in this view, the therapist serves as a temporary substitute for the deceased individual who formerly provided the interpersonal cues (the zeitgebers) of homeostatic regulation for the bereaved survivor. Similarly, friends, relatives, and intimates may serve the same substitutive purpose, although presumably the effect they can have depends in part on the degree of exposure and intimacy of the relationship. Whether it is desirable to use substitutes rather than adjust to the absence of the deceased individual probably depends on the individual; this is also a question for research.

Psychological and Behavioral Mechanisms

Learned helplessness. In the behavioral realm, the learned helplessness model, stemming from research in animals, is a principal paradigm that has utility as a model of pathogenesis for complications of bereavement. In this model, uncontrollable shock and the inability to escape create a state of passivity, impaired learning, neurovegetative symptoms, and social withdrawal. Bereavement approximates this model in many respects. The circumstances caused by a death are unavoidable. Bereaved survivors are subject to severe emotional distress over which they have limited control. Also life experiences in modern society, where extended families and stable communities no longer provide guidance on the tasks of grief, inadequately prepare the bereaved individual for the task of coping with a loss. In short, the irrevocability of a loss by death and the unique coping response that a loss requires for recovery are characteristics of bereavement that make it similar to the learned helplessness model.

For action-oriented individuals who need to feel in control of themselves and who do not understand the nature of grief, the experience of bereavement can be especially stressful. It can lead to a sense of helplessness and low self-esteem (Bibring 1953) as well as the catecholamine depletion, reduction in gamma-aminobutyric acid release, and altered hypothalamic-pituitary-adrenocortical function associated with it, according to laboratory studies in rats (Petty and Sherman 1981; Weiss et al. 1970, 1981), primates (McKinney 1985), and humans (Brier et al. 1987). The depletion of norepinephrine in particular as well as the other changes can lead in turn to a dysregulated depressive state, including dysphoric hyperarousal and vegetative symptoms as discussed above (Siever and Davis 1985). Thus in this framework, the stress of bereavement, the state of helplessness, the low self-esteem caused by the inability to cope with the loss, and the CNS dysregulation can lead to depression, an identified complication of bereavement. Treatment interventions based on the learned helplessness model might address the physiological process directly by using antidepressants or, as an analysis of this mechanism suggests, might aim at reducing the sense of helplessness and poor self-esteem and helping the bereaved individual feel more under control and cope as effectively as possible through psychotherapy or mutual support groups.

The case of Ms. A (in Chapter 1) is the best example to illustrate the behavioral mechanism of learned helplessness among the examples that have been presented thus far. Ms. A had a strong sense of uselessness and failure as a mother. She simply did not understand the type of coping that was required for successful adaptation to her losses. By addressing her disturbed self-esteem through psychotherapy and education about grief and how to cope with it, we were able to avert what I judged to be a decidedly pathologic pattern of grief. (The psychotherapy and mutual support intervention for this patient are described in Chapters 13 and 14.)

Insecure attachments. Another psychological mechanism for the pathogenesis of clinical complications of bereavement is introduced in Chapter 2 within the discussion of the historical development of the concept of pathologic grief. Freud (1917) suggested that there is a mechanism involving anger about a perceived rejection, presumably aimed at the individual who has died, which is turned against the self. This convoluted process occurs as a consequence of a narcissistic object relationship to the departed individual and causes melancholia.

More recently, Bowlby (1980) advanced a cognitive perspective on the pathogenesis of pathologic grief that considers the nature of the attachment to the individual who is lost in different terms. According to this view, cognitive biases about attachment figures cause chronic or absent grief. These cognitive biases, which consist of ideas such as the conviction that attachment figures are above criticism and the self is less worthy, are activated by a death in the family. In a sense, the relationship to the deceased person has held these latent cognitive biases in check. This concept of a relationship holding maladaptive behavior in check is reminiscent of the formulation that latent self-images and role models are activated as the basis of pathologic grief when a loss occurs (Horowitz et al. 1980). Generically, these pathogenetic concepts are founded on the idea that aspects of the relationship to the deceased individual, which are rooted in developmental experiences, reflect flaws in personality functioning that emerge when the particular attachment figure is lost.

Typically in clinical practice, these special interpersonal patterns are played out in the relationship to the psychotherapist. Recognition of the problems guides the therapist's response to various expectations of the patient's need for help. The case of Ms. M (see Chapter 13) is an example of this. As the discussion of her treatment illustrates, bereaved patients who have experienced separations from or the death of a parent in childhood often present these phenomena most intensely. Interpretation of repetitive, maladaptive behavior patterns such as these is a cornerstone of psychodynamically oriented therapies.

Poor health practices. On a more basic level for thinking about behavioral mechanisms, it is conceivable that the neglect of sound health practices leads to illness (Jacobs and Douglas 1979). A regression in health practices can result from several parts of the experience of grief: the aimlessness and disorganization of behavior that is characteristic of the early stages of bereavement, the exhaustion from searching unsuccessfully for the deceased individual in a sustained state of high arousal, or the challenge to adapt to new roles in an environment that is perceived as threatening. Examples of changes in health practices may be the failure to seek help for the early signs of a disease such as cancer, the neglect of proper management of a disease such as hypertension, the reluctance to recognize a depressive syndrome on the assumption that it is all grief, or the excessive use of alcohol, other substances, or prescribed medicines such as benzodiazepines. All of these examples of disease are drawn from the chronic disorders of middle and late life that, according to the epidemiological literature, occur frequently during acute bereavement (Jacobs and Ostfeld 1977). The epidemiological data make the hypothesis that poor health habits play a role in the appearance of new or recurrent illness episodes during bereavement a plausible one. The implication for treatment is an emphasis on giving adequate clinical attention to this obvious, potential mechanism.

Probably the most conspicuous example of unhealthy behavior (or poor health practices) is the abuse of alcohol among the bereaved individuals. Several examples of alcohol abuse are presented in this book: Case 3 (in Chapter 3) and Cases 6 and, perhaps, 7 (in Chapter 7). One of the participants in the open trial of antidepressant drug treatment described below, is another example of a widower for whom pronounced alcohol abuse interfered with the treatment of his major depression; ultimately, his failure to control his drinking required the discontinuation of his antidepressant medicine (Jacobs et al. 1987). Although the evidence I discuss in Chapter 3 does not generally support the idea that there is an increased risk of new cases of alcohol abuse during bereavement, it is quite clear from the clinical examples I give and from clinical experience that bereaved individuals who already have a habit of heavy alcohol use are liable to drink in greater quantities during bereavement. By doing so, they interfere with the process of recovery from bereavement.

Social Mechanisms

Social processes may also serve as pathogenetic mechanisms. In general, they have received less attention, and the mechanisms of their action are less highly developed.

Social isolation. Social isolation is frequently a consequence of bereavement, especially among elderly people, and carries a high risk of mortality via mechanisms that remain obscure (Berardo 1970; Berkman and Syme

1979; Townsend 1957). It is possible that social isolation operates as a risk factor because it reflects the loss of care suffered by a bereaved spouse (Jacobs and Douglas 1979). This can occur in circumstances where the deceased conjugal partner was the medically responsible member of the family and no one assumes this responsibility after the loss. Case 7 (Chapter 7) illustrates this idea of loss of care in that Mr. G felt very needy for the care that his wife used to provide. His wife used to remind him about medical care and good health practices. Following her death, he expressed his neediness repeatedly in terms of his deep gratitude to family and friends who offered to care for him and even to the research staff who looked in on him. His felt need for care may have contributed to alcohol abuse, although we were never able to document this conclusively.

Change in socioeconomic status. In addition to social isolation, bereavement often is associated with socioeconomic misfortune, especially for widowed women (Lehman et al. 1987; Lopata 1973; Zisook et al. 1987). When family income is threatened or health insurance is terminated after a loss, the survivor is tempted to economize in health expenditures as well as in other financial areas. Thus socioeconomic hardship in the context of modern American society, where the highest quality of medical care is on average privately purchased or provided through health insurance coverage in the workplace, can potentially compromise health practices and damage an individual's health status. Although I am unaware of any study that specifically and directly documents such changes, in one study of the social environment during bereavement, Bankoff (1983) found that a decline in health or financial status inhibited customary patterns of seeking and obtaining social support.

Stress of learning new roles. Role strain, a product of the process of psychosocial transition (see Chapter 6), also occurs as bereaved people, particularly widows and widowers, are confronted with providing for all their own needs. This is especially a challenge when, before the loss, a division of labor in the family unit may well have existed. The need to do for oneself, in addition to the loss of economic power for purchasing medical services (as discussed above), can compromise patterns of care and aggravate existing medical problems, conceivably resulting in the onset of new illnesses as well. Furthermore, the role strain inherent in these adjustments can be plausibly linked to an individual's physiological state through repeated challenges to the acutely bereaved individual to attend to new tasks and learn new skills. If the level of separation distress remains high, each attempt to undertake a new role becomes a painful reminder of the loss.

The psychotherapy of Ms. B (Case 2, in Chapter 2), which is described more in Chapter 13, provides an example of this role strain. The hypothalamic/CRH and locus coeruleus–norepinephrine systems are thought to be the physiological substrates in the brain that promote attention, arousal, and aggressive action in confronting these new demands. Thus role strains may contribute to the uncontrolled state of arousal, discussed above. The prolonged arousal potentially raises the risk of depressive complications during acute bereavement. Once again, as in the discussion on learned helplessness, the implication for treatment is not only for pharmacological treatment of the depressions that may occur but also active efforts to facilitate social adjustment.

Perhaps social mechanisms of pathogenesis are not as well developed or specifically related to the clinical complications of bereavement as physiological or behavioral mechanisms. Nevertheless, it is important to keep them in view and not lose sight of future developments in this area. In the meantime, we ought not to ignore existing ways of conceptualizing the social mechanisms by which disease occurs after bereavement as these provide clues for multidimensional intervention.

Mechanisms of Recovery

Although the natural experience of bereavement offers a unique opportunity to study the process of recovery from acute physiological, psychological, and social disturbances in an individual's life, very little has been done to clarify these mechanisms. Perhaps the least has been done in the physiological sphere to elucidate recovery in contrast to pathogenetic mechanisms. The speculation about substitute relationships for maintaining homeostasis discussed above (Reite 1990) seems to hold potential for further investigation to determine how bereaved individuals manage the fundamental biological need to reestablish and maintain homeostasis after a loss occurs.

Working Through Grief

Somewhat more has been written about psychological recovery from grief. Most of this stems from Freud's concept of *grief work* (Freud 1917). By this, Freud meant that the acutely bereaved individual must slowly and painfully give up the emotional investment (cathexis) in the deceased individual while developing new interests and attachments. Others have refined the concept of grief work as a process of giving up the bond to the deceased individual, emphasizing the inevitability of this task (Lindeman 1944; Parkes 1972; Worden 1982). The two most convincing rationales for the unavoidability of grief work derive from attachment theory and cognitive theory.

Attachment theory posits an evolutionary purpose of grief in promoting the survival of individuals separated from social groups and, conversely, the advantage of membership in groups for the purpose of survival (Bowlby 1977). Within this perspective, grief or separation anxiety can be seen as a useful albeit very unpleasant human response, programmed into our genes and biological structure, that discourages separation and promotes affiliation. In the circumstances of a death, separation is painful and, in this sense, is maladaptive in the short run. All the same, its purpose in the life cycle of the individual can still be appreciated. If nothing else, this perspective on the experience can be explained in treatment as part of a psychoeducational process.

Cognitive theory explains the mental processes involved in adjusting to a major change in life (Parkes 1971) as a progressive, integrative operation that takes place over time (Horowitz 1976). This theory explains how fundamental changes in reality, such as the traumatic death of an intimate, must be slowly integrated from active memory into enduring cognitive schemata of the world (Horowitz 1976). Until completed, this process is characterized by the intrusive and avoidant phenomena that are recognized as manifestations of grief. Painful though it can be, the very useful purpose served by the process is the reorganization of the survivor's practical and philosophical assumptions about the world and how he or she functions in it (Parkes 1971). If observations of cognitive processes, which cognitive theory attempts to explain, are precise, then these processes presumably reflect the basic biological workings of memory and perception that inevitably shape our subjective experience after a major change in our lives. This insight into recovery can be used as one of the bases for psychotherapeutic interventions. (In Chapter 13, I return to this idea when the task of restructuring a view of the world and the bereaved individual's place in it is discussed as part of the psychoeducational goals of therapy.)

Even if a satisfactory explanation is found for the inevitability of grief, it does not necessarily follow that the work of grief requires that a bereaved individual must suffer through the emotional distress of acute grief in order to recover. Recently, two groups of researchers have questioned this assumption (Stroebe and Stroebe 1990; Wortman and Silver 1989), but the amount of empirical evidence on the question is still meager. For the most part, it is widely accepted by clinicians that "giving grief words," the expression of grief, and grief work—concepts that are central to psychodynamic theory—are essential to the process of recovery. The concept of grief work seems to underlie another assumption about recovery as well. This is the idea that encouraging the bereaved individual to give up the bond to the dead individual and to "say goodbye" is a useful intervention for individuals who suffer from pathologic grief of the chronic, severe type. (An alternative formulation for psychotherapy, that it is more useful to focus on remembering, consistent with the cognitive tasks of grief work rather than the psychodynamics of affect, is developed in Chapter 13.)

To present a balanced picture of the status of the concept of grief work, it should be pointed out that the recent skepticism about grief work appears to be founded on an operational assumption that equates high levels of emotional distress with grief work on the one hand and avoidance of the loss with the absence of grief work on the other, as if emotional catharsis is going to lead to recovery (Stroebe and Stroebe 1990; Wortman and Silver 1989). This is an oversimplification of the concept of grief work. In this sense, the data against the idea of grief work are far from conclusive; this aspect of recovery will need more clarification from future empirical studies. As a cornerstone of this endeavor, it will be essential to define the elusive concept of grief work with more precision and concreteness than it has been given previously.

Using Multiple Coping Styles

Presumably, future studies of coping will lead to additional insights into the process of recovery. At present, the clinical implications of the small number of studies that are available so far is limited. For example, our study (Jacobs et al. 1991; Kim et al. 1991) indicated that there are advantages to coping by problem-focused planning and coping by making a change (or distancing) and disadvantages to coping by fantasy escape (see also Chapter 7). Even if we could transcribe these observations into useful therapeutic prescriptions, it would be premature to begin to make simple recommendations of this type to bereaved individuals. These observations require confirmation.

Furthermore, the coping styles that predicted good outcome in our study were effective only when measured against the specific outcomes of separation distress and depression. Logically, and as our data suggested, emotion-focused coping, in contrast to problem-focused coping, probably plays an important role in the early stages of grief when the psychological distress is most intense. Problem-focused coping may become preeminent in value later in the course of bereavement when the tasks of social adjustment demand attention. The salient point here is that the complexity of the tasks facing the acutely bereaved individual must be given ample consideration before we begin to prescribe coping styles. In fact, it is conceivable that each coping style inherently carries both benefit and risk with respect to multiple outcomes, and success depends on the right mix and modulation of coping over time.

Additional research on how bereaved individuals cope promises to advance our knowledge of this important aspect of recovery. In the meantime, we can provide opportunities for acutely bereaved patients to understand the full range of coping strategies that others have used successfully in the same circumstances. This can be done through membership in mutual support groups and discussion in psychotherapy. We can encourage patients to learn through trial and error and choose a pattern of coping that is both consonant with their personal strengths and weaknesses and consistent with the general principle of a flexible and complex coping repertory.

Negotiating Social Transitions

The idea of recovery from bereavement as a process of social transition is another concept that has received attention (Silverman 1986). In this framework, taking a widowed individual as an example, the bereaved spouse must come to terms with a new identity as someone who is unmarried and relatively more independent than before the death. Tasks and roles that were formerly the responsibility of the deceased marital partner must be learned or transferred to someone else. Development of new, independent interests and involvement in new friendships is an inevitable step that leads to accommodation to the loss. Ultimately, a predominant orientation toward the future emerges rather than the typical, painful preoccupation with the recent loss that characterizes the early stages of grief or chronic, pathologic grief. Negotiation of the social transitions of bereavement is a process of recovery that must be addressed in cases in which grief is not resolving spontaneously and the bereaved individual seeks help.

This discussion of pathogenetic mechanisms of the clinical complications of bereavement and mechanisms of recovery is intended to create a preliminary, albeit largely theoretical, foundation for practice and, at the same time, emphasize the limits of our knowledge. The basic mechanisms as well as their implications for treatment are summarized in Table 10–1. Until a better understanding of mechanisms is available, and always as a complement to our knowledge of mechanisms, we can turn to studies of treatment interventions to guide our judgments about treatment for our patients.

Studies of Treatment for the Complications of Bereavement

In this section, I review the small, evaluative literature regarding pharmacological and psychotherapeutic interventions, the two main approaches to treatment. With this review, it becomes apparent that there are no randomized, controlled trials of pharmacological treatments and a quite limited number of such studies for psychotherapeutic treatments of the complications of bereavement.

Pharmacological Treatment

Treatment of depressions of bereavement. To date, no randomized, controlled clinical studies on treatment of the major depressions that occur during acute bereavement have been reported. Only small open trials, case reports, and anecdotal information are available that, despite their limitations, indicate that antidepressants and electroconvulsive therapy may be very useful in treating the depressions of bereavement. By definition, these reports are not controlled, and they include a heterogeneous group of depressive illnesses.

Preclinical evidence for the value of antidepressant treatment is provided from animal models in studies of separation and loss in primates.

Table 10–1. Mechanisms of pathogenesis and treatment implications of complications of bereavement

Pathogenesis	Recovery	Treatment
Physiological		
Stress/arousal (corticotropin-releasing hormone, locus coeruleus, norepinephrine)	Homeostasis	Possibly alprazolam Stress management
Norepinephrine dysregulation	Homeostasis Substitution (remarriage) Self-care	Antidepressant drugs Cognitive and interpersonal psychotherapy Mutual supports
Behavioral		
Learned helplessness	Effective coping Mastery	Antidepressant drugs Cognitive and interpersonal psychotherapy Psychoeducation Mutual supports
Insecure attachments	Substitution Growth Grief work	Brief, dynamic psychotherapy
Poor health practices	Healthy life-style	Health education Psychoeducation
Social		
Social isolation/loss of care	New interests New friends	Social services Mutual supports
Decline in socioeconomic status	Work Recognition	Social services Mutual support
Psychosocial transitions	Effective coping New identity New assumptions about the world Future orientation	Psychoeducation Brief, dynamic psychotherapy Mutual supports

For example, imipramine has been effective not only in alleviating the "depressive" behavior and social withdrawal observed in primates who are separated from mothers or siblings but also in preventing the emergence of depressive behaviors in highly aroused primates exposed to the stress of a loss (McKinney 1985, 1986).

The best data available for judging the use of pharmacological treatments come from two open trials of the use of antidepressants to treat the major depressions associated with bereavement (Jacobs et al. 1987; Pasternak et al. 1991). In one study (Jacobs et al. 1987), my colleagues and I completed a small, open trial of tricyclic antidepressants (principally desipramine) in the treatment of the persistent depressions of bereavement. Seven of 10 participants demonstrated moderate to marked improvement of depressive symptoms during the 1-month period of the study at an average dosage level of 119 mg/day of desipramine. Although the intensity of grief declined for all but 1 participant, the reduction was of major proportions in only 3 participants. Thus it was difficult to discern any consistent effect of the antidepressant medicine on the intensity of grief. In general, the medicine was well tolerated. Anticholinergic side effects were the most common, occurring in 4 participants.

The findings of this open trial were only preliminary and must be tested in a controlled, double-blind, crossover study. Still, in support of a pharmacological effect is the fact that the depressive syndromes were deeply entrenched and had not responded to interpersonal interventions. Furthermore, the clinical responses of the participants were notable for their pronounced improvement in sleep disorders and appetite disturbances as well as in mood and cognition, suggesting that a biological process underlies the response to antidepressant medications. In addition, the depressive symptoms that responded to treatment—the depressed mood, guilt, worthless feelings, hopelessness, decreased interests, anhedonia, anergia, anorexia, insomnia, and somatic anxiety—were the same symptoms that responded to antidepressants in other clinical trials of antidepressant drugs for treating melancholic patients (Nelson et al. 1984). Nonspecific, supportive, psychotherapeutic processes were undoubtedly at play also; however, in our experience, psychotherapy alone has not been successful in relieving these depressions. Nevertheless, the question undoubtedly is not one of either pharmacological or psychotherapeutic treatment but rather what is the best combination of these treatments for each patient.

(The issue of integration of treatments is taken up in Chapter 11.)

In another open, noncontrolled trial of antidepressants to treat depressions of bereavement among elderly people (Pasternak et al. 1991), 13 participants received nortriptyline for up to 16 weeks. The criterion for judging response was a reduction in the participants' depression scores that lasted for 3 weeks or more after therapeutic blood levels of nortriptyline were achieved (50–150 ng/ml). All 13 participants had a good response to the medicine by this criterion at a mean dosage level of 49 mg/day and with mean blood levels of 68 ng/ml. The antidepressant response time averaged 9.6 weeks with a median of 6.4 weeks. The intensity of grief declined 9.3% on average, a small reduction that did not reach the lower level of intensity in a nondepressed, bereaved comparison group of 20 individuals. As the authors suggested, the results of their study (Pasternak et al. 1991) point toward the need for controlled studies to assess the relative contribution of different treatment modalities, including psychotherapy, to target the residual pain associated with intense grief.

Although there is a need for controlled trials to demonstrate the efficacy of antidepressant medicines specifically for the depressions of bereavement, the general psychopharmacological literature does document the effectiveness of antidepressants in treating major depressions (Brotman et al. 1987; Potter et al. 1991). This is another major line of evidence that supports the use of antidepressants to treat the depressions of bereavement. Given that most depressions of bereavement present as anxious depressions in the circumstances of unresolved grief, a question might be raised about the choice of antidepressants. In particular, it might be speculated that monoamine oxidase inhibitors would be effective given their superiority in treating atypical depressions typified by anxious as well as depressive symptoms. This is an interesting question on which we have no empirical data and one that is ripe for study. In the meantime, the dietary restrictions associated with and the risks of using monoamine oxidase inhibitors weigh against their use as first-line antidepressants. The newer antidepressants affecting serotonergic transmission may also have a useful role in treating these disorders.

Treatment of anxiety disorders of bereavement. Neither anecdotal nor systematic empirical research has been done on the pharmacological treatment of the anxiety disorders of bereavement. The literature on the treatment of panic disorder using imipramine is relevant insofar as a large subgroup of patients with panic disorder experience the onset of their disorder in the circumstances of a loss (Klein 1964; Jacobs et al. 1990). If it is confirmed in future studies that anxiety disorders are a significant clinical complication of bereavement, the treatment for these disorders would be fertile ground for research.

Psychotherapeutic Treatment

Although psychotherapeutic treatment for complications of bereavement has been studied more than pharmacological treatment, the literature from randomized, controlled trials on the efficacy of psychotherapy for the treatment of the clinical complications of bereavement is also quite limited (see Table 10–2). A review of the available studies indicates that professional therapeutic interventions are effective in helping bereaved individuals judged to be at high risk for developing complications (Gerber et al. 1975; Marmar et al. 1988; Raphael 1977). However, in one study (Polak et al. 1975; Williams and Polak 1979), the authors' results were contrary to these positive findings; they concluded that their psychotherapeutic intervention may have been "harmful."

Table 10–2. Controlled studies of psychotherapy

Type of psychotherapy	Studies
Specific to bereavement	
Crisis intervention	Gerber et al. 1975
	Raphael 1977
	Williams and Polak 1979
Brief psychodynamic psychotherapy	Horowitz et al. 1984c
	Marmar et al. 1988
Behavioral intervention	Mawson et al. 1981
Nonspecific	
Cognitive psychotherapy	Rush et al. 1977
	Murphy et al. 1984
	Simons et al. 1986
	Elkin et al. 1989
Interpersonal psychotherapy	Weissman et al. 1979
	DiMascio et al. 1979
	Elkin et al. 1989

Crisis intervention: studies showing a positive effect. In two of the studies (Gerber et al. 1975; Raphael 1977) in which the authors documented a positive effect, the intervention was considered to be brief, crisis intervention. These clinicians followed the concept of crisis intervention developed by Caplan (1964) within the framework of crisis theory, which is considered to be an active treatment process that is attentive to social supports. In the study by Raphael (1977), a psychiatrist provided the treatment. Raphael described the treatment used as a brief intervention that provided support for the expression of grieving affects and facilitated review of the positive and negative aspects of the lost relationship within the framework of psychodynamically oriented psychotherapy. The outcome of treatment in this study was assessed using a measure of general health status. The success of the intervention was considered to be a result of the therapist's facilitating the expression of normal grief. In the study by Gerber et al. (1975), either a psychiatric social worker or a psychiatric nurse provided the treatment. The investigators used multiple dimensions of health status, the extent to which medicine was used, and the number of doctor's visits as outcome criteria.

In the third study that demonstrated a beneficial effect (Marmar et al. 1988), the intervention was brief, psychodynamic, individual psychotherapy provided by a professional therapist. In this study, the control group was a mutual support group for widows led by a widow trained in the mutual support techniques described by Silverman (1986). Based on the assumption that the beneficial effects of treatment had been demonstrated already, this group of investigators was not funded to include a nontreatment comparison group. Therefore, it is impossible to determine if either treatment, psychotherapy or mutual self-help groups, was more effective than the tincture of time alone. The outcome of treatment was measured in terms of stress-specific symptoms, general psychiatric symptomatology, and social and work functioning. The interventions were judged effective in reducing both the intrusive and avoidant manifestations of bereavement as well as general anxious and depressive symptomatology. Interestingly, professional interventions and self-help groups in this study appeared to be about equally effective, with the exception that the psychotherapy group experienced greater relief of general symptomatology (Marmar et al. 1988). The interventions had a greater impact on symptoms than on work and interpersonal functioning, suggesting to the authors that treatment longer than the 12 meetings provided in the study would be more effective in facilitating social adjustment. (Given the observation of the effectiveness and ubiquity of mutual support groups, as well as their utility to acutely bereaved individuals, the relationship between mutual support groups and treatment interventions is discussed more in Chapter 14.)

A related study of adults bereaved by the death of a parent (Horowitz et al. 1984a), carried out by the same investigators who completed the previous study, was designed to test the effects of individual, time-limited, dynamic psychotherapy during the first 2 years of bereavement. In this study, the authors used a nonequivalent comparison group of bereaved adults whose parents had died at the general hospital where the study was completed. The comparison group was neither randomly assigned to control status nor blindly rated on the measures of outcome. These limitations aside, the nonpatient, comparison group was reasonably comparable to the treatment group in its sociodemographic characteristics other than the severity of distress and the decision to seek treatment. The discrepancies between the treated group and the control group (e.g., the comparison group included more men and older individuals) operated in a way that made it harder to prove the effect of treatment. Measures of psychological distress in the treatment group, which were significantly higher than those in the comparison group, indicated that the treatment group was probably a high-risk group with severe and prolonged pathologic grief. Over 13 months, the treatment group demonstrated a marked decline in psychological distress so that they were comparable to the comparison group on a measure of distress. The major difference between the two groups over time was a decline in the need for the patients to actively and consciously avoid themes and emotions about the parental death. This is an interesting observation because it suggests that the psychodynamically oriented treatment largely affected avoidance of bereavement by the patients. This study of adults bereaved by the death of a parent, along with the study described just before (Marmar et al. 1988), is important because it is one of a series of reports about the psychotherapeutic treatment of the complications of bereavement by a highly experienced group (Horowitz 1976; Horowitz et al. 1980, 1984b, 1984c, 1986; Marmar et al. 1988).

Crisis intervention: studies showing a negative effect. As mentioned above, one controlled study (Polak et al. 1975; Williams and Polak 1979) failed to demonstrate that family-focused crisis intervention was effective in facilitating recovery from grief. In this study, family intervention was provided exclusively, with no individual treatment given. The outcome of treatment was measured by the occurrence of medical illness and psychiatric illness as well as by assessments of social functioning, family functioning, and social costs. Based on their observations, the authors of the family crisis intervention study expressed their doubt that mental health intervention was useful for the unselected, acutely bereaved individual and wondered if their treatment was appropriate.

Several methodological flaws in the study raise questions about whether these authors' conclusions were valid and generalizable to professional treatments in general. One methodological problem involved the success of the randomization procedures for assigning participants to crisis intervention or control status. The bereaved family members in the experimental group who received the intervention retrospectively reported significantly more traumatic deaths and reported significantly more family crises in the year prior to the death; in addition, their family environments were retrospectively rated as significantly more destructive prior to the loss than were those of the control group. In other words, despite random assignment, the treatment group appeared to be at higher risk for poor outcome than the controls. Furthermore, there was a high dropout rate among subjects who were in the control group, conceivably of participants who were faring poorly, which may have created a residual subgroup with favorable outcome, thus making it difficult to show the effect of the crisis intervention.

Another methodological concern with this study was the method used for selecting participants. The authors did not consider risk of poor outcome in selecting their sample. In the most convincing study of the therapeutic value of crisis intervention (Raphael 1977), the procedures provided for identification of high-risk, bereaved individuals who could benefit substantially from the intervention. This methodological step was also instrumental in two studies demonstrating a beneficial effect from mutual support interventions (Parkes 1975; Vachon et al. 1980; see also Chapter 14). The identification of high-risk candidates for intervention is useful in separating out a group of bereaved individuals who preeminently need help in contrast to the general population of bereaved people, most of whom will do fine on their own. The latter group will dilute the effect of an intervention if they are included in the treatment group. Therefore, identification of high risk looms as a central methodological issue that requires attention in controlled trials; it was omitted in this study of family crisis intervention that showed no beneficial effect. The importance of this methodological step also leads to questions about the need and suitability of treatment interventions for low-risk, bereaved individuals.

Another aspect of the family crisis intervention study seems to be salient for clinical practice. The therapeutic intervention, in which telephone contact may have been the predominant means of contact with the families, was unconvincing as a treatment. The intervention was described as a "social systems intervention" (Williams et al. 1972). The type of mental health professional responsible for the intervention was not specified in the articles that described the study. According to the design of the study, the therapists acted "less as a professional and more as a natural resource person" (Williams et al. 1972, p. 68). Within this framework, apparently the clinicians felt like "intruders" in the family. The crisis intervention involved an average of six meetings over the first few months of bereavement, a rather brief course of treatment. In addition, the treatment philosophy was described as an individual-centered cathartic approach in which repression and denial were conceptualized as "ineffective or harmful defenses." In the end, the authors concluded that their intervention may have delayed or interfered with the bereavement process. This description of the treatment stands in rather stark contrast to the descriptions of the skillful, psychodynamically oriented psychotherapy that was provided to high-risk, bereaved individuals in other studies that demonstrated a beneficial effect of intervention (Horowitz 1976; Horowitz et al. 1984a; Raphael 1974). It is worth taking the trouble to describe the family crisis intervention technique because it holds potentially important lessons in what not to do during acute bereavement while illustrating some of the overzealous assumptions of the community mental health movement of the 1960s and 1970s about crisis intervention.

Studies of other forms of brief intervention. While confrontational and cathartic approaches have their limits, particularly in the circumstances of acute grief, they also have their uses in the specific circumstances of chronic grief. One small controlled study of *guided mourning* (Mawson et al. 1981) demonstrated modest benefit from a very brief, behavioral intervention for patients with chronic grief of at least 1 year's duration. In this study, the authors contrasted a treatment lasting six sessions that involved intense exposure to avoided or painful memories of the deceased individual to a control treatment that encouraged avoidance of the painful memories. The treatment effect was modest in comparison to the reports of benefit from several previous uncontrolled trials of similar behavioral interventions (Gauthier and Pye 1979; Hodgkinson 1982; Lieberman 1978). One reason for the modest effect may have been the very short duration of the intervention. In addition, the control group did receive an intervention that may have helped those in it who were experiencing severe, chronic grief. This unintended effect may have occurred even though the authors conceptualized the control situation as nontherapeutic within a theoretical framework that considered pathologic grief as a type of phobic disorder.

A notable observation of the study of guided mourning was a discrepancy in the response of the patients on measures of unresolved grief, for which the treatment had an effect, in contrast to the measures of depression, for which treatment did not have an effect. This observation serves as a counterpoint to the open trials of antidepressants that found no benefit on measures of separation distress but good effects on depressive symptoms. Furthermore, it suggests that different treatment approaches have potentially different benefit in addressing the overall needs of the bereaved patient.

Another notable observation from this study (Mawson et al. 1981) was the salutary effect of treatment on avoidant behavior in the bereaved patients. In a subsequently study of individual, time-limited, dynamic psychotherapy, the most significant treatment effect reported was also on avoidant behavior (Horowitz et al. 1984a). Thus both behavioral and psychodynamic interventions appear to have a prominent effect on avoidance of those aspects of bereavement that are feared by the patient. If this is true, it suggests that this may be a common effect that should be used to evaluate and compare the success of different psychotherapeutic interventions. It also implies that there is a phobic quality in the nature of these disorders of bereavement, an idea that has been advanced by therapists using behavioral treatments (Ramsay 1977). Finally, it provides a potentially useful focus for thinking about common elements in the psychotherapy of the complications of bereavement. (Along this line, in Chapter 13 I develop the idea that a central task of psychotherapy is to address the bereaved patient's demoralization and fear. This task can be accomplished using educational and supportive techniques in a psychotherapeutic process that also includes interpersonal, psychodynamic, and behavioral techniques, which are integrated into a coherent whole, depending on the syndrome of pathologic grief and the stage of bereavement.)

Another study (Cameron and Parkes 1983) demonstrated the beneficial effects of a brief bereavement intervention by a hospice nurse, including home visits and telephone contacts. Unfortunately, for our purposes, the bereavement intervention cannot be separated from the effects of a palliative, terminal care program in which the most salient characteristic was adequate pain management. Nor can it be ignored that the palliative care program also provided counseling about the imminent death for families of the patients. This preparation of the family for the death addressed a risk factor for complicated bereavement (Parkes and Weiss 1983) that presumably affected the outcome of this study. Despite these limitations of the study for our present purposes, the members of the control group were suffering more intense manifestations of grief, had more irritable and angry feelings, were more hostile toward others, were using more tranquilizers, and were sleeping more poorly 1 year after the loss than the intervention group.

In addition to the studies reviewed in this section, which, with two exceptions (Cameron and Parkes 1983; Horowitz et al. 1984a), included random assignment of unselected patients to treatment and control groups, many clinicians who work with acutely bereaved patients will testify to the effectiveness of psychotherapy in the circumstances of a loss and when the patient has taken the initiative to seek help (Lieberman 1978; Melges and DeMaso 1980; Sireling et al. 1984; Volkan and Showalter 1968).

Another line of evidence about the effectiveness of psychotherapy for treating the complications of bereavement stems from research into psychotherapy as a treatment for major depressions. Both cognitive behavioral therapy (Elkin et al. 1989; Murphy et al. 1984; Rush et al. 1977; Simons et al. 1986) and interpersonal therapy (DiMascio et al. 1979; Elkin et al. 1989; Weissman et al. 1979) have proven to be effective treatments for depressions in controlled trials. This evidence provides support for the efficacy of interpersonal and cognitive therapy in treating the depressive syndromes of bereavement.

Conclusions

Although the discussion of the clinical trials of treatment and the various theories of pathogenetic mechanisms in this chapter creates a beginning scientific framework for thinking about therapeutic interventions, the reader will probably agree that our current knowledge is long on theoretical ideas and short on empirical demonstration.

Given the current state of scientific knowledge, I take the liberty in subsequent chapters of presenting a view of the treatment of the clinical complications of bereavement that is anchored in clinical practice as well as clinical science. It is my assumption in the following chapters on treatment that the reader will have some familiarity with the general literature on psychopharmacology and psychotherapy. It is not my intention to be as thorough as other texts in presenting a model for psychotherapeutic treatment or an overview of psychopharmacology. Rather, I highlight conceptual issues that I have found important in using psychotropic drugs and undertaking psychotherapy when working with bereaved patients. Also I discuss the relationship of treatment to self-help efforts, which make an important contribution to the care of bereaved individuals with clinical complications. All these approaches to caring for bereaved patients ought to be integrated into coherent, individualized treatment plans, which is a task of such importance that it will be discussed next before considering the details of each approach to treatment.

References

Adamson JD, Schmale AH: Object loss, giving up, and the onset of psychiatric disease. Psychosom Med 27:557–576, 1965

Bankoff EA: Social support and adaptation to widowhood. Journal of Marriage and the Family 10:827–839, 1983

Bartrop RW, Lazarus L, Luckhurst E, et al: Depressed lymphocyte function after bereavement. Lancet 1:834–836, 1977

Berardo FM: Survivorship and social isolation: the case of the aged widower. Family Coordinator 19:11–25, 1970

Berkman LF, Syme SL: Social networks, host resistance, and mortality: a nine year follow-up of Alameda County residents. Am J Epidemiol 109:186–204, 1979

Bibring E: The mechanism of depression, in Affective Disorders. Edited by Greenacre A. New York, International Universities Press, 1953

Blois MS: Medicine and the nature of vertical reasoning. N Engl J Med 318:847–851, 1988
Bowlby J: The making and breaking of affectional bonds. Br J Psychiatry 130:201–210, 1977
Bowlby J: Attachment and Loss, Vol 3: Loss, Sadness and Depression. New York, Basic Books, 1980
Brier A, Albus M, Pickar D, et al: Controllable and uncontrollable stress in humans: alterations in mood and neuroendocrine and psychophysiological function. Am J Psychiatry 144:1419–1423, 1987
Brotman AW, Falk WE, Gelenberg AJ: Pharmacologic treatment of acute depressive subtypes, in Psychopharmacology: The Third Generation of Progress. Edited by Meltzer HY. New York, Raven, 1987, pp 1031–1040
Cameron J, Parkes CM: Terminal care: evaluation of effects on surviving family of care before and after bereavement. Postgrad Med J 59:73–78, 1983
Caplan G: Principles of Preventive Psychiatry. New York, Basic Books, 1964
Ciocco A: On the mortality in husbands and wives. Hum Biol 12:508–531, 1940
Clayton PJ, Herjanic M, Murphy GE, et al: Mourning and depression: their similarities and differences. Canadian Psychiatric Association Journal 19:309–313, 1974
Das M, Berrios GE: Dexamethasone suppression test in acute grief. Acta Psychiatr Scand 70:278–281, 1984
DeLisi LE, Weber RJ, Pert CB: Are there antibodies against brain in sera from schizophrenic patients? Review and prospectus. Biol Psychiatry 20:110–119, 1985
DiMascio A, Weissman MM, Prusoff BA, et al: Differential symptom reduction by drugs and psychotherapy in acute depression. Arch Gen Psychiatry 36:1450–1456, 1979
Ehlers CL, Frank E, Kupfer DJ: Social zeitgebers and biological rhythms. Arch Gen Psychiatry 45:948–952, 1988
Elkin I, Shea, T, Watkins JT, et al: National Institute of Mental Health Treatment of Depression Collaborative Research Program. Arch Gen Psychiatry 46:971–982, 1989
Engel GL: Is grief a disease? A challenge for medical research. Psychosom Med 23:18–22, 1961
Engel GL: Anxiety and depression withdrawal: the primary affects of unpleasure. Int J Psychoanal 43:89–97, 1962
Engel GL: The need for a new medical model: a challenge for biomedicine. Science 196:129–136, 1977
Engel GL: The clinical application of the biopsychosocial model. Am J Psychiatry 137:535–544, 1980
Freud S: Mourning and melancholia (1917), in The Standard Edition of the Complete Psychological Works of Sigmund Freud, Vol 14. Edited and translated by Strachey J. London, Hogarth Press, 1953, pp 243–258
Gauthier J, Pye C: Graduated self exposure in management of grief. Behavioral Analysis and Modification 3:202–208, 1979
Gerber I, Wiener A, Battin D, et al: Brief therapy to the aged bereaved, in Bereavement: Its Psychosocial Aspects. Edited by Shoenberg B, Gerber I, Wiener A, et al. New York, Columbia University Press, 1975, pp 310–333
Gold PW, Goodwin FK, Chrousos GP: Clinical and biochemical manifestations of depression: relation to the neurobiology of stress (first of two parts). N Engl J Med 319:348–352, 1988a

Gold PW, Goodwin FK, Chrousos GP: Clinical and biochemical manifestations of depression: relation to the neurobiology of stress (second of two parts). N Engl J Med 319:413–420, 1988b

Hodgkinson PE: Abnormal grief—the problem of therapy. Br J Med Psychol 55:29–34, 1982

Hofer MA: Relationships as regulators: a psychobiologic perspective on bereavement. Psychosom Med 46:183–197, 1984

Horowitz MJ: Stress Response Syndromes. New York, Jason Aronson, 1976

Horowitz MJ, Wilner N, Marmar C, et al: Pathological grief and the activation of latent self-images. Am J Psychiatry 137:1157–1162, 1980

Horowitz MJ, Weiss DS, Kaltreider N, et al: Reactions to the death of a parent: results from patients and field subjects. J Nerv Ment Dis 172:383–439, 1984a

Horowitz MJ, Marmar C, Weiss DS, et al: Brief psychotherapy of bereavement reactions: the relationship of process to outcome. Arch Gen Psychiatry 41:438–448, 1984b

Horowitz M, Marmar C, Krupnick J, et al: Personality Styles and Brief Psychotherapy. New York, Basic Books, 1984c

Horowitz MJ, Marmar C, Weiss DS, et al: Comprehensive analysis of change after brief dynamic psychotherapy. Am J Psychiatry 143:582–589, 1986

Irwin MR, Weiner H: Depressive symptoms and immune function during bereavement, in Biopsychosocial Aspects of Bereavement. Edited by Zisook S. Washington, DC, American Psychiatric Press, 1987, pp 159–174

Jacobs SC, Douglas L: Grief: a mediating process between a loss and illness. Compr Psychiatry 20:165–175, 1979

Jacobs SC, Ostfeld AM: An epidemiologic review of the mortality of bereavement. Psychosom Med 39:344–357, 1977

Jacobs SC, Nelson JC, Zisook S: Treating depressions of bereavement with antidepressants: a pilot study. Psychiatr Clin North Am 10:501–510, 1987

Jacobs SC, Hansen FF, Kasl SV, et al: Anxiety disorders during acute bereavement: risk and risk factors. J Clin Psychiatry 51:269–274, 1990

Jacobs S, Kim K, Schaefer C, et al: Conscious and unconscious coping under stress, part 2: relationship to one and two year outcomes after bereavement. Paper presented at the Third International Conference on Grief and Bereavement, Sydney, Australia, June 30–July 4, 1991

Kagan J, Reznick JS, Snidman N: Biological bases of childhood shyness. Science 240:167–171, 1988

Kaufman IC, Rosenblum LA: The reaction to separation in infant monkeys: anaclitic depression and conservation-withdrawal. Psychosom Med 29:648–675, 1967

Kim K, Jacobs S, Schaefer C, et al: Conscious and unconscious coping under stress, part 1: relationship to each other and neuroendocrine function. Paper presented at the Third International Conference on Grief and Bereavement, Sydney, Australia, June 30–July 4, 1991

Klein DF: Delineation of two drug responsive anxiety syndromes. Psychopharmacologia 5:397–408, 1964

Kosten TR, Jacobs SC, Mason JW, et al: The DST in depression during bereavement. J Nerv Ment Dis 172:359–360, 1984

Kronfol Z, House JD, Silva J, et al: Depression, urinary free cortisol excretion and lymphocyte function. Br J Psychiatry 148:70–73, 1986

Lehman DR, Wortman CB, Williams AF: Long term effects of losing a spouse or child in a motor vehicle accident. J Per Soc Psychol 52:218–231, 1987

Leigh H, Reiser MF: The Patient: Biological, Psychological, and Social Dimensions of Medical Practice, 2nd Edition. New York, Plenum, 1985

Lieberman S: Nineteen cases of morbid grief. Br J Psychiatry 132:159–163, 1978

Lindeman EL: Symptomatology and management of acute grief. Am J Psychiatry 101:141–148, 1944

Lindeman EL: Psychiatric factors in the treatment of ulcerative colitis. Archives of Neurology and Psychiatry 53:322–335, 1945

Lopata HZ: Widowhood in an American City. Cambridge, MA, Schenkman Publishing, 1973

Marmar CR, Horowitz MJ, Weiss DS, et al: A controlled trial of brief psychotherapy and mutual help group treatment of conjugal bereavement. Am J Psychiatry 145:203–209, 1988

Mawson D, Marks IM, Ramm L, et al: Guided mourning for morbid grief: a controlled study. Br J Psychiatry 138:185–193, 1981

McKinney WT: Separation and depression: biological markers, in The Psychobiology of Attachment and Separation. Edited by Reite M, Field T. New York, Academic Press, 1985, pp 201–222

McKinney WT: Primate separation studies: relevance to bereavement. Psychiatric Annals 16:281–287, 1986

McKinney WT, Moran EC, Kraemer GW: Separation in nonhuman primates as a model for human depression: neurobiological implications, in Neurobiology of Mood Disorders. Edited by Post RM, Ballenger JC. Baltimore, Williams & Wilkins, 1984, pp 233–245

Melges FT, DeMaso DR: Grief-resolution therapy: reliving, revising, and revisiting. Am J Psychother 34:51–61, 1980

Murphy GE, Simons AD, Wetzel RD, et al: Cognitive therapy and pharmacotherapy. Arch Gen Psychiatry 41:33–41, 1984

Nelson JC, Mazure C, Quinlan DM, et al: Drug responsive symptoms in melancholia. Arch Gen Psychiatry 41:663–668, 1984

Parkes CM: Psychosocial transitions: a field for study. Soc Sci Med 5:101–115, 1971

Parkes CM: Bereavement: Studies of Grief in Adult Life. New York, International Universities Press, 1972

Parkes CM: Determinants of outcome following bereavement. Omega 6:303–323, 1975

Parkes CM, Weiss RS: Recovery From Bereavement. New York, Basic Books, 1983

Pasternak RE, Reynolds CF, Schlernitzauer M, et al: Acute open-trial nortriptyline therapy of bereavement-related depression in late life. J Clin Psychiatry 52:307–310, 1991

Paulley JW: Pathological mourning: a key factor in the psychopathogenesis of autoimmune disorders. Psychother Psychosom 40:181–190, 1983

Petty F, Sherman AD: GABAergic modulation of learned helplessness. Pharmacol Biochem Behav 15:567–570, 1981

Polak PB, Egan D, Bandenbergh R: Prevention in mental health: a controlled study. Am J Psychiatry 132:146–149, 1975

Potter WZ, Rudorfer MV, Manji H: The pharmacologic treatment of depression. N Engl J Med 325:633–642, 1991

Ramsay RW: Behavioural approaches to bereavement. Behav Res Ther 15:131–135, 1977

Raphael B: The management of pathologic grief. Aust N Z J Psychiatry 9:173–180, 1974

Raphael B: Preventive intervention with the recently bereaved. Arch Gen Psychiatry 34:1450–1454, 1977

Reite M: Attachment relationship has impact on patients' physiologic functioning. The Psychiatric Times, February, 1990, pp 41–44

Rush AJ, Beck AT, Kovacs M, et al: Comparative efficacy of cognitive therapy and pharmacotherapy in the treatment of depressed outpatients. Cognitive Therapy and Research 1:17–37, 1977

Schleifer SJ, Keller SE, Camerino M, et al: Suppression of lymphocyte stimulation following bereavement. JAMA 259:374–377, 1983

Schleifer SJ, Keller SE, Stein M: Stress effects on immunity. Psychiatr J Univ Ott 10:126–130, 1984

Schmale AH, Iker HP: The affect of hopelessness and the development of cancer. Psychosom Med 28:714–721, 1966

Shuchter SR, Zisook S, Kirkorowicz C, et al: The dexamethasone suppression test in acute grief. Am J Psychiatry 143: 879–881, 1986

Siever LJ, Davis KL: Overview: toward a dysregulation hypothesis of depression. Am J Psychiatry 142:1017–1031, 1985

Silverman P: Widow to Widow. New York, Springer, 1986

Simons AD, Murphy GE, Levine JL, et al: Cognitive therapy and pharmacotherapy for depression. Arch Gen Psychiatry 43:43–48, 1986

Sireling L, Cohen D, Marks I: Guided mourning for morbid grief. Paper presented at Proceedings of the First International Symposium on Grief and Bereavement in Contemporary Society, Jerusalem, November 11–14, 1984

Stroebe M, Stroebe W: Does "grief work" work? a review and empirical investigation. Reports from the Psychological Institute, University of Tübingen, Number 31, 1990

Townsend P: Isolation, loneliness, and the hold on life, in The Family Life of Old People. Edited by Townsend P. Glencoe, IL, Free Press, 1957, pp 166–182

Vachon MLS, Lyall WAL, Rogers J, et al: A controlled trial of self-help intervention for widows. Am J Psychiatry 137:1380–1384, 1980

Volkan V, Showalter CR: Known object loss, disturbance in reality testing, and "regrief work" as a method of brief psychotherapy. Psychiatr Q 42:358–374, 1968

Ward AWM: Mortality of bereavement. BMJ 1:700–702, 1976

Weiss JM, Stone EA, Harrell N: Coping behavior and brain norepinephrine in rats. Journal of Comparative and Physiological Psychology 72:153–160, 1970

Weiss JM, Goodman PA, Losito BG, et al: Behavioural depression produced by an uncontrollable stressor: relationship to norepinephrine, dopamine, and serotonin levels in various brain regions. Brain Res Brain Res Rev 3:167–205, 1981

Weissman MM, Prusoff BA, DiMascio A, et al: The efficacy of drugs and psychotherapy in the treatment of acute depressive episodes. Am J Psychiatry 136:555–558, 1979

Williams WV, Polak PR: Follow-up research in primary prevention: a model of adjustment to acute grief. J Clin Psychol 35:35–45, 1979

Williams WV, Polak PR, Vollman RR: Crisis intervention in acute grief. Omega 3:67–70, 1972

Windholz MJ, Marmar CR, Horowitz MJ: A review of the research on conjugal bereavement: impact on health and efficacy of intervention. Compr Psychiatry 26:433–437, 1985

Worden JW: Grief Counseling and Grief Therapy: A Handbook for the Mental Health Practitioner. New York, Springer, 1982

Wortman CB, Silver RC: The myths of coping with a loss. J Consult Clin Psychol 57:349–357, 1989

Zisook S, Shuchter SR, Lyons LE: Adjustment to widowhood, in Biopsychosocial Aspects of Bereavement. Edited by Zisook S. Washington, DC, American Psychiatric Press, 1987, pp 51–74

CHAPTER 11

Integrating the Treatment for Complications of Bereavement

Pathologic grief is an acute disorder that can appear shortly after a loss or emerge later in the course of bereavement. It has the potential to become chronic. As several of the treatment studies I review in Chapter 10 indicate, many patients with the complications of bereavement are not identified for treatment until the course of their disorder has become quite prolonged. In these circumstances, most often there is a need not only to treat acute symptoms but also to provide rehabilitation for chronic patterns of maladaptive coping. The acute clinical picture may include unremitting depressive syndromes or incapacitating panic disorders that require pharmacological intervention. In practically all cases, bereaved patients have a limited understanding of normal grief and are confused about what has gone wrong. This is the nature of pathologic grief as a psychiatric disorder, but this description does not present the whole clinical picture.

An adaptive model provides an excellent framework for thinking about the tasks of treating pathologic grief by reminding us that the clinical problems we face as practitioners go beyond a patient's symptomatic and functional disturbance to include vital changes in the social environment. The nature of a death can introduce clinical themes (e.g., traumatic distress in the case of a traumatic loss) that must be recognized and integrated into the treatment strategy. The desolate environment created by a loss will also determine in part the final adjustment of bereaved individuals as they cope with the absence of the deceased family member or intimate. Thus as clinicians we cannot simply treat the symptoms of the clinical disorder; we must also attend to the specific environmental context in which the disorder occurs and the efforts of the bereaved individual to cope.

Given the nature of pathologic grief, the scope of the clinical problems presented by bereaved patients ordinarily calls for multidimensional treatment; furthermore, these various modalities of treatment need to be integrated into a total treatment plan. The wisdom of integrating the major modalities of treatment into multidimensional, individualized treatment plans for particular patients is a fundamental tenet of treatment that guides the discussion of therapeutic interventions in this chapter and Chapters 12–14. In this chapter, I analyze the goals of the following three main treatment and rehabilitative modalities (which are then discussed in more detail in the chapters indicated): psychopharmacological treatments (Chapter 12), psychotherapeutic treatments (Chapter 13), and mutual support interventions (Chapter 14). The goals of these modalities are analyzed for the purpose of developing a rationale for the integration of therapeutic approaches. I realize that it might be more logical to undertake this task after the discussion of each of the treatment modalities, when the details for each approach have been presented. The value of integrating treatment modalities is so fundamentally important, however, that it seems there is merit in leading with a discussion of the goals as an organizing principle. The choice to begin with a discussion of treatment integration is made in part to leave no doubt that simple approaches to treatment are not being advocated.

Another consideration that supports the need for integrated treatment plans is the fact that the nonresponse rate to each of the major interventions for the clinical complications of bereavement is high. For psychotherapy, poor response ranges from 15% to 30% (Rynearson 1987). The nonresponse rate to psychopharmacological treatment is equally elevated (Jacobs et al. 1987; Pasternak et al. 1991; Potter et al. 1991). There is every reason to suspect that the failure rate of mutual support interventions is just as large, although these type of data are seldom reported for these groups. The reported failure rates come from studies that evaluate each intervention as a single modality of treatment. If pathologic grief presents with the spectrum of clinical problems discussed in this book, one modality of treatment that addresses only one aspect of the disorder is less likely to succeed. This consideration points to the need for integrating the various treatment approaches in order to enhance the overall chances of positive response for the particular patient.

The need for integration of treatment approaches is all the more compelling if the thrust and target of each major type of therapeutic intervention is largely independent from that of the others. The following conceptual analysis of the goals of treatment supports this conclusion about the relative independence of treatment approaches. The judgment that each of the major modalities of treatment addresses separate and additive parts of the problems that bereaved patients face provides added incentive for developing a integrated, multidimensional approach to helping the patient.

As a final note, the conceptual analysis in this chapter is not heavily documented and is inevitably somewhat personal because it is based in part on clinical experience. In Chapter 10 and in Chapters 12–14 (in which the specific modalities of treatment are addressed), I include documentation, such as it currently exists, from both systematic studies and clinical practice for the conclusions about the goals of treatment presented in this chapter.

Goals of Treatment

Psychopharmacology

The goal of psychopharmacological intervention is the treatment of major depressions and anxiety disorders that occur during bereavement (see Table 11–1 and Chapter 12). The objective of treatment is the alleviation of symptoms that overwhelm the bereaved individual or that interfere with his or her functioning. Antidepressants promise to be an effective treatment for depressive syndromes during acute bereavement. Both benzodiazepines and antidepressants may have a role in treating incapacitating anxiety disorders. Furthermore, the use of antidepressants and, in some cases benzodiazepines, indirectly, and maybe directly, facilitate the resolution of pathologic grief.

It is important to emphasize that in treating the depressions or anxiety disorders of bereavement, the target of the intervention is not to eliminate the normal manifestations of grief, such as separation distress. In fact, clinical experience and data from the two open trials of antidepressants that have been completed (Jacobs et al. 1987; Pasternak et al. 1991) indicate that the course of separation distress is independent of the course of depressive symptoms. Paradoxically, the successful treatment of major depressions may lead to the reemergence or exacerbation of the severity of grief (see Chapter 12). The therapist can then facilitate this natural process of healing in psychotherapy.

When psychotropic drugs are used to treat complications of bereavement, there is no pretension of cure, just as in all of psychopharmacological practice. The only difference in the case of treating the complications of bereavement is that we know a little more about the natural process of healing, that is, grief. Therefore, while clinicians are alleviating the symptoms, they also ought to help patients understand and adapt to both the challenges of bereavement and the vulnerability defined by the psychiatric disorder under treatment.

Table 11–1. Goals of treating psychiatric complications of bereavement

Modality	Goals
Psychotropic drugs	Treat major depressions and anxiety disorders
	Alleviate symptoms that are subjectively overwhelming or that interfere with functioning
	Facilitate the natural healing of grief
Psychotherapy	Counter demoralization
	Provide psychoeducation
	Solve problems
	Clarify interpersonal problems
	Elucidate maladaptive relationship patterns
	Clarify pessimistic cognitive schemas
	Desensitize the phobic avoidance
Mutual support groups	Provide membership and friendship
	Exchange information about grief, coping, and community resources
	Offer a milieu for practicing social skills
	Empower through publicity and advocacy
	Promote self-esteem

Psychotherapy

The basic goal of psychotherapy during acute bereavement, using both psychodynamic and behavioral techniques, is to reduce the mystery, fear, and sense of helplessness that accompanies the experience of bereavement (see Chapter 13). Psychotherapy provides an opportunity for bereaved patients to formulate the problems and tasks that they face and consider how they will cope with them, thereby fostering personal competence in them. By so doing, psychotherapy encourages bereaved patients to face problems rather than avoid them. By discussing the problems posed by bereavement, the patients increase their chances of successful adaptation. To meet these goals, the concept of psychotherapy during acute bereavement need not be very complicated. It is basically a process of listening and teaching. Bereaved individuals who are at a high risk for developing complications need to talk about their experience to understand their grief; this understanding in turn allows them to cope more effectively with it by solving the problems they face. Psychotherapists are trained to listen carefully with the basic aim of educating bereaved patients about their experience, about themselves, and about potential solutions to their problems.

Therapists educate their patients by means of psychoeducational, psychodynamic, and behavioral psychotherapeutic techniques. Consistent with this concept of psychotherapy and the nature of the complications of bereavement as adaptive disorders, it is useful to emphasize the psychoeducational component of psychotherapy in the treatment of the clinical complications of bereavement (see Chapter 13). Except to the extent that an individual grows by learning from life experiences, acute bereavement is not a time to undertake long-term therapeutic goals such as personality change. It is to be expected that the acute distress of grief will strain the coping resources of most bereaved individuals; thus the emotional strain of the experience makes personality diagnoses unreliable, thereby providing a very unstable basis for their treatment. In any event, bereaved people are capable of personal growth through solving the problems of bereavement, whatever their developmental level of personality functioning.

In addition to the psychoeducational goals of psychotherapy that are specific to the context of bereavement, cognitive and interpersonal psychotherapy serve the goal of treating major depressions, anxiety disorders, and phobic avoidance during bereavement in ways that complement psychopharmacological treatment. Psychotherapy accomplishes this by addressing the pessimistic cognitive schemas and the avoidance that are part of the impairment caused by chronic grief, major depression, or anxiety disorders. Also because it is based on psychodynamic insights, psychotherapy focuses on repetitive, dysfunctional behavior patterns and deficits in interpersonal relationships and social skills that interfere with a bereaved patient's efforts to adapt to a loss.

Mutual Support Groups

The goal of mutual support interventions is to provide membership in a social organization that is designed to meet the needs of acutely bereaved individuals who must adapt to a new social reality (see Chapter 14). Through formal and informal components of mutual support programs, the bereaved individual can learn about the experience of grief, how others cope with it, and what community resources are available for those who are bereaved. In short, the acutely bereaved individual must become more independent or find substitutes for those things that the lost relationship provided. In the case of spousal bereavement, mutual support activities provide an opportunity for the bereaved individual to become socially active again and practice the social skills required of an unmarried individual. In other instances, such as parental bereavement, the group may provide an organized vehicle for social advocacy about the needs of survivors of violent deaths or for research into the disease that claimed the life of their child. This empowers those who have experienced a tragic life event to act constructively and altruistically in the face of horrifying adversity and, sometimes, social neglect of their needs.

When viewed from a medical perspective, mutual support groups primarily serve the rehabilitative goal of reducing the impairment in social functioning or diminishing the risk of disability associated with a loss. When viewed within a social framework, the mutual support group facilitates the transition from nonbereaved to bereaved status with all the attendant changes in role functioning and required skills. It accomplishes this through providing education, advocacy, and friendship. Whereas psychotherapy can help conceptualize the tasks of a psychosocial transition in treatment, only the mutual support group can provide this important medium of action and actual sources of friendship and support outside of a professional office.

Goals of Treatment as Complementary and Synergistic

For the most part, the goals of each of these main components of care for the bereaved patient address different aspects of the problems that bereaved patients face (Table 11–1). Even when the goals of treatment converge, as they do in the case of psychotropic drug treatment and cognitive psychotherapy in the treatment of depressive symptoms, or in the case of psychotherapy and mutual support groups in providing an intervention for psychosocial problems, the effects have the potential for being complementary if not synergistic. The potential for synergy between psychotropic drugs and psychotherapy has been noted in some studies of the treatment of major depressions (DiMascio et al. 1979; Weissman et al. 1979) although not all (Murphy et al. 1984). Furthermore, from the review of psychopharmacological and psychotherapeutic treatment studies of the clinical complications of bereavement in Chapter 10, there is evidence of selective effects. Pharmacological treatment may selectively benefit depressive symptoms (Jacobs et al. 1987; Pasternak et al. 1991) and behavioral psychotherapy may selectively affect symptoms of unresolved grief (Mawson et al. 1981). The potential for synergy between psychotherapy and mutual support groups was appreciated by the authors of a study comparing brief dynamic psychotherapy and mutual support groups (Marmar et al. 1988). These investigators were impressed, obviously due in part to the design of the study, that psychotherapy placed emphasis on recurrent, maladaptive relationship patterns and idiosyncratic obstacles to successful mourning whereas mutual support groups emphasized support, role modeling, and exchange of practical information.

Integration of Treatment

Efficacy of Integrating Treatment Goals

A conceptual analysis of the goals of treatment leads to the conclusion that the aims of each type of intervention are sufficiently different to justify their integration into a treatment plan that comprehensively addresses all the treatment and rehabilitative needs of the patient. For example, there is evidence that pathologic grief overlaps considerably with major depressive syndromes and anxiety disorders (Jacobs et al. 1987; Kim and Jacobs 1991; Zisook and DeVaul 1983). Effective treatment must address all the clinical problems that the patient presents, including the symptomatic disorders, the demoralization, the maladaptive behavior patterns, and the impaired functioning. This is true particularly in light of the clinical impression that the major depressions and anxiety disorders of bereavement interfere with the spontaneous resolution of grief and, conversely, that chronic grief is associated with incipient depressions and anxiety disorders as a reflection of the continuing stress caused by the loss. We must treat the symptoms of the depressive and anxiety disorders and, at the same time, we must undertake the psychotherapeutic tasks of health education and behavioral change. In addition, if rehabilitative tasks are addressed early and integrated into treatment, the disability of chronic impairment in social functioning is reduced. This is important in circumstances of bereavement where the risk of disability is high given the need to at least reactivate old roles if not learn new ones at a time of intense emotional distress.

Simple models of treatment based on a single theory are associated with falsely high expectations that lead to narrow, potentially damaging treatment plans and results (Polak et al. 1975; Williams and Polak 1979; see Chapter 10 for a discussion of this study). Several examples of this fallacy come to mind. One is the prescription of abreactive interventions for chronic, disabling distress because of convictions about "getting it out" and "saying goodbye." Another example is the failure to treat a clearly disabling depressive syndrome because the clinician does not recognize it or is inexperienced with the use of antidepressants during bereavement. Yet another example is the neglect of problems of social adjustment that constrict a patient's life on the assumption that psychosocial rehabilitation does not fall under the responsibility of the treating clinician. The needs of the patient ought to dictate treatment, not the charismatic and perhaps limited treatment perspective of the clinician. Patients have problems as well as diagnoses, and the problems are the currency of treatment. Problems arise as the bereaved individual strives to adapt to the challenges posed by a loss. Treatment that is problem focused and goal oriented succeeds by drawing on a range of treatment strategies that meet the particular needs of a patient faced with specific problems at a particular stage of bereavement and in a particular phase of treatment.

Potential for One Treatment Approach to Interfere With Another

There is no evidence that psychotherapy, pharmacological treatment, and mutual support interventions conflict, particularly if they are part of an overall treatment plan. Hence, this should not be a deterrent to integration of treatment. For example, the patient does not have to be depressed to engage in psychotherapy, a commonly accepted clinical adage in my training as a psychiatrist. On the contrary, pharmacologically treating a major depression may make psychotherapy possible, and psychotherapy may lay the groundwork for compliance with a pharmacological intervention. A derivative of the idea that relief of symptoms interferes with motivation for treatment is the notion that patients must suffer through grief on their own for the purpose of learning from the experience. This assumption is discussed in Chapter 13 where emphasis is placed on learning, not suffering, by the patient.

Similarly, there is no inherent conflict between mutual support interventions and either psychopharmacology or psychotherapy. While it is true that strong attitudes of the partisans of each approach may interfere with an integrated treatment plan (see Chapter 14), the goals of each approach to helping the bereaved individual are basically different and complement each other. There is no friction, beyond proper timing and maintenance of a reasonable psychological load for a particular patient, between treating the emotional and psychological symptoms of pathologic grief while at the same time formulating the problems of social adjustment as well as coping strategies for their solution.

In short, the impression of potential conflict between different approaches to caring for the acutely bereaved individual with clinical complications of bereavement appears to be more a function of false assumptions and overzealous commitment to one point of view or another rather than any inherent antagonism between the treatments themselves. The essential element for managing the various tasks of treatment is a caring, skilled clinician who takes responsibility with the patient for an integrated treatment plan.

A Note on Treatment Conservatism

Treatment for the clinical complications of bereavement should not only be integrated but should be undertaken with a conservative philosophy. The fundamental consideration in this regard is the fact that treatment interventions during bereavement are made at a time when the patient is suffering from an emotional wound and an active mending process is taking place. Care should be taken not to derail the natural healing process of grief, which we still understand in only sketchy terms. The aim of treatment is not to take grief away but rather to trust in it as a process of recovery. An analogy can be made to inflammatory processes that, although potentially painful, promote the healing of a physical injury (Engel 1977, 1980).

In a broader sense, it must be appreciated, as I hope to convey in this book, that the bereaved individual is trying to adapt to a changed, sometimes threatening environment. Counseling and therapeutic interventions are most effective when they are designed to facilitate the resolution of grief. To implement such effective treatment, the clinician must have an intimate knowledge of the normal biological and psychosocial processes of bereavement. In some cases, the natural healing process is obstructed or does not progress. Then we recognize the resulting states as various forms of pathologic grief. When a complication occurs, treatment can be essential in putting the process back on track and giving the bereaved patient a fresh start.

An ancillary consideration supporting a conservative philosophy of treatment is the limited scientific basis (see Chapter 10) for the various treatments that will be discussed in the next three chapters. In the light of this, an appropriate first principle for a philosophy of treatment at the time of acute bereavement is the Hippocratic axiom: first, do no harm. Accordingly, in the discussion of pharmacological treatments, psychotherapy, and mutual supports in subsequent chapters, I try to emphasize not only the indications for treatment but also the risks. Furthermore, in the discussion of guidelines for the integration of treatment that follows, I try to promote a conservative progression of interventions over time that draws on all three main types of intervention (i.e., pharmacological, psychotherapeutic, and mutual support groups) and that respects the natural history of bereaved individuals' efforts to cope with a loss by their own means.

Overview of Treatment That Integrates Psychopharmacology, Psychotherapy, and Mutual Support

Over the years, I have evolved rough guidelines for the integrated treatment of the clinical complications of bereavement. As a basic proposition, all acutely bereaved individuals ought to receive preventive monitoring by a primary care physician, even if they are experiencing uncomplicated bereavement (Jacobs and Ostfeld 1980; Worden 1982). Treatment plans should take into consideration the particular diagnostic formulation of the patient and his or her stage of bereavement.

Treatment During the First Six Months of Bereavement

During the first 6 months of bereavement, careful evaluation, bereavement counseling, and psychotherapeutic intervention in the event of pathologic grief, major depressions, and anxiety disorders ought to be emphasized. During this period, a conservative approach to the use of antidepressants should be followed, unless there is a clinical imperative such as psychotic symptomatology or a high, imminent risk of suicidal behavior as part of a major depression. Panic disorder that is associated with progressive constriction of social activities is another indication for treating with antidepressants in this early period of bereavement. Sparing use of benzodiazepines can be made for the brief treatment of sleep disorders or during a brief period of induction of antidepressant treatment. With regard to psychotropic drugs, for the reasons that are developed in Chapter 12, I believe that the antidepressant drugs are underutilized and antianxiety drugs are used excessively.

It is premature during the first 6 months of bereavement to consider mutual support interventions for the average bereaved individual. Acutely bereaved individuals ordinarily will turn to family and close friends immediately after a loss (see Chapter 14). Furthermore, most acutely bereaved individuals have little or no interest in making new acquaintances when they are intensely preoccupied with their loss and experiencing severe separation anxiety.

During this period, patients who experience patterns of grief that are consistent with pathologic grief of the delayed, inhibited, or severe type ought to be offered brief psychotherapy by a skilled therapist. This intervention is all the more important if the patient is not already receiving counseling from a primary care physician. However, the exclusive use of behavioral interventions at this point is inappropriate, although specific behavioral strategies (e.g., the identification of pessimistic cognitive schemas) may be integrated into treatment. Patients with early occurring syndromes of pathologic grief are not often seen in ordinary clinical practice because they seldom seek treatment on their own. Such patients are more likely to be encountered in bereavement follow-up programs that are part of a hospice or in disaster relief programs that provide early interventions for survivors. The goal of reaching all bereaved individuals in need of professional help is a challenge for preventive psychiatry. I wish to emphasize that patients who exhibit symptoms of pathologic grief need treatment, especially in view of the fact that pathologic grief was ignored as a diagnostic entity in DSM-III-R (American Psychiatric Association 1987). I have written this book in part to counter this oversight by developing evidence indicating that pathologic grief can be considered a definite clinical entity with a reasonably well known symptomatology and course.

Although a careful evaluation of all aspects of a loss is necessary at all times, I especially emphasize assessing the death for any traumatic elements when patients present early in the course of bereavement for treatment. Traumatic losses introduce a dimension into bereavement that must be systematically addressed. The clinician ought to provide patients an opportunity to review the event, slowly come to terms with it, work through their denial, acknowledge their anger, and begin to consider the implications of the experience for their philosophy of life, all within a therapeutic environment that is secure and supportive. Addressing the traumatic distress is the primary focus in early treatment and often interrupts attention to the separation distress that occurs in parallel and must be dealt with concurrently. When the loss is not blatantly traumatic, as in the case of some sudden, unexpected deaths, attention to these issues is less imperative at the start, although they must still be addressed at some point in treatment. In general, the psychotherapeutic strategy for a particular patient depends on the type of pathologic grief (see the discussion in Chapter 13).

Treatment During the Second Six Months Through the Second Year of Bereavement

Some patients will present for treatment later in the course of bereavement, roughly from the second 6 months after a loss and up to the second anniversary of the loss. Sometimes the reason for the delay in presenting for treatment is the traumatic circumstances of the loss, which complicate the process of grief; this must be looked for during the evaluation as mentioned above. Assuming that a careful evaluation has been completed for each patient, treatment planning for patients who present at this time in the course of bereavement is more complicated in general. If the clinical complications persist into the second 6 months of bereavement and beyond, it is time for psychotropic drug treatment and mutual support interventions to be integrated into the treatment plan with psychotherapy. The 6-month time period is not intended as a rigid boundary but rather as a rough guideline that is affected by the clinical situation.

Ms. A (see Chapter 1), who had symptoms of major depression in association with severe, chronic pathologic grief, is an example of the type of patient who presents more than 6 months after a loss. Similar to other patients, she became especially active and insightful in psychotherapy at the time of an anniversary (see Chapter 13).

The psychotherapy during this phase of treatment is primarily psychoeducational and brief, as described in Chapter 13. Six months after a loss, it is still premature to use behavioral strategies as the exclusive thrust of treatment. However, when the patient is approaching the first anniversary of his or her loss, and certainly by the second anniversary of the loss, behavioral techniques can be usefully integrated into the treatment plan when the syndrome of pathologic grief includes prominent avoidant characteristics.

Other patients who present at this time are unable to obtain relief with psychotherapy alone and require vigorous, multidimensional, clinical intervention. While psychotherapy remains a cornerstone for treatment of most patients experiencing a depressive disorder complicating bereavement, antidepressants may be tried concomitantly at this point. If the depressive syndrome is chronic, if it appears to interfere with the expression of grief, if it is associated with severe impairment in functioning, or if psychotic or certain endogenous symptoms are present, the use of antidepressants is often essential in initiating the healing process. This was the nature of treatment for Ms. I (Case 9, in Chapter 9). Also for delusional depressions, such as in the case of Ms. I, an antipsychotic agent may be used before starting an antidepressant (Nelson and Bowers 1978). (A caveat in this regard is to carefully evaluate the symptomatology to establish that severe separation distress is not being misconstrued as psychotic symptomatology, as is discussed in Chapter 12). The guidelines for integrating the treatment of anxiety disorders during bereavement, although less developed, are based on the same kind of rationale as in the case for major depressions.

The primary focus in the early stages of bereavement is the alleviation of symptoms. Once the acute symptomatology is diminished and after the immediate postbereavement adjustment, many patients, such as Ms. E (in Chapter 6), can benefit from mutual support interventions to facilitate their social adjustment. Self-help groups are often instrumental in providing the arena for becoming involved in new social activities, practicing social skills, learning skills for independent living, and making the social transitions of bereavement. Because widowers are less likely to accept these interventions (see Chapter 14), special efforts must be made to clarify the value of social involvement and to design special programs for them. Some bereaved patients will accept referral to a mutual support group in the second 6 months of bereavement; some are still not ready. Following the first anniversary, when patients are isolated, are having difficulty learning new coping skills, or are tied maladaptively to their families or to their in-laws, the situation is ripe for this type of intervention.

Treatment After Two Years of Bereavement

Other patients present for treatment 2 or more years into the course of bereavement. For bereaved patients with chronic, pathologic grief or with chronic dysphoria in the absence of a major depressive episode, more structured, brief, behavioral therapeutic approaches have proven useful (see Chapter 10). In treating these patients, a distinction between the need for abreactive approaches for inhibited grief and the need for goal-oriented approaches fostering autonomy for severe, chronic grief must be recognized (see Chapter 13). Antidepressants may be considered, but as in any patient with dysthymia, medications alone have more limited usefulness than in the treatment of acute, major depressions. Despite this limitation, antidepressants have a role to play in an individualized, multidimensional treatment plan.

Not all patients who present with complications of bereavement can be treated with brief modalities. For some patients the acute loss activates memories of parental losses in childhood that may include a susceptibility to severe depressive reactions as well as lead to the emergence of intense relationship issues in psychotherapy (see Chapter 13). Others will have been subjected to physical or sexual abuse or neglect and abandonment in childhood. Some, but certainly not all (see Chapter 13), acutely bereaved individuals with a history of a major psychiatric disorder, and others with severe personality disorders will require longer-term intervention to treat a reactivation of the underlying psychopathology. Although we do not know for sure, these patients just mentioned probably make up the lion's share of the 20%–30% of patients who do not respond to brief psychotherapy or psychotropic drug treatment. For all these patients, longer-term psychotherapy and pharmacological treatment within the conceptual framework developed in Chapters 12 and 13 is required. For some, longer-term psychotherapy may be required as a rehabilitative intervention to work through the multiple adaptive problems posed by a disorder that has become chronic. Mutual support groups can also be instrumental in helping to address the disability caused by the persistent symptomatic state. Multidimensional, integrated treatment is of the greatest importance in treating these patients, in whom the problems caused by bereavement have become deeply entrenched.

Conclusions

In this chapter, I have presented an overview of treatment for the clinical complications of bereavement and have argued for the need to integrate the main modalities of intervention that are available to help the bereaved patient. To illustrate how treatment can be integrated, I have summarized guidelines for practice. The position on treatment of the complications of bereavement developed in this chapter is based in part on an analysis of the goals of each main type of treatment intervention, showing that there is little overlap, and in part on the results of systematic studies of treatment for the complications of bereavement, which illustrate that different interventions have different effects. The need for integrated, multidimensional treatment is consistent with the concept that the complications of bereavement are complex, potentially chronic disorders of adaptation. Chapters 12–14 discuss the different modalities of treatment and rehabilitation in greater detail for the purpose of elaborating several conceptual issues that are important when implementing treatment.

References

American Psychiatric Association: Diagnostic and Statistical Manual of Mental Disorders, 3rd Edition, Revised. Washington, DC, American Psychiatric Association, 1987

DiMascio A, Weissman MM, Prusoff BA, et al: Differential symptom reduction by drugs and psychotherapy in acute depression. Arch Gen Psychiatry 36:1450–1456, 1979

Engel GL: The need for a new medical model: a challenge for biomedicine. Science 196:129–136, 1977

Engel GL: The clinical application of the biopsychosocial model. Am J Psychiatry 137:535–544, 1980

Jacobs SC, Ostfeld A: The clinical management of grief. J Am Geriatr Soc 28:331–335, 1980

Jacobs SC, Nelson JC, Zisook S: Treating depressions of bereavement with antidepressants: a pilot study. Psychiatr Clin North Am 10:501–510, 1987

Kim K, Jacobs SC: Pathologic grief and its relationship to other psychiatric disorders. J Affect Disord 21:257–263, 1991

Marmar CR, Horowitz MJ, Weiss DS, et al: A controlled trial of brief psychotherapy and mutual help group treatment of conjugal bereavement. Am J Psychiatry 145:203–209, 1988

Mawson D, Marks IM, Ramm L, et al: Guided mourning for morbid grief: a controlled study. Br J Psychaitry 13:185–193, 1981

Murphy GE, Simons AD, Wetzel RD, et al: Cognitive therapy and pharmacotherapy. Arch Gen Psychiatry 41:33–41, 1984

Nelson JC, Bowers MB: Delusional unipolar depression. Arch Gen Psychiatry 35:1321–1328, 1978

Pasternak RE, Reynolds CF, Schlernitzauer M, et al: Acute open-trial nortriptyline therapy of bereavement-related depression in late life. J Clin Psychiatry 52:307–310, 1991

Polak PB, Egan D, Bandenbergh R: Prevention in mental health: a controlled study. Am J Psychiatry 132:146–149, 1975

Potter WZ, Rudorfer MV, Manji H: The pharmacologic treatment of depression. N Engl J Med 325:633–642, 1991

Rynearson EK: Psychotherapy of pathologic grief. Psychiatr Clin North Am 10:487–499, 1987

Weissman MM, Prusoff BA, DiMascio A, et al: The efficacy of drugs and psychotherapy in the treatment of acute depressive episodes. Am J Psychiatry 136:555–558, 1979

Williams WV, Polak PR: Follow-up research in primary prevention: a model of adjustment to acute grief. J Clin Psychol 35:35–45, 1979

Worden JW: Grief Counseling and Grief Therapy: A Handbook for the Mental Health Practitioner. New York, Springer, 1982

Zisook S, DeVaul RA: Grief, unresolved grief, and depression. Psychosomatics 24:247–256, 1983

CHAPTER 12

Pharmacological Treatment of the Complications of Bereavement

As the review in the Chapter 10 revealed, our current knowledge about pathogenetic mechanisms of the clinical complications of bereavement is rudimentary. Moreover, data from controlled clinical trials are quite limited. In these circumstances, the pharmacological treatment of the clinical complications of bereavement is a controversial issue. While acknowledging the controversy and trying to respond to concern about the use of psychotropic drugs during acute bereavement, in this chapter I take the position that these drugs are an important part of the clinician's therapeutic armamentarium. By discussing several conceptual issues that arise in clinical practice, I develop guidelines for pharmacological interventions to treat clinical complications during this time in a patient's life.

The Controversy Over the Use of Psychotropic Drugs

In part, the controversy over the use of psychotropic drugs during acute bereavement exists because two tasks—counseling about the acute, typical manifestations of grief and treatment of psychopathological syndromes—have been confused. This ought to be a conflict that is easy to resolve. No one, to my knowledge, has advocated the use of drugs to manage normal grief, aside from the brief use of antianxiety or hypnotic drugs for the immediate emotional shock and alarm that is typical of the first few days of unexpected bereavement (Hollister 1972; Klein and Blank 1969; Osterweis et al. 1984). Secondly, if in this book I have been successful in creating a wider understanding that 1) the normal resolution of grief is derailed for many bereaved individuals, 2) clinical complications occur for a significant minority of bereaved individuals, and 3) these complications meet criteria for syndromes such as major depressions and anxiety disorders, then the rationale for using psychopharmacological agents will be more convincingly established. In this way, the controversy over the judicious use of pharmacological treatment will be reduced.

Reluctance to implement appropriate pharmacological treatment also stems from inadequate knowledge and experience in the differential diagnosis of the normal manifestations of grief and the psychopathology associated with bereavement. Chapter 9 on differential diagnosis is designed to alleviate this problem by clarifying the best, currently available criteria for diagnosing psychiatric complications. It is my hope that the discussion in Chapter 9 sets the stage for this chapter and Chapters 13 and 14.

The attitudes of our patients also affect the decision to treat. Often, clinicians meeting with mutual support groups for bereaved individuals to discuss clinical complications and their treatment encounter resistance. Opposition occurs not only to the idea that adverse reactions may arise to bereavement but also to the use of medicine during this time in an individual's life. As one woman once said to me, "I don't want the medicine to take my grief away." This concern must be respected and addressed through health education about the effects of psychotropic drugs. As an illustration, the psychiatrist can respond by saying that the antidepressant drugs certainly do not take grief away, no more than they diminish or alter normal emotional reactivity among other patients who use them. On the contrary, as the section below on the treatment of major depressions illustrates, antidepressants seem to allow the expression of grief in some patients whose depression interferes with experiencing normal sadness.

It is important to acknowledge that some observers believe that antianxiety agents have the potential for causing "frozen grief" (Hamlin and Hammersley 1988; Tyrer 1983; see also Marmar's discussion in Rynearson et al. 1990). Most clinicians are attuned to the idea that sedative abuse has the potential for interfering with the normal progression of grief or any psychological process. Yet there is little or no evidence for the idea that the supervised use of antianxiety agents interferes with the resolution of grief in carefully screened patients. The potential for psychological dependence is ever present whenever drugs with sedative properties are used. This is a consideration that argues for their short-term, rather than long-term, use in conjunction with other psychosocial interventions.

Finally, by way of response to bereaved individuals who have doubts about psychotropics, an analogy that can be used in health education to describe the role of a psychiatrist during bereavement is the role of the internist in observing, and intervening when necessary, in the normal process of healing from a physical injury (Engel 1961). Equally useful is the example of the obstetrician who assists the normal process of childbirth. In both cases, judicious intervention can avert a potential complication of the natural physiological process or correct a dysfunctional process if it occurs.

On the one hand, because of the controversy over the use of pharmacological treatments, it is my impression that proper and adequate pharmacological treatment is denied many acutely bereaved individuals who could benefit from it. On the other hand, given the absence of randomized, controlled clinical trials of psychotropic drugs during bereavement, I believe that it is wise to be conservative and careful in the use of these drugs. In an attempt to steer a middle course through this dilemma, I will emphasize the undesirable or adverse effects of using psychopharmacological drugs while presenting the indications for their use.

For the two major classes of medicine that will be discussed—the antianxiety agents and the antidepressants—I believe that the treatment philosophy should be different. Regarding antidepressant drugs, I want to lend cautious encouragement to their use, based on my impression of their benefit, apparent underutilization, and relative safety. With respect to antianxiety drugs, I urge a more conservative attitude, given their limited benefit, their widespread usage, and the higher risks associated with their usage, particularly if unsupervised. Although the conclusions in this chapter are based more on clinical experience than systematic study, that is the current state of the art.

Treatment of Alarm, Emotional Arousal, and Anxiety Disorders

No randomized, controlled clinical trials have been done regarding the use of benzodiazepines to treat the clinical complications of bereavement.

While waiting for these studies to be implemented, in particular for the anxiety disorders associated with bereavement, it is reasonable to seek relevant rationales for their use in the general psychopharmacology literature. In this regard, numerous studies have demonstrated that benzodiazepines are indicated as brief treatments for anxiety disorders such as panic disorder and disabling, generalized anxiety disorder (for a review of the use of benzodiazepines, see Rickels and Schweizer 1987). Another rationale for using benzodiazepines for treating complications of bereavement derives from the literature on the treatment of posttraumatic stress disorder (PTSD) and other stress-related disorders (Forster and Marmar 1991; Tyrer 1983). There is growing evidence from patients with PTSD that benzodiazepines are effective treatment for the emotional and autonomic arousal, severe anxiety, and intrusive symptoms of this syndrome (Forster and Marmar 1991). Related to this clinical experience, there is preclinical evidence that the benzodiazepines reduce the dysregulation in neurophysiological function caused by severe stress and that they can prevent the maladaptive behavioral states associated with experimentally induced traumatic disorders (Bremner et al. 1991; Forster and Marmar 1991). Hence, there is a potential therapeutic role for these drugs in averting the occurrence of posttraumatic stress syndromes. This rationale is applicable to bereavement particularly in the circumstances of traumatic losses. Insofar as sudden, unexpected deaths often cause the same symptomatology as traumatic losses (an issue discussed in Chapter 5), this class of drugs is useful in these circumstances also.

The antianxiety drugs ought to be used during acute bereavement as short-term treatments for subjectively overwhelming symptoms (Hollister 1972; Klein and Blank 1969; Tyrer 1983). They can be used for 3–6 weeks in the framework of an overall plan of treatment that includes behavioral interventions and psychotherapy. Within this framework, the benzodiazepines are indicated as one choice for treating panic disorder, if it emerges during acute bereavement and does not respond to reassurance or psychosocial interventions. The other choice is tricyclic antidepressants, which is the class of drugs that is used for the long-term treatment of panic disorder without incurring the risk of psychological dependence that exists for the benzodiazepines. In some cases, the side effects of tricyclic antidepressants simply cannot be tolerated by a particular patient, or occasionally there are contraindications to the use of tricyclics on an ambulatory basis, such as cardiac conduction defects. It is in these circumstances that benzodiazepines are a useful alternative for the treatment of panic disorder. When using benzodiazepines, not only the panic anxiety but also the anticipatory anxiety regarding specific situations associated with the panic are the target symptoms. Generalized anxiety disorder alone occurs so seldom during acute bereavement (Kim and Jacobs 1991) that it is not practically useful as an indication for treatment. Ordinarily the anxiety symptoms of bereavement coexist as part of a depressive syndrome, and the primary approach to treatment is to decide whether or not to use antidepressants, as is discussed below.

In addition, the benzodiazepines can be used for managing the traumatic distress that intrudes, overwhelms, and incapacitates the survivor and does not respond to psychosocial interventions (Forster and Marmar 1991). Symptoms of arousal and intrusive symptoms such as intrusive imagery, nightmares, startle reactions, hypervigilance, tremor, tachycardia, palpitations, sweating, and difficulty falling and staying asleep are the target symptoms that respond best. Symptoms of avoidance such as emotional numbing, emotional constriction, and feeling stunned and dazed are less likely to improve with this treatment.

Benzodiazepines with an intermediate to long half-life and a rapid onset of action used in customary dosage ranges are the most effective choices for treatment. If the aim is to target insomnia as a symptom, shorter-acting drugs are an alternative.

Risks of Using Benzodiazepines

Although there is potential benefit from using benzodiazepines for bereaved individuals who have developed anxiety disorders as clinical complications, there are also risks. The following five side effects of benzodiazepines should be considered when they are prescribed for use during acute bereavement: 1) sedation, 2) disinhibition of behavior, 3) interference with cognition and memory functions, 4) the risk of becoming dependent on the drug, and 5) the risk of prolonging grief by interfering with its spontaneous resolution.

Sedation. The first concern involves the risk of sedation, which is the most common side effect that occurs with the use of antianxiety drugs.

Accidents are the most worrisome consequence of the sedative effects of these drugs. In this regard, patients must be routinely cautioned about drowsiness while taking benzodiazepines, particularly with regard to driving or using machinery. This is a basic concern in the use of these drugs in any situation.

Disinhibition of behavior. Disinhibition of behavior is an occasional adverse effect of benzodiazepines that can compound the difficulties of managing an acutely bereaved individual in a state of shock. This is illustrated in the following case example of a widow whose husband died suddenly. She had contemplated suicide at other times in the past while intoxicated by alcohol without ever making a suicidal gesture. The prescription of diazepam after confirmation of her husband's death in an emergency room probably contributed to her self-destructive actions by disinhibiting her behavior.

Case 10

Ms. J was a 49-year-old widow whose husband died unexpectedly from an asthma attack in the middle of the night. While in the hospital emergency room after her husband's death, she was prescribed diazepam for sedation. On returning home, she made an attempt to stab herself and, shortly thereafter, to take an overdose of pills. She was prevented by her sons who lived with her. She was taken back to the emergency room where she was severely agitated and reported fleeting auditory and visual hallucinations of her husband. Because of persistent suicidal ideation, she was admitted to the hospital on an emergency certificate. Although there was initial clinical concern about a psychotic illness, the hallucinations subsided shortly after admission during which time she was treated with lorazepam (1 mg bid). She remained sad, tearful, hopeless, helpless, ruminative about the loss of her husband, angry with God for taking him from her, anorectic, fatigued, and insomniac with difficulty falling asleep and middle of the night awakening. No antidepressants were prescribed, although careful consideration was given to doing so. Within a week, Ms. J reported some improvement in her mood, as well as increase in her appetite and energy level.

Ms. J reported abusing alcohol in the past, although she had stopped 5 years earlier when her husband became ill. She also reported a history of a possible anxiety disorder. This was suggestive of agoraphobia with anticipatory anxiety and with constriction of activities but without panic attacks. She was discharged to ambulatory care after 2 weeks with a diagnosis of adjustment disorder with depressed mood and generalized anxiety disorder.

The type of disinhibited reaction shown by Ms. J is most commonly observed if a death is sudden and unexpected or traumatic. The family doctor or consulting psychiatrist is asked to prescribe something to calm down the bereaved individual and facilitate sleep. The frequency of this practice is documented in the repeated observation that about a quarter of acutely bereaved individuals use some sedative or hypnotic at about 2 months after a loss (Zisook et al. 1990). Few people question the intervention because it is usually short term and benign. Indeed, it helps the acutely bereaved individual to settle down and may even serve a preventive purpose (as noted above).

In retrospect there was a failure, admittedly understandable, to provide bereavement counseling to Ms. J in the middle of the night in addition to medication. The opportunity for her to spend the night with a therapist and talk might have averted the suicidal gesture as an expression of her despair. Also there was possibly a failure to appreciate the history of alcohol abuse and of a histrionic character style in this patient (which was not elaborated on in the brief summary above). Both of these histories are risk factors that may be associated with a higher risk of disinhibition of behavior on benzodiazepines (Forster and Marmar 1991).

Interference with cognition and memory functions. Amnestic reactions may also complicate an already difficult process of grief, as the following case illustrates:

Case 11

Ms. K, a 42-year-old acutely bereaved widow, was admitted to a psychiatric inpatient unit after an overdose of Bellergal (phenobarbital 40 mg, ergot 0.6 mg, and belladonna 0.2 mg). Late one night, several hours after her husband was due home from a trip to their summer cottage where he was gardening, a police officer came to her home and told her that her husband had died suddenly from a heart attack. When she heard the news, Ms. K became upset and "combative," requiring restraint by the officer. Her family and clergyman were immediately called and made themselves available to her.

After consultation with her internist, Ms. K was given 2 mg of alprazolam in an attempt to calm her. She reported feeling confused and developing a migraine headache after taking the medicine. She began to take Bellergal for the headache. She took an undetermined amount of Bellergal that was sufficient to cause respiratory depression. The following morning she was discovered semicomatose by her daughter and was brought to the emergency room. Her condition was grave enough to require admission to a medical intensive care unit.

In the first few days after the overdose, Ms. K could neither remember nor explain her intention in taking the Bellergal, although she did not believe that it was suicidal. Moreover, she maintained complete denial of her husband's death. Coincident with the progressive metabolism of the drug, her sensorium improved and the denial of the loss resolved.

Ms. K had no psychiatric history. She did report a history of "sensitivity" to sedative drugs, although the exact meaning of this was unclear. She was kept in the hospital for observation and received a diagnosis of an adjustment disorder with depressive features. No suicidal ideation was noted. A week and a half after admission, she was discharged to an outpatient therapist for counseling.

The use of alprazolam at a high dose apparently complicated this patient's initial reaction to news of the unexpected loss. Her immediate emotional response was characterized by loss of control and amnesia, resembling a dissociative state. It is impossible to sort out the extent to which this response was attributable to the drug and the extent to which it was a function of this patient's acute emotional state and typical style of coping. The absence of a history of emotional dyscontrol or dissociative behavior supports the conclusion of a drug effect.

The magnitude of the risk for these disinhibiting and amnestic reactions to the use of benzodiazepines is difficult to determine. They are not frequently encountered except in the emergency room, and they are probably underreported because they are transient and written off to stress. Nevertheless, these reactions are a reason for caution, particularly in the circumstances of sudden or traumatic losses (Tyrer 1983). Alternate means of comforting the acutely bereaved individual and containing emotions that are out of control must be considered in the form of brief psychotherapy or mutual support. (These are the topics of Chapters 13 and 14.)

Psychological and physical dependence. Yet another risk associated with the use of benzodiazepines is psychological and physical dependence on the drug (Forster and Marmar 1991; Tyrer 1983). As bereaved individuals increasingly seek help in withdrawing from these drugs in special drug dependence units (Hamlin and Hammersley 1988), there is nascent concern about the problem of dependence. On the other hand, longitudinal data on the use of sedatives and hypnotics during acute bereavement do not suggest that they are abused or that dependence occurs (Zisook et al. 1990). While I have never personally encountered a case of dependence that actually began during acute bereavement, I have treated a few patients where I was concerned, because of a history of alcohol or sedative use, about the risk of dependence if such drugs were prescribed.

It seems logical that the risk of becoming dependent is higher when a medicine with addictive potential is used during acute bereavement without careful medical supervision. This is true because the period of emotional distress of bereavement will be predictably prolonged. It will exceed the brief periods of treatment that are routinely recommended for benzodiazepines to minimize concern for the development of tolerance. Therefore, the need to discontinue the benzodiazepine during acute bereavement will ordinarily occur during a time of continuing severe distress. Stopping the medicine compounds the difficulty of dealing with the ongoing distress and postponing termination of the drug runs the risk of psychological dependence.

If a patient's anxious symptoms do not respond to the use of benzodiazepines within 6–8 weeks, thereby leading to their discontinuation, a switch to tricyclic antidepressants should be considered as a way out of this dilemma. The rationale for this strategy rests in the small amount of evidence that tricyclic antidepressants are effective in treating the symptoms of generalized anxiety (Kahn et al. 1986) and PTSD (Frank et al. 1988). It is strengthened if a depressive syndrome is superimposed on the prolonged stress reactions.

As a routine precaution, bereaved patients should be screened and monitored for the risk of dependence when clinicians consider the use of benzodiazepines. Risk factors for dependence are not well established but may include a history of dependence on these drugs and a history of alcohol or substance abuse. When these risk factors are identified, extra caution ought to prevail about the use of these agents.

Prolongation of grief. In addition to the problem of psychological dependence, protracted use of a benzodiazepine during acute bereavement may prolong grief, resulting in what has been referred to as "frozen grief" (Hamlin and Hammersley 1988; Tyrer 1983; see also Mamar's discussion in Rynearson et al. 1990). The mechanism for this reaction is unclear, although it may be related to interference with cognitive processing of the loss or the promotion of greater use of denial and avoidance as coping strategies.

Most psychiatrists can remember substance abusers from their training in psychotherapy who sentimentally expressed their feelings about their problems without progressing in their resolution. This persisted as long as they were locked in a pattern of substance abuse. These patients fail to learn from the experience and adapt by working through it as a problem. This pattern of behavior may underlie the clinical picture of "frozen grief." Such patients can be helped only by engaging them in therapy while concomitantly addressing the substance abuse and withdrawing them from the substance on which they depend. This is an issue that we must be alert to in treating acutely bereaved patients.

There is also some room for skepticism about the potential problem of frozen grief. In an informal survey of colleagues who treat patients with the complications of bereavement, none reported a case of frozen grief secondary to benzodiazepines if the drug was used as part of a comprehensive treatment plan. Furthermore, it is not reported as a problem in the clinical experience of psychiatrists treating posttraumatic stress syndromes (Forster and Marmar 1991). Still, it is sufficiently worrisome as a possible adverse effect of benzodiazepines that it deserves to be monitored.

In summary, there are indications for using benzodiazepines in the symptoms of anxiety disorders (e.g., PTSD and panic disorder) that complicate bereavement. No controlled clinical trials have been completed that definitively establish the benefit of their usage. If they are used in treatment, there are several potential adverse reactions that must be considered. In general, we know that the usage of benzodiazepines during acute bereavement is high. Given the risk of undesirable effects, the use of these medicines must be carefully monitored and included in a total treatment plan in which psychosocial interventions complement the pharmacological treatment. Furthermore, given the absence of proven efficacy of benzodiazepines in treating the complications of bereavement and the relatively high risk of adverse reactions during acute bereavement by comparison with tricyclic antidepressants, I believe that the philosophy about their use ought to be cautious and conservative for the time being.

Treatment of Major Depressions

As was the case for antianxiety agents, no randomized, controlled trials of the use of antidepressants in the treatment of the major depressions of bereavement are available. While psychopharmacologists have recognized the indications for antidepressant medicine during acute bereavement, they have recommended a conservative approach to their use (Hollister 1972; Klein and Blank 1969; Osterweis et al. 1984). Two open trials have been recently completed that support the use of antidepressants. One was a small, noncontrolled clinical series by us (Jacobs et al. 1987), and the other was an open trial of nortriptyline by Pasternak et al. (1991). Beyond these open trials, case reports and anecdotal information, despite their limitations, have indicated that not only antidepressants but also electroconvulsive treatment may be useful in treating depressions during acute bereavement. By definition, the anecdotal reports are not well controlled.

Observations from animal models for studying separation and loss in primates are of some use in bolstering the rationale for using antidepressants to treat depressions of bereavement. Imipramine has been effective not only in reversing the "depressive" behavior and social withdrawal observed in primates who were separated from mothers or siblings but also in preventing the emergence of depressive behaviors in highly aroused primates exposed to the stress of a loss (McKinney 1985). These preclinical studies (cited in McKinney 1985) suggest that antidepressant interventions will be effective in treating depressions of bereaved individuals.

The target symptoms for antidepressants are a depressive mood disturbance, depressive cognition, and the neurovegetative symptoms of major depression. In our small, open trial (Jacobs et al. 1987) it was just these symptoms, similar to the symptoms of major depression in other circumstances that respond to antidepressant treatment, that responded to the psychotropic medicine. In addition, it is my impression that clinical response occurs promptly. There is alleviation of the neurovegetative symptoms, in particular the sleep disorder, within 1 week. Incipient reduction of other symptomatology follows within 2 weeks. These are uncontrolled conclusions that must be tested in randomized, controlled trials. They are consistent with the idea that many of the depressive syndromes seen in our study were first episodes of major depression. The depressions were not chronic syndromes nor as severe as many seen in general clinical practice, and the treatment intervention was made early in the course of illness. These facts distinguish the treatment of the major depressions of bereavement from the treatment of severe major depressions in the hospital and in the psychiatric clinic. They suggest that the treatment of major depressions of bereavement may have unique parameters.

There are interesting issues to consider in the choice of antidepressant medicine. Typically, the depressions of bereavement present as anxious depressions. This is apparent a study (Kim and Jacobs 1991) of the overlap between the depressions and anxiety disorders of bereavement. It is also conspicuous in the series of bereaved, depressed patients that we treated with antidepressants in which 8 of the 10 participants had anxious depressions (Jacobs et al. 1987). These observations lead to a question about whether monoamine oxidase inhibitors (MAOIs), which have been proven effective in the treatment of atypical depressions with anxious and phobic symptomatology, may have special value in treating the anxious depressions of bereavement (Quitkin et al. 1979; Ravaris et al. 1980).

Another salient aspect of atypical depressions for bereavement is rejection sensitivity. This is defined as a personality trait characterized by sensitivity to rejection by others that endures throughout adulthood, resulting in depression with functional impairment (Quitkin et al. 1979). The relationship between this trait and the depressive complications of bereavement is not clear. Conceivably it is a trait that contributes, if present, to the risk of complications in an acutely bereaved individual. Therefore, it is conceivable that MAOIs have a unique role in treating the anxious depressions of bereavement. This interesting issue deserves study. In the meantime, given the dietary restrictions associated with their use and the risk of tyramine reactions if a dietary lapse occurs, the routine use of MAOIs as the first option for treating the depressions of bereavement is not a wise choice.

Another agent recommended for the treatment of anxious depressions is alprazolam (Rudorpher and Potter 1989). There is so little experience using this drug as an antidepressant during bereavement that it is difficult to comment on its importance in treatment. In the broadest sense, its use is discussed in the previous section on using benzodiazepines to treat anxiety disorders. It is probably prudent to be cautious about using alprazolam to treat major depressions of bereavement because of the risks discussed in that section.

Desipramine is also a good choice for treating the depressions of bereavement. Desipramine is a well-established tricyclic antidepressant with known, essentially standardized, efficacy and an advantageous side effect profile (Potter et al. 1991). If it is poorly tolerated, a switch to nortriptyline, which has the same pharmacological advantages, is reasonable. There is no reason to suspect that other tricyclic drugs are not just as useful although they may be associated with a higher risk of undesirable effects. Side effects are not a trivial consideration as bereaved patients may be more reluctant than others to accept antidepressant medicine. The occurrence of side effects can lead to discontinuation of the medicine in a patient ambivalent about its use. When there is no response to a tricyclic antidepressant, MAOIs should be considered, although I have never had to resort to their use in treating depressions of bereavement. The question of whether newer classes of antidepressants, such as selective serotonin reuptake inhibitors like fluoxetine, will prove useful for treating depressions of bereavement will be answered ultimately on the basis of more experience and controlled clinical trials.

When using tricyclic antidepressants, the dosage guidelines are basically the same as those in routine clinical practice (Potter et al. 1991). Regarding dosage, I am impressed that a good clinical response is obtained at moderate dosage levels. For example, it is seldom necessary to raise dosage of desipramine above 150 mg. Regarding duration of treatment, it is my impression that it is possible for the majority of patients to reduce the dosage of desipramine to a maintenance level within a few months. The antidepressant can be successfully discontinued usually within 6 months.

It is important to emphasize once again that these impressions need to be tested in controlled trials. Nevertheless, they are consistent with the nature of the depressions of bereavement as moderately severe, first episodes of illness for which treatment is provided early in the course of illness. As many as 15% of patients may not respond to treatment for depression and develop chronic depressions (Akiskal 1983). During bereavement such patients may be those who present later in the course of bereavement with more deeply entrenched depressive syndromes and those who, for whatever reason (such as concurrent stresses or histories of depressive illnesses), are afflicted with severe, persistent symptomatology. These patients cannot be tapered off medicine quickly. They require longer-term treatment with antidepressants to alleviate their chronic depressions. Dosage should be pushed to therapeutic levels based on blood levels of the antidepressant. At the present time, we do not have the knowledge to predict who will respond to antidepressants. This judgment has to be made by clinical trial and error.

There is a special consideration involving the use of antidepressant medicine to treat depressive symptoms when grief is concurrently an active process. In 20–30 individual patient consultations and in the small systematic series of 10 patients mentioned before (Jacobs et al. 1987), I have repeatedly had the impression that the appropriate use of antidepressant medicine is a crucial intervention for a bereaved individual with prolonged, unresolved grief. The antidepressants, when effective, reduce the depressive symptomatology and seem to free bereaved individuals to resume and work through their grief. Paradoxically, the grief may appear to intensify. The case of Ms. I (originally presented in Chapter 9) illustrates this point.

Case 9 (*continued*)

Ms. I, a 51-year-old widow, was admitted to a psychiatric hospital for the second time since the death of her husband, 2 1/2 years before. She met criteria for major depression (see summary in Chapter 9). She was practically unable to discuss her husband's death, although the unavoidable fact of her loss would repeatedly break through into consciousness. She distinguished between a depressed mood "that goes down to your toes," which she was currently experiencing, and a depressed mood or sadness that occurred in association with intense separation distress.

Ms. I was treated solely with desipramine, with progressive relief of her depressive symptoms over the next 2 weeks. Because her "hallucinations" were atypical and were understood as a severe form of separation distress, antipsychotic drugs were not used. About 3 weeks after beginning the antidepressant treatment she began to report the reemergence of pangs of grief. This coincided with the Thanksgiving and Christmas holidays, events that contributed to the intensification of her feelings. It also coincided with the antidepressant effect of the medicine. The manifestations of grief were no longer subjectively overwhelmingly while she was on the antidepressant and in the supportive context of psychotherapy.

Obviously, the indication for antidepressants were not subtle in this case as it is in some others. This example was chosen to illustrate two points: the salutary effect of the antidepressant medicine and the interplay between depressive symptoms and separation distress, not only throughout the course of this patient's illness (see Chapter 9) but also during treatment. When the separation distress became overwhelmingly severe and unrelenting, depressive symptoms would supervene. When the depressive symptoms were successfully treated, the separation distress reemerged. It was as if alleviation of the depression allowed the normal expression of grief to prevail. In this sense, Case 9 illustrates how a major depression interferes with the normal expression of sadness, reflected perhaps in this patient's report of the distinct quality of mood during the depression. Other patients may describe the disturbance of mood during depression as emptiness or numbness. When the depressive symptoms supervened in the course of Ms. I's illness, she felt she was losing control and going out of her mind. This is a clinical theme that was introduced in Chapter 9 and that is picked up again in Chapter 13. Case 4 (in Chapter 5) illustrated the same effect of adequate treatment of depressive symptoms on the expression of grief and Mr. D's sense of control, although in his case the traumatic aspects of the loss also may have interfered with his grief.

The complex, poorly understood interaction between depression and grief may lead to the suboptimal use of antidepressants. This underutilization may occur secondary to a theoretical concern that the use of medicine to reduce depressive symptoms will interfere with the work of grief. It is presumed that it will interfere with the bereaved individual's opportunity to learn from the challenges posed by the loss and thereby profit from the experience. In my judgment, this is a false concern with respect to antidepressant medicine. It is perhaps some residuum of the hydraulic notion that if feelings are not expressed they will emerge later in another problematic form such as a conversion symptom. As mentioned above and as illustrated in Ms. I's case, on multiple occasions I have seen the opposite of interference result from use of tricyclic antidepressants. Instead, the use of antidepressant medicines is associated with a renewed expression of grief, ordinarily at a level of severity that is not experienced as overwhelming, making the grief available for discussion in psychotherapy. This helps the bereaved individual learn about the grief and how to cope with it.

In many instances, the reemergence of the grief can be deceptive and appear at first as a relapse of the depressive symptoms. Only a careful history will clarify the typical manifestations of separation distress (see Chapter 2). A meticulous examination is essential to avoid the assumption that it is necessary to increase the dosage of antidepressant medication or perhaps stop the medicine based on the judgment that it is not helping. The vicissitudes of separation distress and depressive mood during treatment can be confusing to bereaved individuals if they are left to understand them on their own. With help, the patient will typically recognize the difference between the depressive symptoms and the separation distress. They frequently report that they feel better able to cope with the latter in the absence of the disabling depressive symptoms, as the next case example illustrates:

Case 12

Ms. L, a 43-year-old married mother of two children, presented for evaluation 22 months after her mother's death. Her father had been killed in an automobile accident when she was 13 years old. Ms. L reported her chief complaints as "I can't get over my mother's death" and "I'm depressed." Her grief over the loss of her mother began intensely in the first month of bereavement and had continued without relief.

Ms. L became pregnant shortly after the loss of her mother and delivered her second child about 1 year before the evaluation. The family also moved into a new home shortly after the birth. The demands of the move to a new house and child care after the second birth were oppressive to her. She described a depressive syndrome including melancholic mood, crying, guilt over not loving her husband whom she felt had not been supportive since her mother's death, sleep continuity disturbance, chronic fatigue, loss of interest in social activities, and excessive appetite with a weight gain of 15 pounds. She had had suicidal ruminations 1 year before, which had subsided spontaneously. She expressed fear of losing control, giving up, and becoming crazy.

Ms. L's symptoms failed to respond to psychotherapy alone, despite some early relief. She began treatment with desipramine, which was discontinued

1 week later because she experienced severe sweating as a side effect. One week after starting amitriptyline (eventually reaching a dosage of 100 mg) she began to notice improvement in her sleep pattern and began to feel more rested and energetic. She reported more emotional resilience, illustrated in her capacity to watch the movie *Terms of Endearment*. She began to discuss an ambivalent relationship to her mother.

Two weeks after starting the amitriptyline, Ms. L became concerned that she was relapsing. After a careful assessment of her history and an examination, the story that emerged was one of intense anger toward her mother and reactivation of symptoms of separation distress. Paradoxically, the grief appeared to be intensifying and became the focus of the psychotherapy. The next week she felt as if she wanted "to build a wall around myself," an attitude that was viewed in the light of the imminent anniversary of her mother's death. She acknowledged that she wanted to avoid the anniversary and viewed her grief as self-pity, as her mother would have seen it. With encouragement, she focused on the anniversary. Her distress over it subsided before the actual day. Six weeks after starting the antidepressant treatment, the symptoms of depression were virtually gone with the exception of difficulty falling asleep. Ms. L then began to critically examine her relationship to her husband and his family, her relationship to her sister strained by a dispute over the estate of her mother, and childrearing issues.

As this case example illustrates, the reemergence or apparent intensification of separation distress while using antidepressants can be a source of confusion not only to the patient but also to the physician. This phenomenon can lead to the false conclusion that the antidepressants are ineffective and to the decision to raise dosage or discontinue the medicine.

Risks of Using Tricyclic Antidepressants

Generally speaking, the risk of adverse reactions from the use of a tricyclic antidepressant drug such as desipramine is minimal if usage is well monitored by a physician. Aside from routine caution about anticholinergic side effects, cardiac conduction effects, and postural hypotension, two special considerations about the use of tricyclic antidepressants during bereavement have arisen in my practice. One is pushing dosage too high, thereby exaggerating the risk of general side effects, and the other is the occurrence of pharmacological panic reactions.

Prescribing too high a dosage. The first concern was illustrated as a potential problem in Ms. L's case, where the successful use of amitriptyline was associated with the intensification of separation distress. Unless the nature of the symptomatology is clarified, there is a tendency to increase the dosage of the antidepressant when it is not necessary in my experience. Two strategies can counteract this tendency. One is to carefully evaluate the symptoms and proceed slowly. The other is to use drug blood levels, if they are available, to affirm that the patient is in a therapeutic range. Having reassured themselves, clinicians can then avoid the tendency to push dosage to a level associated with a higher risk of side effects. In most cases, clinical judgment of the symptoms alone is adequate without drug levels.

Occurrence of pharmacological panic reactions. Tricyclic antidepressants that affect norepinephrine systems can also precipitate or aggravate panic attacks during the initial phase of treatment in patients vulnerable to panic disorder. Clinical suspicion of an increased risk of this complication ordinarily comes from a careful psychiatric history.

Case 2 (in Chapter 2) as an example of pathologic grief related to the sudden, unexpected death of a spouse, illustrates this adverse reaction. Because of a recurrent depressive syndrome that occurred 2 years after her husband's death, Ms. B was started on nortriptyline. This antidepressant caused essentially the same adverse reaction that desipramine had produced the year before. Ms. B described it as a state of episodic alarm and panic over her depressive symptoms. This state was associated with the fear that she would lose control and need hospitalization. In retrospect, there were clues that this patient might have been at risk for this complication, such as the occurrence of nighttime panic attacks early in her grief (Mellman and Uhde 1989). Sometimes these episodes of panic were associated with reunion dreams of her deceased husband and sometimes not. The medicine was discontinued after a short, inadequate trial, and Ms. B was treated with psychotherapy alone.

Another example that comes to mind is a case of pharmacological "mania," according to the medical records that accompanied the patient when she was referred for consultation. This patient had a strong history of separation anxiety, including school phobia, inability to leave home until she married, and extreme unhappiness in her marriage until she adopted children, whose care gave her vicarious pleasure. This history suggested to me that the adverse reaction may have been pharmacological panic masquerading as mania because of the presence of severe agitation and the appearance of pressured speech as part of the symptomatology. This type of adverse reaction to antidepressants has been observed in patients with panic disorder, and it is recommended that dose be increased slowly to avoid it. It is not commonly described in patients with major depression or anxious depressions. In the circumstances of bereavement, which increase the risk not only of major depressive syndromes but also panic disorder (see Chapter 2), perhaps it is not surprising to find patients with dual vulnerability, if not actual mixed depressed and anxious syndromes. While pharmacological panic reactions can be observed with the use of antidepressant drugs during bereavement, they are not common in my experience.

In conclusion, probably the most salient issue with regard to the use of tricyclic antidepressants for treating unremitting depressions of bereavement is their underutilization given their relative safety. It is my impression from referrals for consultation that many bereaved individuals who have depressive syndromes are being treated inadequately or are not being treated at all with antidepressant medicine. Controlled studies still need to be done to prove the efficacy and establish the specific parameters of this relatively safe treatment during bereavement. The underutilization of tricyclic antidepressants is related in part to the poorly understood relationship between grief and depression, which causes practitioners to be too conservative in their application. The suboptimal treatment of depressions of bereavement is also probably related to uncertainty about when it is appropriate to prescribe antidepressants, an issue in differential diagnosis that I review in detail in Chapter 9. Antidepressant treatment is not without risks and must be undertaken by a skilled psychopharmacologist, optimally as part of an overall treatment plan that includes psychotherapy. In these circumstances, this class of medicines is reasonably safe, and I believe that our treatment philosophy should be positive but cautious.

Treatment of Pathologic Grief

Pathologic grief, diagnosed by the criteria that are discussed in Chapter 9, may occur in the absence of a major depressive syndrome or an anxiety disorder. Although this is uncommon according to one study (Kim and Jacobs 1991), occurring only once in 16 cases of pathological grief (6%), it is a possibility. Is there a rationale for treating such patients with drugs?

Pathologic grief is not an official or universally agreed upon diagnostic entity. Under the circumstances it is not surprising that no systematic studies of pharmacological interventions have been carried out. Nevertheless, it is useful to consider the idea that antidepressants may be an effective treatment when separation anxiety is severe, persistent, and incapacitating. The evidence is inferential and anecdotal. By inference, it is reasonable to consider pathologic grief as a form of separation anxiety disorder in adults with some relationship to panic disorder (Gittelman and Klein 1984). There is no reason to expect that separation anxiety disorder just disappears after age 18, as it is defined in DSM-III-R (American Psychiatric Association 1987). Furthermore, there can be little doubt that bereavement is a potential precipitant of separation anxiety disorder in adult life just as school matriculation is in childhood (Bowlby 1977). Controlled clinical trials of antidepressants for treating separation anxiety disorder in children have been promising (Gittelman and Klein 1971). It is reasonable, therefore, to consider that antidepressants will be helpful in treating severe separation distress as part of pathologic grief.

There is some anecdotal evidence that antidepressants are effective in treating severe separation distress in adults. In one report (Shuchter 1982), the cases of two patients with severe separation distress are described; one patient was successfully treated with doxepin and the other with amitriptyline. One of the cases had a "secondary depression" that also responded to the medicine; the other case did not have a major depression.

The coexistence of depression is an important issue because data from the series of patients that my colleagues and I treated with desipramine do not support the idea of a direct effect of antidepressants on separation distress (Jacobs et al. 1987). In our study, we measured separation distress at two times—before and after treatment—in 7 of the 10 participants. Six of the 7 had substantial reductions in the intensity of separation distress while taking the antidepressant. However, this effect was not independent of an antidepressant effect because all had reductions in depression scores as well.

Also as discussed above, I have often noted that patients report continuing if not renewed grief while under treatment with antidepressants. In regard to the present discussion, the salient point is that the separation distress is experienced at a subjectively more manageable level of intensity following usage of antidepressants whereas previously it was experienced as overwhelming. These observations suggest that the effect of antidepressants is primarily on the depressive symptoms. In the final analysis, controlled studies will need to be done to separate the effect of antidepressants on depressive symptoms from their effect on separation distress.

Treatment of Psychotic Symptoms

Two cautionary notes on the use of antipsychotic drugs during acute bereavement are necessary.

Treating chronically ill, psychotic, bereaved patients. The first caution regards the inappropriate use of antipsychotic medication to "protect" chronically ill, psychotic patients during this time of stress. Usually there is an assumption that any acutely bereaved individual with a history of psychotic illness will need to have an augmented dosage or resume antipsychotic drugs during bereavement, based on the belief that chronically ill patients with a severe mental disorder are more vulnerable at this time in their lives. However, a search of the literature on bereavement in schizophrenic patients uncovers no evidence to either support this assumption or to guide clinicians when treating chronically ill, psychotic patients during bereavement.

In my own practice, I do not have the clinical impression that psychotic decompensation is common after a loss. I have been consulted a few times about the management of acutely bereaved, chronically ill, psychotic patients and have routinely recommended that there be no automatic change in dosage of medicine. Instead, I have recommended that the early signs of psychotic decompensation be monitored as they ordinarily would be. In each case, the course of illness did not warrant increased dosage. At the same time, to more usefully focus the issue of how to help, I recommended bereavement counseling to assist these chronically ill individuals to learn what to expect about the adjustment that they face in the immediate future. This type of treatment is more to the point and is the same type that would be recommended for other bereaved patients.

Treating symptoms that appear to be psychotic. The second issue about antipsychotic drugs involves the use of these agents to manage severe manifestations of separation distress that are misconstrued as psychotic symptoms. This confusion is more likely to arise if there is an exaggerated quality to the emotional expression of the patient. The following case of Mr. H (presented originally in Chapter 8) illustrates this issue:

Case 8 (*continued*)

Mr. H, a 47-year-old personnel director whose partner had died from complications due to acquired immunodeficiency syndrom (AIDS) 9 months before, was referred for outpatient follow-up. He had just been discharged from a 3-month psychiatric hospitalization. He was being treated with perphenazine (24 mg at bedtime), lithium carbonate (300 mg qid), tranylcypromine (10 mg bid), and diazepam (10 mg at bedtime). On my first examination of him in the hospital, in addition to the dramatic and importuning quality of his presentation, I was impressed with two processes: his severe separation distress (or pathologic grief) and his major depression (see Chapter 8). The auditory hallucination of his lover's voice was not a convincing psychotic symptom in my judgment, not only because it was not experienced as coming from outside of him but also because of it existed as an isolated symptom of psychosis. In other words, the agitation and auditory hallucinations could be viewed as severe manifestations of separation distress that coexisted in relationship to an atypical depressive syndrome. In addition, I was immediately struck by his style of relating to me, which had dependent and histrionic qualities.

Mr. H was discharged to my care. I began to interpret his symptoms in the light of my evaluation and attachment theory. Acknowledging the dramatic quality of his symptomatic picture, I clarified for him my belief that a great loss deserved no less a grief, an idea that resonated with his feelings. After I conveyed to him that I understood the intensity and specificity of his distress, the psychotherapy appeared to reduce the flamboyance of his emotional expression. In addition, by accepting him into treatment and emphasizing my commitment to help him, his need to depend on an expert was addressed. At the same time, I established a short-term framework for therapy and focused the tasks of recovery on his becoming independent again. Although I never told him that his continued treatment was contingent on his making progress, it was strongly implicit, as I was firm about an expectation that he take care of himself and make improvement. Gradually, I tapered the lithium carbonate, then the antipsychotic drug, and finally the benzodiazepine over a period of 3 months. The tapering of the antipsychotic drug was delayed by an exacerbation of the intensity of the deceased partner's voice at the first anniversary of his death. Eventually, the antidepressant was successfully discontinued 6 months after referral without relapse of the depressive symptoms. I am not aware of Mr. H's having any relapses in the past 4 years.

The treatment response of this bereaved man is not unique either in the effectiveness of an attachment perspective for treatment (discussed more in Chapter 13) or the discontinuation of the medications. In one study (Lieberman 1978), all 19 patients, including schizophrenic and endogenously depressed patients, were removed from somatic therapies by the end of a brief, behaviorally oriented psychotherapy for pathologic grief.

Another example is the case of Ms. I (originally presented in Chapter 9 and further discussed above). She might have been considered psychotically depressed given her "bizarre" thinking that she was communicating with her husband, her conviction about his spirit entering her, and the auditory "hallucinations" of his voice. On this assumption, she might have been treated with antipsychotics. Nevertheless, antipsychotic treatment would not be indicated if these same symptoms were viewed as severe separation distress. The fact that all her symptoms concerned her deceased husband was a clue to their nature. Actually, she did well on antidepressants alone.

Yet another example is the case of Ms. K (presented above) whose denial of her husband's death in the first few days of bereavement was so complete that her attending physician was worried about psychotic disorganization. When I was consulted, I recommended that the antipsychotics be withheld for the time being. As described above, the denial and dissociative state resolved spontaneously, perhaps coincident with the metabolism of the benzodiazepine that she had been given.

It should be emphasized that illusions and hallucinations are common during conjugal bereavement, occurring in 47% of cases (Rees 1971). Typically, the illusions of bereavement involve feeling the presence of the deceased spouse. Hallucinations per se are less common. Fourteen percent of bereaved individuals report visual hallucinations and 13% report auditory hallucinations. Often these hallucinations are not frightening, although they are considered to be peculiar by most of the patients that have reported them to me. In elderly, bereaved individuals who have visual impairment, visual hallucinations may be related to sensory deprivation in a pattern recognized as Charles Bonnet syndrome (Adair and Keshavan 1988; Alroe and McIntyre 1983). These phenomena do not require pharmacological treatment, but rather the opportunity to discuss the loss and recognition of the sensory deprivation.

Conclusions

Given the absence of randomized, controlled trials of pharmacological treatments for the depressive and anxious complications of bereavement, it is reasonable for the time being to follow a cautious middle ground in thinking about the use of psychotropic drugs for treating patients who are recently bereaved. Despite this conservative stance, it is important to emphasize a basic thesis in this chapter: that pharmacological interventions can make a crucial difference in helping bereaved individuals who have clinical complications and whose grief is not resolving spontaneously. Judicious pharmacological treatment in conjunction with skillful psychotherapy and mutual support interventions is an important part of the therapeutic armamentarium that we have as psychiatrists to help bereaved patients.

The two main classes of psychotropic drugs that may be indicated during bereavement are the antidepressants and the antianxiety agents. Antidepressants, though reasonably safe, tend to be underutilized and ought to be considered as part of treatment for depressions of bereavement. Antianxiety agents, despite widespread use, are associated with several undesirable side effects and have a more limited application to treating the arousal and anxiety disorders of bereavement. These conclusions, based on current practice and the limited literature on clinical trials during bereavement, ought to be tested systematically in randomized, controlled trials.

In Chapter 13, I discuss psychotherapeutic interventions that ought to be integrated into the overall treatment plan for patients receiving pharmacological treatment.

References

Adair DK, Keshavan MS: The Charles Bonnet syndrome and grief reaction (letter). Am J Psychiatry 145:895–896, 1988

Akiskal HS: Dysthymic disorder: psychopathology of proposed chronic depressive subtypes. Am J Psychiatry 140:11–20, 1983

Alroe CJ, McIntyre JNM: Visual hallucinations: the Charles Bonnet syndrome and bereavement. Med J Aust 2:674–675, 1983

American Psychiatric Association: Diagnostic and Statistical Manual of Mental Disorders, 3rd Edition, Revised. Washington, DC, American Psychiatric Association, 1987

Bowlby J: The making and breaking of affectional bonds. Br J Psychiatry 130:201–210, 1977

Bremner JD, Southwick SM, Charney DS: Animal models for the neurobiology of trauma. PTSD Research Quarterly 2:1–7, 1991

Engel GL: Is grief a disease? A challenge for medical research. Psychosom Med 23:18–22, 1961

Forster P, Marmar CR: Benzodiazepines in acute stress reactions: benefits, risks and controversies, in Benzodiazepines in Clinical Practice. Edited by Byrne PR. Washington, DC, American Psychiatric Press, 1991

Frank JB, Kosten TR, Giller EL, et al: A randomized clinical trial of phenelzine and imipramine for posttraumatic stress disorder. Am J Psychiatry 145:1289–1291, 1988

Gittelman R, Klein DF: Controlled imipramine treatment of school children. Arch Gen Psychiatry 25:204–211, 1971

Gittelman R, Klein DF: Relationship between separation anxiety and panic and agoraphobic disorders. Psychopathology 17:56–65, 1984

Hamlin M, Hammersley D: Benzodiazepines following bereavement. Paper presented at the International Conference on Grief and Bereavement in Contemporary Society, London, July 12–15, 1988

Hollister L: Psychotherapeutic drugs in the dying and bereaved. Journal of Thanatology 2:623–629, 1972

Jacobs SC, Nelson JC, Zisook S: Treating depressions of bereavement with antidepressants: a pilot study. Psychiatr Clin North Am 10:501–510, 1987

Kahn RJ, McNair DM, Lipman RS, et al: Imipramine and chlordiazepoxide in depressive and anxiety disorders, II: efficacy in anxious outpatients. Arch Gen Psychiatry 43:79–85, 1986

Kim K, Jacobs SC: Pathologic grief and its relationship to other psychiatric disorders. J Affect Disord 21:257–263, 1991

Klein DF, Blank HR: Psychopharmacological treatment of bereavement and its complications, in Death and Bereavement. Edited by Kutscher AH. Springfield, IL, Charles C Thomas, 1969, pp 299–305

Lieberman S: Nineteen cases of morbid grief. Br J Psychiatry 132:159–163, 1978

McKinney WT: Separation and depression: biological markers, in The Psychobiology of Attachment and Separation. Edited by Reite M, Field T. New York, Academic Press, 1985, pp 201–222

Mellman TA, Uhde TW: Sleep panic attacks: new clinical findings and theoretical implications. Am J Psychiatry 146:1204–1207, 1989

Osterweis M, Solomon F, Green M (eds): Bereavement: Reactions, Consequences and Care. Washington, DC, National Academy Press, 1984

Pasternak RE, Reynolds CF, Schlernitzauer M, et al: Acute open-trial nortriptyline therapy of bereavement-related depression in late life. J Clin Psychiatry 52:307–310, 1991

Potter WZ, Rudorpher MV, Manji H: The pharmacologic treatment of depression. N Engl J Med 325:633–642, 1991

Quitkin F, Rifkin A, Klein DL: Monoamine oxidase inhibitors. Arch Gen Psychiatry 36:749–760, 1979

Ravaris CL, Robinson DS, Ives JO, et al: Phenelzine and amitriptyline in the treatment of depression. Arch Gen Psychiatry 37:1075–1080, 1980

Rees WD: The hallucinations of widowhood. BMJ 4:37–41, 1971

Rickels K, Schweizer EE: Current pharmacotherapy of anxiety and panic, in Psychopharmacology: The Third Generation of Progress. Edited by Meltzer HY. New York, Raven, 1987, pp 1193–1203

Rudorpher MV, Potter WZ: Antidepressants: a comparative review of the clinical pharmacology and therapeutic use of the "newer" versus the "older" drugs. Drugs 37:712–738, 1989

Rynearson EK, Jacobs SC, Marmor CR: Pathologic grief. Psychiatric Update, 10:1–9, 1990

Shuchter SR: The depression of widowhood reconsidered: the role of antidepressants. Paper presented at the annual meeting of the American Psychiatric Association, Toronto, May 11–15, 1982

Tyrer P: The place of tranquilizers in the management of stress. J Psychosom Res 27:385–389, 1983

Zisook S, Shuchter SR, Mulvihill M: Alcohol, cigarette, and medication use during the first year of widowhood. Psychiatric Annals 20:318–326, 1990

CHAPTER 13

Psychotherapy of the Complications of Bereavement

In beginning a discussion of psychotherapy for bereaved patients, it is useful to distinguish between routine bereavement counseling for all newly bereaved individuals and psychotherapy for bereaved individuals with clinical complications (Worden 1982). (For more on routine counseling for the purpose of facilitating normal grief, see Worden 1983.) Volunteers supported by professionals, trained counselors associated with funeral homes, or self-help group programs most often provide routine bereavement counseling. Psychotherapists with professional training ordinarily take responsibility for psychotherapy for bereaved individuals with clinical complications. This division of labor is consistent with the complicated, multidimensional treatment tasks, the sophisticated content of therapy concerning coping and unconscious functioning, and the subtle relationship issues inherent in the therapeutic task. In this chapter, I focus on psychotherapy for acutely bereaved individuals with identified psychiatric complications of bereavement.

Several books and articles are available on psychotherapy that have varying degrees of specificity for treating the complications of bereavement. In one book, Worden (1982), an experienced therapist, outlines a problem-oriented, psychodynamic approach to psychotherapy for patients with complications of bereavement. In another book (Horowitz et al. 1984a) and a series of articles (Horowitz et al. 1984b; Marmar et al. 1988), the authors describe a strategy of brief, dynamic psychotherapy for patients with stress-response syndromes. By definition, these patients are faced with current stressors, many of which are bereavements. These two approaches to psychotherapy were developed rather specifically as treatments for the psychiatric complications of bereavement.

Other books and related articles are available that develop models of treatment for major depression that are less specifically related to the circumstances of bereavement. These include cognitive behavioral therapy (Beck et al. 1979; Elkin et al. 1989; Murphy et al. 1984; Rush et al. 1977; Simons et al. 1986) and interpersonal psychotherapy (DiMascio et al. 1979; Elkin et al. 1989; Klerman et al. 1984; Weissman et al. 1979). Of the two, interpersonal therapy (IPT) seems to have special application to depressions of bereavement, which was apparently evident to the developers of IPT themselves. For example, they include in their manual an extended case example of a depressed widow confronting the death of her husband (Klerman et al. 1984).

The application of IPT to depressions of bereavement is not surprising when the aims and techniques of the therapy are reviewed. In IPT, grief is one of four problem areas identified as being a situational context commonly associated with major depressions. In fact, all the problem areas identified by IPT commonly arise in treating patients with complications of bereavement: 1) grief, 2) role disputes (such as residual conflicts involving the deceased individual), 3) role transitions (as bereaved individuals adjust to their new status), and 4) interpersonal deficits (usually because certain social skills of the bereaved individual have become rusty). The goal of IPT is to facilitate recovery from acute, major depression by relieving the depressive symptoms and by helping the patient develop more effective strategies for dealing with the current, interpersonal problems and social maladjustment associated with the acute depressive symptoms. In this perspective, IPT is less nonspecific for bereavement than it would seem on first appraisal.

Another book (Frank 1973) provides a cornerstone for contemporary thinking about the fundamental elements of psychotherapy. According to the view expressed by this author, psychotherapy is an art of persuasion and healing for individuals who are failing in their efforts to adapt to life's challenges and who have become demoralized and fearful. Through clarification of the problem, exploration of solutions, and explanation of the emotional response to the crisis, the psychotherapist supports the patient and facilitates his or her adaptation to the challenge.

All of the psychotherapeutic models represented in the literature reviewed above either incorporate concepts of adaptation as background theory or emphasize the identification of current problems and their solution as a task of therapy. All of them emphasize brief, active treatment. These treatment models, based on therapeutic strategies whose efficacy has been proven in controlled trials, are consistent with the concept of the clinical complications of bereavement as disorders of adaptation and provide basic concepts for developing an approach to the brief psychotherapy of the complications of bereavement.

Using this literature on psychotherapy as background, in this chapter I emphasize the psychoeducational tasks of psychotherapy during bereavement. A psychoeducational approach is recommended with the caveats that 1) the approach is integrated into a psychodynamically sophisticated appreciation of the patient's adaptation to the loss, 2) attention is given to interpersonal problems, and 3) it is understood that cognitive-behavioral interventions are often useful as specific therapeutic strategies at certain points in the course of bereavement, particularly when grief has become chronic. Before entering a discussion of the psychoeducational tasks of psychotherapy for pathologic grief, it is important to emphasize the principle of individualized treatment.

Matching Different Psychotherapeutic Approaches With Different Syndromes

Much of the early psychotherapy literature on the treatment of pathologic grief assumed that effective treatment is counterphobic and confrontational. Although these studies originated from the disparate theoretical backgrounds of psychoanalysis (Volkan and Showalter 1968) and behavioral psychology (Hodgkinson 1982; Lieberman 1978; Mawson et al. 1981; Melges and DeMaso 1980; Ramsay 1977), they all emphasized the necessity of facing up to the irrevocability of the loss. For behaviorally oriented clinicians, the treatment is predicated on the presumed similarity of chronic unresolved grief and phobias (Ramsay 1977). The therapists presumably accomplish their goals by helping the patient face up to the feared experience of bereavement, which, in the expression of grief, is ordinarily a painful process. These treatment approaches are designed as brief interventions for chronic, unresolved grief, and clinicians employ *guided* or *forced mourning* procedures. Often, the intervention culminates in a gesture of giving up the attachment and saying goodbye. While this literature has interesting lessons for psychotherapeutic interventions, counterphobic and cathartic techniques do not meet the needs of every bereaved patient by any means.

The essential issue gleaned from a review of the literature and clinical experience is that no single approach to therapy serves the needs of all patients (Horowitz 1976; Horowitz et al. 1984a; Lieberman 1978; Parkes and Weiss 1983; Rynearson 1987a). Eventually treatment will become more tightly connected to our growing knowledge of mechanisms of pathogenesis and specific syndromes of pathologic grief. These different mechanisms and syndromes are discussed next.

Type of Pathologic Grief

Parkes and Weiss's formulation (1983) of the treatment of bereaved patients provides an example of greater specificity. These authors emphasized the need for different therapeutic interventions for the different types of pathologic grief that they identified in their study of middle-aged and younger widows and widowers. For sudden, unexpected grief syndromes they recommended supportive and pacing strategies to address the overwhelming reality of the loss and the feelings engendered by it. For ambivalent, delayed grief they recommended more confrontational or counterphobic strategies to address the avoidance of grief. For dependent, prolonged grief, they recommended therapeutic strategies that were sympathetic but also goal oriented and insistent on the development of autonomy. For dependent grief syndrome, the continuation of therapy itself becomes contingent on efforts by the patient to try new approaches to coping independently, rather than becoming dependent on the therapist as the current object in a series of such dependencies (Parkes and Weiss 1983). Each strategy is styled to the particular problems and the course of bereavement for each syndrome. The differentiation of the treatment tasks provided by these authors is useful to counteract the impression given in the literature on behaviorally oriented treatment of chronic, pathologic grief that the universal problem is avoidance of a feared experience, irrespective of the nature of the syndrome of pathologic grief or the personality style of the patient.

Nature of the Death

Rynearson's formulation of treatment (1987b) builds on our evolving model for understanding and treating pathologic grief that results from traumatic losses. This formulation emphasized the necessity of recognizing the difference in needs of bereaved individuals who are suffering from traumatic losses. After a traumatic loss, the survivor must cope not only with the sense of desolation but also with the consequences of the trauma. These are feelings of victimization caused by the trauma; a fear of recurrent violence expressed as a heightened, perceived threat of personal violation; and, in the case of suicide, the existential problem of choice of death over life by an intimate. These three "V's" of traumatic deaths—victimization, violation, and volition (choice of death over life)—cannot be ignored when helping the bereaved survivor (Rynearson 1987b). Thus the psychotherapy of clinical complications after a traumatic death must attend not only to the loss but also to the sequelae of the trauma. In fact, therapists who have worked extensively with those who have experienced trauma have suggested that these are sequential tasks, with the need to address the trauma and its consequences taking precedence (Lindy et al. 1983; Pynoos and Nader 1992).

Patients' Character Traits

By enlarging the therapeutic model to include character traits, a group of psychotherapists interested in traumatic neuroses (Horowitz 1976; Horowitz et al. 1984a, 1984b, 1984c, 1986; Marmar et al. 1988) amplified the concern for personality style apparent in the study discussed above (Parkes and Weiss 1983). As a result, they described a therapeutic approach specifically designed for each patient. They defined pathologic grief as a maladaptive ego state produced by the activation of latent self-images. According to these authors, the therapist evaluates the need for expressive or mitigatory interventions in order to help the patient modulate his or her affective experience and examines the maladaptive ego state in the context of the clinical relationship. Thus these authors considered not only the level of emotional distress with which a patient must cope for the purpose of regulating the affect that emerges in therapy, but also the ego state, typical character traits, latent self-images, and role models that shaped the patient's means of coping (Horowitz et al. 1980, 1984a).

Different character styles require different therapeutic techniques (Horowitz 1984a). For example, bereaved individuals with an obsessional style may easily find intellectual explanations for their experience as the therapist poses obvious questions about the loss, thereby enhancing their sense of control. On the other hand, the same patients may need to be more insistently encouraged to explore the emotional aspects of the experience. Bereaved individuals with a hysterical cognitive style may have little difficulty expressing the emotional aspects of their experience, at least superficially. These patients may require more insistent interpretation of the meaning and conceptual implications of the loss, which are often more obvious to the therapist or the family than to the patient. Furthermore, these authors (Horowitz et al. 1980, 1984a) clarified that each patient will interact with the therapist in a way that reflects the self-images and role relationships that govern his or her behavior with intimates and authority figures. Attachment theory, which uses the idea that cognitive biases about attachment are activated by a loss and predetermine the risk of pathologic grief, provides a perspective on treatment that is similar to that of Horowitz and colleagues, though it is less well spelled out as a therapeutic approach (Bowlby 1977a, 1977b, 1980).

The implication of these concepts is that the patient will treat the therapist as if he or she were the parent or spouse that has been lost and try to work out attachment issues that were unsettled between them. This is particularly true in two circumstances, according to my experiences. One is the instance of acutely bereaved individuals who have experienced a loss in childhood. In this case, feelings about the remote loss are activated by the recent loss (see discussion below on past losses). The other is the instance of sudden, unexpected losses in which no opportunity was available to address unresolved conflicts with the individual who died; these conflicts are then played out in the relationship with the therapist. By including an understanding of latent role relationships or cognitive biases and how they affect the therapeutic alliance, the therapist can introduce a new dimension of learning about the attachments of the patient into the experience and treatment of grief.

Implications of Different Types of Intervention

The basic principle under consideration in this section is the idea that different patients require different approaches to psychotherapy depending on the nature of the pathologic grief and their character style. Moreover, the same patient needs different approaches depending on the stage of bereavement and the course of his or her adaptation to the loss (see the discussion in Chapter 11). While individualized psychotherapy emphasizes a supportive, interpersonal, interpretive, insistent, or behavioral technique, depending on the needs of the patient, it also integrates all these strategies over time for particular patients.

Another fundamental implication of this discussion is the idea that psychotherapy ought to be individualized to conform to the unique personality style and past experiences of the patient. A developmental history with a special focus on attachments, caregiving, and losses provides a cornerstone for understanding the current problem of a patient in the context of that patient's life history. In addition to understanding the patient's developmental history, the recognition of the patient's character traits along with a knowledge of the vicissitudes of grief, an understanding of the individual's unique coping style, and an appreciation of the current social dynamics of the patient's family life provide the foundation for a psychodynamically informed therapy. Psychotherapy individualized in this manner offers the best hope of compliance and also provides opportunities for therapeutic interpretations of maladaptive (or successful) behavior patterns that can clarify the reaction to the current loss.

Psychoeducation as a Cornerstone of Therapy

The discussion of the tasks of grief in Chapter 7 sets the stage for considering the psychoeducational objectives of psychotherapy. These objectives are introduced in that chapter within the discussion of adaptation in order to illustrate the challenges with which a bereaved individual must cope. The tasks of grief include emotional tasks, such as experiencing the pain of the loss; cognitive tasks, such as changing one's assumptions about the world in light of the absence of the individual who has died; and social tasks, such as developing new skills and role models (Raphael 1975; Shuchter 1986; Worden 1982). These are the tasks that therapists must assist bereaved individuals to accomplish when their grief does not resolve spontaneously. The therapist does this by using a variety of techniques, not the least of which is to teach about bereavement.

It is fundamental, in my judgment, to emphasize psychoeducation as a cornerstone of the therapeutic endeavor. Psychoeducation in therapy involves helping the patient learn about the inevitable life experience of a loss and the various steps that can be taken to cope with it. One therapist has emphasized education as a major part of grief counseling for the general population of bereaved individuals (Worden 1982). It is also my position that psychoeducation is central to the treatment task. I believe that it is hard to place enough emphasis on the value of reducing the mystery and fear of the experience of grief. This demystifying is accomplished through health education about normal grief and its complications as well as an exposition of the tasks of social adjustment over the longer haul. A basic task for the therapist is to provide reasonable expectations for the patient based on current knowledge of bereavement and to offer professional support. Knowledge of the course of grief provides a framework for weathering the distress and a context for the symptomatic treatments indicated.

On the one hand, the psychoeducational, therapeutic task may seem obvious. On the other hand, there are aspects of grief that routinely require some explanation but that are ignored unless the therapist has a thorough knowledge of normal and pathologic grief. For example, many bereaved people feel angry at the individual who has died and left them behind. They worry that this feeling is unreasonable and irrational. It is useful to acknowledge these frequently encountered feelings, even if it is only to say that many others have experienced the same thing, thereby validating their occurrence as a common experience. In addition, these angry feelings can be placed in the context of normal grief as a manifestation of an innate human tendency to protest unexpected, potentially threatening, and sometimes blatantly traumatic separations.

The Tasks of Psychoeducation

In a sense, a wide spectrum of counterphobic therapeutic strategies are encompassed by the rubric of psychoeducation. These range from straightforward teaching to gradual or direct confrontation with feared situations or things. The nature of this effort is consistent with the impression obtained from the literature on the psychotherapy of bereavement that psychotherapy is most effective in addressing the tendency of many bereaved patients to avoid their grief. The pace varies according to the patient; for example, it is slow for those bereaved patients who feel overwhelmed. While the major thrust of psychotherapy is counterphobic and carried out at a supportive pace, a short-term framework for psychotherapy creates incentive for the patient to achieve as much autonomy as possible during the opportunity that the treatment provides (see discussion below on the length of therapy).

Learning About Separation Distress

In my experience, the most consistently puzzling aspects of grief that require some explanation are the manifestations of separation distress. Often, bereaved individuals are rapt students of separation behavior and will acknowledge it readily. Ms. I (in Chapter 9), rather typically testified after several appointments "I didn't realize it but I was grieving for my dead husband." This realization came after two hospitalizations and a major depressive illness associated with the chronic emotional distress of the loss.

Another example is Ms. A (in Chapter 1). She was at a loss for what to do for her grieving children after her eldest son had died. As a consequence, she felt helpless and useless as a mother, a role from which she ordinarily derived considerable gratification. After the deaths of her son and mother, she was fascinated with an explanation of the nature of her distress in light of attachment theory. She achieved a greater sense of control over herself because she had a new framework for interpreting how she felt. She also used her new knowledge to teach her adult children about grief. This gave her distinct satisfaction with a renewed sense of being an effective mother for her remaining children, despite the loss of her first child.

The following anecdote illustrates how even though she had begun to understand separation distress, it was still a challenge for Ms. A to recognize all of its manifestations. At the time of the first anniversary of her son's death, she had a strong impulse to take a bowl of strawberries and cream to her son's grave. She initially viewed this desire as an irrational and psychologically threatening idea. Then, it was clarified in psychotherapy that this was a favorite treat of her son and was understood as an aspect of an ongoing attachment to him in the framework of severe separation distress. In this context, the impulse lost its threatening and irresistible quality and was experienced with more detachment. She visited her son's grave with a bowl of strawberries as a memorial, and it was a deeply gratifying anniversary observance.

In the case of Mr. H (in Chapters 8 and 12), the framework of attachment theory set a whole new course for understanding the symptomatology of his experience. Until he was evaluated by a psychiatrist knowledgeable about bereavement, Mr. H understood his auditory hallucinations of his deceased lover's voice as a psychotic symptom. Subsequently, by interpreting the same symptom within the perspective of attachment theory, he comprehended the hallucinations as a severe manifestation of separation distress and his yearning to be reunited with his partner. This is not to gainsay that the hallucinations had some of the qualities of a psychotic symptom and that Mr. H seemed to derive benefit from taking antipsychotic medicine, which it took 3 months longer to discontinue after the evaluation.

Nevertheless, Mr. H was originally skeptical and then fascinated with the insight offered by an understanding of separation distress. Ultimately, it gave him a greater sense of control over the hallucinated voice as well as more optimism that the symptom would subside over time. (Perhaps, it is more precise to say that the symptom would change rather than subside over time, as Mr. H remembered his deceased lover in a mode that was different from his initial way of remembering him [see the discussion of remembering below].) This was a fundamentally transformed perspective from the view that the hallucination was a severe symptom that was part of a psychotic illness, one that presumably carried a grave prognosis. (It is worth noting that the treatment response of this patient was not unique. Others have also noticed that dramatic treatment results are possible even when patients with diagnoses of schizophrenic disorder [Lieberman 1978; Volkan and Showalter 1968] and endogenous depression [Lieberman 1978] are treated with psychotherapeutic techniques aimed at the complications of bereavement.)

Learning About Trauma

When bereavement is the result of a traumatic death, psychoeducation about trauma and traumatic distress is another aspect of psychotherapy that serves to reduce the fear and enhance the feelings of mastery of the survivor. A review of the circumstances of a death will often lead to a discussion of the terminal disease process, the nature of treatment, the decision making of the attending doctors, and death itself. Practitioners are not extensively prepared in medical or graduate school to have informational and philosophical discussions with patients about these topics. The discussion of death raises feelings of fear, helplessness, survivor guilt, and anger over the death for not only the patient but also the therapist. This is a good example of how the therapist can use his or her own feelings to get in touch with the patient's response. This process was part of the treatment of Ms. B (in Chapter 2) and Mr. D (in Chapter 5). It was also instrumental in the treatment of Ms. M (see below).

Clarifying Tasks of Social Adjustment

It is also useful to clarify the tasks of social adjustment that will be created by a loss, particularly the death of a spouse (Silverman 1986). This is a longer-term objective that can be acknowledged early without having to be immediately acted upon during acute bereavement. Typically, patients who understand the nature of the emotional distress of bereavement and no longer feel threatened by it are better able to adjust to the status of being unmarried and accommodate to new roles, such as being a single parent. This is true because the tasks of social readjustment, just like the "empty situations" that are encountered early on in bereavement, inevitably involve reminders about the absence of the deceased individual. If the emotional distress is severely intense, subjectively overwhelming, and incapacitating, social readjustment is avoided because it is so painful.

If social readjustment is not an explicit issue at the end of brief treatment, often the patient will return for another brief series of psychotherapy. Ms. B (in Chapter 2) was an example of this. It was not until her third return to a period of brief treatment that social readjustment was the primary focus of therapy. At that time separation distress was still as prominent as it had been when she had her first dinner party at home as an unmarried woman. Having set the table and prepared the dinner, she reflexively expected her deceased husband to enter and not only compliment the preparations but also assume the lead role of host, as was his manner. His absence was once again brought forcefully home to her. Typically, in the later stages of bereavement, as this case illustrates, it is the attempt to resume life in a new status rather than the relatively unconscious searching behavior or random reminders from others, which are so characteristic of early bereavement, that provoke separation distress.

Appraising the Nature of the Life Event

There is something to teach the acutely bereaved patient about coping as well, although it remains relatively nonspecific given our current state of knowledge (see Chapter 7). If nothing else, the basic psychoeducational approach advocated in this chapter is consistent with the idea of intervening in the primary and secondary appraisal of the life event of bereavement. During appraisal, the affected individual judges whether the recent event is irrelevant, benign, threatening, or challenging. Secondarily, the individual makes a judgment about his or her capacity to cope with the event. This concept of appraisal is of central importance within one theoretical framework for understanding coping (Lazarus and Folkman 1984). The idea that psychoeducation can address appraisal is illustrated in the next example. Psychotherapy was successful in changing Ms. M's appraisal of the loss of her mother, which was initially experienced as very threatening but was subsequently viewed as sad but not dangerous (see below).

Evaluating the Patient's Coping Strategies

Unfortunately, our current understanding of effective coping with bereavement is in its infancy. This part of psychotherapy is, therefore, rather nonspecific. The therapeutic task is to evaluate the repertory of coping strategies that an individual has. It is useful for the therapist to examine the bereaved patient's coping for obvious gaps or limitation in range. In general, it is agreed, admittedly not on much evidence, that using a wide range of coping skills—including both instrumental and emotion-focused coping—in a flexible manner is the most promising strategy for successful adaptation. Also there is probably wide agreement that mature ego defenses, as part of a wide spectrum of ego defensive mechanisms, are preferable for adaptation to a challenge such as bereavement rather than rigid, narrow, relatively immature ego defenses. Based on my and my colleagues' studies (see Chapter 7), it is reasonable to believe that excessive suppressive coping may be associated with and even lead to delayed or absent grief, that limited and rigid repertoires of coping may lead to severe grief, and that ineffective coping (e.g., inadequate use of problem-focused strategies) will lead to prolonged grief. Until more evidence is available, these assumptions can cautiously guide our thinking.

When we begin to consider ego defenses and the association of neurotic coping with a risk of depression (see Chapter 7), we move from the relatively conscious sphere of coping to the relatively unconscious sphere of ego mechanisms that may be less amenable to purely educational interventions. The complexity of coping and the need to teach about it establish another rationale—in addition to the skill that is required to recognize latent, reactivated role relationships (see above)—for placing responsibility for the psychoeducational tasks of treating bereaved patients in the hands of skilled psychotherapists. The alternative is to settle for the typical, packaged distillates of many stress reduction programs.

Special Issues in the Psychotherapy of Bereaved Patients

Understanding the Fear of Losing Control

Clayton et al. (1971) first suggested that the fear of losing control was a signal of a poor, long-term outcome for bereavement. A fear of losing control, of going insane, of coming apart, or of becoming nonfunctional and requiring institutionalization is prominent in many individuals with pathologic grief. It may be particularly prominent in bereaved patients who have suffered traumatic losses and in those bereaved individuals who seek help on their own initiative, which is the most common avenue into treatment. Ms. L (in Chapter 12) is an example of someone who said that she feared she would lose control. When she was asked to clarify her meaning, she said that she feared that she would give up and become crazy. This was true for several other patients whose cases have been presented in this book, including Ms. A (in Chapter 1), Ms. B (in Chapter 2), Mr. D (in Chapter 5), and Ms. I (in Chapter 9). Ms. M, whose case is presented here, is another example.

Case 13

Ms. M was a 38-year-old, married social worker and mother of two children—an 8-month-old son and a 6-year-old daughter. She presented with the chief complaint that she was having trouble functioning from day to day in meeting her household and child-rearing responsibilities since her mother's death 4 months earlier. She reported intense separation distress and the feeling that she could not accept her mother's death from metastatic cancer. In her words, she could not "trick the grief away." She was quite angry over the "dehumanizing care" that her mother received at the end of her life. (It had become necessary in the course of her mother's illness to insert an intracerebral shunt to treat elevated intracranial pressure from brain metastases.) She felt that it would have been better for her mother to have died in a coma. The suffering and the ugly wasting of her mother caused by the disease frightened her.

During the evaluation, Ms. M acknowledged an impulse to hurt her 8-month-old son. She was terrified of losing control. She said that she resented the new child, who was conceived during her mother's terminal illness, from the time that the family began to suggest that he was a replacement for her mother. Her feelings of helplessness, her efforts to manage her anger, and her obsession about hurting her infant son were the focus of therapy. She had a subclinical depressive syndrome with depressed, irritable mood; guilt over decisions she had made about her mother's care; and strong feelings of resentment about how her mother had died. She reported that she was "uncertain" if she was suicidal.

Ms. M denied any personal history of psychiatric disorders. Her mother had been hospitalized with a "nervous breakdown" and abused multiple medicines after the death of Ms. M's father in a car accident when Ms. M was 16 years old. She said that she missed having a father but did not notice any severe difficulty in adjustment. A year after her father's death, Ms. M's mother, who was a career woman, sent her daughter away to boarding school. Ms. M said that she soon learned to be "on my own" and "depend on myself," and developed a pattern of vicarious caregiving in which she would experience gratification in helping others. She said that she approached her grief over her mother's death as "something to be avoided" for the reasons above. She blamed her mother for never teaching her about bereavement at the time of her father's death.

This young mother needed to talk about the circumstances of her mother's death. The nature of her mother's terminal illness, the reason for the treatment recommendations, and the details of her mother's death were all topics of intense interest and sources of anger for her that needed to be directly, carefully, patiently, nonjudgmentally, and empathically reviewed. As she did this the intensity of her anger and obsession began to subside. In addition, as she learned more about the nature of grief, particularly the intense separation distress that she was experiencing, she began to feel more in control and less threatened. Her new knowledge provided her an opportunity to teach her daughter about death, something she had not been able to do before and that her mother had reportedly neglected for her. This was a fundamental change in her ability to cope with the loss. Slowly and progressively, as she talked through these issues and felt more under control in general, the impulse to hurt her infant son subsided completely. She began to bond more intimately with the infant. Over the course of six visits, her depressive symptoms subsided.

Psychoeducation about death and bereavement was the cornerstone for providing this patient a greater sense of control and a reduced sense of vulnerability. The clinical effectiveness of explaining the nature of separation distress to this bereaved patient, acknowledging her anger over the loss, and discussing means of coping with bereavement can be understood as a function of changing the cognitive appraisal of the experience. In this case the patient used her new understanding to help her daughter, thereby correcting a perceived deficiency in her own mother's care for her when she was younger and her father died. Typical of many cases where fear of losing control is prominent, there was a traumatic element in the losses that this patient had suffered, first in the accidental death of her father and its consequences for her, then in the frightening confrontation with death as her mother was ravaged by cancer.

The effectiveness of psychoeducation about the nature of bereavement is reminiscent of the importance of the cognitive appraisal of first panic attacks with patients with panic disorder and agoraphobia (Brier et al. 1986). In this interesting, retrospective study, those patients who understood their panic attack as a form of anxiety or had some other, plausible explanation of its nature, such as it being a manifestation of pregnancy, rather than interpreting the attack as an obscure, inchoate threat to life, were considerably less likely to develop avoidant behavior and agoraphobia within a year. Those patients with panic disorder who had no plausible explanation of the panic attack were more likely to feel that they were going insane or to attribute the symptoms to a heart attack or life-threatening illness. Their risk of becoming avoidant was high. Similarly, in bereavement, as the case of Ms. M illustrates, a cognitive appraisal of the symptomatic experience of bereavement in the framework of attachment theory leads to a greater sense of control and less avoidance. This occurs not only because the experience is no longer mysterious and threatening but also because bereaved individuals with a proper understanding begin to see how to cope more effectively on their own. In doing so, they achieve a growing sense of mastery.

Sometimes psychotherapy alone is not enough to help a patient feel more under control. Case 4 (in Chapter 5) and Case 9 (in Chapters 9 and 12) illustrate the necessity in some cases for effective treatment of incapacitating depressive symptoms by pharmacological interventions. In both cases, antidepressants were prescribed in conjunction with psychotherapy that employed the strategies that are being described here.

Developing a Different World View

Much of psychotherapy during bereavement is devoted to helping patients restructure their view of the world. This perspective on the experience of bereavement stems from Parkes's original thesis (1971) about psychosocial transitions and his recommendation about its usefulness in understanding the bereaved individual (Parkes 1988). After the death of a spouse, for example, the bereaved partner must come to terms with his or her new status as a widower or widow. A microanalysis of what has been lost discloses that there are multiple ramifications of the death (Parkes 1988). A surviving spouse may suffer multiple deprivations, including the loss, among other things, of a parental partner, a sexual partner, companionship, protection, reassurance, income, social status, and a certain type of home. We all make assumptions about these ingredients of our lives, creating what Parkes (1971) calls our *assumptive world*. When a death occurs, we can no longer accept the assumptions by which we have lived. As a corollary, we must reestablish or revise our assumptions for the future. These serve as internal, cognitive models for making decisions as we lead our lives.

The process of restructuring a world view goes hand in hand with the process of social adjustment as bereaved individuals are forced to learn new roles to provide for themselves. It is facilitated ordinarily by the rituals that our culture prescribes to structure bereavement as a major transition of life, beginning with the wake and concluding with the resumption of normal membership in society. The latter occurs after a period of time, usually a year or so. Ordinarily, the development of a new world view after bereavement is a step-by-step process with progressive resolution. Sometimes, the damage to old assumptions about oneself as a competent individual or about living in a safe and secure world appears to be a stumbling block to progress in social readjustment and resolution of the grief. In this event, focusing on the process of restructuring a view of the world and the bereaved individual's place in it is a useful tool for working out the clinical problem posed by the patient.

Among the clinical examples already introduced, there are several examples of the value of this perspective. Ms. A (in Chapter 1), who profited from health education about separation distress, was helped in these terms by understanding the reason for her shaken confidence in herself as a resourceful mother. Similarly, Mr. D (in Chapter 5), who was struggling with his sense of impotence over being unable to prevent or avenge his daughter's murder, was helped to gain some philosophical perspective by examining the damage done to his self-image and his world view by the traumatic event. It is important to acknowledge that this alone did not control his episodic feelings of revenge or despair. But it did give him some measure of distance from his feelings, and it provided him an opportunity to begin to test his working assumptions after the death that he could no longer trust himself or others. Ms. B (in Chapter 2) needed an opportunity in psychotherapy to test her assumption that she would not be able to control her feelings on her own. She needed to explore her reactions to her new role as a single parent and grandparent. Typically, survivors of sudden, unexpected, or traumatic deaths that abruptly shake the survivor's assumptions about themselves and the environment, benefit the most from the introduction of a psychosocial transition perspective into psychotherapy. Still, it is a model for understanding the experience of bereavement that may be useful for everyone.

Learning How to Remember and Continue a Relationship With the Deceased Individual

As yet another psychoeducational objective, it is worthwhile to discuss the task of teaching bereaved individuals how to maintain a relationship with the individual who has died. This is useful for the purpose of reorienting our clinical thinking about another commonly identified task in the bereavement literature—saying goodbye. Many writers on the treatment of complications of bereavement emphasize the importance of saying goodbye to the individual who has died and getting on with life's challenges and opportunities. This task is most specifically relevant when grief is severe and prolonged, which is the most common clinical picture that bereaved patients present. On the other hand, it is not clear that there is a need to focus specifically on this task. An alternative strategy is to focus on remembering (Shuchter 1986; Vaillant 1985; Weisman 1973). The advantage of this approach is that it is relevant throughout the course of grief. Also it does not contain the same latent threat to the bereaved individual.

Before discussing the process of remembering, it is important to distinguish between saying goodbye during bereavement and the process of leave-taking during a terminal illness. The latter is another matter; further, there is evidence that failure to provide an opportunity for family and intimate friends to say goodbye to a patient during his or her terminal illness raises the risk of complicated bereavement (Lundin 1984; Parkes and Weiss 1983). This issue is addressed as an aspect of prevention in Chapter 15. The focus in this chapter is on the treatment of the complications of bereavement after the individual has already died.

Placing emphasis on remembering provides the potential for a continuing attachment to the deceased individual that is more reassuring to the bereaved survivor than the recommendation to say goodbye. The failure to give up the grief can be viewed either as a resistance to saying goodbye or a failure to understand how to remember in a new mode. Often, the resistance to saying goodbye in therapy is rooted in the bereaved individual's assumption that saying goodbye is tantamount to saying "forget about it." This creates the impression that the bereaved individual is in jeopardy of losing the deceased individual twice, usually before they are ready to not only physically but also psychologically. For example, Ms. L (in Chapter 12; also see below) originally needed to justify her involvement in therapy to herself because of her conviction that her deceased mother would exhort her to "forget about her and get on with life." She remarked when she began to remember her mother with less distress, "I fear that I will forget my mother, and then I will feel guilty." The alternative idea she would eventually remember in a different, less painful mode was reassuring.

There is much to learn about remembering during bereavement, and this knowledge furnishes a fresh perspective on separation distress. Typically, reminders of the individual who has died are painful at first. This is what we define as separation distress. Yet even at this stage, many patients will recognize that the memories are comforting. Ms. B (in Chapter 2) repeatedly commented on this and distinguished between the acceptable anguish of the separation distress and the much more threatening torment of anxious depression. Bereaved individuals appreciate reassurances that there is no reason to expect that the painful recollection early in bereavement is harmful or that it will get out of control. In addition, it benefits them to understand the natural history of these distressful memories. Typically, the distress subsides over time and memories of the deceased individual become more compartmentalized in relationship to obvious reminders such as holidays. Also the memories become more bittersweet than painful. In this sense they become progressively more comforting than distressful. In addition, for reasons that are not well understood, memories become more graphic and vivid over time. Often, acutely bereaved individuals complain that they cannot evoke in their mind's eye a visual image of the deceased individual. This is a source of frustration and disappointment for some. It is reasonable to reassure them that this capacity to visualize the deceased individual will probably develop over time, usually toward the end of the first year. Finally, memories become more balanced and integrated with time in contrast to initial recall when the deceased individual is remembered, on the average, in an embellished way. There are exceptions such as when the relationship has been ambivalent. In this case, the above pattern does not hold although with skilled intervention there is a progression to a more integrated rather than an ambivalent view.

With these perspectives, the acutely bereaved individual usually finds it easier to accept the immediate suffering associated with separation distress and is reassured that he or she can weather it. In addition, it is consoling that it is through memory, rituals, memorials, adoption of interests of the deceased (referred to as *internalization* in psychological literature), and internal dialogues that a continuing relationship with the deceased individual is maintained. Many bereaved individuals do not want to give this up, nor should they. On the contrary, the majority of bereaved individuals report a gratifying sense of presence of the individual who has died that grows over time. It is notable that this sense of presence is associated with a history of long and satisfactory relationships (Rees 1971).

Understanding Anger and How to Forgive

In many instances, the ongoing relationship to the deceased individual is complicated by anger over a multitude of issues. These issues may include long-standing grievances, the fact of being left behind, or the fact of not being adequately provided for. Unresolved anger is one of the ingredients of ambivalence. When this is recognized in therapy, there is value in providing an opportunity for expressing these feelings with the aim of achieving a greater integration of the bereaved individual's internal representation of the other (Raphael 1975). In addition, it is useful to focus on the task of forgiving and being forgiven for the purpose of addressing the feelings of guilt that often go hand in hand with the anger (Colgrove et al. 1991). Ms. L (in Chapter 12; also see below) was an example of this.

A fundamental implication of forgiving for the therapeutic process is untying bereaved individuals from the past for the purpose of reorienting them toward the future (Colgrove et al. 1991). Forgiving another individual is an intrapersonal and interpersonal process. Intrapersonally, bereaved individuals must let go of their anger about past conflicts and no longer let it govern them as a central part of their life. They must forgive themselves for omissions of care or long-standing disputes with the deceased individual and give up the guilt associated with these. Interpersonally, forgiving lets the relationship with the deceased individual go forward on a new footing instead of the bereaved individual holding on, often in a guilty manner, to what has been lost, which is often a dynamic of chronic grief. The incentive for bereaved individuals is to get beyond the painful reminiscences that are typical of a relationship that has stalled because of conflict. Alternatively, they can trust in the evolution of a less distressing connection to the deceased individual as described above. Usually the anger is a reflection of the need to hold on to something that bereaved individuals fear giving up. Patients need help in understanding what to expect as they relinquish painful memories and how to do it. They also need to learn how to give to themselves what the other individual used to give. In these ways and by emphasizing the almost universal need or tendency for reconciliation at the end of a life, the therapist can be instrumental in fostering a forgiving attitude.

Past Losses and Clinical Relationship Issues

To the extent that object relations are concrete or sensorimotor, in a Piagetian sense, rather than more developed, abstract, and integrated (Blatt et al. 1979; Lane et al. 1987), the means of remembering is more nonverbal and behavioral rather than verbal. Everyone incorporates more or less conscious and unconscious ways of remembering in their response to a loss. It is the unique mixture of these ways that characterizes each individual. The point is that the acutely bereaved individual will engage others in relationships that serve as partial substitutes for what has been lost. Perhaps it is misleading to characterize this as an aspect of remembering insofar as it is unconscious and behavioral. Yet the two types of behavior, verbal and nonverbal, are related insofar as they are both aspects of maintaining a relationship with the deceased individual. The basic concept in this regard is that developed by Horowitz et al. (1980) (see above and Chapter 2) who attributed pathologic grief to the reactivation of latent self-images and role relationships after a loss. It seems to me that this basic idea applies to everyone in the circumstances of a loss. It is only when there is a desperate, importuning quality to the interpersonal demand and the role relationships are maladaptive that we recognize them as pathologic grief.

Although it is true that transference issues are always active in the psychotherapy of the bereaved patient, it is my impression that they are particularly important in treating those patients who have experienced separations from or losses of parents or other caregiving individuals in childhood. This phenomenon is illustrated in the next example, which continues the case history of Ms. L. It was equally true for Ms. B (in Chapter 2), Ms. M (described above), and others that I have not had an opportunity to introduce in this book. As the brief review of childhood losses in Chapter 8 suggests, the transference issues involve both supplicating and angry sentiment about the trauma of the loss suffered as a child and also complex feelings about the quality of care and support that other adults provide in intimate relationships.

An example of a maladaptive self-image and role relationship emerged between Ms. L (in Chapter 12) and me during the course of her treatment. She sought evaluation for an unremitting depressive syndrome during acute bereavement over the death of her mother. The clinical relationship issues seemed to be related to unresolved feelings about the death of her father when she was younger.

Case 12 (*continued*)

Ms. L had entered treatment with a depressive syndrome about 2 years after the death of her mother. She was having problems during bereavement despite a history of very high functioning prior to the loss. Her father died when she was 13.

Without being able to specify what it was, Ms. L was repeatedly insistent that I had more to give her than she was getting from the treatment. She was angry with her husband "who had not supported me enough" after her mother's death. She also repeated that "there were things that my mother could not give me." As my understanding of this theme developed, I interpreted this general statement about her mother to refer to her mother's failure to give her support while she grieved over her father's death. This theme was reflected in the inner voice of her mother that she currently heard telling her to "forget about me" and the patient's assumption that her mother would deplore her need for psychiatric help.

Ms. L reported an event that occurred when she was 21 and was attending a wedding with her mother and grandmother. At one point, she became tearful over the realization that her father would not be at her own wedding to give her away in marriage. Her grandmother harshly reprimanded her for being "silly" and her mother did not intervene to reassure her. I viewed her insistence that I was holding something back in this context and repeatedly explained the ways in which I could and could not help. In addition, I clarified the developmental themes rooted in the death of her father. She weathered her frustrations at my not giving her what she felt she needed with mild to moderate disappointment in me.

Eventually, Ms. L committed herself, almost in a businesslike fashion, to getting as much out of therapy as she could while the time lasted. In parallel with this evolution of the therapeutic relationship, she was encouraged to reevaluate her mother's deficiencies concerning how to cope with the loss of her husband. I also encouraged her finally to forgive her mother for the past insults, placing her ongoing relationship with her deceased mother on a new footing that was less distressing.

In this case it was apparent that the death of Ms. L's mother unleashed the self-image of a needy, young woman who had been deprived of the support and wisdom of her father and who felt cheated by his untimely death. Her mother's stoic attitude toward the loss of her husband and daughter's father had contributed to this state. At the same time, the mother's caring and support for her daughter in other ways had kept this needy self-image in check until her death.

Understanding Identification Symptoms

Acutely bereaved individuals often present to psychiatrists with multiple somatic complaints (see Chapter 2). It is essential to evaluate these somatic symptoms in the light of the terminal illness of the deceased individual, as the symptoms sometimes will be closely related to those of the terminal illness. When a resemblance occurs, it is interpreted as a type of identification with the deceased individual that presages a poor outcome (Parkes 1972; Zisook and DeVaul 1977). This ominous implication distinguishes identification symptoms from other identification processes that are considered to be part of normal recovery from grief (Parkes 1972).

There is another perspective on these symptoms that has more to do with traumatization than identification. The genuine fear of illness and death among acutely bereaved patients with such somatic symptoms has impressed me. Some diseases cause wasting and ugly, physical changes during the terminal phase of illness. Other deaths are patently traumatic and grotesque. These same qualities of a death, when witnessed by combat veterans, have been identified as risk factors for chronic posttraumatic stress syndromes (Green et al. 1990). In this light, the "identification" symptoms of bereavement can be viewed as a reflection of a repetition compulsion, as survivors try to internally master the threat that took the life of their intimate. The death of and intimate confronts survivors with their own mortality and raises questions about body integrity.

The somatic symptoms of the survivors can be seen as an expression of their concern. In other words, the symptoms are a residual manifestation of traumatic aspects of the loss. In clinical practice with bereaved individuals who have pathologic grief syndromes, the patients who have identification symptoms are typically those who have been frightened by the exposure to death. This was true, for example, for Ms. E (in Chapter 6) and Ms. L (in Chapter 12 and above). When these symptoms are recognized, the psychotherapist can encourage the bereaved individual to work out his or her philosophy of life and the place of death in life. Providing information on causes of death, how people die, how to relieve pain, where people die, what happens to them after death, and so on is important in this regard; these are tasks that are added on to the basic objectives of psychotherapy already discussed.

Recognizing the Impact of Anniversaries and Significant Holidays

A theme that deserves more emphasis than it has received recently in the treatment of the complications of bereavement is the importance of anniversaries and holidays. These are times when the distress of a loss is aggravated. They are also times that serve as opportunities for concerted and concentrated therapeutic effort. This was true, for example, for Ms. A (in Chapter 1), Ms. B (in Chapter 2), and Ms. E (in Chapter 6). The ability to take advantage of these critical junctures depends on a thorough knowledge of the dates of death and the most meaningful holidays for the bereaved individual.

Although no systematic data are available, clinicians have noted that patients tend to present for treatment around anniversaries more often than would be expected (Cavenar et al. 1977; Pollock 1970). A careful history of the dates of death will demonstrate this. A careful history of the reaction to the first anniversary of a loss is also a useful index of the status of the patient's recovery (Jacobs et al. 1987). Some intensification of distress at the time of the first anniversary is to be expected. When this period of distress exceeds a few days, however, it is often associated with demoralization, depression, and unresolved grief (Jacobs et al. 1987). In some cases, recurrent difficulties around holidays can be misconstrued as cyclical disease and misdiagnosed as manic depressive disorder (Cavenar et al. 1977). Despite the impression created by clinical anecdotes, there is little systematic evidence of an association between anniversaries of losses and psychotic illness or psychosomatic disease (Birtchnell 1981) as some clinical investigators have claimed (Bressler 1956; Bunch and Barraclough 1971; Engel 1975; Hilgard and Newman 1959; Musaph 1973; Pollock 1970). Even if anniversaries do not cause psychiatric disorders, they appear to be powerful organizers of illness behavior and presentation for treatment, as noted above.

Stigmatization

A virtually inevitable task in the early phase of treatment is to deal with bereaved patients' fears of stigmatization stemming from their need to consult a psychiatrist or mental health professional. This is a particularly important issue in the treatment of bereaved patients who are consulting a psychiatrist for the first time. The fear that the distress of bereavement will be construed as a mental illness often serves as an excuse for not accepting treatment. It is especially salient as a means of avoidance in those who fear losing control and seize on this excuse for averting the risk of opening up in therapy. The status of being acutely bereaved offers the patient a logical, alternative explanation for the symptomatic disturbance that otherwise would impel the individual to seek help.

This issue of stigmatization, often latent, ought to be recognized explicitly in therapy. The clinician can counterbalance the negative effect of stigma by offering a commonsense explanation of conclusions he or she has reached at the end of a thorough evaluation and detailing a plan for treatment. Specifically, if the clinical problems are conceptualized as maladaptations to a loss, it often serves to distinguish them from other psychiatric syndromes that the patient may know and fear. Even if the euphemism of an adaptive disorder is accepted by the patient, the facts of a psychiatric diagnosis and treatment remain. Therefore, another type of reassurance about the safety of treatment to the patient is a strong affirmation of clinical confidentiality.

In treating patients with complications of bereavement, the therapist often encounters the attitude that "you need to suffer through" the pain of bereavement. Often this attitude coexists with the fear of stigmatization and becomes a basis for refusing treatment. The same attitude is encountered not only in patients but also in clergy, primary care physicians, and occasionally in mental health professionals, despite their being more attuned in general to the concept and treatment of emotional disorders (Wortman and Silver 1989). The question of the appropriateness of treatment during bereavement is certainly an issue with which I wrestled when I began to work with acutely bereaved patients.

This attitude of "suffering through a loss" is difficult and controversial to discuss because it goes to the heart of many religious and cultural assumptions of Western civilization. Many of us accept the basic postulate that we must accept the emotional pain of a loss. By struggling with an adverse experience, we are presumably toughened through learning to tolerate the affliction. We are rendered more mature through learning about life's experiences as well as our own strengths and weaknesses. Moreover, we are made more noble, provided that we learn to suffer with dignity. The problem is that this attitude can insidiously undermine the chances for treatment in circumstances when it is necessary. It is an issue that is best addressed directly with the patient.

There is something to be said for the emotional fitness and wisdom gained from enduring life's hardships, such as the loss of a family member. In the final analysis, though, it is not only the capacity for suffering but also the degree of learning that determines whether the adaptation to bereavement is successful or not. The critical issue for the therapist is how to help patients mitigate the pain of bereavement for the purpose of pacing themselves through the experience and learning from it. By pacing themselves, bereaved individuals remain emotionally fit as they continue to fulfill other essential roles in life that simply cannot be put on hold.

A therapist can effectively advance the goals of developing emotional fitness and personal confidence in the bereaved individual in several ways. As discussed above, these include active efforts to educate the acutely bereaved patient about grief and the meaning of death, to aid the bereaved individual to find an appropriate pace at which to work through the experience, to teach various strategies of coping with the challenges of bereavement that are specifically useful to the grieving individual, and to search in concert with the bereaved individual for opportunities to grow from of the experience. In this way, clinicians can espouse educational, habilitative, and growth-promoting objectives while still attending to the treatment task of alleviating the emotional pain of bereavement.

Frequently, patients will report their frustration with others who advise them that they must just suffer through it. The case of Ms. E (in Chapter

6) is an example of estrangement from the church, which occurred after a new clergyman in the parish asserted that she must learn to accept her suffering because it "was God's will." Until the new clergyman arrived, Ms. E had been getting along, bearing her chronic grief (admittedly without much progress in the direction of recovery). The change in parish priest played a part in her seeking professional help. After consultation with me, the assumption that something could be done to help her suffering through brief psychotherapy and entrance into a mutual support group gave enormous hope and impetus to this widow's recovery. Her response illustrated the effect of a positive and sophisticated attitude toward helping. (The contribution of the mutual support group to her treatment, complementary to the psychotherapeutic endeavor, is discussed more in Chapter 14.)

Family Treatment

There are often indications for inviting families into treatment (Kosten et al. 1985). Family intervention may be particularly salient for the surviving parents and siblings of children who have died; it can be instrumental in averting the marital dysfunction and poor school performance that often follow the loss of a child.

Two important considerations from the general psychiatric literature emerge with regard to the usefulness of family treatment. One is that excessive amounts of expressed emotion can contribute to the relapse of patients with schizophrenic and affective disorders (Vaughn and Leff 1976). The other is that psychoeducational approaches with families can be instrumental in preventing relapse of psychiatric disorders (Leff et al. 1982). In addition, clinical experience teaches us that family therapy is often crucial in identifying family conflict or structural problems that, if addressed, are instrumental in the treatment and rehabilitation of the individual patient. In Chapter 7 I note that different members of the family will respond to a loss in different ways and at a different pace. (In Chapter 14, the case of Ms. A [Chapter 1] is used to illustrate this point.) Basic psychoeducation about the process and the range of normal response to a loss as well as the identification of family members with specific clinical problems are fundamental to the process of the family therapy. It should be noted that the only controlled study of family crisis intervention for bereaved adults concluded that such an intervention early in bereavement may have been harmful (Polak et al. 1975; Williams and Polak 1979; see discussion in Chapter 10). The main implication of this study, in my judgment, is that family therapy must be accomplished by well-trained, skillful therapists who are knowledgeable about therapeutic process.

Family treatment for bereaved children is another example of the role of family involvement in treating the complications of bereavement. The value of family treatment in this circumstance has been demonstrated convincingly in one study (Black 1979).

Determining the Beginning, End, and Duration of Treatment

The essential first step in beginning treatment is to complete a thorough assessment of the patient. This includes determining the chief complaint and the current psychiatric illness and completing a personal history and mental status examination. The assessment also ought to incorporate a history of the death, the bereaved patient's reaction to the death since it occurred, a review of previous losses, and an evaluation of ways the patient has coped with similar problems in the past (Raphael 1975, 1983).

There is an important message in this evaluative process. It is the communication that the clinician, for one, is able to talk about death and grief and does not shy away from the contingency of death or the crisis in the structure and meaning of life when a loved one dies. Furthermore, the clinician's office is identified as a place where the task of addressing these existential issues (Yalom 1980; Yalom and Vinogradov 1988) can be undertaken, if no other opportunities exist in the patient's life or perhaps in preference to other settings. The initial assessment also lays the groundwork of knowledge for clarifying the patient's unique, personal experience of the loss, including anniversary reactions.

Preparation for the end of treatment begins with setting the duration of treatment. This task is essential, particularly in the treatment of dependent grief syndromes (Parkes and Weiss 1983) or for patients with preexisting psychiatric disorders. Generally, the treatment programs that have been described in the clinical literature are brief in duration, meaning that treatment may involve 10–15 meetings or less. Setting a limit on the duration of treatment for the complications of bereavement, which is consistent with the tasks that are discussed in this chapter, clarifies for the patient that the long-term rehabilitation of personality dysfunction or other chronic disabilities is not the task of this particular treatment. It also provides the incentive of a deadline for the bereaved individual to address the problems of bereavement.

It is necessary to go even further when treating dependent grief syndromes (Parkes and Weiss 1983; Weisman 1973). Dependent grief syndromes often include persistent feelings of guilt that usually signal that the patients are holding on to their grief, sometimes for secondary gain (Weisman 1973). In treating these patients, the continuation of brief treatment becomes contingent on the patient's progress in achieving increased autonomy. The contingency is established for the purpose of keeping treatment in a short-term perspective (Parkes and Weiss 1983). Alternatively, the therapist can abandon the short-term treatment goals for treating complications of bereavement and undertake long-term, psychotherapeutic rehabilitation (see below).

When a patient's maladaptation to bereavement has become chronic, a question arises about whether the basic strategies recommended in this chapter are still useful. I would emphasize from my experience that the brief, psychoeducational strategy of treatment that is described above is applicable to the treatment of chronic, unresolved grief also. This is true as long as the focus of treatment is on the loss and its consequences and the task is not redefined in terms of personality change or other long-term goals. The literature on psychotherapy of the psychiatric complications of bereavement supports this view, suggesting that either a brief, psychodynamic approach is effective most of the time (Horowitz et al. 1984a) or a brief, confrontational, and behavioral approach to psychotherapy is useful (Mawson et al. 1981).

At the end of treatment, taking the time to review the treatment process and explore the patient's feelings about the conclusion of the therapeutic relationship is meaningful for many patients. This task is particularly pertinent in the instances where there has been an intensive activation of latent self-images and role models that confound the therapist with the deceased individual (Horowitz et al. 1980). As noted above, this is often the case when the acutely bereaved individual has a history of earlier losses that are still unresolved. Saying goodbye to the deceased individual, a technique which is often recommended at this juncture, is just one way of conceptualizing the end of treatment and acute bereavement. Conceptualizing the ongoing relationship in memory to the departed individual is equally, if not more, effective.

Longer-Term Treatment

The emotional crisis of acute bereavement and its clinical complications may provide the impetus for some patients with severe character pathology or chronic, subclinical dysphoria to seek treatment. Keeping to short-term goals with these patients will be more difficult than is usually the case with bereaved individuals. In my judgment, it is still valuable to compartmentalize the short-term goals of brief psychotherapy and the special considerations in treating bereaved patients that are discussed above. The longer-term task of psychotherapy for the purpose of treating impairments in personality function is more effectively addressed as a separate task that the current therapist, or conceivably another therapist, can undertake. Approximately 20%–30% of patients may benefit from longer-term or alternate forms of treatment (Rynearson 1987a). Some patients, such as Ms. B (in Chapter 2) or Mr. D (in Chapter 5) will return to therapy after a hiatus to focus on newly defined tasks for treatment related to bereavement. This option can be explained to patients at the end of a period of acute treatment. This strategy is just as effective in my experience as long-term therapy for treating the complications of bereavement.

Failed Treatment or Ambiguous Outcome

We must always remain alert to the possibility that treatment is not working. As one experienced therapist has reminded us, it is often our patients who tell us that there is no progress, if only we do not interpret their opinion as resistance (Rynearson 1987a). Specifically, when no headway is being made in pursuit of the basic pharmacological (see Chapter 12) and psychotherapeutic tasks (as discussed in this chapter), there is reason to believe that the acute treatment is stalled and may fail. This is sometimes a subtle judgment; nonetheless, this is a judgment the therapist cannot avoid. Otherwise, false, illusory, and unilateral expectations for treatment by the patient enter the process and ultimately undermine it. This becomes manifest in early terminations or prolonged therapy where sight of the end has become lost and the character of specific treatment is missing.

On the other hand, some tolerance of ambiguity about the goals and progress of psychotherapy is justified. One case comes to mind of an adult patient (Ms. N) whose mother had died a year earlier. Shortly after the anniversary of her mother's death, Ms. N's husband fell gravely ill. The patient was under a lot of stress and certainly met criteria for an adjustment disorder, although no other psychopathology was evident. She was determined to come regularly to meetings. She seemed to have an agenda that I never quite fathomed. I worried throughout the treatment, which I was determined to keep in a brief mode, that the goals of the therapy were not well defined. Because of my concern, I periodically questioned the progress. She ended treatment after 10 appointments with my agreement. By that time I had perceived a vague glimmer of role-relationship issues involving her father that she was working out through me. I believed that I had done my best to evaluate the state of her adjustment to bereavement and teach her about grief. Truthfully, however, I was uncertain how to characterize the outcome.

I learned from the physician who originally referred Ms. N to me that she was quite content with the experience and felt it had been helpful. Experience as a psychotherapist helped me to ride out this therapy and trust my faint intuition. On the other hand, knowledge of the failure rates in helping patients with complicated grief served as a reminder of the limitations of our current psychotherapeutic approaches. Confidence in my skills as a psychotherapist and humility about the power and efficiency of therapy were basic attitudes that helped with this patient. While they conveyed to the patient that brief psychotherapy can be an effective treatment, they also acknowledged that psychotherapy cannot help everyone nor solve every problem, and that this fact is no one's fault.

Conclusions

Caregiving is complementary to attachment behavior, and there is some evidence that the way parental caregivers discharge their responsibility determines the attachment behavior and future mental health of the recipient of care (Bowlby 1977a, 1977b). The psychotherapist becomes a critical caregiver for the patient in the circumstances of complicated bereavement where attachment behavior has been acutely activated by a loss, and therapy, along with other treatment interventions, plays a decisive role in determining the outcome. There is even some speculation that the therapeutic relationship may transiently and substitutively contribute to the homeostasis of the bereaved patient (Reite 1990). Knowledge of attachment, separation, and loss are therefore essential for a professional who offers psychotherapy during bereavement (Bowlby 1977a, 1977b).

The discussion in this chapter is a distillation of several concepts that are useful in forming a therapeutic alliance and undertaking psychotherapy for the complications of bereavement. The patients who seek help from professionals present with very complex problems, considerable psychological distress, and disability. They require the most experienced, informed, empathic, and professional care that we can provide. A cornerstone of psychotherapy is careful listening to the acutely bereaved patient. By paying close attention, the therapist is able to understand and clarify the patient's personal experience of grief and the clinical complications that may have occurred.

My intent in this chapter has been to supplement this basic tenet of psychotherapy by highlighting specific issues regarding the treatment task with bereaved patients. I have suggested that psychoeducation about bereavement is essential in the treatment process. Moreover, a thorough knowledge of normal and pathologic grief can direct the clinician's attention to several other special issues such as anniversaries, identification symptoms, past losses, and the process of remembering that are uniquely significant at this time in an individual's life.

Although listening and psychoeducational goals are the cornerstones of psychotherapy, they are not the only therapeutic objectives. I make this comment as a reminder that the concepts discussed in this chapter ought to be placed in the context of the broader psychotherapy literature. The therapist will have to attend to the interpersonal problems, such as those identified by IPT, which are usually part of the nuclear content of therapy. In addition, the clinician with well-rounded education and experience will use cognitive techniques to treat dysfunctional, automatic thoughts, and pessimistic or fearful schemas (Beck et al. 1979). Clinicians also will use psychodynamic insights and interpretations to clarify repetitive, maladaptive behavior patterns or complicated, clinical relationship issues that thwart recovery from a loss (Horowitz et al. 1984a; Klerman et al. 1984). In some cases psychotherapy must become contingent on the patient's progress toward explicitly defined goals and personal autonomy (Parkes and Weiss 1983). Collectively, these psychotherapeutic interventions serve to reduce hopelessness, helplessness, and avoidance of the experience of bereavement and its clinical complications, hence addressing the core symptoms of demoralization that characterize patients in psychotherapy (Frank 1973).

References

Beck AT, Rush AJ, Shaw BF, et al: Cognitive Therapy of Depression. New York, Guilford, 1979
Birtchnell J: In search of correspondences between age at psychiatric breakdown and parental age at death—"anniversary reactions." Br J Med Psychol 54:111–120, 1981
Black D: The bereaved child. J Child Psychol Psychiatry 19:287–292, 1979
Blatt S, Wien S, Chevron E, et al: Parental representations and depression in normal young adults. J Abnorm Psychol 88:388–397, 1979
Bowlby J: The making and breaking of affectional bonds, I: aetiology and psychopathology in the light of attachment theory. Br J Psychiatry 130:201–210, 1977a
Bowlby J: The making and breaking of affectional bonds, II: some principles of psychotherapy. Br J Psychiatry 130:421–431, 1977b
Bowlby J: Attachment and Loss, Vol 3: Loss, Sadness and Depression. New York, Basic Books, 1980
Bressler B: Ulcerative colitis as an anniversary symptom. Psychoanal Rev 43:381–387, 1956
Brier A, Charney DS, Heninger GP: Agoraphobia and panic disorder: development, diagnostic stability, and course of illness. Arch Gen Psychiatry 44:1029–1036, 1986
Bunch J, Barraclough B: The influence of parental death anniversaries on suicide dates. Br J Psychiatry 118: 621–626, 1971
Cavenar JO, Nash JO, Maltbie AA: Anniversary reactions masquerading as manic depressive illness. Am J Psychiatry 134:1272–1276, 1977
Clayton PJ, Halikas JA, Maurice WL: The bereavement of the widowed. Diseases of the Nervous System 32:597–604, 1971
Colgrove M, Bloomfield HH, McWilliams P: How to Survive the Loss of a Love. Los Angeles, CA, Prelude Press, 1991
DiMascio A, Weissman MM, Prusoff BA, et al: Differential symptom reduction by drugs and psychotherapy in acute depression. Arch Gen Psychiatry 361450–1456, 1979
Elkin I, Shea T, Watkins JT, et al: National Institute of Mental Health Treatment of Depression Collaborative Research Program. Arch Gen Psychiatry 46:971–982, 1989
Engel GL: The death of a twin: mourning and anniversary reactions. British Journal of Psychoanalysis 56:23–39, 1975

Frank J: Persuasion and Healing: A Comparative Study of Psychotherapy, Revised Edition. Baltimore, MD, Johns Hopkins University Press, 1973

Green BL, Grace MC, Lindy JD, et al: Risk factors for PTSD and other diagnoses in a general sample of Vietnam veterans. Am J Psychiatry 147:729–733, 1990

Hilgard JR, Newman MF: Anniversaries in mental illness. Psychiatry 22:113–121, 1959

Hodgkinson PE: Abnormal grief—the problem of therapy. Br J Med Psychol 55:29–34, 1982

Horowitz MJ: Stress Response Syndromes. New York, Jason Aronson, 1976

Horowitz MJ, Wilner N, Marmar C, et al: Pathological grief and the activation of latent self-images. Am J Psychiatry 137:1157–1162, 1980

Horowitz M, Marmar C, Krupnick J, et al: Personality Styles and Brief Psychotherapy. New York, Basic Books, 1984a

Horowitz MJ, Weiss DS, Kaltreider N, et al: Reactions to the death of a parent: results from patients and field subjects. J Nerv Ment Dis 172:383–392, 1984b

Horowitz MJ, Marmar C, Weiss DS, et al: Brief psychotherapy of bereavement reactions: the relationship of process to outcome. Arch Gen Psychiatry 41:438–448, 1984c

Horowitz MJ, Marmar C, Weiss DS, et al: Comprehensive analysis of change after brief dynamic psychotherapy. Am J Psychiatry 143:582–589, 1986

Jacobs SC, Schaefer CA, Ostfeld AM, et al: The first anniversary of bereavement. Isr J Psychiatry Relat Sci 24:77–85, 1987

Klerman GL, Weissman MM, Rounsaville BJ, et al: Interpersonal Psychotherapy of Depression. New York, Basic Books, 1984

Kosten TR, Jacobs SC, Kasl SV: Terminal illness, bereavement, and the family, in Health, Illness, and Families. Edited by Turk DC, Kerns RD. New York, Wiley, 1985, pp 311–337

Lane RD, Jacobs SC, Mason JW, et al: Sex differences in prolactin change during mourning. J Psychosom Res 31:375–383, 1987

Lazarus RS, Folkman S: Stress, Appraisal, and Coping. New York, Springer, 1984

Leff J, Kuipers L, Berkowitz R, et al: A controlled trial of social intervention in the families of schizophrenic patients. Br J Psychiatry 141:121–134, 1982

Lieberman S: Nineteen cases of morbid grief. Br J Psychiatry 132:159–163, 1978

Lindy JD, Green BL, Grace M, et al: Psychotherapy with survivors of the Beverly Hills Supper Club fire. Am J Psychother 27:593–610, 1983

Lundin T: Morbidity following sudden and unexpected bereavement. Br J Psychiatry 144:84–88, 1984

Marmar CR, Horowitz MJ, Weiss DS, et al: A controlled trial of brief psychotherapy and mutual help group treatment of conjugal bereavement. Am J Psychiatry 145:203–209, 1988

Mawson D, Marks IM, Ramm L, et al: Guided mourning for morbid grief: a controlled study. Br J Psychiatry 138:185–193, 1981

Melges FT, DeMaso DR: Grief-resolution therapy: reliving, revising, and revisiting. Am J Psychother 34:51–61, 1980

Murphy GE, Simons AD, Wetzel RD, et al: Cognitive therapy and pharmacotherapy. Arch Gen Psychiatry 41:33–41, 1984

Musaph H: Anniversary disease. Psychother Psychosom 22:325–333, 1973

Parkes CM: Psychosocial transition: a field for study. Soc Sci Med 5:101–105, 1971

Parkes CM: Bereavement: Studies of Grief in Adult Life. New York, International Universities Press, 1972

Parkes CM: Bereavement as a psychosocial transition: processes of adaptation to change. Journal of Social Issues 44:53-65, 1988
Parkes CM, Weiss RS: Recovery From Bereavement. New York, Basic Books, 1983
Polak PB, Egan D, Bandenbergh R: Prevention in mental health: a controlled study. Am J Psychiatry 132:146–149, 1975
Pollock GH: Anniversary reactions, trauma, and mourning. Psychoanal Q 39:347–371, 1970
Pynoos RS, Nader K: Issues in the treatment of posttraumatic stress in children and adolescents, in The International Handbook of Traumatic Stress Syndromes. Edited by Wilson JP, Raphael B. New York, Plenum, 1993, pp 535–544
Ramsay RW: Behavioural approaches to bereavement. Behav Res Ther 15:131–135, 1977
Raphael B: The management of pathological grief. Aust N Z J Psychiatry 9:173–180, 1975
Raphael B: The Anatomy of Bereavement. New York, Basic Books, 1983
Rees WD: The hallucinations of widowhood. BMJ 4:37–41, 1971
Reite M: Attachment relationship has impact on patients' physiologic functioning. The Psychiatric Times, February, 1990, pp 41–44
Rush AJ, Beck AT, Kovacs M, et al: Comparative efficacy of cognitive therapy and pharmacotherapy in the treatment of depressed outpatients. Cognitive Therapy Research 1:17–37, 1977
Rynearson EK: Psychotherapy of pathologic grief. Psychiatr Clin North Am 10:487–499, 1987a
Rynearson EK: Psychological adjustment to unnatural dying, in Biopsychosocial Aspects of Bereavement. Edited by Zisook S. Washington, DC, American Psychiatric Press, 1987b
Shuchter SR: Dimensions of Grief: Adjusting to the Death of a Spouse. San Francisco, CA, Jossey-Bass, 1986
Silverman P: Widow to Widow. New York, Springer, 1986
Simons AD, Murphy GE, Levine JL, et al. Cognitive therapy and pharmacotherapy for depression. Arch Gen Psychiatry 43:43–48, 1986
Vaillant GE: Loss as a metaphor for attachment. Am J Psychoanal 45:59–67, 1985
Volkan V, Showalter CR: Known object loss, disturbance in reality testing, and "regrief work" as a method of brief psychotherapy. Psychiatr Q 42:358–374, 1968
Vaugh CE, Leff JP: The influence of family and social factors on the course of psychiatric illness. Br J Psychiatry 129:125–137, 1976
Weisman AD: Coping with untimely death. Psychiatry 36:366–378, 1973
Weissman MM, Prusoff BA, DiMascio A, et al: The efficacy of drugs and psychotherapy in the treatment of acute depressive episodes. Am J Psychiatry 136:555–558, 1979
Williams WV, Polak PR: Follow-up research in primary prevention: a model of adjustment to acute grief. J Clin Psychol 35:35–45, 1979
Worden JW: Grief Counseling and Grief Therapy: A Handbook for the Mental Health Practitioner. New York: Springer, 1982
Wortman CB, Silver RC: The myths of coping with loss. J Consult Clin Psychol 57:349–357, 1989
Yalom ID: Existential Psychotherapy. New York, Basic Books, 1980
Yalom ID, Vinogradov S: Bereavement groups: techniques and themes. Int J Group Psychother 38:419–446, 1988
Zisook S, DeVaul RA: Grief related facsimile illness. Int J Psychiatry Med 7:329–336, 1977

CHAPTER 14

Mutual Support Groups

As part of the surprisingly rapid proliferation of self-help efforts in recent times, mutual support groups for the acutely bereaved have developed extensively in the past 20 years. It is important, therefore, to consider both the role of mutual support groups in caring for the acutely bereaved individual and the role of the professionally trained clinician in mutual support programs. Furthermore, for clinical purposes, it is useful to understand the relationship of the educational and supportive services of mutual support programs to the treatment that is provided by a clinician. When viewed in a clinical perspective, mutual support services, given their nature and the timing of their application, are essentially rehabilitative in nature. This type of psychosocial rehabilitative intervention addresses the disabilities in social role functioning that are associated with complicated bereavement and potentially complements the treatment of acute symptoms associated with episodes of psychiatric illness during bereavement.

There are several potential roles for professionals in mutual support programs. At the most basic level of collaboration, the clinician can take responsibility for bereaved individuals who are identified in these programs as having clinical complications. In addition, professionals have an important role in supervising volunteer caregiving programs that reach out to newly bereaved individuals. In some instances, professionals have a role in the leadership of mutual support, small group meetings, usually as a coleader with a bereaved caregiver. These small groups are often part of the overall social programs of mutual support organizations. Finally, the clinician can consult with mutual support programs to help them enhance their organization and the content of their services.

The foundation of a mutual support program is the idea that people who share an experience have much to offer to each other. For example, bereaved individuals who have lived through the psychosocial transition of bereavement and who have integrated the experience of loss into their lives organize a mutual support program to help newly bereaved members. The assumption is that the newly bereaved individual enters uncharted waters when a death occurs and can benefit from guidance. This is presumably true because in contemporary society, with its breakdown of stable communities and extended families, the bereaved individual is ill prepared for coping with a loss. These social changes have diminished the opportunity for the bereaved individual to learn how to cope with loss from families and lifelong friends. Bereaved individuals who already have been through the experience themselves can serve as guides, for which there is no substitute, professional or otherwise.

Using these ideas as a starting point, in this chapter I review the nature of mutual support programs for acutely bereaved individuals and consider the professional's role in consulting with them.

How Mutual Support Groups Help

Over the past 10 years, social scientists have both described the functioning of mutual support groups and, in a few cases, evaluated their effectiveness (Galanter 1988; Osterweis et al. 1984). There is a growing appreciation of the several mechanisms by which mutual support programs work. These mechanisms include providing a sense of belonging through membership and companionship in a group, allowing members to learn about a particular experience through the exchange of information, facilitating coping and adaptation, and enhancing members' self-esteem. In addition, mutual support programs empower their membership through political advocacy of the group's needs and agenda.

Mutual support programs provide support of several types, which consist of emotional support for a member's point of view, the provision of new information to a member, the creation of a social framework for appraising how a member is doing in comparison with others in similar circumstances, and instrumental support in the form of providing a hot meal in an emergency or providing resources to a needy member. Mutual support programs also pursue policy goals. Advocating for the needs of survivors of violent deaths is an example. Survivors of a death in the family caused by negligence or homicide often encounter the criminal justice system for the first time. Frequently they become frustrated with a process that appears more concerned about the rights of the alleged perpetrator than with the horror and distress of the surviving family. To counteract this, mutual support groups organize legislative agendas that gain recognition for the rights of those who have been victimized by crime and their families.

The types of social support that an individual requires under stress probably vary over time. For example, sometimes it is the family and sometimes it is a mutual support organization that best serves the need of a bereaved patient (Walker et al. 1977). As I note in Chapter 7 and as my colleagues and I found in a pilot study of widowers' attitudes towards social support (D. L. Snow, J. K. Tebes, S. C. Jacobs, unpublished analyses, 1987; see below), the family appears to play the most important role in supporting the newly bereaved individual during the earliest stages of grief. At this point in time, it may be necessary to advise a mutual support group to refrain from its well-intentioned but premature and overzealous efforts to help. Later on, it may be essential for bereaved individuals to turn to new interests, friendships, and organizations in order to find encouragement for establishing a new social structure for their lives. At this point, it is the family that must step back. Mrs. E (Chapters 6 and 13) is an example of how a mutual support group can be instrumental in helping an individual cope with bereavement. The group activities provided her friendships with other individuals having the same experience, supported her self-esteem, taught her various approaches to emotion-focused and problem-focused coping, and offered her a new range of interests.

Evaluations of Mutual Support Programs

Although the acid test of a program in the community is whether it works and solves a problem, it is appropriate in the framework of clinical science to pose a question about the proven efficacy of mutual support interventions. On the one hand, the proliferation of self-help programs strongly suggests that they are meeting a need. On the other hand, what are the evaluative data, if any, that justify a more reasoned conclusion about their usefulness and their role in helping bereaved individuals? When the literature is reviewed, there is some systematic evidence for the effectiveness of mutual support interventions. Also as is usually the case when interventions are systematically tested, the evidence is not uniformly supportive of a therapeutic effect.

Investigators in two studies (Marmar et al. 1988; Vachon et al. 1980) found that mutual support intervention reduces the psychological distress of bereavement and facilitates the social adjustment of the bereaved individual to the loss. In the controlled study by Vachon et al. (1980), the mutual support intervention included paired widow-to-widow relationships followed by an invitation to join a mutual support group. The groups were led by widows specifically trained for helping newly bereaved widows who were considered to be at high risk for pathologic grief by virtue of having severe emotional distress. This intervention began to have a advantageous effect on social adjustment within 6 months. The intervention's effect on emotional distress appeared later, at 24 months.

In the other controlled study (Marmar et al. 1988), mutual support groups—led by widows specially trained in mutual support techniques described by Silverman (1986) and used by Vachon et al. (1980)—met regularly for 12 weeks. These groups were found to be as effective as brief psychotherapy for treating complicated bereavement in widows who were bereaved for 54 weeks on the average (range 16–158) at the time of the intervention. This was true when both symptom reduction and improvement of social functioning were considered, although the latter occurred more slowly for both interventions (Marmar et al. 1988). The absence of a nonintervention control group for this study (Marmar et al. 1988) makes it hard to conclude definitively that both interventions were superior to the healing effects of time alone. When the findings of this second study are placed in the context of the first study (Vachon et al. 1980) and other evidence for the efficacy of brief psychotherapy, it is reasonable to conclude that the evidence of the second study supports the effectiveness of mutual support and brief psychotherapy.

Another salient feature of the Marmar et al. (1988) study was the high dropout rate from the mutual support groups in comparison with that from the one-to-one psychotherapy. The attrition occurred despite the fact that the participants were equally satisfied whether they were assigned to a mutual support group or to brief psychotherapy at the beginning of the study. This observation raises a question about the appropriateness of mutual support group interventions during the early stages of treatment in contrast to individual approaches that customize help provided to bereaved individuals when their distress is most intense.

The findings from three other studies are less convincing about a therapeutic effect of mutual support interventions. In one study (Barrett 1978), the author found that self-help, among several psychosocial interventions, was the least effective intervention for improvement in physical, emotional, and social functioning of widows. The other interventions included consciousness-raising groups, relationships with confidants, and a waiting list control group. Further, when Lieberman and Borman (1979) evaluated a large sample of members of They Help Each Other Spiritually (THEOS), a mutual support group for widows, they found that only members who had an intense involvement in the mutual support group reported lower levels of depression and higher levels of self-esteem. Another evaluation done by Videka-Sherman and colleagues (Lieberman and Videka-Sherman 1986; Videka-Sherman 1982) of Compassionate Friends (a mutual support group for bereaved parents) found no difference in depression scores according to the degree of involvement in the mutual support group, although more involvement in the group was associated with greater self-reported personal growth.

The last two studies discussed had two flaws. Neither study addressed the question of whether their sample was representative of bereaved individuals in general, and neither reported what the true positive response rates were. Also in both studies, the absence of control groups made it impossible to appreciate whether the interventions were more effective than the improvement that would have naturally occurred over time. Both studies suggest, however, that the more committed and involved a bereaved individual is in the mutual support activity, the greater the potential benefit is, a lesson that is consistent with clinical experience in psychotherapy.

One additional study (Parkes 1980) of a volunteer bereavement outreach service is relevant to our discussion. This particular volunteer service was provided through a hospice; however, volunteer outreach services are often components of multidimensional, mutual support programs. The volunteer service in this study serves as a model of collaboration between professional and mutual support approaches to helping. In this study, trained widowed volunteers, who were supervised and supported by a psychiatrist, offered friendship and crisis intervention to bereaved family members considered to be at high risk for poor adjustment (Parkes 1980). Risk was defined by a composite rating of high emotional distress; heavy child care responsibilities, and a global clinical rating of need for help completed by the hospice nurse. The outreach did not have a demonstrable effect until after a 1-year implementation period for the new program. Subsequently, the treated group demonstrated significantly lower scores on autonomic symptomatology and the use of drugs, alcohol, and tobacco by comparison with a control group that was randomly assigned to no intervention. The outcomes were measured 20 months after the loss. The treated group also tended to report a better state of health and less deterioration in health, although these differences were not statistically significant ($P<.05$) unless they were used as part of an overall score. Thus this study modestly affirmed the value of this special type of mutual support, in particular for high-risk bereaved individuals. This conclusion ought to be confirmed with additional studies, perhaps with attention to comparing individual and group approaches to helping acutely bereaved individuals.

It is worth noting the relationship between this study of a one-to-one, volunteer intervention (Parkes 1980) and the study discussed above (Marmar et al. 1988) that included a comparison group for which widowed volunteers led mutual support groups. Given the questions that are emerging about the appropriateness of a group format for mutual support during acute bereavement (see the discussion of widowers below), it would be worthwhile for a systematic study to contrast the two approaches. Review of these studies raises an interesting question about whether one-to-one mutual support interventions might be more effective than group modalities at least in the initial stages of contact with the acutely bereaved individual (Barrett 1978; Marmar et al. 1988). Perhaps, a sequence of one-to-one, then group membership, or both at once would make the most sense.

Another question that arises is whether the combination of mutual support interventions with treatment interventions such as brief psychotherapy is not the most effective approach to helping acutely bereaved individuals. This is a possibility because mutual supports and psychotherapy seem to address different aspects of the bereaved individual's needs

(Marmar et al. 1988). These are questions that require attention in future evaluative research, not to mention the need to bolster in general the evidence for the effectiveness of these interventions.

The state of knowledge from controlled studies of mutual support interventions is no worse than that for other therapeutic interventions for the clinical complications of bereavement. Still, the demonstration of efficacy for mutual support interventions for bereaved individuals is of special importance given the absence of convincing evidence (reviewed in Chapter 6) that social networks and social supports are variables that affect the outcome of bereavement. In the meantime, there are reasons to continue to consider social network variables within a clinical framework because they logically play an important role in an environmental model of disease. Moreover, inferences from other studies about the contribution of social supports to health status encourage investigators to search for their specific role in the circumstances of bereavement (Berkman and Syme 1979; Cassel 1976; Cobb 1976).

A final issue about mutual support interventions concerns their application to the needs of widowers (American Association of Retired Persons 1984). Widowers are notably absent from the two most convincing evaluative studies of self-help (Marmar et al. 1988; Vachon et al. 1980). Because little is known about the needs of widowers, two colleagues and I (D. L. Snow, J. K. Tebes, S. C. Jacobs, unpublished analyses, 1987) undertook a pilot study with 22 widowers to clarify their attitudes about self-help efforts. One group of 10 widowers, who ranged in age from 29 years to 82 years and who had been bereaved for a range of 1 to 9 years, were identified because of their extensive participation in mutual support groups since the death of their wives. Above anything else, these men valued the companionship provided by the mutual support groups as a means of combating loneliness as well as the opportunity to confide in others about their experience. At the same time, they emphasized the importance of frequent contacts with family and friends both by telephone calls and through visits or invitations to dinner. Their reactions about their mutual support experiences were very favorable and underlined their active role in seeking out social activities as the most important coping strategy that they used. Yet they emphasized that they were receptive to joining such groups no earlier than 3 months after their loss. Before then, they relied on their families and close friends. They felt that the groups should be composed of both widows and widowers and should be aimed at providing the members with skills for living alone.

The other group of 12 widowers included 6 who were bereaved for 2–4 months and 6 who were bereaved for 7–9 months, all of whom had been identified systematically by screening death certificates from the local health department. None of them, as chance would have it, had an affiliation with a mutual support group. They ranged in age from 55 years to 88 years. Without exception, all of these widowers rejected the idea of a group format for mutual support and preferred that outreach on a one-to-one basis come from another widower rather than a widow. Contact with a widow was considered threatening insofar as it included a potential for intimacy. These widowers were receptive to the idea of emotional and instrumental support depending on who offered it. The younger and more recently bereaved men preferred this help from family. Those bereaved from 7 to 9 months were prepared to accept help from both family and friends, including other widowers.

Summarizing these two pilot studies, there was a distinction between the attitudes of a small but representative sample of 12 acutely bereaved men and those of the sample of 10 widowers selected because of their established involvement in mutual support groups. Those widowers who were not already committed to participation in mutual support groups were considerably more skeptical about the value of the groups than those who had already joined. Nevertheless, there was some agreement between the groups on the benefit of interpersonal contacts outside of the family and with close friends. The widowers from both groups believed that these outside contacts ought to begin sometime toward the end of the first year of bereavement. The findings from this small survey of attitudes not only highlighted the special issues of mutual support services for bereaved men but also illustrated the complicated issues involved in designing mutual support services for representative groups of acutely bereaved individuals.

Providing mutual supports for elderly widowers may be a particularly important task. The incentive for solving the problem of reaching widowers comes from observations such those from our study (C. F. Mendes de Leon, S. V. Kasl, S. C. Jacobs, unpublished observations, December 1992) using Established Populations for Epidemiologic Studies of the Elderly (EPESE; Cornoni-Huntley et al. 1986) data, which indicated that elderly widowers with low levels of instrumental and emotional support appear to have persistently high levels of depressive symptoms (also see Chapter 6). Our cross-sectional analyses suggested that the availability of social supports may protect widowers from unremitting depression.

The Clinician's Role in Mutual Support Programs

Many members of mutual support organizations, fearing the risks associated with the introduction of a clinical model, consider the professional irrelevant for their purposes. As a counterpoint to these apprehensions, I would argue that the exclusion of professionals is a short-sighted decision. In my judgment, the role of the professional in mutual support programs is quite important if not essential. Just what are the roles for the professional?

On the most basic level of collaboration with mutual support programs, the clinician plays an important part in recognizing and treating the clinical complications of bereavement that inevitably become obvious to the sophisticated members of these programs. This consultant role is not essentially different from that of a psychiatric consultant in a general hospital, with the exception that there is no attending physician who makes the referral from the mutual support group. Rather, mechanisms of referral are established through the leadership of the mutual support program, who may be mental health professionals or trained bereavement volunteers. In addition, the professional serves as an educational consultant to mutual support programs about the nature of bereavement and its clinical complications. The professional can also advise about the design of the supportive services that make up the organization's program (Caplan 1974). The professional's knowledge of bereavement bolsters the health education provided by supportive groups by providing education based on scientific understanding and knowledge of human behavior rather than on assumptions that may be oversimplified or even misguided. Also the professional's knowledge of coping and the social environment to which the bereaved individual must adapt contributes to the teaching of psychosocial rehabilitation through these groups.

In some instances, professionals serve as coleaders of mutual support groups (Yalom and Vinogradov 1988). In this role, they draw directly on their knowledge of therapeutic group process as well as their knowledge of grief. Not surprisingly, the content of supportive group meetings for bereaved individuals is similar in many respects to the content of individual psychotherapy (Yalom and Vinogradov 1988). This similarity speaks for the need for psychoeducational strategies of the type I discuss in Chapter 13 in groups as well as in individual interventions.

These are the main ways in which a professional serves a mutual support organization. In return, the mutual support organization can be a source of tremendous interest for the professional. There is much for the professional to learn about the techniques—cognitive approaches, ideological indoctrination, self-control techniques, means of reinforcing self-esteem, and means of empowerment—that are useful to the members of these groups in adapting to the problems posed by bereavement. Knowledge of this sort rounds out a clinician's understanding of the clinical complications of bereavement and the way that bereaved individuals cope with these complications in the community.

If a mutual support organization becomes involved in one-to-one, volunteer caregiving services, the professional can play a critical role in training and supervising the volunteer caregivers as bereavement counselors (Parkes 1980).Lest we begin to slip into a polarized way of thinking about professional help on the one hand and self-help on the other, it is instructive to consider this type of service as one of the most useful examples of collaboration. In the findings from three studies reported by Parkes (see Parkes 1980), there is preliminary and limited evidence for the efficacy of this type of service (see above). Volunteer caregivers' service takes advantage of the unique qualifications of the bereaved individual who has successfully adapted to grief, a qualification of great import to other bereaved individuals, and combines it with the therapeutic expertise, scientific knowledge of grief, and an understanding of the clinical complications that the clinician provides.

Relationship Between Professional Treatment and Mutual Support Efforts

The success of caring for the patient often depends on the quality of the cooperation between the professional and the nonprofessional support groups. Sometimes, professionals and mutual support groups view each other with distrust and stay at arm's length. Yet despite the inevitable disparity in some of the goals of each party, there is much that they share in common for the purpose of serving the acutely bereaved individual. For the professional, the deciding consideration is this: if the clinician encourages the patient to take an active role in his or her own treatment, the patient will often find a path to self-help activities in pursuit of this goal. Assuming this assumption is valid, the quality of the relationship between the two helping agencies is essential to the active involvement of patients in treatment and its successful outcome.

One stumbling block to successful collaboration between professionals and mutual support organizations stems from the problem of stigmatization. Stigmatization touches not only psychiatric patients but also those who treat them. As a rule, the same stereotypes of psychiatrists and psychiatric treatment that are found in American society are also found in the general membership of mutual support organizations. This underlies in part the distrust and antagonism that sometimes characterize the relationship between the psychiatrist and the mutual support group. It is essential for professionals to address this issue squarely. They can do this by taking the initiative to meet with mutual support organizations for the purposes of getting to know the organization's program, demonstrating their own professional knowledge, and showing how they can help. Frequently, on first meeting with a mutual support group, a question will be raised about whether the clinician has personally suffered a recent bereavement, which is the basic credential for entry into the mutual support program. There is a presumption that if the clinician does not know about bereavement he or she cannot help. The counterpoint to this theme is a clear exposition by the professional of the roles that he or she can play in a mutual support organization (discussed above), using as many examples or even personal anecdotes as are appropriate. The simple process of getting to know each other usually cuts through the stereotypic barriers that are encountered.

If the professional wins the friendship of the mutual support organization, the organization will then play a vital part in identifying individuals in its membership who are experiencing severe, clinical complications. Typically, the leadership of the organization plays a lead role in encouraging bereaved members who are not doing well to seek an evaluation as well as supporting the treatment for which a professional is highly trained to provide. Mrs. A (Chapter 1) is an example of a patient who needed treatment that would not have been possible without the support of the mutual support, aftercare program of the hospice in which her mother died. A more detailed description of her treatment is given below to illustrate the collaboration between the two agencies of care, the mutual support group and the therapist.

Conflict sometimes arises in these shared clinical endeavors because the clinician, whose primary commitment is to his or her patient, may or may not agree completely with the other caregivers on the objectives of treatment. For instance, many self-help organizations will have strong beliefs about the use of medicine, which may conflict with an individual's need for treatment. In addition, the issue of confidentiality of the clinical relationship potentially interferes with the collaboration between a professional and other, nonprofessional caregivers when it inhibits the exchange of information.

Confidentiality is a cornerstone of the treatment endeavor, which professionals accept because of its clinical importance and because it becomes a principle of practice that is almost second nature. Yet in order to collaborate with caregivers providing psychosocial rehabilitation, often the clinician will have to take the initiative to point out to the patient the advantages of the collaboration. This is done for the purpose of ultimately obtaining the patient's approval to disclose information and to share decisions with the group, even in the circumstances of potential disagreement between the patient and the group. The professional can offer to arbitrate the differences as a way of encouraging disclosure. If the group's involvement in rehabilitation is essential, clinicians may even indicate that they will disqualify themselves from treatment responsibility if the patient refuses. These compromises are essential in providing care for some bereaved patients, in particular those with chronic interpersonal problems that underlie the acute psychopathology. Patients like this have various degrees of disability and run a high risk of relapse that can be reduced with rehabilitative support.

Another dimension to the relationship between mutual support endeavors and the professional emerges in the task of social and political advocacy for the needs of bereaved individuals who require clinical services. One thesis of this book is that the clinical complications of bereavement are generally underrecognized and undertreated. This is a problem that is especially true for special bereaved groups, such as the survivors of

AIDS deaths, who suffer not only from bereavement overload but also from the progressive destruction of their social supports, not to mention the risk of being ill themselves (Lennon et al. 1990). By joining with mutual support organizations in advocating the needs of patients, clinicians serve the broader goal of gaining services for patients. The advantage of the collaboration is not insignificant. The professional has a unique opportunity to collaborate with bereaved individuals advocating the need for services and research without running the risk of being in an apparent conflict of interest. Often in the past, in the absence of organized patient groups, the unfortunate professional, however altruistic his or her motive, was accused of being primarily self-serving in his or her advocacy.

Just as there is great potential for collaboration in striving for mutually important policy goals, there is, as always, real potential for conflict. The conflict derives from the fact that different groups have different goals that they would like to put forward. One example of potential conflict involves the issue of treatment confidentiality, which was introduced above. Confidentiality is of fundamental importance to the therapeutic undertaking of the professional. On the other hand, telling the story of mental illness, in this case the psychiatric complications of bereavement, requires communication of important clinical information. The more personal the story that is told, the more appeal it has for fund-raising efforts or for the media. This problem can often be solved as courageous spokespersons for the needs of the bereaved individuals and patients emerge from the ranks of the bereaved themselves, thereby skirting the problem of disclosure.

Another area of potential conflict in regard to advocacy exists in different research and service agendas. The agenda of mutual support organizations tends to be oriented more toward rehabilitation and the agenda of professionals more toward treatment. These are differences that must be addressed and worked out in any collaboration with a self-help group for the purpose of advocacy. These differences sometimes thwart a collaborative effort, but in most cases common ground can be found in shared policy agendas.

The potential differences between professionals and mutual support, advocacy groups are overshadowed by their many shared goals, founded on the desire to help bereaved individuals in general and bereaved patients in particular. For example, one shared goal is the need to combat stigmatization of bereaved individuals with psychiatric disorders, not to mention the subtle stigmatization of the unmarried individual. Furthermore, there is a basis for a shared interest in psychological and mental health education. In addition, there is a shared commitment to increase funding not only for the treatment and rehabilitation of the clinical complications of bereavement but also for research into the causes of and new treatments for these disorders. There is much to be done to bring to the attention of the American public that psychiatric disorders associated with bereavement are common and that treatment exists to alleviate the suffering associated with them. This is but a part of the task of calling to the attention of society that services for psychiatric disorders in general are underfunded by comparison with other chronic medical diseases and that research into their nature is equally neglected, an illustration perhaps of the ultimate stigmatization.

The case of Ms. A, originally presented in Chapter 1, illustrates a productive collaboration between a mutual support group, to which I consulted as the psychiatrist in a hospice program, and myself as the treating psychiatrist. The clinical anecdote that follows also provides a concrete example of the ways in which a mutual support group can help.

Case 1 (*continued*)

Ms. A was referred for evaluation by both her children, who urged her to get help, and the leaders and members of the mutual support group she attended as part of the bereavement follow-up program of the hospice where her mother had died. With regard to the mutual support program, I communicated exclusively with a social worker and a nurse who led the mutual support group for the hospice.

Both the experienced members of the bereavement support group and I agreed that Ms. A needed professional help because of a depressive syndrome that was interfering with her functioning. The depression might have required pharmacological treatment if she had not responded to the combined, collaborative mutual support and psychotherapeutic interventions that we made.

Ms. A had organized herself around the impending anniversary of her son's death, which she regarded as a nemesis. Both the mutual support group and I recognized that she had been stunned by the death of her son. With the death of her mother shortly after the death of her son, she was overloaded with losses. She no longer trusted her own judgment, feeling that she had failed her son, nor could she sustain the belief that she lived in a reasonably predictable and benign world. She currently viewed her environment as threatening, if not hostile, because of her recent experiences.

To help her with these traumatic aspects of her loss and its consequences for how she felt—the disbelief, the philosophical crisis, and her sense of guilt—the mutual support group provided her an opportunity to review her recent experiences and test her reactions against the shared and accumulated wisdom of the group. I supported this objective in psychotherapy. At the same time, as she placed the events of her life in new perspective with the help of others, she was encouraged to forgive herself for the death of her son for which she felt in some way responsible. The group and I challenged this emotionally determined assumption by examining the details of the death and the logic of her feelings as well as bearing witness to her state of mind.

In addition, both the mutual support group and I undertook the psychoeducational task of helping Ms. A understand more about the desolation and separation distress that she felt. This task was predominantly mine along with the support of the group. Ms. A was not accustomed to intense levels of distress over which she had little control. Her characteristic, active style of coping was not particularly useful in helping her to come to terms with the high levels of distress. In fact, she felt useless as a mother, not only as a legacy of her son's death, which she felt she could not prevent, but also because she did not know what to do to help her surviving children to cope with the loss of their brother. As she learned about the nature and course of separation distress in herself as well as the role of the imminent anniversary of her son's death in intensifying her distress, she became more accepting of herself. In addition, she began to teach her surviving children about their reaction to the death of their brother, which provided deep gratification to her and restored in small measure her sense of being an efficacious mother.

This bereaved mother's exposure to the range of techniques used by others in her mutual support group to cope with their losses, and her discussion of these coping strategies with me in psychotherapy and others outside the group, provided her with considerable information about community resources and psychological means of coping. She was an apt student. She seemed to learn quickly about emotion-focused coping, such as expressing her feelings and pacing herself through the bereavement. It was as if she were just waiting for someone to show her how to do it and make helpful suggestions. She was perfectly capable of making use of the opportunity to do something with the right tools, as she had demonstrated in the past.

As a final point, both the mutual support group and I recognized the potential for conflict between Ms. A and her second husband, who was less severely affected by the losses than she. Furthermore, Ms. A was very concerned about her surviving children and how they were coping with the death of their brother. In turn, they were concerned about her. In principle, we recognized that different members of a family go through grief at their own pace, at varying levels of intensity and in their own way. Optimally, we would have invited the husband, and perhaps the children, into the mutual support group or into conjoint meetings with me. This would have been the most direct means of addressing the marital conflict and the family worries. Unfortunately, both Ms. A and her husband resisted this recommendation. Nevertheless, by pointing out to her the wide range and variability of human responses to a loss, the marital conflict seemed to dissipate. In addition, as she improved and passed her new knowledge on to her children, both her concern for them and theirs for her diminished.

This example is not typical of most bereaved individuals who enter a mutual support group. Most do not become directly involved with a mental health professional or even a volunteer caregiver. I chose this example because it demonstrates not only many of the interventions that mutual support groups can make on their own, in most cases, but also the collaboration between the group and a professional.

Mutual Support: Prevention, Treatment, or Rehabilitation

Mutual support interventions for bereaved individuals were developed in the Laboratory of Community Psychiatry at the Massachusetts Mental Health Center in the 1960s. This program focused on bereavement and other life stresses as risk factors for psychiatric disorders (Caplan 1964; Silverman 1986; Silverman et al. 1974). Mutual support interventions were originally conceptualized as a type of preventive intervention within a theoretical framework taken from public health. Coincident with their preventive intent, mutual support interventions serve treatment and rehabilitative goals. In a public health model these are provided for as secondary and tertiary preventive interventions (see Chapter 15).

Taking Ms. A above as an example, the mutual support intervention primarily served treatment and rehabilitative goals. To the extent that the intervention was early in the course of bereavement, the emphasis was on treatment. Ms. A had a severe major depressive syndrome that was not resolving spontaneously. The combination of psychotherapy and the mutual support intervention was effective in the early treatment of her depression. The therapeutic effort probably averted a chronic depression, which might have included the need to use antidepressant medicine. The therapy also possibly averted the development of deeply entrenched maladaptive coping. Insofar as the intervention was early, the information on coping skills and resources that Ms. A received was more facilitative of ongoing and future adaptation than rehabilitative. Rehabilitation more appropriately is conceptualized as an intervention for maladaptive coping that has established itself as a persistent pattern of impairment in interpersonal functioning. Still, the main effect of the mutual support intervention for Ms. A was to minimize the risk of disability associated with the major depression. This tertiary prevention was accomplished through the friendship and education provided by the group with the aim of helping Ms. A cope more effectively.

There was no primary preventive aspect to the interventions for Ms. A. This is true by definition because the major depression afflicting her was already well established as a clinical complication at the time of therapy. It is conceivable that many bereaved individuals make use of mutual support interventions to facilitate their adaptation to bereavement early enough in the course of events to avoid the occurrence of clinical complications. In these cases, the mutual support intervention is truly preventing a disorder, and this is primary prevention. Clinicians do not see many of these bereaved individuals unless they serve as consultants to mutual support organizations. Given the rarity of direct clinical experience, it would be helpful to turn to systematic studies to demonstrate a preventive effect of mutual support during bereavement. Unfortunately, at the present time, no studies of this nature are available. In any event, it does not appear that bereaved individuals become involved in mutual support groups early enough in the course of grief for the mutual support intervention to have a primary or even secondary preventive effect on the acute clinical complications of bereavement.

It is also conceivable that many bereaved individuals with chronic, pathologic grief take part in mutual support programs by way of self-referral. In some cases the referral is made by a therapist, such as Ms. E (in Chapter 6). In these cases, the mutual support intervention is plainly rehabilitative, although this may not be appreciated by the mutual support organization. Generally, the members of mutual support groups lack the clinical acumen to reach a conclusion about maladaptation and clinical complications, though they may dimly perceive that something is not right.

When pathologic grief becomes chronic, the distinction between treatment, rehabilitation, and primary prevention of comorbidity is useful for conceptualizing the nature of the clinical work; however, clinical practice is characterized by the integration of all three. For that matter, this is the case for all chronic diseases. It is truly hard to separate the tasks. Even if the major responsibility for rehabilitation is delegated, it is the clinician's responsibility to integrate all the tasks of therapy into a particular treatment plan for the bereaved individual.

Conclusions

The benefits of collaboration outweigh the disadvantages of conflict in the relationship between the professional and mutual support endeavors or organizations. Involvement by the professional individual in self-help activities fosters appropriate humility about the limits of professional expertise and appreciation of the possible contributions of the patient with a clinical disorder to his or her own care. Ignorance of and noninvolvement in mutual support efforts, either out of fear of the risk of conflict or because a particular therapeutic ideology does not provide for it, fosters a professional self-satisfaction that is ultimately illusory. Professional apathy about involvement in self-help programs leads to a failure to appreciate the problems of noncompliance, the limitations of our treatments, and the potential of mutual support organizations to contribute to the long-term treatment and rehabilitation of our patients. An analysis of mutual support programs indicates that their contribution to the care of bereaved individuals is potentially substantial through promoting successful adaptation and fostering self-esteem.

The skills that the professional individual needs for collaboration are basic social and political adeptness, ability as a teacher, knowledge of the consultant's role, and a collaborative attitude. Probably the initiative for professional and self-help collaborations appropriately lies with us, the professionals, although open-mindedness and goodwill on the part of mutual support organizations are essential also. The paramount goal is to provide a comprehensive program of care for patients with clinical complications of bereavement.

References

American Association of Retired Persons: The forgotten men. Ideas for Action 1:1–4, 1984
Barrett CJ: Effectiveness of widows' groups in facilitating change. J Consult Clin Psychol 46:20–31, 1978
Berkman LF, Syme SL: Social networks, host resistance, and mortality: a nine year follow-up of Alameda County residents. Am J Epidemiol 109:186–204, 1979
Caplan G: Principles of Preventive Psychiatry. New York, Basic Books, 1964
Caplan G: Support Systems and Community Mental Health. New York, Behavioral Publications, 1974
Cassel J: The contribution of the social environment to host resistance. Am J Psychiatry 104:107–123, 1976
Cobb S: Social support as a moderator of life stress. Psychosom Med 38:300–314, 1976
Cornoni-Huntley J, Brock DB, Ostfeld AM, et al (eds):Established Populations for Epeidemiologic Studies of the Elderly: Resource Data Book (NIA USDHHS, PHS, NIH, NIH Publication No 86-2443). Bethesda, MD, National Institutes of Health, 1986
Galanter M: Research on social supports and mental illness. Am J Psychiatry 145:1270–1272, 1988
Lennon MC, Martin JL, Dean L: The influence of social support on AIDS-related grief reaction among gay men. Soc Sci Med 31:477–484, 1990
Lieberman MA, Borman LD: Self-Help Groups for Coping With Crises. San Francisco, CA, Joffey-Bass, 1979
Lieberman MA, Videka-Sherman L: The impact of self-help groups on the mental health of widows and widowers. Am J Orthopsychiatry 56:435–439, 1986
Marmar CR, Horowitz MJ, Weiss DS, et al: A controlled trial of brief psychotherapy and mutual help group treatment of conjugal bereavement. Am J Psychiatry 145:203–209, 1988
Osterweis M, Solomon F, Green M (eds): Bereavement: Reactions, Consequences and Care. Washington, DC, National Academy Press, 1984
Parkes CM: Bereavement counseling: does it work? BMJ 281:3–6, 1980
Silverman P: Widow to Widow. New York, Springer, 1986
Silverman PR, MacKenzie D, Pettipas M, et al (eds): Helping Each Other in Widowhood. New York, Health Sciences Publishing, 1974
Vachon MLS, Lyall WAL, Rogers J, et al: A controlled trial of self-help intervention for widows. Am J Psychiatry 137:1380–1384, 1980

Videka-Sherman L: Effects of participation in a self-help group for bereaved parents: Compassionate Friends. Prevention in Human Services 1:69–77, 1982

Walker KN, MacBride A, Vachon MLS: Social support networks and the crisis of bereavement. Soc Sci Med 2:35–41, 1977

Yalom ID, Vinogradov S: Bereavement groups: techniques and themes. Int J Group Psychother 38:419–446, 1988

CHAPTER 15

Prevention

The study of life events repeatedly identifies familial bereavement as one of the most stressful human experiences (Holmes and Rahe 1968; Murrell et al. 1984; Paykel et al. 1971). According to the estimates from one epidemiological study of adults over age 55 (Murrell et al. 1984), 3% of women and 1.6% of men in this age group experience conjugal bereavement each year. The large sample in this study was representative of the adult population of Kentucky in this age range and an accurate reflection of the population of the United States. Using the same sample, the authors estimated that 14% of women and 12% of men experience some death in the family each year. Given bereavement's ranking as the most undesirable life experience and the evidence reviewed in previous chapters and elsewhere for both the mental and physical health consequences of the experience, it should be a prime target for prevention in mental health programs (Murrell et al. 1984).

Not surprisingly in light of these considerations, for four decades, since Lindeman and Caplan developed their ideas in the 1940s and 1950s, bereavement has served as one of the most important models for conceptualizing the tasks of prevention in psychiatry. Caplan, building on Lindeman's study (1943) of bereavement caused by the Coconut Grove fire, was the architect of crisis theory (Caplan 1964). Based on crisis theory, crisis intervention was developed as a brief, psychotherapeutic modality for the treatment of acute, emotional crises associated with environmental stressors, such as the death of a family member. In treatment, emphasis was placed on the involvement of family and close friends in order to arrange a social environment that supported the individual in crisis. This tradition of thinking about prevention has a long line of development that can be traced down the years through Maddison's studies in Boston (Maddison and Walker 1967) and in Sydney, Australia, (Maddison and Viola 1968) to a major study of crisis intervention as a preventive intervention for pathologic grief completed by Raphael (1977) in Sydney. The tradition of using bereavement as a model for prevention also can be tracked through Silverman's work with widows' and widowers' groups in the United States (Silverman 1986; Silverman et al. 1974) to studies of mutual support as an intervention for acutely bereaved individuals (Marmar et al. 1988; Vachon et al. 1980). Mutual support interventions provide a new social medium for working on the problems of social adjustment that arise after a loss. These interventions may avert the occurrence and persistence of severe symptomatology if offered in a timely way.

It is useful for the psychiatrist and the mental health professional interested in helping acutely bereaved individuals to learn more about concepts of prevention for the purpose of intervening early in the course of illness. In some instances, there is the opportunity to head off the occurrence of mental disorders. Many clinical interventions during bereavement can be effectively conceptualized as forms of prevention. Furthermore, preventive concepts create a basis for considering the consultative and collaborative relationship of the professional to community-based services (Caplan 1974). The content of the consultations centers around the clinical complications of bereavement, about which the professional is an expert, that are inevitably discovered in some participants in community-based programs for bereaved individuals.

Concepts of Prevention

Before entering a discussion of prevention in bereavement, it is worthwhile to introduce a few concepts about prevention drawn from a general public health framework. In public health programs, three types of prevention are recognized. The ultimate goal of any public health program is *primary prevention*, which involves the elimination of the causes of disease. Success in this endeavor is measured by a reduction in the incidence of new cases of the disease. *Secondary prevention*, which involves early, efficient treatment intervention for incipient illness, is usually accomplished through screening for disease in high-risk populations. Its purpose is to reduce mortality and disability as consequences of disease. The expediency of secondary prevention is measured in a reduction in the prevalence of a disease. *Tertiary prevention* involves early, efficient rehabilitation and health education. These interventions are made for the purpose of reducing the risk of chronic disability as a consequence of disease. Included in tertiary intervention is professionals' consultation with institutions and agencies that provide health services to the population. This public health framework is used to organize the discussion of preventive interventions below.

At first, a public health perspective may seem like an alien approach to conceptualizing interventions for clinicians. Ordinarily, practitioners are preoccupied with treatment and rehabilitation. It is my hope that, through the discussion in this chapter, the perspective that a preventive model in the broadest sense provides for both treatment and rehabilitation will become better appreciated. It does this by providing for primary prevention while concomitantly placing emphasis on available methods for early, efficient interventions using public health strategies. This strategy is preferable to just waiting for the patient to present in the doctor's office for treatment. Also a preventive model formally introduces the task of preventing illness (i.e., reducing incidence) to round out the responsibilities of the physician. Indeed, I would agree with an epidemiologist who exhorted his medical colleagues to take a broad view of their responsibilities to their patients when he wrote "prevention and control constitute the ultimate business of health professionals" (Susser 1981, p. 7).

It is true that a lack of knowledge about the specific etiology of psychiatric disorders and the pathogenetic heterogeneity of psychiatric syndromes handicap the development of preventive strategies in psychiatry. Yet this is no more true of psychiatry than other parts of chronic disease medicine. In chronic disease medicine, disease entities are understood as products of complex, multifactorial etiologies. In the case of chronic diseases, typically both clinical knowledge and epidemiological knowledge of the diseases are brought to bear in developing preventive approaches. For example, the strategies for reducing the incidence of myocardial infarctions, intervening early with treatment to prevent disability after an infarction occurs, and efficient rehabilitation to prevent relapses and minimize chronic disability from coronary disease do not differ materially from the preventive interventions for the complications of bereavement that I discuss below. In the case of the clinical complications associated with bereavement, a case can be made that at least the psychopathological syndromes are homogeneous by virtue of their relationship to loss as a stressor, even if we do not yet understand the etiological mechanism precisely.

In psychiatry, there are several examples of the ways in which existing knowledge of psychiatric disorders can be used to develop preventive models and interventions. These include perinatal and early child care interventions for children of schizophrenic mothers (J. McGrath, "The Brisbane Schizophrenia High Risk Intervention Study," unpublished manuscript, 1991). Such a program is designed to avoid neurodevelopmental damage to the child that may be the basis of some forms of schizophrenia. Another example is the preventive use of thiamine to reduce the incidence of alcoholic dementias. Other examples include special interventions for those who have experienced trauma and thus are at high risk for developing posttraumatic stress disorder (B. Raphael, "Prevention of Post Traumatic Stress Disorder in Caregivers for Disaster Victims," unpublished manuscript, 1991); health education programs for primary care physicians, such as the Depression/Awareness, Recognition, and Treatment (DART) program, for the purpose of the early recognition and treatment of major depressions (National Institute of Mental Health 1986); psychoeducational programs for families of severely ill patients to teach about expressed emotion and reduce the risk of relapse into acute psychosis (Leff et al. 1982; Vaughn and Leff 1976); the use of lithium to prevent relapses of bipolar illness (Fleiss et al. 1978); and psychotherapies for neuroticism as a personality trait, a risk factor for anxiety disorders, to reduce the risk of occurrence of anxiety disorders in young adults (Jorm 1989).

Many examples of clinical interventions during bereavement can also be understood in a preventive context. These include pharmacological interventions, psychotherapeutic interventions conceptualized in terms of crisis intervention, and mutual support interventions. In the remainder of this chapter, the treatment and rehabilitative interventions that I discuss in Chapters 11 through 14 are reviewed within a preventive perspective. This perspective serves as another strategy, supplementary to the analysis of the tasks of treatment in Chapter 11, for thinking about a comprehensive and integrated approach to patient care. Drawing on the same line of reasoning used in Chapter 11, it is apparent that no single intervention for treating the complications of bereavement is sufficiently powerful or sweeping in scope that we can depend entirely upon it. This fact serves as an incentive to search for more effective treatments as well as an encouragement to integrate the treatments that are currently available. The synthesis of preventive thinking into a clinical perspective provides an added measure of power in our treatment model.

A final note is necessary concerning the nature of prevention. It is important to emphasize that the discussion in this chapter is about prevention of psychiatric disorders rather than the promotion of mental health or human growth. The latter objective is a legitimate one for public health programs; however, it sets virtually no limits on the nature and scope of prevention. Practically anything that is good and positive—whether in the domain of parental responsibilities, education, politics, or economics—can be understood as preventive in the perspective of promoting mental health. Mental health programs that promote personal growth and development through teaching coping skills or consulting to institutions to make them more conducive to these aims have proliferated. But promoting mental health is too loose a definition of prevention and too far removed from medical practice for the present purpose. It is preferable to emphasize the role of the physician in prevention and to place some constraint on what is considered appropriate for clinical psychiatry and medicine to accept responsibility for. Therefore, the emphasis is on the prevention of psychiatric disorders.

Primary Prevention

One convincing example of an opportunity for primary prevention related to bereavement springs from the evidence that sudden, unexpected deaths are associated with poorer outcomes (Lundin 1984). Complementing this evidence, Parkes and Weiss (1983) observed that sudden death is associated with unexpected grief, one pattern of pathologic grief in their study. The implication of these observations for prevention of the clinical complications of bereavement is that attending physicians or other clinical staff should discuss the diagnosis of terminal illness with family members. This provides the family the opportunity to come to terms with the terminal illness and take leave of the patient in the final phase of the individual's life. The discussion with the family may or may not lead to subsequent conversations with the patient regarding his or her diagnosis and prognosis. The latter is a task that has been advocated in many hospice programs for which the patient will be more or less prepared. What is essential for our consideration is that the surviving family be advised of the imminent loss. This should not be optional. In some cases, the family may need counseling to come to terms with the threatened loss. Presumably, the time and effort invested in this step before the death occurs will reduce the risk of later complications of bereavement in surviving family members. This is a type of preventive intervention that has not been systematically tested and ought to be examined to prove its usefulness.

Crisis intervention for high-risk bereaved individuals provides another example of primary prevention in bereavement. In this case, the intervention stands somewhere between primary and secondary prevention, depending on how the emotional disturbance immediately after a loss is conceptualized. For example, if the bereaved individual already has a major depressive syndrome at the time that crisis intervention is provided, it would be appropriate to consider this as secondary prevention. If the early, ubiquitous depressive disturbances of bereavement are viewed as nonspecific dysphoria, then the crisis intervention is justifiably considered primary prevention. This is true insofar as the intervention reduces the risk of major depressions and other clinical complications of bereavement that might occur later. This is an open issue that has not been systematically tested and requires study. I follow the assumption made in the published studies of crisis intervention that the identification of individuals who are at high risk for developing clinical complications of bereavement and eligible for this type of intervention occurs before the onset of recognized psychopathology. Assuming that this is the case for the time being, crisis intervention is an example of legitimate primary prevention in psychiatry.

Within the framework of crisis theory, it is accepted that the high-risk individual will be in a state of emotional crisis following the death (i.e., he or she will be highly emotionally aroused, psychologically distressed, more or less confused in thinking through the problems posed by the loss, and uncertain what to do) (Caplan 1964). Theoretically, such an individual is at higher risk for pathologic grief, depressions, or anxiety disorders than other bereaved individuals. This risk is reduced if an effective preventive intervention is provided. One major, well-controlled study of crisis intervention during bereavement convincingly demonstrated the efficacy of preventive intervention in reducing prolonged distress or chronic grief among high-risk bereaved spouses (Raphael 1977).

In a broad sense, the study of crisis intervention provides a cornerstone for recommendations about bereavement counseling for uncomplicated grief (Worden 1982). It should be noted, however, that counseling is distinguished from crisis intervention insofar as the former is recommended for everyone, not only individuals at high risk for developing complications of bereavement. The value of general counseling, though intuitively promising and perhaps obvious as a fundamental education task for the clinician who encounters an acutely bereaved patient, needs to be tested.

Secondary Prevention

Early intervention for the major depressions of bereavement serves as a good example of secondary prevention for the clinical complications of bereavement. Increasingly, there is an awareness of the importance of early intervention and maintenance treatment with antidepressants for patients with affective disorders. Such treatment should be done to prevent the transformation of the affective illness process into more accelerated cycles, the development of autonomous episodes, and the potential for drug refractoriness (Post 1991).

To illustrate this example of prevention during bereavement, it is necessary to develop the rationale for it in some detail. In short, the rationale is based on evidence indicating that the major depressive syndromes of bereavement that occur shortly after a loss and do not remit 4–6 months later ought to be treated. If untreated, the depressive state may persist (Bornstein et al. 1973; Jacobs et al. 1989), the symptoms of the depressive syndrome may evolve into melancholic features and a disturbance of self-esteem (Blanchard et al. 1976; Clayton and Darvish 1979), and the unresolved grief may coexist as a reflection of the chronic stress of the loss (Jacobs et al. 1987b; Zisook and DeVaul 1983). Furthermore, the epidemiological profile of these unremitting depressions is comparable to that of clinical depressions observed in psychiatric clinics, including a higher risk in women and some evidence that personal and family histories of depression increase the risk (see Chapter 4).

In contrast, the depressive syndromes that occur early in the course of bereavement and subside in a few months do not appear to be similar to clinical depressions. Rather, converging lines of evidence suggest that remitting depressive symptoms that occur early in bereavement, even those that are severe in intensity, appear to be a reflection of the intensity of the separation distress caused by the loss. The bases for this conclusion are manifold. In bereaved individuals, early separation distress is also intense and correlates with depression (Hays 1991). In addition, depressive symptoms are ubiquitous as manifestations of grief, occurring in at least one-third of acutely bereaved individuals in the first month, and therefore have a nonspecific character (Bornstein et al. 1973; Zisook and Shuchter 1991). Moreover, the content of the remitting depressive symptoms is typically focused on the death of the spouse rather than generalized to a pervasive, pessimistic attitude (see Chapter 9). Autonomic arousal, which is associated with neurovegetative symptoms, is conspicuous in the early stages of bereavement, providing an alternative to depression as an explanation for the neurovegetative symptoms that are observed (Clayton and Darvish 1979; Nelson and Charney 1981). Also nonsuppression on the dexamethasone suppression test, which occurs in 10%–20% of acutely bereaved individuals, is positively correlated with anxiety scores rather than depression scores (Shuchter et al. 1986). Finally, the depressive syndromes seen in acutely bereaved individuals are transient over a few months for 80% or more of these individuals (Bornstein et al. 1973). In other words, for most acutely bereaved individuals, these depressive symptoms are part of uncomplicated bereavement and subside spontaneously in a few months.

Unfortunately, our ability to predict those bereaved individuals with a major depression who will get better naturally and those who will not is limited. As I note in Chapter 4, female gender and, perhaps, a positive history of major depressions predict a higher risk of unremitting depressions of bereavement (Jacobs et al. 1989). The most powerful predictor, however, is the occurrence of depressive symptoms early in the course of bereavement. Whereas 80% of individuals with depressions early in bereavement will improve spontaneously as noted above, the other side of the coin is that 20% will not (Bornstein et al. 1973). Therefore, the relative risk of a persistent depression of bereavement is six or more for a bereaved individual for whom a depressive syndrome occurs in the first few months. This is a substantial relative risk, exceeding by far the relative risk associated with being female and bereaved.

The best timing for a secondary preventive intervention is difficult to ascertain. A consensus is growing that it should take place 4 months after a loss. This is the time when, for the majority of bereaved individuals, the intensity of emotional distress including depressive symptoms is subsiding (Clayton 1988; Windholz et al. 1985). There is additional evidence that rates of depression in acutely bereaved samples fall off steeply over the first 4–6 months, subsequently becoming rather stable (Bornstein et al. 1973; Clayton 1988; Jacobs et al. 1989). It appears, therefore, that this is the time when the depressive states of early bereavement begin to become entrenched, chronically disabling, and clinically significant. Hence, this is the strategic time for early intervention with antidepressant treatment or a psychosocial intervention. An intervention at this time will efficiently relieve the symptoms of major depression and minimize the risk of chronic disability. The findings from two open clinical trials that I discuss in Chapter 12 (Jacobs et al. 1987a; Pasternak et al. 1991) create a basis for considering psychotropic drug treatment as a type of secondary prevention. Studies of crisis intervention, cognitive therapy, and interpersonal therapy furnish a foundation for considering a psychosocial intervention (Elkin et al. 1989; Raphael 1977). These are examples of secondary, preventive interventions that ought to be systematically tested in order to prove their usefulness.

The types of interventions that have been discussed in this chapter thus far are also considered from different perspectives in Chapters 12 and 13; the discussion in this chapter has been selective for the purpose of illustrating the concepts of prevention. So far, these interventions are appropriately the responsibility of a trained mental health professional, preferably a psychiatrist who has knowledge of both pharmacological treatment and psychotherapy. The discussion of tertiary prevention involves the professional in a relationship to nonprofessional caregivers.

Tertiary Prevention

When mutual support programs are implemented early during a period of emotional crisis and before a psychopathological syndrome appears (i.e., in the first few months of bereavement), they have the potential for habilitative and primary preventive effects also. However, ordinarily acutely bereaved individuals do not choose to enter mutual support groups at this time in the course of their bereavement and thus the opportunity for primary prevention is rare. Therefore, mutual support groups are more appropriately considered tertiary prevention.

The single, best example of early rehabilitation and health education for bereaved individuals is the mutual support, widow-to-widow program described by Silverman and her colleagues (Silverman 1986; Silverman et al. 1974). Mutual support groups have been defined as "groups in which people with a common problem come together for the mutual support and constructive action that will lead to the achievement of shared goals" (Marmar et al. 1988, p. 204). The widow-to-widow program is one in which widowed individuals, who have lived through and integrated the experience, reach out to newly widowed individuals and provide a range of social, supportive, and educational activities. A program of social support achieves its goals through programs of social activities as well as through multiple modalities: the exchange of information and experiences, facilitation of the bereaved individual's ability to cope and adapt to a new status, the process of effecting changes in the social environment of the bereaved individual, and the enhancement of the bereaved individual's self-esteem through a sense of belonging and emotional support.

Concomitant with the pioneering work in developing a self-help program for widows and widowers, several other mutual support programs, such as Candlelighters, Compassionate Friends, and They Help Each Other Spiritually (THEOS), have emerged (Osterweis et al. 1984). Although mutual support programs have developed extensively, presumably because of their success in meeting the needs of their membership, only a few controlled studies have been done to evaluate their effectiveness. The concepts in the original widow-to-widow program (Silverman 1986; Silverman et al. 1974) have served as the background for the two most convincing evaluative studies that have been done to demonstrate a salutary effect of mutual supports during bereavement (Vachon et al. 1980; Marmar et al. 1988). As was the case in discussing primary and secondary preventions above, more systematic research is needed to affirm the value of these interventions for tertiary prevention.

Conclusions

Historically, bereavement provided a model for thinking about prevention in psychiatry. Modern research, beginning with the development of recent life event scales and contemporary studies of bereavement, has reinforced earlier impressions based on clinical acumen that bereavement is a severe stress. Contemporary studies also continue to support the idea that bereavement is an important model for thinking about psychiatric prevention. The early study of bereavement contributed directly to the development of two of the more important preventive interventions in psychiatric practice: crisis intervention and mutual support intervention. More recently, additional ideas about bereavement counseling for the families of terminally ill patients, early interventions for depressions of bereavement, and refinements in program ideas for mutual support interventions have contributed to our concepts of primary, secondary, and tertiary prevention during bereavement.

To the extent that a well-defined event such as the death of a family member opens a finite period for the survivors in which they may be at higher risk for psychiatric disorders, an opportunity exists to conceptualize preventive tasks. The public health concepts of primary, secondary, and tertiary prevention provide a framework for integrating preventive work into clinical practice. A preventive perspective not only introduces the opportunity to prevent the occurrence of pathologic grief, major depressions, and, perhaps, anxiety disorders but also encourages the clinician to make early treatment and rehabilitative interventions to reduce the risk, extent, and duration of disability associated with a psychiatric disorder caused by bereavement. The integration of preventive tasks into clinical practice with concern for the efficiency of intervention techniques is a valuable step in the direction of achieving the most effective approach to helping our patients. The potential for integrating prevention and clinical practice stems from a perspective that places bereaved individuals in an environmental context, recognizes the death of an intimate as a vector of disease, and considers the effects of the loss not only on individuals but also on the social milieu around them. These are the elements of an adaptive model that I adopt in Chapter 5 for thinking about the clinical complications of bereavement.

References

Blanchard CG, Blanchard EB, Becker JV: The young widow: depressive symptomatology throughout the grief process. Psychiatry 39:394–399, 1976

Bornstein PE, Clayton PJ, Halikas JA, et al: The depression of widowhood after thirteen months. Br J Psychiatry 122:561–566, 1973

Caplan G: Principles of Preventive Psychiatry. New York, Basic Books, 1964

Caplan G: Support Systems and Community Mental Health. New York, Behavioral Publications, 1974

Clayton PJ: Preventing depression: the symptom, the syndrome, or the disorder, in Depression Prevention: Research Directions. Edited by Munoz R. Washington, DC, Hemisphere Publishing, 1988, pp 31–43

Clayton PJ, Darvish HS: Course of depressive symptoms following the stress of bereavement, in Stress and Mental Disorder. Edited by Barrett JE, Rose RM, Klerman GL. New York, Raven, 1979, pp 121–136

Elkin I, Shea T, Watkins JT, et al: National Institute of Mental Health Treatment of Depression Collaborative Research Program. Arch Gen Psychiatry 46:971–982, 1989

Fleiss JL, Prien RF, Dunner DL, et al: Actuarial studies of the course of manic depressive illness. Compr Psychiatry 19:355–362, 1978

Hays JC: Psychological distress, social environment, and seeking social support following conjugal bereavement. PhD dissertation, Yale University, School of Epidemiology and Public Health, 1991

Holmes TH, Rahe RH: The social readjustment rating scale. J Psychosom Res 11:213–218, 1968

Jacobs SC, Nelson JC, Zisook S: Treating depressions of bereavement with antidepressants: a pilot study. Psychiatr Clin North Am 10:501–510, 1987a

Jacobs SC, Schaefer CA, Ostfeld AM, et al: The first anniversary of bereavement. Isr J Psychiatry Relat Sci 24:77–85, 1987b

Jacobs SC, Hansen F, Berkman L, et al: Depressions of bereavement. Compr Psychiatry 30:218–224, 1989

Jorm AF: Modifiability of trait anxiety and neuroticism: a meta-analysis of the literature. Aust N Z J Psychiatry 23:21–29, 1989

Leff J, Kuipers L, Berkowitz R, et al: A controlled trial of social intervention in the families of schizophrenic patients. Br J Psychiatry 141:121–134, 1982

Lundin T: Morbidity following sudden and unexpected bereavement. Br J Psychiatry 144:84–88, 1984

Maddison DC, Viola A: The health of widows in the year following bereavement. J Psychosom Res 12:297–306, 1968

Maddison DC, Walker WL: Factors affecting the outcome of conjugal bereavement. Br J Psychiatry 113:1057–1067, 1967

Marmar CR, Horowitz MJ, Weiss DS, et al: A controlled trial of brief psychotherapy and mutual help group treatment of conjugal bereavement. Am J Psychiatry 145:203–209, 1988

Murrell SA, Norris FH, Hutchins GL: Distribution and desirability of life events in older adults: population and policy implications. Journal of Community Psychology 12:301–311, 1984

National Institute of Mental Health: Depression/Awareness, Recognition, and Treatment Campaign (DART). Washington, DC, National Institute of Mental Health, 1986

Nelson JC, Charney DS: The symptoms of major depressive illness. Am J Psychiatry 138:1–13, 1981

Osterweis M, Solomon F, Green M (eds): Bereavement: Reactions, Consequences and Care. Washington, DC, National Academy Press, 1984

Parkes CM, Weiss RS: Recovery From Bereavement. New York, Basic Books, 1983

Pasternak RE, Reynolds CF, Schlernitzauer M, et al: Acute open-trial nortriptyline therapy of bereavement-related depression in late life. J Clin Psychiatry 52:307–310, 1991

Paykel ES, Prusoff BA, Uhlenhuth EH: Scaling of life events. Arch Gen Psychiatry 15:340–347, 1971

Post RM: Transduction of psychosocial stress into the neurobiology of recurrent affective disorder. Paper presented at the Third Annual Bristol-Myers Squibb Symposium on the Neurobiology of Depression. New Haven, CT, October 25–26, 1991

Raphael B: Preventive intervention with the recently bereaved. Arch Gen Psychiatry 34:1450–1454, 1977

Shuchter SR, Zisook S, Kirkorowicz C, et al: The dexamethasone suppression test in acute grief. Am J Psychiatry 143:879–881, 1986

Silverman PR, MacKenzie D, Pettipas M, et al (eds): Helping Each Other in Widowhood. New York, Health Sciences Publishing, 1974

Silverman P: Widow to Widow. New York, Springer, 1986

Susser M: The epidemiology of life stress. Psychol Med 11:1–8, 1981

Vachon MLS, Lyall WAL, Rogers J, et al: A controlled trial of self-help intervention for widows. Am J Psychiatry 137:1380–1384, 1980

Vaughn CE, Leff JP: The influence of family and social factors on the course of psychiatric illness. Br J Psychiatry 129:125–137, 1976

Windholz MJ, Marmar CR, Horowitz MJ: A review of the research on conjugal bereavement: impact on health and efficacy of intervention. Compr Psychiatry 26:433–437, 1985

Worden JW: Grief Counseling and Grief Therapy: A Handbook for the Mental Health Practitioner. New York, Springer, 1982

Zisook S, DeVaul RA: Grief, unresolved grief, and depression. Psychosomatics 24:247–256, 1983

Zisook S, Shuchter SR: Depression through the first year after the death of a spouse. Am J Psychiatry 148:1346–1352, 1991

CHAPTER 16

Conclusions

Having discussed the nature, the diagnosis, and the treatment of the clinical complications of bereavement, in this final chapter I briefly review the major questions raised about pathologic grief in the book and tie together the major themes that appear throughout it.

Risks and Benefits of Attachment

One of the characteristics that distinguishes humans from other animals, in addition to their upright ambulation, hands with opposing thumbs, large brains, and use of symbols and language, is their unique sociability. And one of the great insights of contemporary epidemiology and biology is the recognition that our social relationships serve an essential biological function and convey evolutionary advantage in the struggle for survival.

One of the noblest characteristics of humans is their conscious awareness and acceptance of the finiteness of their existence. This consciousness becomes evident in their attachment to other individuals despite the fact that the cost of commitment, as well as the evolutionary advantage, is high (Parkes 1972). Most of us do not think of attachment as a conscious choice in our lives; we make decisions about attachment for other reasons, such as the need for intimacy or the desire to have children, and we deny the inevitability of change and loss. When we begin to contemplate the question of loss, it becomes clear that attachment is the essence of a very private heroism and tragedy in each of our personal, social lives.

Of course, the gratification and satisfaction from intimacy are immense. The formation and maintenance of attachment bonds that confer an evolutionary advantage are described as the joys of falling in love and being in love (Bowlby 1977). The safety and security provided by attachments are known as the comforts of the home. The long-term advantages of caring for others and being cared for by them in return is experienced as the satisfaction of enduring commitments to others. All these counterbalance the risks of intimacy and ultimately motivate us to make new attachments when old relationships are lost or shattered. Thus attachment obviously has its benefits, which are part of the engine and deep gratification of life. But attachment also has its risks, which are the main focus of this book. When attachment behavior activated by the death of an intimate becomes maladaptive, we recognize it as pathologic grief.

Pathologic Grief

Pathologic grief is a clinical disorder associated with bereavement that can appear first during the early stages of bereavement or can emerge later and that has the potential to become chronic. It has been described in various forms throughout most of the 20th century and it was even recognized for centuries before that. The clinical complications originate in a desolate social environment; the environment itself is fundamentally altered by the death of an intimate.

There is a growing consensus about how to diagnose pathologic grief. Contemporary criteria identify at least three variants of pathologic grief, including delayed, inhibited, and chronic syndromes. A severe grief syndrome is probably another variant. In the absence of studies of the natural history of these syndromes, their relationship to each other is poorly understood. In clinical practice, the most common presentation is chronic grief because bereaved individuals are not inclined to seek professional help early in the course of grief (at which time delayed and inhibited grief may be present). When bereaved individuals do present early for evaluation, the complications of normal grief are probably underrecognized.

Multiple dimensions of symptoms contribute to the clinical picture of pathologic grief. Manifestations of separation distress and symptoms of depression are part of the clinical syndrome in the majority of cases. In light of this, two concepts of the nature of the disorder seem relevant. One is that pathologic grief is an adult variety of separation anxiety disorder, which is ordinarily seen in children. The other is that pathologic grief is an ecologically specific, affective disorder. Panic disorder and occasionally major depressions occur independently of pathologic grief during bereavement, but ordinarily these syndromes overlap. In relationship to other psychiatric disorders, pathologic grief appears to be a type of stress-related disorder. Pathologic grief is common, occurring in as many as 20% of acutely bereaved individuals. Given the magnitude of the rates of occurrence and the scope of pathologic grief as a clinical disorder, it is a significant public health problem.

Normal and Pathologic Grief

Claude Bernard (1957), the French physiologist, taught us that a true understanding of pathology cannot be gained without a knowledge of normality: "Knowledge of pathological or abnormal conditions cannot be gained without previous knowledge of normal states, just as the therapeutic action of abnormal agents, or medicines, on the organism cannot be scientifically understood without first studying the physiological action of the normal agents which maintain the phenomena of life" (p. 2).
Although the discussion in Chapter 2 is largely on a psychosocial rather than a physiological level, the value of knowing about normal grief is a premise that was accepted with little discussion for the purpose of understanding the clinical complications of bereavement. This principle serves reasonably well in considering these complications as it suggests that we be alert for disturbances in the multidimensional processes of normal grief, including separation distress, mourning and dysphoria, and traumatic distress.

The historical review of the concept of pathologic grief identified delayed, inhibited, prolonged, and possibly severe variations in the evolution of separation distress as the main manifestations of the clinical complications of a loss. In addition, major depressions, posttraumatic stress disorders, and perhaps anxiety disorders were all recognized as potential complications of bereavement.

Diagnosis of Pathologic Grief

We are at a point in thinking about the clinical complications of bereavement where we are beginning to conceptualize pathologic grief in categorical terms. This is an important start for advancing our understanding of this stress-related disorder. In the long run, however, it may prove to be more useful to conceptualize pathologic grief in functional and dimensional terms. Modern criteria for pathologic grief include the vicissitudes of separation distress and mourning as the central, essential elements. A dimensional model of pathologic grief more easily includes multiple dimensions such as depression, anxiety, and traumatic distress, as well as separation distress.

The advantages of a dimensional model are considerable (Strauss 1973). Within the context of the present discussion, a dimensional model provides a conceptual framework for considering the relationship of normal to abnormal phenomena. It encourages us to think about the relationship between the common illusory experiences and hallucinations of bereavement and the psychotic hallucinations of affective or schizophrenic disorders. In addition, it fosters a comparison of the common, transient depressive syndromes of bereavement with major depressions. Moreover, a dimensional model facilitates the investigation of the relationship among dimensions by providing an opportunity to ask how an increase (or decrease) in one dimension ("x") affects another dimension ("y") and vice versa rather than investigators being limited to the more rudimentary, unidirectional question of whether x causes y. For example, what is the interplay between separation distress and depression? A dimensional system of psychopathology also makes it easier to describe individual patients and fit them into a model of psychopathology rather than forcing patients into procrustean diagnostic beds. Finally, analogous to hypertension or other functional diseases, a dimensional model makes it possible to consider thresholds or cutoffs for intervention. These serve as more flexible cues to the clinician for when treatment is indicated and facilitate the task of accomplishing early interventions for the purpose of secondary prevention.

Treatment of Pathologic Grief

Given the multiaxial nature of the clinical problems posed by pathologic grief, it is logical to consider a multidimensional approach to treatment. Psychopharmacological, psychotherapeutic, and mutual support interventions all have potential as effective interventions. The number of studies that have specifically tested these interventions during bereavement is small. Nevertheless, in the main, the studies of treatment methods that are available have indicated that those methods are effective. Also the specific problems of treating the complications of bereavement can be illuminated by the general psychiatric literature on treatment of major depressions and anxiety disorders.

Treatment ought to be integrated into individualized treatment plans for specific patients. Also there is an excellent opportunity during bereavement to make treatment more efficient than usual by intervening early. This is possible because mechanisms for identifying the at-risk population are available and feasible. In fact, it is conceivable that the complications of bereavement can be prevented if interventions such as crisis therapy or mutual support interventions are made early enough. These types of intervention are considered primary and secondary prevention within a public health model.

Regarding pharmacological treatment, antidepressants are probably underutilized for treating the major depressions that occur during bereavement. I have developed guidelines for their use in this book. In order to provide a better foundation for their utilization, more randomized, controlled trials of antidepressant treatment at the earliest, reasonable point in the course of bereavement need to be completed. Benzodiazepines are probably used excessively during bereavement. Nevertheless, they have a useful role in the brief treatment of intense autonomic arousal and panic disorder that occur during bereavement.

Psychotherapy is effective in treating pathologic grief, major depressions, and anxiety disorders. In this book I have developed the view that the essential goal of therapy ought to be to educate the patient about the specific problems posed by bereavement. This psychoeducation ought to be integrated with interpersonal, psychodynamic, cognitive, and behavioral strategies that are available to help bereaved individuals cope more effectively and adapt successfully to the environment left desolate by the loss. Brief therapy is ordinarily adequate, although special, longer-term treatment is necessary for some patients whose maladaptation to a loss has become chronic or who were chronically impaired before the bereavement occurred.

Mutual support interventions are also powerful interventions for pathologic grief and for rehabilitative purposes. They may be just as effective as psychotherapy; to be more precise, they probably provide a distinct service for bereaved patients who need to learn about how others in similar circumstances cope with their problems. Mutual support groups also provide an opportunity for bereaved individuals to practice rusty social skills. It is probably useful for professionals to take initiative in establishing collaborative relationships with mutual support organizations for the purpose of integrating this aspect of caring for bereaved patients into treatment.

The Humanity of the Patient

The reader probably appreciates a preoccupation on my part, on the one hand, with the scientific basis of treatment. On the other hand, I want to emphasize the influence of a famous essay by Francis Peabody (1977) about the importance of appreciating the humanity of the patient when accepting responsibility for treatment. As one of the first in a series of distinguished medical teachers on this point (e.g., see Engel 1977, 1980; Leigh and Reiser 1985), Peabody reminded us that our ultimate concern in medical practice is the sick individual, not an abstract pathologic entity. People get sick; diseases do not just happen to them and exist in a vacuum. Peabody's dictum was "the secret of the care of the patient is in caring for the patient." This is a wonderful double entendre that properly focuses the tasks of treatment as a counterpoint to the scientific tasks of trying to better understand the nature of pathologic grief, which is the primary focus of the first half of this book, and to find effective treatments for the clinical complications of bereavement, which is the primary focus of the second half.

Important Questions That Will Advance Our Understanding

Several questions remain at the edge of our current knowledge of pathologic grief and its treatment. As future research addresses these questions, our understanding of bereavement and its complications will progress. Some of these questions, which I have raised throughout the book, are the following:

- What is the relationship between pathologic grief and major depressions and anxiety disorders?
- What are the mechanisms of pathogenesis of the complications of bereavement?
- What is the relationship between personality traits and the occurrence of pathologic grief?
- To what extent do losses account for major depressions among elderly individuals?
- What is the relationship between trauma and loss?
- What are the most effective treatments for the major depressions of bereavement?
- Do social networks play an important role in the recovery from bereavement?
- What are the coping strategies that work most effectively at different stages of bereavement?
- Is primary prevention possible through crisis intervention or mutual support interventions or, perhaps, the use of benzodiazepines for excessive arousal?
- When is the best time to treat major depressions of bereavement for effective secondary prevention?
- Is psychotherapy just as effective as psychotropic drugs for treating the depressions of bereavement? Is it more effective or synergistic with pharmacological treatment?
- Are mutual support interventions just as effective as psychotherapy?

This is a personal list, and I imagine that readers have many questions of their own.

Stress-Related Disorders

The knowledge of bereavement can be applied in many challenging life experience situations where the theme of loss is relevant. These situations include loss of a marital partner through divorce, loss of health or functional capacity, loss of a home or community, loss of personal possessions through fires or theft, and so on. Although the aspects of each loss are unique, comprehension of the grief over the loss is facilitated by an understanding of bereavement, and interventions that are similar to those used during bereavement are useful.

Knowledge of bereavement also has application to understanding other stress-related disorders. Differences among stress-related disorders highlight the disorders' unique characteristics, and similarities among them illustrate common aspects that unite the group of stress-related disorders.

There is a fascinating relationship between trauma and loss, two stressful experiences. Although most traumatic experiences involve loss of some sort, and the experiences of trauma and loss are inseparable, the element of loss is minimal in some traumatic situations. Conversely, although it might be argued that losses that lead to pathologic grief are traumatic by definition, certainly there are many losses that are not traumatic. Therefore, it is possible to conceptualize trauma and loss as separate experiences and distinct processes. For example, except in times of war, great social upheaval, or disasters, trauma is not universal and inevitable like bereavement. Dissociation is conspicuous in trauma but rare in bereavement, although less severe attenuating processes such as transient numbness and disbelief and the use of psychological ego defenses are common after a loss. The content of the intrusions after trauma is horrifying and frightening rather than desolate and empty, as is typical of bereavement. The essential affective experience in a traumatic situation is fear. In bereavement, it is separation distress characterized by yearning and pining. Therefore, each experience is distinctive and potentially leads to a unique type of clinical complication.

However, in some ways loss and trauma resemble each other, and the study of one clarifies the other. For example, loss and trauma are similar in the intrusive quality of the distress and the mitigating processes employed by the afflicted individual to cope. Also both loss and trauma are associated with major depressions and anxiety disorders if they do not, in fact, increase the risk of their occurrence. These similarities establish common ground for both loss and trauma that argues for their inclusion together as stress-related disorders.

The authors of DSM-IV (*Diagnostic and Statistical Manual of Mental Disorders, 4th Edition*), being developed by the American Psychiatric Association, are considering the introduction of a new category of disorders called stress-related disorders, in part in order to conform with ICD-9 (World Health Organization 1991) and in part as a function of the immense, current interest in posttraumatic stress disorder. This category of disorders would include the etiological implication that an environmental stressor causes the disorders. This assumption is justified as much for pathologic grief as for traumatic disorders, and therefore pathologic grief ought to be included as a category of acute stress disorder.

An Adaptive Model

An adaptive model for understanding the clinical complications of bereavement places the disturbances of bereavement in a proper context. While certainly there are personal vulnerabilities that contribute to the risk of falling ill, there are also social contextual issues as well. In addition, characteristics of a death itself, which can be conceptualized as a vector of disease, contribute to the nature of the grief and the risk of clinical complications as sequelae. An adaptive model reminds us that we must ask questions and learn more about these important environmental elements of the clinical problems presented by patients with the clinical complications of bereavement.

Two basic implications of an adaptive model for treatment have emerged in this book. One is the need to address not only the symptomatic disturbance and functional impairment of our patients when they present for treatment, but also the nature and circumstances of the loss. I would argue that this need exists even if the death is peaceful and apparently benign, because, prospectively, the details of a death are never known for sure. This need is particularly relevant when the loss is traumatic, as was discussed in Chapter 5 on the adaptive model. In this case, the practitioner must attend to the traumatic distress that occurs as an independent dimension of emotional disturbance in addition to the separation distress associated with the desolation caused by the loss. In addition, the practitioner must monitor the evolution of a traumatic bereavement for the emergence of posttraumatic stress disorder. Furthermore, the psychotherapy of the complications of bereavement is certainly more specific and conceivably more effective if the therapist gives special consideration to the context created by a loss. In other words, the treatment of the clinical complications of bereavement is optimal if the disorders are understood in a specific, environmental context.

Another implication of an adaptive model is the need for sophisticated psychotherapeutic and psychopharmacological skills in treating the clinical complications of bereavement. In approaching the clinical complications of bereavement, two perspectives ought to be integrated to the extent possible: that pathologic grief is a maladaptation to a loss and that depressive disorders, anxiety disorders, and posttraumatic stress disorders may be the manifestations of a complicated bereavement. When both perspectives apply concurrently, which is often the case (see Chapter 4), the indications for treatment include both psychotherapeutic and psychopharmacological interventions. When these maladaptations go unrecognized and become chronic, which unfortunately is also often the case, there is a need for rehabilitation to address the residual impairment and disability. These disorders are not easy to treat, although often the treatment may be brief; the need for help may go beyond self-help and the important, however limited, measures it offers. Therefore, the treatment of clinical complications of bereavement calls for broadly trained, knowledgeable, and experienced practitioners who can integrate the multiple elements of treatment into a coherent, individualized treatment plan.

Dialogue Between Clinical Practice and Clinical Science

I trust that the reader is impressed, as I am, with the challenging task ahead of learning more about normal and pathologic grief. I also trust that the reader is humbled, as I am, by the limitations of our understanding of pathologic grief and our ability to help the bereaved patients who seek our advice and care. At least one clinician has noted the latter, and called for a vigilant watch for novelty in the treatment setting when there is no progress toward recovery (Rynearson 1987). By virtue of an openness to novelty, we will gain insights into the nature of bereavement, its complications, and processes of recovery as our patients teach us about this stressful experience and how they cope with it. These insights will provide questions for researchers to investigate for the purpose of scientifically testing ideas that arise in the crucible of clinical experience.

In combination with an attitude of clinical humility, a commitment to the scientific study of normal grief, pathologic grief, and the other complications of bereavement, as well as the treatment of these complications, promises to advance our understanding. With the development of knowledge, we will become more effective clinicians. Thus there is a closed circle between the observations and insights of the clinician and the new knowledge gained from scientific study.

There is a contrast between the scientific skepticism of investigators who are hopeful of advancing knowledge and the therapeutic pragmatism and optimism of clinicians who are primarily committed to helping their patients. This contrast in styles gets played out internally in clinical investigators. In fact, I suspect that this book reflects this internal dialogue between the clinical scientist and the practicing clinician within myself. It is a dialogue that is essential to the ongoing progress of the field and must continue.

This same dialogue is played out between researchers and therapists in professional meetings on grief and bereavement. While both sides are interested in the whole picture, the researchers are strongly if not principally interested in the scientific advancement of knowledge. The therapists eagerly want to hear from master clinicians and learn about new domains of practice, which are often anecdotal and experiential. The sentience of each group, as well as the need for recognition and the competition for time on the program, frequently obscure the dialogue. There is an impression that never the twain will meet. But, of course, the dialogue must continue in these professional forums. By listening to clinicians, the researchers can learn what is important for the care of patients and for clues to the nature of the disorders being studied. Clinical scientists can also contribute to the vertical reasoning that is the unique characteristic of medical practice (Blois 1988). By listening to the scientists, the therapists can learn more about the nature of the disorders they treat as it is revealed in the scientific process and about the value of treatments that have been scientifically tested in randomized, controlled trials.

More succinctly, as Osler reminded us at the turn of the century when medicine was poised to understand many disorders because of the availability of multiple, new scientific techniques, "the practice of medicine is an art, based on science" (Osler 1951, p. 123). He urged us to listen to our patients because they are telling us the diagnosis. We must also maintain the scientific basis of our practice because that is the foundation on which our clinical work is built.

Dialogue Between the Writer and the Reader

A book is a special type of communication with others, between the author and the readers. Sometimes the experience of writing is like a long monologue. At other times, it is truly a dialogue with previous authors who have written on the same topic and an extension of discussions with colleagues and bereaved individuals. The value of this book will be determined by the extent to which it stimulates interest and a continuing dialogue between clinical scientists and clinicians, among mental health professionals, and between mental health professionals and bereaved individuals. This is the kind of attention that the complications of bereavement deserve because of their scope and severity as clinical problems. Needless to say, if this book contributes to the recognition and effective treatment of pathologic grief, I would feel that I have repaid a debt of gratitude to the bereaved individuals who have taught me so much about their experience. Beyond that, I would hope that this book is another stimulus, among many other recent contributions, for the scientific study of the interesting group of problems that we denote as pathologic grief and a clinical discussion of their nature and treatment.

References

Bernard C: An Introduction to the Study of Experimental Medicine. New York, Dover Press, 1957

Blois MS: Medicine and the nature of vertical reasoning. N Engl J Med 318:847–851, 1988

Bowlby J: The making and breaking of affectional bonds, I: aetiology and psychopathology in the light of attachment theory. Br J Psychiatry 130:201–210, 1977

Engel GL: The need for a new medical model: a challenge for biomedicine. Science 196:129–136, 1977

Engel GL: The clinical application of the biopsychosocial model. Am J Psychiatry 137:535–544, 1980

Leigh H, Reiser MF: The Patient: Biological, Psychological, and Social Dimensions of Medical Practice, 2nd Edition. New York, Plenum, 1985

Osler W: Aphorisms From His Bedside Teachings and Writings. Edited by Bean WB. Springfield, IL, Charles C Thomas, 1951

Parkes CM: Bereavement: Studies of Grief in Adult Life. New York, International Universities Press, 1972

Peabody FW: The care of the patient. Psychiatric Annals 7:264–273, 1977

Rynearson EK: Psychotherapy of pathologic grief. Psychiatr Clin North Am 10:487–499, 1987

Strauss JS: Diagnostic models and the nature of psychiatric disorders. Arch Gen Psychiatry 29:445–449, 1973

World Health Organization: International Classification of Diseases, 9th Edition, Geneva, Switzerland, World Health Organization, 1991

APPENDIX

Diagnostic Criteria for Pathologic Grief

Normal Grief

A. Normal grief commences within a 2-week time frame after a major loss of a significant attachment figure. It may occur in less intensive form following lesser losses.
B. The bereaved individual demonstrates a phasic response that involves a general but not fixed progression of phenomena. These phenomena can be seen in terms of the following multiple dimensions:
  B1. Numbness and/or disbelief lasting from a few hours to several days (usually 2–5 days, but no longer than 2 weeks) (not invariably present)
  B2. A focus, affectively, cognitively, or behaviorally on the lost individual:
    a. Attachment feelings and behaviors reflecting and specific to the bereaved's attachment bonds to the lost individual:

    - Searching for the lost individual
    - Looking for the lost individual in familiar places
    - Acting as though the lost individual were still alive

    b. A perceptual set for the lost individual

    - Sense of the presence of the lost individual
    - Preoccupation with the image of the lost individual
    - Hallucinatory experiences of the lost individual

Adapted from Raphael B: "Diagnostic Criteria for Bereavement Reactions." Paper presented at the International Symposium on Pathologic Bereavement, Seattle, WA, May 1989.

- Thoughts of the lost individual coming spontaneously to the mind
- Dreaming of the lost individual as if still alive

    c. Arousal—higher levels of arousal and associated features but focused on cues relevant to the lost individual
    d. Distress—generalized and associated with physical sensations, which may occur in waves or pangs stimulated by the absence of the lost individual[1]

B3. Nonspecific affects and behaviors that are usually high initially in the first 4–6 weeks and that progressively diminish over that time (may be increased by reminders of the loss):

- Anxiety
- Anger
- Depression
- Guilt
- Crying

B4. Specific grief-loss reactions to acceptance of the reality of the loss in the second and third months and diminishing:

- Yearning and pining for the lost individual
- Need to talk about the lost individual
- Recurring memories and/or relationship with the lost individual
- Sadness
- Distress at reminders of the loss
- Nostalgia

C. There is a "recovery" as evidenced by lessening of the B2 through B4 dimensions progressively over the first year.

All the B2 items generally are diminished or absent or appear transiently and are not perceived as disturbing the bereaved individual's functioning.

---

[1]Note that B2 a, b, c, and d occur in the early weeks and lessen, usually after first 2–3 months.

Marked decrease of B3 items, although they may appear transiently, but are not perceived as disturbing to the bereaved individual.

B4 items lessened substantially, but may still be present to some degree and particularly at times of the anniversary. These are the residual manifestations of normal grief.

All these items improve significantly over the first year and diminish progressively over subsequent years. Normal bereavement is to be differentiated from depressive disorders, anxiety disorders, and posttraumatic stress disorders.[2]

Delayed and Absent Grief

The definition of *delayed grief* is dependent on the time after a loss. However, the judgment is made on cross-sectional assessment of phenomenology. Thus this diagnosis can be made by two variables—the time after loss and the relative level of appropriate response to that time frame. Thus, it may present as a clearly delayed form (i.e., occurring late) but present as appropriate, or as a delayed form occurring late but not yet present (i.e., an absent form). Whereas there may be a question about whether or not delay of grief is in itself pathologic, the "absence" of grief is usually thought to be pathologic.

A. Delayed grief follows within the time frame after a major loss. (Time frame defined in terms of days, weeks, months, or years after loss). This time frame must be at least greater than 2 weeks after the loss. (The loss would be of a spouse or partner, child, or close or primary attachment figure; the grief may be delayed weeks, months, or years after the loss, or may not have occurred at all at the time of presentation.

---

[2]Note that a general progression of reduction in distress and lessening preoccupation with the lost individual and acceptance of the loss, plus the return of some capacity for reinvestment in new or other interests and activities, should gradually occur. Although some losses (e.g., the death of a child or spouse) may bring more intense phenomena, the general components above should be present, at least once at some time.

B. The bereaved individual demonstrates a phasic response that is delayed more than 2 weeks at the time of assessment or may have appeared later, at the time of assessment, or not at all.
   B1. Numbness and/or disbelief lasting from a few hours to several days (usually 2–5 days), but has not appeared more than 2 weeks after the death
   B2. Affective process and cognitions and behaviors reflecting a focus on the lost individual
      a. Attachment feelings and behaviors specific to the bereaved individual's attachment to the lost individual (see above)
      b. A perceptual set for the lost individual (see above)
      c. Arousal focused on cues relevant to the lost individual (see above)
      d. Distress related to the absence of the lost individual (i.e., separation distress or pangs of grief continue)
   B3. General affective response initially, which may include (to varying degrees) affects of anxiety, depression, anger, and guilt and which may be associated with crying
   B4. Specific grief reactions related to acceptance of the reality of the loss (see above)
C. There is "recovery" as evidenced by diminution of B2 and B3 items, but a lesser diminution of the B4 items.

These various aspects are delayed in their occurrence. The bereaved individual may appear to be acting as though nothing has happened or the reactions may appear but after a substantial time. In particular there is a lack of attachment behaviors, perceptual set, focused arousal, and distress and the bereaved individual may carry on normal activities or even extra activities. A general affective response may be delayed or absent. Specific grief reactions do not appear or are delayed. The characteristic multidimensional pattern of phased progression may not occur or may be delayed or slowed in progression. The delay may reflect the bereaved individual's "carrying on as though nothing had happened" as a mechanism of avoiding the implications of the loss. Alternatively the delay or absence may be related to the presence of other phenomena (e.g., posttraumatic stress reaction or disorder phenomena that are associated with trauma experienced in the circumstances of the death). Or the bereaved individual may not grieve, or grieving may be delayed because of the bereaved individual's own struggle for psychological or physical survival, so that the bereavement process is delayed partially or totally because of this (e.g., in the circumstances of a disaster, war, or terrorist situation or following accidents in which the bereaved individual was seriously injured).

In some instances, other disorders (e.g., manic reactions, somatic or psychological complaints or disorders) may appear in place of grief.

Inhibited (or Distorted) Grief

This pattern of pathology has been suggested by a number of investigators and represents a diminution of all or part of the bereavement process, to such an extent that it is considered this may interfere with adjustment to the loss.

A. Inhibited grief follows within 2 weeks of a major loss (e.g., of a significant attachment figure).
B. The bereaved individual demonstrates some aspects of a phasic response along multiple dimensions. Any of these dimensions may be inhibited or diminished, whereas others appear to occur to the full extent, or all may be diminished.
    B1. Numbness and/or denial possibly prolonged
    B2. Affect and cognition focused on the lost individual (may be diminished, absent, or may occur, but there may be a failure of progression):
        a. Attachment behaviors
        b. Perceptual set
        c. Arousal focused on the lost individual
        d. Distress related to the absence of the lost individual
    B3. General affects possibly diminished or occurring (e.g., depression)
    B4. Specific grief reactions unlikely to appear with any frequency or intensity
C. Recovery may not occur as there may be an inability to adjust to or come to terms with the loss. However, affects may appear and continue (e.g., depression, anxiety, and anger). They are not focused. Evidence that the bereavement process is still active may be in a perceptual set,

attachment and ongoing focus on the lost individual, and the fact that the bereaved individual has been unable to negotiate or reach the dimension of specific grief (i.e., he or she does not show sadness, nostalgia, yearning, or pining for the lost individual, or if so, to only a very minor degree).

Chronic Grief

A. Chronic grief follows within 2 weeks of the major loss of a primary attachment figure or relationship.
B. The bereaved individual fails to demonstrate a phasic response with progression through the bereavement process. The individual may become locked into any one of several of these phenomenological patterns and not progress into further areas or to diminution of intensity of the response with time. The phenomena that appear continue with an intensity that is at the level, which would normally only be expected in the first 2–3 months of the acute phase after the loss. Although some of these phenomena occur throughout the first year, it is generally agreed that they decrease markedly after the first few months toward the end of the first year. The high level of intensity carries on for 6 months or more and may be present 1, 2, 5, or many years later.
B1. Numbness not prolonged (brief or lasting only a few days)
B2. Affective and cognitive focus on the lost attachment figure:
   a. Attachment behaviors intense and profound, for example:

   - Searching for the lost individual
   - Looking for the lost individual in familiar places
   - Acting as though the lost individual were still alive or shortly to return (e.g., keeping the room ready and untouched, setting a place at the table)

   b. Perceptual set for the lost individual:

   - Profound and ongoing intense preoccupation with the lost individual who is often idealized
   - Sense of presence of the lost individual, which may be profound and involves talking to or seeing him or her

c. Arousal—high levels of arousal that are focused on the lost individual and often to the exclusion of other individuals and other facets of the bereaved individual's life
d. Distress—general (continues at a high level, aggravated by reminders)

B3. General affects intense; particularly common affects:

- Intense anger and bitterness toward those who did not prevent the death
- Intense guilt over what the bereaved individual did to or was unable to do for the individual who has died (guilt may be intense and out of proportion to any real events)
- Crying likely to be profuse, intense, and easily triggered (depressed feeling may be profound, but other criteria for depressive disorder are not met; anxiety feelings may be intense, but are not as frequent as depressive and do not reach diagnostic criteria for disorder)

B4. Some aspects of specific grief

- Yearning and pining for the lost individual
- Need to talk about the lost individual
- Recurring memories, which are usually idealized
- Distress at reminders may be intense

C. Failure to recover as evidenced by the above, particularly the ongoing focus on the lost individual, the ongoing distress, and the failure of diminution of this over time. The bereaved individual fails to accept the death at some level and is unable or unwilling to give up the lost individual. The bereaved individual may be unable to visit the grave or may go daily or very frequently, as though an ongoing attachment to the lost individual exists. The bereaved individual's whole existence is dominated by the ongoing grief for and focus on the lost individual, often to the extent that other relationships and functioning are significantly impaired.

Index

A

Absent grief
  diagnostic criteria for, 13, 26, 27, 175–176, 365–367
  differential diagnosis of, 176, **180**
  disordered mourning and, 22
  as pathologic grief variant, 19–20
Accidents, benzodiazepines and, 258
Acquired immunodeficiency syndrome (AIDS), 104, 147, 204, 326–327
Adaptation
  definition of health and, 78–79
  to loss, 115
  to social environment, 108
  understanding, approaches to, 75–76
Adaptive model
  adaption challenge of loss and, 77–78
  as clinical framework, 235–236
  concept of, 89
  course of bereavement and, 79–81
  crisis theory and, 77
  death characteristics and, 81–82
  deficit model and, 77
  definition of, 78–79
  diagram of, **76**
  environment and, 77
  implications for treatment, 7, 357–358
  purpose of, 75
  usage, argument for, 6
Adler, A., 21
Adrenocortical activity, 68, 162, 164, 209
Advocacy groups, 326–328
Affective disorders, 305
Age
  complications of bereavement and, 142–144
  traumatic death and, 144
Agoraphobia, 71, 293
Alarm, treatment of, 255–263
Alcohol abuse, 52, 211
Alcohol use, 50–52
Alcoholic dementias, 338
Alprazolam, 260
Ambivalence, 144–145
Amitriptyline, 268–269, 270, 272
Amygdala, 14
Anger, 298–299
Animal models
  norepinephrine dysregulation in, 205
  for separation and loss, 263
Anniversaries of death
  evaluation of bereavement and, 181–182
  impact of, 302–303
"Anophelia," 105
Antianxiety drugs
  for acute bereavement, 253, 256
  "frozen grief" and, 254
  treatment philosophy for, 255
Anticipatory anxiety, in panic disorder, 257

Page numbers printed in **boldface** type refer to tables or figures.

Antidepressants
   for acute bereavement, 237
   for complications of bereavement, 207–208
   duration of treatment, 265
   expression of grief and, 254
   indications for, 245
   for major depression, 217–220, 263–271
   for separation anxiety, 272
   separation distress and, 268–269
   for sleep disorders, 263
   suboptimal use of, 267
   target symptoms for, 263
   treatment philosophy for, 255
   tricyclic. *See* Tricyclic antidepressants
Antipsychotic drugs, inappropriate use of, 273, 274–276
Anxiety disorders, 21. *See also* Panic disorder; Posttraumatic stress disorder (PTSD); Separation anxiety
   in acute bereavement, 25
   alcoholism and, 50
   benzodiazepines for, 255–256, 262
   catecholamines and, 163
   as complication of bereavement, 44–45
   congruence with other bereavement syndromes, 60–64
   dysregulation of norepinephrine and, 205–206
   ego defenses and, 121–122
   epidemiological profile for, 64–67, 65
   evolution, longitudinal studies of, 63–64
   family history of, as risk factor, 191
   implication of diagnosis, 173
   with major depression, 31
   neuroendocrine function in, 68
   normal apprehensions and, 188
   overlap with depression, 264
   in panic disorder, 257
   pathophysiology of, 14
   personal history, as risk factor, 191
   pharmacological treatment of, 220–21
   rates during bereavement, 45
   severe grief and, 178
   in traumatic bereavement, 83
   treatment integration and, 242
   tricyclic antidepressants for, 261
   as variant of pathologic grief, 21, 80
Anxious depression, 264–265
Apprehensions, normal, 188
Arousal, 257
Assumptive world, 294–295
Attachment
   anxious, 153
   benefits of, 349–350
   bereavement complications risk and, 144–148
   caregiving and, 309–310
   formulation, personality traits and, 149
   insecure, 209–210
   intense, 1
   maladaptive, 80
   as motivational system in brain, 9–10, 14
   neurological aspects of, 9
   risks of, 349–350
Attachment theory
   environment and, 77
   framework
      learning about, 288
      psychoeducation on, 294
   grief work and, 214
   normal grief and bereavement and, 77
   psychological distress dimensions and, 16
   risk period for major depression and, 160

separation distress and, 84
Auditory hallucinations, 275, 288
Autonomic arousal, 342
Avoidance, symptoms of, 257
Avoidant personality disorder, 153
Axis I disorders, 154
Axis II disorders, 154

B

Behavioral interventions, 208
Behavior disinhibition,
    benzodiazepines and, 258–259
Benzodiazepines
    abuse of, 53–54
    for anxiety disorders, 237,
        255–256, 262
    "frozen grief" and, 53
    for panic disorder, 257
    for posttraumatic stress disorder,
        256
    risks, 257–263
        for disinhibition of behavior,
            258–259
        for interference with cognition,
            258–259
        for interference with memory
            functions, 258–259
        for physical dependence, 261
        for prolongation of grief,
            262–263
        for psychological dependence,
            261
        for sedation, 257–258
Bereavement
    acute
        biological assessments of, 191
        range of psychiatric disorders
            in, 30
        symptomatology of, personality
            traits and, 155–158
    anxiety symptoms of, 257
    biological aspects of, 142, 162–165

clinical interventions for, 338–339
clinical perspective, 4–5
complications. *See* Complications
    of bereavement
coping during. *See* Coping
course of, adaptive model and,
    79–81
depressive syndromes of. *See*
    Depressive syndromes
disorders of, 31–32
immunological function in, 165
kinship and, 145–148
maladaptive consequences of, 1, 19
mortality risk, 109
nature of, psychoeducation on,
    291–294
purpose of, 1
saying goodbye during, 296
    resistance to, 296
    versus leave taking during
        terminal illness, 296
stage of, social support for, 97
suffering through pain of, fear of
    stigmatization and, 303–305
tasks of, 133–135
Bereavement overload, 194
Biological assessments, of acute
    bereavement, 191
Biological psychiatry, 40
Biological research, versus
    epidemiological research, 166
Biopsychosocial model, 108
Bipolar disorder, 64, 338
Borderline personality disorder,
    widowhood and, 153
Bowlby, J., 21–23
Brain development, 9

C

Candlelighters, 344
Cardiovascular mortality, 109
Catecholamines, 163, 209

Cathexis, 214
Cattell 16 Factor Personality
    Questionnaire, 149
Center for Epidemiologic Studies
    Depression Scale (CES-D),
    45–46, 47, 117, 132
Central nervous system, homeostatic
    disturbance of, 203
Character traits, psychotherapy
    approach and, 282–283
Charles Bonnet syndrome, 276
Childhood losses, long-term
    consequences of, 159–165, 284
Children, personality traits of,
    outcome of bereavement and,
    150–151
Chronic depression, development of,
    265–266
Chronic grief
    clinical example of, 194–195
    with delayed grief, 176
    diagnostic criteria for, 178–179,
        368–369
    differential diagnosis of, **180**
    manifestations of, 23, 26, 28
    as pathologic grief variant, 27, 350
    severe grief and, 29
    versus normal grief, 178–179
Chronic mourning, 22
Circumstances of death, 81–83, 179,
    181
Clayton, P. J., 24–25
Clinical practice, dialogue with
    clinical science, 358–359
Clinical relationship issues, 299–301
Clinical science, dialogue with clinical
    practice, 358–359
Clinician, professional
    collaboration. See Collaboration
    effectiveness of intervention,
        consumer challenge of, 39
    mutual support programs and,
        323–324, 324–330
    skills for collaboration, 332–333
    treatment agenda of, 327
Clomipramine, 69
Cognition interference,
    benzodiazepines and, 258–259
Cognitive appraisal, 293–294
Cognitive theory, 22, 214–215
Collaboration
    benefits of, 332
    confidentiality in, 326, 327
    disadvantages of, 332
    professional skills for, 332–333
    successful, 328–330
Comorbidity of syndromes, 60
Compassionate Friends, 319, 344
Complications of bereavement, 4, 18
    anxiety. See Anxiety disorders
    attention to, decline in, 39–40
    clinical studies data, problems
        with, 45–47
    comorbidity of, 60
    conceptualization of, 3
    congruence of, 60–64, **61**
    depression. See Depression
    diagnostic dimensions of, 191–194
    differential diagnosis
        clinical examples of, 194–197
        criteria for, 174
    impact of, 4
    longitudinal studies of, 63–64
    neurobiological comparisons,
        67–71
    obstacles to understanding, 54
    pathologic grief. See Pathologic
        grief
    posttraumatic distress disorder. See
        Posttraumatic stress disorder
        (PTSD)
    rates of occurrence
        epidemiological studies of,
            41–42
        significance of, 47–50
    relationships among, 59–72

risk factors for, 65
risk of, 42, 43
sociodemographic characteristics of, 65
symptomatic criteria of, 174–188
treatment of. *See* Treatment
Confidentiality, in collaboration, 326, 327
Conflicted grief, 23
Conscious coping, 115, 122–126
Consciousness-raising groups, 319
Consumer movement, questioning of professional competence and, 39
Control
   fear of losing
      pathologic grief and, 181
      psychoeducation about death and bereavement, 291–294
   low internal sense of, 149
Coping
   behaviors of, 76
   during bereavement, 135–137
      evolution of, 124–125
      versus coping with severe illness, 117–120
   case example of, 116–120
   conscious, 115, 122–126
   cross-sectional studies of, 123
   definition of, 122
   ego defenses and, 120–122
   emotion-focused, 125, 131–132, 135
   empirical studies of, 124–133
   immature, 115–116
   longitudinal studies of, 123
   mature, 115
   motives for study of, 116
   neuroendocrine function and, 126–127
   problem-focused, 132, 216
   social environment and, 107–111

   styles or strategies, 31, 80, **121**
      adaptive outcomes and, 189
      complex, 132
      evaluating, 290–291
      with good mental outcome, 127–130
      multiple, use of, 215–216
      multiple factors in determination of, 122–123
      prediction of outcome and, 130–133
      by suppression-activity substitution, 126
      unconscious, 115, 125–126
Corticotropin-releasing hormone (CRH), 203–204, 213
Cortisol, serum, 126, 162, 164
Counseling, 279. *See also* Psychotherapy
Crisis intervention, 345
   for high-risk bereaved individuals, 340–341
   negative effects of, 223–225
   positive effects of, 222–223
   techniques, 40
Crisis theory, 155
   adaptive model and, 77
   crisis intervention development and, 335–336
Crowne-Marlowe Scale, 163

D

Death. *See also* Loss
   from acute versus chronic illness, 82
   anniversaries of, 181–182, 302–303
   characteristics of, 30–31
      responses to loss and, 81–89
      as risk factor for bereaved person, 81
   of child, 145–146
   circumstances of, 81–83, 179, 181

Death (continued)
  denial of, 81
  multiple ramifications of, 294
  nature of, 75, 81, 283
  of spouse, 145–146
  sudden
    clinical complications of bereavement and, 79–80
    primary prevention and, 339
    severe emotional numbing and, 175
    survivors of, 295
    traumatic dimension of bereavement, 88
    and unexpected, 87–89, 175, 295, 339
    versus anticipated, 82
  timely versus untimely, 82
  traumatic. See Traumatic death
  unnatural, 82
Decathectation, 134
Deceased, relationship to, 31
Defense mechanism, denial as, 151
Defensiveness, measure of, 163
Defensive work, 133
Deficit model, adaptive model and, 77
Delayed grief
  clinical example of, 194–195
  diagnostic criteria for, 175–176, 365–367
  differential diagnosis of, 176, **180**
  major depression and, 63
  manifestations of, 23, 26, 27
  posttraumatic stress disorder and, 179
  versus absent grief, 176
Denial, as defense mechanism, 151
Dependent grief syndromes, 282, 306–307
Dependent personality disorder, 154

Depression, 18
  alcoholism and, 50
  anxious
    alprazolam for, 264–265
    monoamine oxidase inhibitors for, 264
  anxious personality traits and, 167
  during bereavement
    overlap with anxiety disorders, 264
    prevention of, 341–343
  bipolar, 64, 338
  catecholamines and, 163
  chronic, development of, 265–266
  delayed, severe grief and, 1, 2
  desipramine for, 265
  family histories of, as risk factor, 159
  immune function and, 68
  kinship and, 146–147
  major, 29, 31, 45
    in acute bereavement, 41
    with anxiety disorder, 44
    borderline personality disorder and, 154
    childhood loss or separation of parent and, 160–161
    as complication of bereavement, 43–44
    congruence with anxiety disorders and pathologic grief, 60–64
    delayed grief and, 63
    differential diagnosis of, **183**, 184
    epidemiological profile of, 64–67, **65**
    evolution, longitudinal studies of, 63–64
    family history of, 190
    functional impairment of, 189
    history of, 342
    implication of diagnosis, 173

longitudinal perspective of, 185–186
normal depressive mood of bereavement and, 182–188
normal expression of sadness and, 267
personal history, as risk factor, 190
pharmacological treatment of, 217–220
physiological mechanisms of, 203–208
psychological and behavioral mechanisms of, 208–211
risk factors for, 24–25, **65**, 161
severe grief and, 29
sociodemographic characteristics of, **65**
successful treatment of, 238
suicidal risk and, 187–188
symptomatic criteria for, 48–50, 182, 184–185
timing of, 186–187
in traumatic bereavement, 83
treatment integration and, 242
treatment of, 263–271
in women, 143
maladaptation to loss and, 80
neuroendocrine function in, 68
pathogenesis
dysregulation of norepinephrine and, 205–206
homeostatic disturbances secondary to interpersonal loss, 206–208
pathophysiology and mechanisms of, 201–213
separation and loss as model for, 202
social mechanisms of, 211–213
stress response system disturbances and, 203–204
pathophysiology of, 14
personal histories of, as risk factor, 159
rates
age variations in, 46
in bereaved children, 44
methodological variations in, 47
sex variations in, 46
risk for, 149
separation distress and, 267
severe grief and, 178
sleep physiology and, 69
of uncomplicated bereavement, differential diagnosis, **183**, 184
unipolar, 64
vulnerability to, 141
Depression/Awareness, Recognition and Treatment (DART), 338
Depressive syndromes, 193
clinical example, 195–197
duration and timing of, 186–187
evolution of symptoms over time, 185–186
major depression and, 182–188
symptomatic criteria of, 182, 184–185
Descriptive psychiatry, 3
Desipramine
for depression, 265
grief intensification and, 266–267
for major depression in bereavement, 69
for persistent depression, 219
separation distress and, 272
side effects of, 269
Deutsch, H., 19–20
Dexamethasone suppression test (DST), 162, 191, 204, 342
Diagnostic and Statistical Manual of Mental Disorders, 3rd Edition, Revised (DSM-III-R), 40
Diagnostic and Statistical Manual of Mental Disorders,, 4th Edition, (DSM-IV), 356–357

Dimensional approach, to clinical evaluation and treatment planning, 191–194, **192**
Distorted grief. *See* Inhibited grief
Doxepine, 272
Dysthymia, in acute bereavement, 41

E

Eating disorders, risk of, 160–161
Ecological model of psychopathology, 31–32
Ego defenses
  in bereaved versus nonbereaved spouses, 125
  conceptualization of, 121
  in coping, 120–122
  definition of, 120
  endocrine system and, 163–164
  mature, 118–119, 291
  neurotic, 126, 132–133
  outcome and, 132–133, 151–153
Ego functioning, personality traits and, 151–153
Ego states, maladaptive, 24
Elderly, antidepressants for, 220
Emotional arousal, treatment of, 255–263
Emotional constriction, 257
Emotional crisis theory, 40
Emotional fitness, 304
Emotional numbing
  avoidance and, 257
  in delayed grief syndrome, 175
  in grief, 14, 17, 18
  progression to separation distress, 33–35
Emotional trauma, separation distress and, 24
Emotion-focused coping, 125, 131–132, 135
Empty situations, 93, 289
Environment
  adaptive model and, 77, 78
  attachment theory and, 77
  in bereavement, 79–80, 93
  complications of bereavement and, 75
  social, support from. *See* Social support
  social transition theory and, 77
Epidemiologic Catchment Area (ECA) study, 41–42
Epidemiological studies
  age variations in, 46
  of complications of bereavement, 41–42
  methodological variations of, 47
  sex variations in, 46
Epinephrine, 164
Established Populations for Epidemiologic Studies of the Elderly (EPESE), 46, 103, 322
Estrogen, 14
Eysenck Personality Inventory, 149

F

Failure to grieve, family history of, 190
Family
  as support, 93
  treatment for, 305–306
Family history, risk for bereavement complications and, 158–159, 190, 191
Fantasy, 119
Fear of losing control, 181, 291–294
Fluoxetine, 265
Forced or guided mourning, 225–227, 282
Forgiveness, 298–299
Freud, S., 19, 40, 134
Friends, as support, 93
"Frozen grief"
  antianxiety agents and, 254
  benzodiazepines and, 53, 262–263

G

Gamma-aminobutyric acid release, 209
Gender, bereavement complications and, 142–144
Generalized anxiety disorder
  in acute bereavement, 25, 257
  benzodiazepines for, 256, 257
  diagnosis of, 188
  in pathologic grief, 29, 62
  personal and family histories of, 191
  risk
    childhood loss or separation of parent and, 160–161
    factors for, **65**, 66
    sociodemographic characteristics of, **65**
  symptoms of, 48–50
Goodness of fit, 106
Grief
  biological substrate of, 14
  chronic. *See* Chronic grief
  conflicted, 23
  definition of, 9
  delayed. *See* Delayed grief
  dimensions of, **17**
  duration of, 110
  evolutionary purpose of, 214
  intensification, antidepressants and, 266–267
  maladaptive, 18
  manifestations of, 14, **15**
  normal, 13–18, 27
    diagnostic criteria for, 363–365
    differential diagnosis of, **180**, 254
    progression of, 18, 29
    psychotropic drugs and, 253
    symptomatic criteria for, 174–179
    versus pathologic grief, 174–179, 351
  pangs of. *See* Pangs of grief
  phases of, 18
  prolongation of, benzodiazepines and, 262–263
  psychiatric disorders in, 39
  psychological distress in, 16–18
  separation distress in, 14–16
  severe. *See* Severe grief
  symptoms of, **15**
  tasks of, 75–76
  unanticipated, 23
Grief work
  attachment theory and, 214
  cognitive theory and, 214–215
  concept of, 214
  meaning of, 134
Growth hormone, 162–163
Guided mourning, 225–227, 282

H

Hallucinations, 185, 275–276, 288
Health, definition of, 78–79
Health practices, poor, 210–211
Holidays, impact of, 302–303
Homeostasis, substitute relationships and, 213
Horowitz, M. J., 23, 24
Hospice movement, 81
Hospice nurse, brief bereavement intervention by, 227
Humanity of patient, treatment and, 354
17-Hydroxycortisol excretion, 163
Hypervigilance, 257
Hypnotic drugs, 253
  abuse of, 52–54
Hypothalamic-pituitary-adrenocortical function, 209. *See also* Adrenocortical activity

I

Identification symptoms, understanding, 301–302

Illusions, 275
Imagery, intrusive, 257
Imipramine, 69, 219, 221, 263
Immune function
   in bereavement, 68, 165
   etiology of depression and, 207
Impact of Event Scale, 24, 88
Inhibited grief, 29
   absence of separation distress and, 28
   diagnosis of, 27–28
   diagnostic criteria for, 23, 27, 176–177, 367–368
   differential diagnosis of, **180**
   manifestations of, 26, 176–177
Internalization, 298
Interpersonal therapy (IPT), 280
Intrusive symptoms, 257
Isolation call, development of, 9

K

Kinship, bereavement and, 145–148

L

Learned helplessness, 205, 208–209
Learning, from pain of bereavement, 304
Learning model, conceptualization of tasks of bereavement, 134–135
Leiden Bereavement Study, adaptation and, 77–78
Life event, appraising nature of, 290
Limbic system, 14
Lithium, 338
Locus coeruleus–norepinephrine system, 203–206, 213
Loneliness, states of, 105
Longitudinal studies, of social supports and networks, 100–102
Loss. *See also* Death
   adaptation challenge of, 75–76
   in childhood, long-term consequences of, 159–165, 284
   maladaptations to. *See* Anxiety disorders; Depression; Pathologic grief
   past, 299–301
   risk for alcohol use and abuse, 50–52
   sudden, unexpected, 284
   suffering through, fear of stigmatization and, 303–305
   trauma and, 24

M

Major depression. *See* Depression, major
Mania, pharmacological, 270–271
Marital conflict, 145
Melancholia
   mourning and, 40
   symptoms of, 185
   versus mourning, 19
Memory, benzodiazepines and, 258–259
Minnesota Multiphasic Personality Inventory (MMPI), 151, 161
Monoamine oxidase inhibitors (MAOIs), 220, 264, 265
Mortality risk, in bereavement, 109
Mothers, 146
Mourning, 18
   chronic, 22
   depressive features of, 16
   disordered, variants of, 22
   guided or forced, 225–227, 282
   melancholia and, 40
   tasks of, 134
   versus melancholia, 19
Mourning-depressive phenomena, in grief, 18
Mutual support groups, 332–333, 345. *See also* Self-help

agenda of, 327
clinician's role in, 323–324
collaboration with psychiatrist, successful, 328–330
definition of, 344
dropout rate, 318–319
efficacy of, 222–23
evaluations of, 317–323
foundation of, 316
goals of, **238**, 240–241
nonresponse rate for, 236
one-to-one volunteer intervention, 320
for pathologic grief, 353–354
prevention and, 330–332
professionals in, 315
professional treatment and, 324–330
rationale for, 316–317
rehabilitation and, 330–332
role of, 96–97
during second 6 months to second year, 248
synergy with psychotherapy, 241
treatment and, 330–332

N

Narcissism, 144–145
Network stress, 96
Neuroendocrine system, 207
in bereavement, 67–68, 162–164
coping and, 126–127
Neurotic disorders, 105
Neuroticism, 149
Neurovegetative symptoms, 185, 263, 342
Nightmares, 257
Nighttime panic attacks, 270
Nonsupportiveness, perceived, 104–106, 149
Norepinephrine, 163, 205–206, 209
Nortriptyline, 69, 220, 265, 270

O

Occupational functioning, impairment of, 189–190
Outcome of bereavement, 48–54
clinical studies of, 42–45
ego defenses and, 132–133
pathologic grief as, 42–43
prediction using coping variables, 130–133
Oxytocin, 14

P

Palpitations, 257
Pangs of grief
in delayed grief syndrome, 27, 175
description of, 16
in early grief, 17
empty situations and, 93
separation anxiety and, 22
Panic disorder, 25, 293–294
with agoraphobia, separation anxiety and, 71
anticipatory anxiety in, 257
benzodiazepines for, 256, 257
diagnosis of, 188
norepinephrine and, 163
in pathologic grief, 29
personal and family histories of, 191
pharmacological treatment of, 221
risk
childhood loss of parent and, 160–161
factors for, **65**, 66
separation anxiety syndrome and, 63
sociodemographic characteristics of, **65**
symptoms of, 48–50
Panic reactions, pharmacological, 270–271
Parent(s)
bereaved, 146
death of, 147–148

Parental separation, in childhood, adult psychopathology and, 161
Parkes, C. M., 21–23
Pathogenesis mechanisms, treatment implications for, **218**
Pathologic grief, 235, 350–351
   absent grief as, 19–20
   as adaptive disorder, 30
   affective syndromes of, risk for, 150
   anxiety disorders and, 59, 60–64
   clinical attention and, 3–4
   clinical examples of, 2–3, 32–36, 194
   congruence of syndromes, 60–64
   delayed, psychotherapy approach for, 282
   dependent, prolonged, psychotherapy approach for, 282
   depression and, 59–64
   descriptions of, 25–26
   diagnosis, 350, 351–352
      implication of, 173
      manifestations of separation distress and, 28
   diagnostic criteria for, 23, 27–31, 54, 363–369
      development of, 26–27
      separation distress and, 62–63
   differential diagnosis of, 254
   as ecologically specific disorder, 31–32
   epidemiological profile of, 64–67, **65**
   fear of losing control and, 181
   functional impairment in, 30
   historical development of concept, 18–27, **26**, 36
   longitudinal studies of, 63–64
   with major depression, 184
   maladaptation to loss and, 80
   maladaptive ego states and, 24
   multidimensional model of, 352
   nature of, 28, 350–351
   nosology for, 30–31
   occurrence of, 42–43, 45
   pathogenesis of, 210
   patterns of, 1
   pharmacological treatment of, 271–273
   posttraumatic stress disorder and, 179, 181
   psychosocial functioning and, 30
   recent studies of, 25–27
   risk factors for, **65**
   as separation anxiety disorder form, 272
   sociodemographic characteristics, 65
   sudden, unexpected, psychotherapy approach for, 282
   symptoms, 60
      criteria, 174–179
      multiple dimensions of, 350
   treatment. *See* Treatment
   typology, 31
      personality characteristics and, 151
      psychotherapy and, 282–283
   understanding, questions for, 354–355
   variants of, 13, 22, 350. *See also* Absent grief; Chronic grief; Delayed grief; Inhibited grief
   versus normal grief, 351
Pathologic mourning concept, 19, 40
Peptidergic transmitter systems, 14
Personal characteristics, 165
Personal history, as bereavement risk factor, 158–159, 190, 191
Personality disorder, definition of, 154
Personality traits
   acute symptomatology and, 155–158

assessment of, intrinsic problem in studies, 148–149
of bereaved individuals, 148–158
as bereavement risk factors, 166–167
in children, outcome of bereavement and, 150–151
ego functioning and, 151–153
in pathologic grief diagnosis, 153–155
risk for affective syndromes of pathologic grief, 150
Personal values, 107
Personal vulnerability, 141
Pharmacological treatment. *See also* Psychotropic drugs; *specific drugs*
adaptive model and, 358
for anxiety disorders of bereavement, 220–221
for complications of bereavement, 69–70
for depressions of bereavement, 217–220
during first six months of bereavement, 245
goals of, 237–238, **238**
nonresponse rate for, 236
for pathologic grief, 271–273, 353
for psychotic symptoms, 273–276
synergism, 241
Philosophical acceptance, in coping, 130
Phobia, risk, childhood loss of parent and, 160–161
Physical dependence, benzodiazepines and, 261
Political advocacy, collaboration and, 326–327
Positivist philosophical attitude, 118
Posttraumatic stress disorder (PTSD)
absent grief and, 175
benzodiazepines for, 256
implication of diagnosis, 173

pathologic grief and, 179, 181
risk, 83, 338
risk factors for, 301
sudden, unexpected death and, 88
Prefrontal cortex, 14
Prevention, 335
concepts of, 336–344
primary, 40, 336, 339–341
secondary, 341–343
tertiary, 343–344
Problem-focused coping, 132, 216
Professional clinician. *See* Clinician, professional
Psychiatric disorders, 305, 338
Psychiatrist
role in bereavement, 255
in successful collaboration, 328–330
Psychoanalysis, 3, 40
Psychoanalytic theory, 77, 134
Psychoeducation
in psychotherapy, 239, 285–286
on remembering and continuing relationship with deceased, 296–298
on separation distress, 287–288
social adjustment and, 289–290
tasks of, 286–291
on trauma, 289
Psychological dependence, benzodiazepines and, 261
Psychological distress
course in bereavement, 109–110
in grief, 16–18
mourning-depressive dimension, 17
Psychomotor retardation, 184
Psychopathology. *See also specific psychopathologic disorders*
dimensional approach for, 191–194, **192**
ecological model of, 31–32
Psychopharmacology. *See* Pharmacologic treatment

Psychosocial functioning, pathologic grief and, 30
Psychosocial transitions, 108–113, 294
Psychotherapist, as caregiver, 309–310
Psychotherapy, 310–311
　adaptive model and, 358
　approaches, matching with syndromes, 281–285
　beginning, determination of, 306–309
　books and articles on, 279–280
　brief intervention, studies of, 225–227
　for complications of bereavement, 221, 221–227
　controlled studies of, 221, 221, 221
　for crisis intervention
　　negative effects, 223–225
　　positive effects, 222–223
　duration, determination of, 306–309
　end, determination of, 306–309
　family interventions, 305–306
　fundamental elements of, 280–281
　goals of, **238**, 239–240
　individualized, 285
　intervention types, implications of, 285
　nonresponse rate for, 236
　for pathologic grief, 353
　psychoeducation in, 281, 285–286
　during second 6 months to second year, 247–248
　synergy with other treatments, 241
　understanding fear of losing control, 291–294
Psychotic decompensation, 273
Psychotic symptoms,
　pharmacological treatment of, 273–276

Psychotropic drugs. *See also* Pharmacologic treatment
　classes of. *See* Antianxiety drugs; Antidepressants
　clinical trials, absence of, 255, 265
　controversy, 253–255
　synergy with other treatments, 241
　treatment goals for, 237–238, **238**
PTSD. *See* Posttraumatic stress disorder (PTSD)
Public health, framework for prevention, 336–338

R

Rapid-eye-movement sleep (REM sleep), 69, 164–165, 206, 207
Recent life event schedules, 81
Recovery
　mechanisms of, 213
　　negotiating social transitions, 216–217
　　using multiple coping styles, 215–216
　　working through grief, 214–215
　normal progression of grief and, 18
　process of, 17, 202–203
　psychosocial transitions of, 108–109
Rejection sensitivity, 150, 264
Religious beliefs, 107
Remembering, during bereavement, 296–297
Role relationship, maladaptive, 300–301
Role strain, 212–213

S

Sadness, normal expression of, major depression and, 267
Schizophrenia, 273, 288, 305, 338
Searching behavior

in delayed grief syndrome, 175
in early grief, 17
in loss, 21–22
in separation anxiety, 22
in separation distress, 16
Secondary prevention, 40, 336–337, 341–343
Sedation, from benzodiazepines, 257–258
Sedative abuse, 52–54, 254–255
Self-blame, 131
Self-destructive actions, 257–258
Self-esteem
  assessment of, 149
  disturbance of, 131
  low, 209
  morbid disturbance of, 184
  social support and, 107
Self-help, 39. See also Mutual support groups
  evaluation of social support network, 94
  mutual support groups, 96–97
  programs for, 344
  for widowers, 321
Self-image, maladaptive, 300–301
Separation, parental, in childhood, adult psychopathology and, 161
Separation and loss model of depression, 202
Separation anxiety disorder, 31, 80. See also Separation distress
  antidepressants for, 272
  in bereavement, 22
  bereavement as precipitant, 272
  and panic disorder with agoraphobia, 71
  pathologic grief as, 272
  terminology, 14–15
  traumatic distress and, 24
Separation distress. See also Separation anxiety disorder
  absence of, 28

course of, 238
as criterion for recognizing pathologic grief, 33–35
definition of, 15–16
delay in onset, 175
depression and, 267
duration of, 60
fear of losing control and, 181
in grief, 18
intensification, antidepressants and, 268–269, 270
intensity of, 342
learning about, 287–288
manifestations of, 28, 350
natural history of, 111
in pathologic grief, 28, 62–63, 70
physiological substrates of, 68–69
prolonged. See Pathologic grief
psychoeducation on, 295
remembering and continuing relationship with deceased, 297–298
in severe grief, 177
severe manifestations of, antipsychotic drugs and, 274–276
terminology, 14–16
traumatic distress and, 83–87, 89
vicissitudes of, 36, 109
versus traumatic distress, 83–84
Separation pain, 15. See also Separation distress
Serotonin reuptake inhibitors, 265
Severe grief
  chronic grief and, 29
  clinical example of, 194–195
  with delayed grief, 176
  differential diagnosis of, **180**
  symptomatic criteria of, 26, 177–178
  traumatic death and, 83
Sisters, bereaved, 147–148

385

Sleep disorders, 257, 263
Sleep physiology, during
   bereavement, 69, 164–165
Social adjustment
   clarifying tasks of, 289–290
   facilitation, by mutual support
      groups, 318
   natural history of, 111
Social advocacy, professional–mutual
   support group collaboration and,
   326–327
Social change process,
   conceptualization of, 108
Social environment
   bereaved individual and, 95
   deficit in, 106
   personal means of coping and,
      107–111
   as risk factor, 93
   support from, 93–94
Social functioning
   impairment, as psychopathology
      criterion, 189–190
   symptoms and, 136–137
Social interventions, 208. *See also*
   Mutual support groups
Social isolation, 105, 211–212
Social networks
   cross-sectional studies of,
      102–104
   evaluation of, 94
   importance to recovery, case
      example of, 98–100
   longitudinal studies of, 100–102
   size of, 94, 101
   social support from, 94–95
   stress in, 95–96
Social support, 93–94
   availability of resources, 75
   concept of, 94
   cross-sectional studies of,
      102–104
   longitudinal studies of, 100–102

as moderating or mediating factor,
   97–98
perceived deficit in, 100–101,
   104–106
perceptions of, 107
seeking, 130
from social network, 94–95. *See
   also* Social networks
stage of bereavement and, 97
types of, 317
Social systems intervention, 225
Social transition, recovery and,
   216–217
Social transition theory, 77
Social zeitgeber theory of depression,
   206
Socioeconomic status, changes in,
   108, 212
Sociological perspective, versus
   medical perspective, 108–111
Somatic complaints, 149
Spouses, bereaved versus
   nonbereaved, coping styles of,
   124–125
Startle reactions, 257
Stigmatization
   collaboration and, 325
   combating, 327–328
   psychiatric disorders in grief and,
      39
   psychotherapy and, 303–305
   of widows, 96
Stress-diathesis model, 141
Stress reduction programs, 115
Stress-related disorders
   benzodiazepines for, 256
   knowledge of bereavement and,
      355–357
Stress response systems, disturbance
   of, 203–204
Substitute relationships, for
   homeostasis, 213
Suicide risk, 109, 147, 187–188

Survivors
   of acquired immunodeficiency
      syndrome death, 104, 147,
      204, 326–327
   empty situations for, 93
   social environment and, 95
   of traumatic losses, 83
Sweating, 257
Symptoms, social functioning and,
   136–137

T

Tachycardia, 257
Terminal illness
   leave taking during, 296
   primary prevention and, 339
Tertiary prevention, 337, 343–344
Texas Inventory of Grief, 24
They Help Each Other Spiritually
   (THEOS), 319, 344
Thiamine, 338
Thyroid system, during bereavement,
   162
Time, needs of bereaved and, 97
Transference, 299–300
Trauma
   degree of exposure, risks and,
      84–87
   emotional, loss and, 24
   learning about, 289
Traumatic death
   age and, 144
   consequences, case example of,
      85–87
   occurrence of, 89
   response to loss and, 82–83
   severe emotional numbing and, 175
   three "V"'s of, 283
   traumatic distress and, 83–87
   untimely death and, 87
   versus nontraumatic, 82
Traumatic distress, 89, 194

in complications of bereavement,
   24
in separation distress, 18
traumatic death and, 83–87
versus separation distress, 83–84
Traumatic loss, 21
Traumatic stress theory, 77, 84
Treatment, 5–6, 228. *See also specific*
   treatment modalities
   conservatism, 244
   controlled trials of, 201
   failed or ambiguous outcome,
      308–309
   goals, 237–241, **238**
      as complementary and
         synergistic, 241
      integrating, efficacy of,
         241–243
   integration, 249–250
      after 2 years, 248–249
      efficacy of, 241–244
      during first 6 months,
         245–246
      interference or conflict
         potential, 243
      need for, 235–237
      during second 6 months to
         second year, 247–248
   longer-term, 308
   mechanisms of pathogenesis and,
      218
   of pathologic grief, 352–354
   pharmacological, 217–221,
      253–276
   psychotherapeutic, 221–227
   synergism, 241
Tremor, 257
Tricyclic antidepressants. *See also*
   specific tricyclic antidepressants
   for anxiety disorders, 261
   dosage
      guidelines for, 265
      too high, 270

Tricyclic antidepressants *(continued)*
  for major depression, 219
  risks, 256–257, 265, 269–271
  underutilization of, 271

U

Unanticipated grief, 23
Unconscious coping, 115, 125–126
Unipolar depression, 64

V

V code, for uncomplicated
  bereavement, 40
Victimization, in traumatic death, 282
Violation, in traumatic death, 282
Visual hallucinations, 275–276
Volition, in traumatic death, 282
Volunteer outreach services, 279,
  319–320, 324

W

Ways of Coping measure, 118, 122, 124
Widowers, mutual support
  interventions and, 321–322
Widows
  borderline personality disorder
    and, 153
  depressive symptoms of, 46
  mutual support programs for,
    318–319
  psychosocial transition of,
    108–109
  stigmatization of, 96
Widow-to-widow program, 344
World view, restructuring of,
  108–109, 294–295

Z

Zietgebers, 206, 208